A Search of African American Life, Achievement and Culture

First Search

John C. Cothran

Published by
Stardate Publishing Company
P.O. Box 112302
Carrollton, Texas 75011ñ2302

Cover design by John C. Cothran

Library of Congress
Catalog in Publication Number
92-61350

Hard Cover
ISBN-13: 978-0-9634002-0-8
ISBN-10: 0-9634002-0-7

Paperback
ISBN-13: 978-0-9634002-1-5
ISBN-10: 0-9634002-1-5

Please send feedback regarding this book to:
Stardate Publishing Company
info@stardatepublishing.com
or
P.O. Box 112302
Carrollton, Texas 75011-2302

This book is dedicated to the memory of my sister, Gwendolyn Louise Cothran,
my parents Willie Floyd and Qutesta Bell Cothran,
my maternal grandparents, Carter and Anna Lee Bell, Jr.,
my paternal grandparents, John Leonard and Mattie McBride Cothran,
my maternal great grandparents Anna Montgomery Bell and Carter Bell, Sr.,
my paternal great grandparents Lorenzo and Fannie Braxton Cothran,
the victims and surviving family members of the September 11, 2001 attacks
near Shanksville, Pennsylvania, the Pentagon in Arlington, Virginia,
and the World Trade Center in New York, New York,
the victims, their surviving family members, and evacuees of natural disasters,
especially Hurricane Katrina, which devastated the Gulf Coast of Alabama,
Mississippi, and Louisiana and the subsequent flooding of
the city of New Orleans in August and September 2005,
and to all the members of the 54 National Guard units, who come from all 50 states,
Guam, the District of Columbia, Puerto Rico, and the Virgin Islands, and
all members of the armed forces of the United States of America.

Table of Contents

Preface vii

Sources ix

Acknowledgments xi

Introduction 1

Chapters, Questions & Answers

    1—Adolescence . . . . 3 – A23

    2—Art . . . . 27 – A59

    3—Business and Professional Associations . . . . 63 – A76

    4—Children . . . . 81 – A103

    5—Education . . . . 107 – A121

    6—Entertainment . . . . 127 – A165

    7—Geography . . . . 171 – A182

    8—History and Civil Rights . . . . 185 – A218

    9—Literature . . . . 223 – A235

    10—Military History . . . . 239 – A257

    11—Science . . . . 265 – A282

    12—Sports . . . . 287 – A308

Select Bibliography 313

Index 335

Preface

The purpose in writing this book is to create a source that covers several aspects of African American culture and life without the reader having to use several sources at one time. In other words, this is a small encyclopedia in a different format.

The term "African American" as used in this book pertains to people of African descent from North America and South America.

The author's mission is to develop a positive book that touches on major African American contributions and at the same time does not offend other readers. Unfortunately, it was not possible to include all deserving African Americans in this endeavor.

The chronology of the material covered begins in some cases with Europeans of African ancestry, and with the early days of the first explorers in America, to the present day. Each chapter is in chronological order.

Many text and history books do not contain detailed information on the contributions of African Americans. This book explores the contributions of African Americans in the areas of adolescence, art, business and professional associations, children, education, entertainment, geography, history and civil rights, literature, military history, science and sports.

This is also an attempt to create a book that parents or grandparents and children will discuss together; or it can be reviewed by an individual or group.

The question-and-answer format was chosen for most of the book to get as much information as possible into a limited number of pages.

Finally, I want to thank people of all races who have helped African Americans in their endeavors to contribute to society over the years.

Sources

Many art sources assisted in the endeavor to create this book. I would like to express my sincere appreciation to the Art Institute of Chicago; Bowdoin College Museum of Art; Dallas Museum of Art; Detroit Institute of Art; Library of Congress; Library of the Boston Athenaeum; Los Angeles County Museum of Art; Milwaukee Art Museum; the Museum of Fine Arts, Houston; National Archives; National Museum of Art, Smithsonian Institution; National Portrait Gallery, Smithsonian Institution; New Orleans Museum of Art; the Newark Museum; the Pennsylvania Academy of the Fine Arts; Philadelphia Museum of Art; the Phillips Collection; Providence Art Club; San Francisco Museum of Modern Art; Schomburg Center for Research in Black Culture; State Historical Society of Iowa; the Taft Museum of Art; the Toledo Museum of Art; and the Whitney Museum of American Art.

Many historical and other sources assisted in the creation of this book. I would like to thank Dr. Harold Amos; the Academy of Motion Picture Arts and Sciences; the Air and Space Museum of the Smithsonian Institution; Arkansas History Commission; American Express Corporation; the Arizona State Library; the Atlanta Braves; the Bancroft Library, University of California, Berkeley; the Baseball Hall of Fame and Museum; Vernon J. Biever; Birmingham, Alabama Mayor's Office; Brown University; the Boston Celtics; the California State Library; Carrollton Public Library, Carrollton, Texas; Chapel Hill, North Carolina Mayor's Office; the Chicago Bears; the Chicago Bulls; the Chicago Historical Society; the Colorado Historical Society; Corbis, Inc.; the Cowboy Hall of Fame; the Dallas Cowboys; the Dallas Public Library; the Denver Public Library; Fisk University; Governor's Office, Commonwealth of Virginia; William P. Gottlieb; the Green Bay Packers; IBM Corporation; interviews; IOC/Olympic Museum; Jackson State University; Barbara Jordan; Kansas State Historical Society; James J. Kriegsmann; Library of Congress; Lincoln University, Pennsylvania; Los Angeles, California Mayor's Office; Markus Weiner Publishing, Inc.; Massachusetts Historical Society; MichaelOchsArchives.com; Minnesota Historical Society; Mississippi Department of Archives and History; Missouri Historical Society; Montana Historical Society; Moorland Spingarn Research Center, Howard University; National Archives; National Cowboy Hall of Fame and Western Heritage Center; Natural History Museum, Los Angeles County Museum of Natural History; Seaver Center for Western History Research; Naval Photographic Center; New York City Mayor's Office; North Carolina Mutual Life Insurance Company; the Oakland Athletics; Oregon Historical Society; Patton Museum; pension records of states that participated in the Civil War; the Philadelphia 76ers; the Pittsburgh Steelers; Pro-Line Corporation; Dick Raphael Associates; San Francisco Giants; San Francisco State University Library; the *Saturday Evening Post*; Schomburg Center for Research in Black Culture, New York Public Library; Smithsonian Institution; State Historical Society of Iowa; State of Arkansas; State of California; State of North Carolina, Department of Cultural Resources; Supreme Court of the United States; Texas Memorial Museum; University of California at Los Angeles; University of Chicago Library; University of Iowa; University of Memphis; University of Memphis Library; University of Memphis Special Collections Department; University of Mississippi, Delta Blues Museum; U.S. Army Military History Institute; U.S. Census Bureau; U.S. Department of the Navy; U.S. Mint; U.S. Naval Academy; the U.S. Pentagon; U.S. Postal Service; U.S. Senate; Virginia Historical Society; Walker Collection of A'Lelia Perry Bundles; Washington State Historical Society; and the Western Reserve Historical Society.

Acknowledgments

My wife Brenda, whose father is Charles Russ, Sr. and mother is Geneva Russ, edited the manuscript and gave valuable encouragement and assistance.

I'd like to thank my sister-in-law Betty and my brother William Cothran, Jr., who served in Vietnam, and my niece Dr. D. Lisa Cothran, who edited the manuscript and made useful suggestions. Betty, William, and Lisa are educators and William is a former member of the Army's 82nd Airborne Division, Fort Bragg, North Carolina. My sister-in-law Anita and my brother Charlie provided constant encouragement. Anita and Charlie are educators and Charlie is also a corporate employee. Both William and Charlie are deacons of Central Baptist Church in Memphis, Tennessee (Pastor, Reverend Dr. Ruben Green, whose wife is Dr. Mildred Green). My sister-in-law Samra and my brother Samuel reviewed the manuscript and made useful suggestions. Samuel is a former E7 Sergeant First Class in the Army stationed in Germany, South Korea, and Turkey. My sisters Glenda, a corporate employee, and Juanita, a county employee, also provided constant encouragement. Also, I want to thank my cousins Carrie Gaines Bell, a member of the Lane Tabernacle Christian Methodist Episcopal Church of St. Louis, Missouri (the church was named in honor of Bishop Isaac Lane; the pastor is Reverend Dr. James T. Morris); Helen Gaines Bennett of Detroit, Michigan; Charline Davis and Russie Mae Madlock of Memphis, Tennessee; Calvin Claggs, Jr., of Covington, Georgia, who served in Vietnam; and Troy Claggs of Arlington, Texas. Finally, I'd like to thank my brother-in-law Calvin D. Ousby, Sr. and his wife, Dr. Barbara Ousby, of Madison, Mississippi; and my aunt Minnie Cothran Fears Smith of Memphis, Tennessee, for their encouragement and motivation.

Other individuals were essential in the effort. Lee Gilman was invaluable in proofreading the manuscript. Bill Hence edited the manuscript and made valuable suggestions and gave valuable assistance. Michele Fagan, University of Memphis Library, was very helpful in researching photographs. Ed Frank, University of Memphis Special Collections, was very knowledgeable and helpful in obtaining excellent photographs. Jim Huffman was invaluable in obtaining photographs from the Schomburg Center for Research in Black Culture. Beth M. Howse, Fisk University Library, helped immensely. Also, Karen L. Jefferson, Howard University, was outstanding in photographic research. Finally, I am deeply indebted to Kimberly Cody, National Museum of American Art, Smithsonian Institution, for assistance in obtaining photographs. I could not have finished this book without the assistance I received from Elaine Dawson of Norfolk, Virginia, who scanned most of the images into the book, and prepared the camera-ready copy of the manuscript.

Introduction

As an African American growing up in the United States, I was not aware of significant accomplishments of African Americans. Moreover, I wondered if we made any contributions to this country. After researching, I am amazed that in spite of the odds, we made many contributions.

This book is a result of years of intermittent research. I am attempting to share the discovered facts, and a comprehensive approach to the facts, with African Americans and others. At the beginning of the effort, I envisioned a game, and later decided to abandon the original game. However, due to the question and answer format, this book can still be used to play a game. My vision of the game includes up to twelve participants, based on the twelve chapters. Each question would be worth 5 points. The first team to reach 100 points (or any agreed-upon goal) would be the winner.

A brief synopsis of the twelve chapters is as follows:

The purpose of the Adolescence chapter is to focus on the adolescence of major African American contributors. Reviewing some aspects of major contributors as adolescents may interest all, especially young adults.

> *Many are aware of Mary McLeod Bethune, but few are aware of her life during adolescence.*

Artists, including painters, sculptors, and photographers are covered in the Art chapter.

> *Many are aware of the painter Georgia O'Keeffe, but few are aware of Henry O. Tanner.*

Information for the Business and Professional Associations chapter was difficult to obtain due to the scarcity of written documentation on this topic.

> *Many are aware of J. Pierpoint Morgan, but few are aware of Maggie Lena Walker.*

The chapter on Children concentrates on the major African Americans as children.

> *What was a memorable event in the childhood of Benjamin O. Davis, Sr.?*

> *Many are aware of Goldilocks and the Three Bears, but few are aware of the story of John Henry.*

The Education chapter covers the strides made in education by African Americans. Special emphasis is placed on education by African American schools, colleges, and universities.

> *Many are aware of Horace Mann, but few are aware of John Hope.*

In the Entertainment chapter, accomplishments of African Americans are highlighted.

> *Many are aware of Vivien Leigh, but few are aware of Ethel Waters.*

In the Geography chapter, the contributions of African Americans are reviewed, along with significant locations of interest for African Americans.

> *Many are familiar with Lewis and Clark and their exploration of the midwestern United States, but few are aware of York, who traveled and explored with them.*

In the History and Civil Rights chapter, historical and civil rights contributions of African Americans are reviewed.

> *Many are aware of George Washington crossing the Delaware River, but few are aware of Prince Whipple, an African American oarsman, also in the boat.*

> *Many are familiar with the Bill of Rights, but few are aware of the Civil Rights bill of 1875.*

The Literature chapter covers significant contributions of African Americans in the field of literature.

> *Many are aware of Sinclair Lewis, but few are aware of Richard Wright.*

In the Military History chapter, important contributions of African Americans are reviewed.

> *Many are aware of General Patton and the Battle of the Bulge, but few are aware of the 761st and its contributions during the battle.*

The Science chapter reviews the significant contributions of African Americans in the field of science.

> *Many are aware of Thomas Edison, but few are aware of Lewis Latimer.*

The Sports chapter reviews the contributions of African Americans in the field of sports.

> *Many are familiar with Babe Ruth, but few are familiar with Oscar Charleston.*

Following the chapters are a selected bibliography and an index.

1 —Adolescence

1. Early African American poet Phillis Wheatley (1753–1784) grew up in what city, where as an adolescent she wrote her first poems, *Poems on Various Subjects*, in 1773?

2. Born in Africa, what Revolutionary War hero as a young adult was sent by his wealthy father to America to be educated, but was sold into slavery by the ship's captain?

3. Who spent his youth on a farm in New Jersey and later spent six distinguished years in the Revolutionary War?

4. Who grew up as a free adolescent in Andover, Massachusetts, and later was cited for heroics during the Battle of Bunker Hill in 1775?

5. Haitian volunteers of African descent, including Henri Christophe (1767–1820)—who was twelve years old at the time—fought the British at what battle during the Revolutionary War?

Contributors To The Cause...
Salem Poor · Gallant Soldier · U.S. 10¢

Figure 1—Salem Poor. Copyright © U.S. Postal Service. Reproduced with permission of the U.S. Postal Service.

6. Who grew up in New Orleans, Louisiana, and later donated her estate to establish the Catholic Indigent Orphan's School to provide for underprivileged, free African American orphans, many of whom had Caucasian fathers? ("Free" refers to individuals (children or adults) not held in bondage as property.)

7. Paul Cuffee (1759–1817), a wealthy African American of early America, went to work at sea as a teenager, later struggled for African American rights, and advocated the return to what continent?

8. As a teenager, who converted his master to Christianity, purchased his freedom, and later founded the African Methodist Episcopal Church?

9. Who served in the Continental Army at age 14 as a waiter, then enlisted two years later and served until the end of the war?

10. Who grew up in Charles County, Maryland, and was the "Uncle Tom" in Harriet Beecher Stowe's *Uncle Tom's Cabin*?

11. Who was a slave as an adolescent and later became the principal interpreter and counselor of the Seminole Indians?

12. Who was born a slave in Northampton County, North Carolina, later earned money writing for students at the University of North Carolina, and tried without success to purchase his freedom with the proceeds from his published volume of poetry, *The Hope of Liberty* (1829)?

13. As a slave, Sojourner Truth (1797–1883) was separated at what age from her mother, and later became an evangelist and abolitionist?

14. What engraver and lithographer began drawing professionally at the age of thirteen, and made a notable drawing of DeWitt Clinton (1769–1828)?

15. Who spent his adolescence as a house slave in Baltimore, Maryland, and later became a noted abolitionist and orator? He was born Frederick Augustus Washington Bailey in February 1817 in Maryland. His mother was a slave and his father was an unknown White man. At age 16, he was beaten by his master to break his spirit. But his spirit was not broken. At the age of 21 he escaped slavery dressed as a sailor. He later settled in New Bedford, Massachusetts with his new bride and a new name, Frederick Douglass.

Figure 2—Sojourner Truth. Copyright © U.S. Postal Service. Reproduced with permission of the U.S. Postal Service.

16. At the age of 13 Harriet Tubman (1820–1913) was struck by a rock thrown by her master and suffered occasional blackouts for the rest of her life. She was known for leading slaves to what?

17. Who was born a free African American in Fayetteville, North Carolina, attended school in Indiana and Ohio, and in 1870 became America's first African American senator representing the state of Mississippi? He assumed the seat held by Senator Jefferson Davis, who became President of the Confederate States of America.

18. Who was raised in Cincinnati, Ohio, became a teacher and civil rights activist, and was known for the book *The Black Brigade of Cincinnati* (1869)?

Figure 3—Harriet Tubman. Copyright © U.S. Postal Service. Reproduced with permission of the U.S. Postal Service.

19. Who was raised in New Orleans, Louisiana, and later became a noted composer and pianist whose best known work is *La Bamboula*, a composition based on the scenes and sounds of New Orleans' Congo Square?

20. Who grew up as a slave in Virginia, moved to Chicago, and in 1871 during the Great Fire, opened the vaults at the Chicago Board of Trade and saved

as many valuable papers as possible? A portrait hangs in his honor in the Hall of Celebrities at the Chicago Board of Trade.

21. Who settled in Chicago, Illinois in 1854 at age 14, and due to the help she provided during Chicago's great fires of 1871 and 1874, was referred to as the "Fire Angel" and "Chicago's Grand Old Lady"?

22. Who acquired the skill of a printer as an adolescent slave, and later became the first African American to serve a full term as U.S. Senator representing the state of Mississippi?

23. What adolescent, under the patronage of an abolitionist, was educated and became a well-known African American sculptor?

24. Who remained a slave until age 16 when Union forces captured Natchez, Mississippi, and later became a U.S. Congressman representing a district from the state of Mississippi?

25. Who passed as her mother's slave as a young child, becoming a teacher and community worker in Memphis, Tennessee, sometimes referred to as the "Angel of Beale Street"?

26. Who grew up in Raleigh, North Carolina and later became a writer, with one of her books entitled *A Voice from the South: By a Black Woman from the South*?

27. Who, as an adolescent, attended Hampton Institute and later became a well-known educator?

28. Who grew up near Orangeburg, South Carolina, studied for a short time at the then-integrated University of South Carolina (1875), received an M.D. degree from Howard University, and became Collector of Customs for the port of Charleston, South Carolina?

29. In 1880, who worked at the age of 13 in the cotton fields around Vicksburg, Mississippi, and became a well-known hair care businesswoman? She was born in 1867, in Delta, Louisiana and her parents died when she was 7. At age 14, she married and had a daughter A'Lelia, who was a noted philanthropist during the Harlem Renaissance. Walker died in 1919.

30. Who attended public school in Washington, D.C., then Howard University, and established Day Home Clubs (which were later adopted by other organizations) in the early 1900s in Nashville, Tennessee, to provide care for children left at home by their parents?

Figure 4—Madam C.J. Walker. Copyright © U.S. Postal Service. Reproduced with permission of the U.S. Postal Service.

31. Ida Bell Wells-Barnett (1862–1931) began teaching at a country school in Mississippi at the age of 14, and later became a crusader against lynching while teaching at Woodstock School (near Memphis, Tennessee). For what Memphis newspaper did she write?

32. Who grew up in Macon, Mississippi, was a supporter of women's clubs and a noted educator, and became the third wife of Booker T. Washington?

Figure 5—Ida B. Wells. Copyright © U.S. Postal Service. Reproduced with permission of the U.S. Postal Service.

33. Who grew up in La Grange, Georgia, and later established the traditions at Spelman College of training young women to work as missionaries in Africa and also educating African women at Spelman? She was born on August 25, 1866, in Columbus, Georgia. She graduated from Spelman Seminary (now Spelman College) in 1888, attended missionary school in London, England, and later worked in the Congo. Gordon died on January 26, 1901.

34. Who, in his early teens, played the piano at churches and socials in Texarkana, Texas, and became a well-known composer and pianist? He was born about 1867 near Linden, Texas. Around 1872, the family moved to Texarkana, Texas. His mother was able to purchase a piano for him to practice and he received piano lessons from a German piano teacher, Julius Wiess, who taught him classical music. Joplin attended George Smith College in Sedalia, Missouri, where he studied musical composition. He is best-known for the composition "Maple Leaf Rag" and the ragtime opera *Treemonisha*. Joplin was married twice. He was married to Belle Hayden from 1901 to 1903; they had a daughter who died as an infant. Joplin married Lottie Stokes around 1909. He died in the Manhattan State Hospital in New York City in 1917.

Figure 6—Scott Joplin. Copyright © U.S. Postal Service. Reproduced with permission of the U.S. Postal Service.

35. Who attended high school in Worcester, Massachusetts, and became a renowned educator at Atlanta University? He was born in 1868 in Augusta, Georgia. His parents probably never married because interracial marriage was illegal in many states. He could have passed as White, but was proud of his African American heritage. In 1907, he became the first African American president of Atlanta Baptist College (later called Morehouse College). In 1912, he visited his father's homeland, Scotland, and other areas of Europe. In 1929, he became the first president of the Atlanta University System. Hope died in Atlanta, Georgia, in 1936.

36. James Weldon Johnson (1871–1938), who grew up in Jacksonville, Florida, changed his middle name from William to Weldon and was a noted poet, author, and lyricist, attended high school in what city?

Figure 7—James Weldon Johnson. Copyright © U.S. Postal Service. Reproduced with permission of the U.S. Postal Service.

37. What clergyman attended high school in Dallas, Texas, and wrote the novel *Imperium Imperico*, which he self-published and sold door to door? He was born in 1872 in Chatfield, Texas, and attended Dallas public schools and Bishop College. He served as pastor of First Baptist Church of East Nashville, Tennessee, Tabernacle Baptist Church in Memphis, Tennessee, and Hopewell Baptist Church of Denison, Texas. He eventually returned to the Tabernacle Baptist Church. In 1914, he established the National Public Welfare League to promote interracial cooperation and community efficiency among African Americans. His novel was subsequently embraced by the African American community. Griggs died on January 5, 1933.

38. Who attended school in Florence, Alabama, as an adolescent and whose autobiography is entitled *Father of the Blues*?

Figure 8—W.C. Handy. Copyright © U.S. Postal Service. Reproduced with permission of the U.S. Postal Service.

39. Who worked on his father's farm as an adolescent, later moved to Durham, North Carolina, and became a well-known insurance executive?

40. Who, at the age of 15, quit school to take the place of her family's deceased mule "Ole Bush" to plow the field, and later founded a college in Florida?

41. Who left home at the age of 13 to work in a lumber camp near Surry, Virginia, later attended high school in Petersburg, Virginia, and became a noted educator?

42. Who, at the age of 14, lived and worked in Cincinnati, Ohio, moved to Cleveland, Ohio, and later invented the automobile traffic light?

43. Who danced in the streets of Washington, D.C. as an adolescent, and later starred in movies with Shirley Temple?

44. Who studied the violin at the age of 14, later became a noted band leader, and was buried with military honors in Arlington National Cemetery?

45. At the age of 17, who worked on a boat in New York City to earn enough money to enter Kimball Academy in Meridian, New Hampshire, and later entered Dartmouth College to become an outstanding marine biologist?

46. Who spent her youth with a touring show company, later becoming the first African American woman to record the blues? One of her songs is entitled "That Thing Called Love."

47. Who attended high school in Cambridge, Massachusetts, and in 1902, founded the Palmer Memorial Institute, a school for African American women?

Figure 9—Ernest E. Just. Copyright © U.S. Postal Service. Reproduced with permission of the U.S. Postal Service.

48. Who moved to New York City as an adolescent, and became a recognized actress with her appearance in the play *Deep River* (1926)?

49. Who started out as a Pullman porter at age 17, and later became a pioneer movie producer whose first production was entitled *The Homesteader* (1919)?

50. Who grew up in Florida and later became a baseball player whom Babe Ruth regarded as the greatest baseball player he had ever seen?

51. Who lived in Ypsilanti, Michigan as an adolescent, and later developed 42 patents, including a patent for treads on tires?

52. Who was born in 1885 in Mooringsport, Louisiana, spent his youth there, and later became a blues musician?

53. Who spent her adolescence near Jackson, Mississippi, and later became a philanthropist, humanitarian, and founder of an African American women's club in Memphis, Tennessee?

Figure 10—Leadbelly. Copyright © U.S. Postal Service. Reproduced with permission of the U.S. Postal Service.

54. Who suffered from rheumatic fever, began to read books as an adolescent, and later wrote *The Negro and His Music*?

55. Who grew up in Little Rock, Arkansas and Chicago, Illinois, and became a noted woman composer? One of her works is entitled *Symphony No. 3 in C Minor*.

56. Who, as an adolescent, held various jobs in Goshen, New York, and later became a well-known artist?

57. Who attended high school at Clark University in Atlanta, and later became the first African American surgeon to be admitted to the American College of Surgeons?

58. Who secured a position as an apprentice mechanic at age 16, and later invented the refrigerated truck?

59. Who attended East Side High School in Aurora, Illinois, and later devised methods to sterilize food and medical supplies?

60. Who was born and grew up in Chattanooga, Tennessee, and later became known as the "Empress of the Blues"?

61. Who attended public school in Brooklyn, New York, and was the first African American professional librarian in the New York Public Library? She was educated at Howard and Columbia. In 1920, she became reference librarian at the 135th Street branch of the New York Public Library and was there when Arthur Schomburg became curator.

Figure 11—Bessie Smith. Copyright ©U.S. Postal Service. Reproduced with permission of the U.S. Postal Service.

She managed the Negro literature and history collection until 1939. Her protégé, Ernest D. Kaiser, put together the *Ernest D. Kaiser Index to Black Resources*, a tool for locating information on people of African descent.

62. Who, at the age of 14, worked as a maid and wardrobe girl for a Gilbert and Sullivan traveling show, and later authored the novel *Mules and Men*? She was born on January 7, 1891 to John Hurston and Lucy Ann Potts. Her mother died in 1904. She grew up in Eatonville, Florida, was an early town founded by African Americans, where her father was elected mayor three times. She left Eatonville at age 14, supporting herself by working as a maid. She

Figure 12—Zora Neale Hurston. Copyright © U.S. Postal Service. Reproduced with permission of U.S. Postal Service.

entered Howard University in 1918, taking college preparatory courses, and in 1928, she received her B.A. degree from Barnard College. Some of the novels by Hurston included: *Jonah's Guorde Vine* (1934), *Tell My Horse* (1938), *Moses, Man of the Mountain* (1939) and *Seraph on the Suwanee* (1943). She died in poverty on January 28, 1960.

63. Who left school at the age of 13, supported herself by doing domestic work, and became a well-known singer and actress in the 1920s? She was born in 1896 in Chester, Pennsylvania, the result of her 12-year-old mother's rape by a Caucasian man. Her songs included "Memories of You," "Am I Blue," "Heat Wave," "Suppertime," and "Stormy Weather." She spent the last years of her life touring with Billy Graham, although she was a devout Catholic, and died in 1977 in Chatsworth, California.

Figure 13—Ethel Waters. Copyright © U.S. Postal Service. Reproduced with permission of U.S. Postal Service.

64. Who became interested in entertainment at the age of 14 by appearing in a talent show, and was later known as the "Mother of the Blues"?

65. Who graduated at the age of 16 as high school valedictorian in Little Rock, Arkansas, and later became a noted composer?

66. Who, when she was 13, joined the Union Baptist Church Senior Choir in Philadelphia, Pennsylvania, and later became a noted contralto?

Figure 14—"Ma" Rainey. Copyright © U.S. Postal Service. Reproduced with permission of the U.S. Postal Service.

67. What athlete and actor attended high school in Somerville, New Jersey, where his Glee Club music teacher, Miss Vosseller, helped train his voice?

68. Who grew up in South Carolina and became a community activist, fighting for desegregation of public schools in Columbia and central South Carolina?

69. Who grew up in Washington, D.C., later becoming a noted playwright, with one of her plays entitled *Stranger in the Dust*?

70. Who, though encouraged by her mother to study medicine, instead studied art, and designed the portrait of President Franklin Roosevelt that appears on the dime?

Figure 15—Paul Robeson. Copyright © U.S. Postal Service. Reproduced with permission of the U.S. Postal Service.

71.   What author of the novel, *Southern Road*, as an adolescent attended Dunbar High School in Washington, D.C., where he edited the school magazine and began to write poetry?

72.   Who was an adolescent in Crescent City, Florida in the early 1900s, and became a labor leader? He was born in 1889, in Crescent City, Florida. In 1911, Randolph traveled to Harlem hoping to become an actor at City College of New York. His parents objected and he changed to politics. In 1925, he organized the Brotherhood of Sleeping Car Porters. It was ten years before the Pullman Company negotiated with the Brotherhood, but in 1937, an agreement was reached. Randolph organized the League on Non-violent Civil Disobedience to protest discrimination in the military. President Truman issued Executive Order 9981 in 1948, banning discrimination in the armed forces. Randolph helped organize the 1963 march on Washington, D.C. for jobs and freedom. He died in 1979.

Figure 16—A. Philip Randolph. Copyright © U.S. Postal Service. Reproduced with permission of the U.S. Postal Service.

73.   Who left high school at the age of 14 in Bay St. Louis, Mississippi to get a job, and later became an outstanding sculptor? He was born on January 28, 1901, in Bay St. Louis, Mississippi. At age 17, he began working as a butler for Mr. Harry Pond, who recognized his artistic talent and helped further his education as a painter. Later, as a student at the Art Institute of Chicago, he developed a deep interest in sculpture. Two of his noted sculptures, *Blackberry Dancer* (1932) and *African Dancer* (1933) became part of the permanent collections of the Whitney Museum of American Art. He died on March 5, 1989.

74.   Who was sent at the age of 13 to a school for wayward boys in New Orleans, where he began to learn music, and later was called "Satchelmouth" (eventually shortened to "Satchmo")? He was born August 4, 1901, in New Orleans, Louisiana and grew up in New Orleans' Third Ward. He was sent to a school for wayward boys after firing a gun during a New Year's Day celebration. At the school, he learned to play the tambourine, the bugle, and the coronet. He considered his year and a half at the school as making the best of a bad situation and laying the foundation of his musical career.

Figure 17—Louis Armstrong. Copyright © U.S. Postal Service. Reproduced with permission of the U.S. Postal Service.

75. Who grew up in St. Paul, Minnesota, with his aunt and uncle, and became executive secretary of the National Association for the Advancement of Colored People (NAACP) in 1955? He was born August 30, 1901, in St. Louis, Missouri and attended integrated schools, and later attended the University of Minnesota. His parents were Mayfield and William D. Wilkins. Later he married Aminda Badeau. He became a writer for the African American newspaper, the *Kansas City Call*, and served as an assistant to Walter White at the NAACP. He was also an editor of *Crises* magazine. He became executive secretary of the NAACP after the death of Walter White in 1955, and served until 1965. Then he became the executive director of the NAACP from 1965–1975. Wilkins died September 9, 1981. His autobiography, *Standing Fast: The Autobiography of Roy Wilkins*, was published posthumously in 1982.

Figure 18—Roy Wilkins. Copyright © U.S. Postal Service. Reproduced with permission of the U.S. Postal Service.

76. Who was an adolescent in Washington, D.C. around 1915 to 1920, later became a noted educator at the University of Chicago, and challenged the testing of African American students? He was born William Allison Davis on October 14, 1902, in Washington, D.C. to Gabrielle and John Davis. He grew up on a farm in Virginia and his family later moved back to Washington, D.C., where he was the valedictorian of his class at Dunbar High School. Afterwards, he attended Williams College in Massachusetts, and in 1924 was the valedictorian of his college class. In 1925, he earned his master's degree in English from Harvard and went on to teach English at Hampton Institute. He was not satisfied with his contribution and what he wanted to accomplish, so he went back to Harvard and graduated with a master's degree in anthropology in 1932. From 1935 to 1939 he taught at Dillard University, then became head of the department of education at Atlanta University. In 1941, after he completed a study in Mississippi, he was motivated to write *Deep South: A Social Anthropological Study of Caste and Class*. This book was later used as a reference in the U.S. Supreme Court decision in the 1954 case, *Brown v. Board of Education, Topeka, Kansas*. His last book, *Leadership, Love and Aggression* (1983), is a psychological study of Frederick Douglass, Richard Wright, W.E.B Du Bois, and Martin Luther King. He died on November 21, 1983.

Figure 19—Dr. Allison Davis. Copyright © U.S. Postal Service. Reproduced with permission of the U.S. Postal Service.

77. Who was taught piano by his mother, by Fats Waller, and by James P. Johnson, and later became a well-known piano player and band leader? He was born William Basie on August 24, 1904, in Red Bank, New Jersey. His parents were Lilly Ann and Harvey Lee Basie. As a child, his instrument of choice was the drums, but later he changed to the piano. He was noted for some of the following hits: "One O'clock Jump" (1937), "Jumpin' at the Woodside" (1938), and "Taxi War Dance" (1939). There are several

Figure 20—Count Basie. Copyright © U.S. Postal Service. Reproduced with permission of the U.S. Postal Service.

accounts as to how he received the nickname "Count." According to his autobiography, *Good Morning Blues*, the name was the result of Basie wanting to be a part of the perceived royalty—"Duke" Ellington, King Oliver, Barron Lee, and "Earl" Hines—a "Count" would add to the Barons of Rhythm. After Basie was voted the leader of a band, replacing Buster Moten, the band assumed a new name—"Count Basie and his Barons of Rhythm." Basie died April 26, 1984.

78. Who attended Jefferson High School in Los Angeles, California, and received the Nobel Peace Prize in 1950? He was born in 1904 in Detroit, Michigan, to Fred and Olive Johnson Bunche. The family moved in 1914 to Albuquerque, New Mexico for his mother's health. In 1917, after the death of his parents, his grandmother moved the family to Los Angeles, where he graduated valedictorian of his class. Bunche attended UCLA, starred on three championship basketball teams, majored in political science, and was elected Phi Beta Kappa. In 1928, he received his master's degree from Harvard and was appointed an instructor at Howard University, where he established the Department of Political Science. In June 1930, he married Ruth Ethel Harris

Figure 21—Ralph Bunche. Copyright © U.S. Postal Service. Reproduced with permission of the U.S. Postal Service.

of Montgomery, Alabama, who had been his student at Howard. He earned his Ph.D. at Harvard in 1934, and in 1936 was appointed co-director of the Institute of Race Relations at Swarthmore College in Pennsylvania. In 1944, Dr. Bunche transferred to the State Department's Division of Territorial Studies and in May 1946, went to work at the United Nations "on loan" from the State Department. He helped secure an armistice in the Holy Land in 1949 and for his efforts, he was awarded the 1950 Nobel Peace Prize. He later worked for the United Nations, and died December 9, 1971.

79.   Who grew up in Brooksville, Mississippi, and St. Louis, Missouri, later founded the Ira Aldridge Players and the American Negro Theater, and starred in the movie *Anna Lucasta*?

80.   Who attended the Industrial School for Negro Children in Mount Meigs, Alabama, where he was a star pitcher? Later he became known as "Satchel" and was an all-time baseball pitching great. Accounts vary as to the origin of the nickname. In one account, a neighbor, Wilber Hines, claimed to have given him the nickname when they carried bags for money as children at a railroad station. The nickname was bestowed by Hines after Paige tried to pilfer a satchel.

Figure 22—Satchel Paige. Copyright © U.S. Postal Service. Reproduced with permission of the U.S. Postal Service.

81.   What author attended school in Jackson, Mississippi, and after graduating moved to Memphis, Tennessee, where he obtained his first job and borrowed books from the Memphis library on the library card of a friendly Caucasian?

82.   As an adolescent, who danced in Noble Sissel's Broadway play *Shuffle Along*, and later was a star at the Folies Bergères in Paris, France?

83.   Who spent his youth in Birmingham, Alabama, and Chicago, Illinois, and is a well-known jazz vibraphonist and drum player?

84.   Who attended high school in Joliet, Illinois, and was called the mother of African American dance? She was born in 1909 in Glen Ellyn, Illinois, to Fanny and Albert Dunham. After her mother died, she moved to Joliet, Illinois when her father purchased a dry-cleaning business. In the 1920s she attended the University of Chicago and received two Rosenwald Fellowships to study the anthropological origins of African American dance. She studied the Jamaican Maroon Dance and the Haitian Vodoun dance rituals, visited Martinique to study fighting dance called "Ag' Ya," and studied dance in the island of Trinidad. As a result of her research, Dunham earned her bachelor's degree in social anthropology from the University of Chicago. Her works include: the book *Journey to Accompany* (1946), *The Dances of Haiti* (her master's thesis, 1947), and *Island Possessed* (1969). Some the films in which she appeared are: *Carnival of Rhythm* (1939), *Star-Spangled Rhythm* (1942), *Stormy Weather* (1943), *Casbah* (1948), *Je Suis de la Revue* (1951), *Mambo* (1954), and *In the Mirror of Myra Deren* (2002). In 1964, Dunham became the Visiting Artist in the Fine Arts Division at Southern Illinois University. Her successful reviews include: *Tropics and Le Jazz Hot* (1940), *Tropical Review* (1943), *Caribbean Rhapsody* (1950), and *Bamboche* (1962).

85. W.E.B. Du Bois (1868–1963), who attended high school in Great Barrington, Massachusetts, and later edited *The Crises Magazine*, was one of the founders of the Niagara Movement and what other prominent organization?

Figure 23—W.E.B. Du Bois. Copyright © U.S. Postal Service. Reproduced with permission of the U.S. Postal Service.

86. Who began writing at age 12, and her only book is entitled *The Negro Trail Blazers of California*? She was born in 1872 in Cincinnati, Ohio, grew up there, published a column in the *Cincinnati Enquirer*, and moved to California in 1910. Her only book had an effect on newspaper writing in California, such as spelling the word "Negro" with a capital "N," and discontinuance of the word "darkie." She did research on early African Americans in California at Berkeley, California. For about 10 years she wrote a Sunday column entitled "Activities among Negroes," for the *Oakland Tribune*. Beasley died in 1934.

87. What blind musician played harmonica at an early age, played in a group at age 14, and was called the greatest blues harmonica player? Born Saunders Terrell in Terrell, North Carolina in 1911, he was blind by age 18 due to eye injuries. He learned to play harmonica from his father and played for money in Shelby, North Carolina. He teamed with Blind Boy Fuller in 1937 and in 1938 played at the "From Spirituals to Swing" concert at New York City's Carnegie Hall. After Fuller's death in 1940, Terry teamed with Brownie McGhee and they became a popular duo in the 1940s, 1950s, and 1960s. Terry died in 1986.

Figure 24—Sonny Terry. Copyright © U.S. Postal Service. Reproduced with permission of the U.S. Postal Service.

88. Who attended Lindblom High School in Chicago, Illinois, and later became known as the "First Lady of the Black Press"?

89. Who spent her youth in Rankin, Pennsylvania, and later served as president of the National Council of Negro Women, and member of the board of the Young Women's Christian Association (YWCA)?

Figure 25—Ethel L. Payne. Copyright © U.S. Postal Service. Reproduced with permission of the U.S. Postal Service.

90. Who attended Central High School in Cleveland, Ohio, and led the 99th Fighter Squadron during World War II?

91. In 1927, who graduated from Frederick Douglass High School in Baltimore, Maryland, and later became the first African American woman to practice law in the state of Maryland?

92. Who sang in the choir at her father's church as an adolescent, and is considered to be the "Queen" of gospel music? Born in 1911 in New Orleans, she lost her mother at age 4. In 1916, she lived with her aunt Mahalia "Duke" Paul and sang at Plymouth Rock Baptist Church. She moved to Chicago in 1927 and sang gospel music at the Greater Salem Baptist Church. During the 1940s she toured with Thomas Dorsey. Her autobiography *Movin' on Up*, written with Evan McCleod Wylie, was published in 1966. She died in 1972 and was inducted posthumously into the Gospel Music Hall of Fame in 1978.

Figure 26—Mahalia Jackson. Copyright © U.S. Postal Service. Reproduced with permission of the U.S. Postal Service.

93. What Detroit adolescent used money intended for violin lessons to hire a boxing coach, and later became one of the greatest boxing heavyweight champions? He was born Joseph Louis Barrow in 1914, in Chambers County, Alabama. When he was 5, his mother married Pat Brooks and the family moved to Mt. Sinai, Alabama and in 1926, to Detroit. When his mother learned what he had done with the money for violin lessons, she offered to work to help him in his boxing career. Instead, Louis quit school and took a job to support his boxing. In 1932, he lost his first amateur match to Johnny Miller, a 1932 Olympian, who knocked Louis down seven times. Louis quit boxing and got a job at a Ford plant, but the lure was too great and he eventually returned to the sport. Over the next two years he won 50 of his 54 amateur fights. He hired John Roxborough and Julian Black to manage his professional career for half the proceeds after expenses. Black

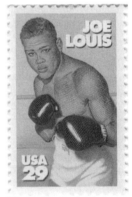

Figure 27—Joe Louis. Copyright © U.S. Postal Service. Reproduced with permission of the U.S. Postal Service.

and Roxborough felt Louis could be champion, with careful management and matches with successively more highly rated boxers, until he could challenge for the heavyweight championship. In 1936, Max Schmeling defeated Louis at Yankee Stadium, exploiting a weakness in Louis's defense, but Blackburn worked with Louis to correct the weakness, and Louis won the world heavyweight championship in June 1937, knocking out Jim Braddock. In 1938, Louis defeated Schmeling in a rematch at Yankee Stadium. After serving almost 4 years in the U.S. Army during World War II, Louis returned to boxing but his reflexes were off and he did not have the same power. He retired from boxing in 1949, but came out of retirement in 1950 to fight Ezzard Charles, who beat him badly. In 1951, a bout with Rocky Marciano ended his career. His professional record was 68 wins and 3 defeats. Louis died April 12, 1981.

94. Who was raised in Greenville, South Carolina, and later became a blues folk singer?

95. Who was orphaned at an early age, at the age of 16 won an amateur contest at the Apollo Theater in New York City in 1934, and became a well-known jazz singer?

96. Who attended Booker T. Washington High School in Tulsa, Oklahoma, became a noted historian, and wrote, among other books, *From Slavery to Freedom*?

Figure 28—Josh White. Copyright © U.S. Postal Service. Reproduced with permission of the U.S. Postal Service.

97. I.C. Wiley, a mathematics teacher at Mayo High School in Darlington, South Carolina, motivated what future San Francisco dental surgeon to improve his math grade and become an excellent student?

98. Who, at age 13, was not allowed to enter New York City's Apollo Theater weekly amateur contest because he had won too many times, and later became a well-known jazz musician?

99. Who was born in Atlantic City, New Jersey, received early training at the Harlem Art School, and later became a well-known African American painter?

Figure 29—Thelonious Monk. Copyright © U.S. Postal Service. Reproduced with permission of the U.S. Postal Service.

100. Who was born in 1917, attended Booker T. Washington High School in Memphis, Tennessee, and later became a recording artist, disc jockey, and entertainer?

101. At age 16, who attended Lincoln University in Jefferson City, Missouri, and later became the first African American woman to serve as Justice of the Supreme Court of Pennsylvania?

102. What famous jazz musician attended Crispus Attucks Grammar
School in Kansas City, Kansas, and
was inspired by his Alonzo Lewis,
his Lincoln High School music
teacher? He was born on August 29,
1920, in Kansas City, Kansas. His
father was Charles Parker, Sr., a
traveling vaudeville song-and-dance
man from Memphis, and his mother
was Addie Boyley Parker from Kansas City, Kansas. When Parker was
8 or 9, his family moved to Kansas
City, Missouri. His first musical instrument in high school was the

Figure 30—Charlie Parker. Copyright ©
U.S. Postal Service. Reproduced with
permission of the U.S. Postal Service.

tuba, and his mother purchased a used saxophone for him to play in a dance
band. He began playing in clubs around Kansas City as a teenager (he was
large for his age and thought to be much older), and left high school to
pursue his musical career. He traveled to New York City and worked as a
dishwasher at Jimmy's Chicken Shack in Harlem. Art Tatum played the
piano there and Parker studied his playing intensely and included Tatum's
rhythmic patterns in his saxophone music. At some point, he acquired the
nickname "Yardbird" (because chicken is a yard bird and he really liked
chicken). "Yardbird" was eventually shortened to "Bird." Some of Parker's
numbers included: "Ornithology," "Yardbird Suite," "Swingmatism,"
"Scrapple from the Apple," and "Moose the Moche." Parker died on March
12, 1955. He was only 34 years old.

103. Who was born in Lincoln Ridge, Kentucky, in
1921, attended Lincoln Institute (a boarding
school run by his father where his mother also
taught), and served as the executive director of
the Urban League from 1961 to 1971?

104. Who began dancing at the age of 16 in the Cotton
Club in New York City, and later starred in the
movie *Carmen Jones*?

105. Who spent her youth in Philadelphia,
Pennsylvania, and later became the first African
American appointed Poet Laureate for the state
of Louisiana?

Figure 31—Whitney Moore
Young. Copyright © U.S.
Postal Service. Reproduced
with permission of the U.S.
Postal Service.

106. Who attended Public School 28 in New York
City, whose most admired heroine was Harriet
Tubman, and later became the first African
American woman U.S. Representative? She
subsequently became the ambassador to Jamaica.

107. In 1977, who became the first African American woman to hold a presidential cabinet position (Secretary of Housing and Urban Development)? Born in 1924, she graduated from Howard University in 1945 and in 1960, earned her law degree from George Washington University. Harris was also the first African American woman to be named to a U.S. ambassadorship (1965, Ambassador to Luxemburg). Harris died in 1985.

108. Who attended Arts High School, sang at the Mount Zion Baptist Church in Newark, New Jersey, and became a well-known singer, sometimes referred to as "The Divine"?

109. Who grew up in New Orleans, Louisiana, and later became a noted art historian, greatly enhancing the art department at Florida A&M University?

Figure 32—Patricia Roberts Harris. Copyright © U.S. Postal Service. Reproduced with permission of the U.S. Postal Service.

110. Who was born in Harlem in 1924, attended DeWitt Clinton High School (New York City), where he edited a literary magazine, and wrote the novels *The Fire Next Time* and *Go Tell It on the Mountain*? His mother married David Baldwin in 1927, and he adopted his stepfather's surname. He edited his junior high school newspaper and one of his teachers was Countee Cullen. He was editor-in-chief of his high school's literary magazine. He died in 1987.

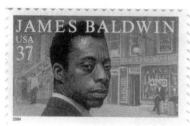

Figure 33—James Baldwin. Copyright © U.S. Postal Service. Reproduced with permission of the U.S. Postal Service.

111. Who was born in Omaha, Nebraska, attended Mason Junior High School in Mason, Michigan, and later became a dynamic speaker for the Black Muslims?

112. Who attended Oak Park High School in Laurel, Mississippi, sang in the high school choir, and later became a well-known operatic soprano?

113. Who was born in Silver, South Carolina, attended high school in the Bronx, New York, and won the women's world tennis championship at Wimbledon in 1957?

Figure 34—Malcolm X. Copyright © U.S. Postal Service. Reproduced with permission of the U.S. Postal Service.

114. Who attended Hudson High School in Macon, Georgia, in the 1950s, dropped out to support his family financially, and became a well-known singer?

Figure 35—Otis Redding. Copyright © U.S. Postal Service. Reproduced with permission of the U.S. Postal Service.

115. Who was raised in Marion, Alabama, graduated from Antioch College, worked in the community, and later became the wife of Martin Luther King, Jr.?

116. Who grew up in New York City and became the first African American woman to be licensed as an architect in the state of New York? Some of her works are Terminal One at Los Angeles International Airport, the City Hall of San Bernardino, California, and the U.S. Embassy in Tokyo, Japan.

117. Who attended an Atlanta University-sponsored school for gifted students, and later led the 1965 Selma to Montgomery, Alabama civil rights march?

118. At age 14, who began writing a teenage social column for the Philadelphia edition of the *Pittsburgh Courier*, and later wrote the novel *Soul Brothers and Sister Lou*?

119. What comedian ran track at Sumner High School in St. Louis, Missouri, and ran for president of the United States in 1968?

120. Noted for his humanitarian efforts, who was the youngest of four children, spent his adolescence (1947–1952) in Carolina, Puerto Rico, and became a baseball player for the Pittsburgh Pirates?

121. Who grew up in Los Angeles, California, attended California State College, and later became a ceramic sculptor, with one of her works entitled *Black American*?

122. Who played baseball for the Black Bears as an adolescent, and later hit 755 career professional home runs?

Figure 36—Roberto Clemente. Copyright © U.S. Postal Service. Reproduced with permission of the U.S. Postal Service.

123. A leading figure in psychiatry, who moved to New York City at age 14, attended Wadleigh high school for girls and Columbia University, and wrote two books, one of which is entitled *Young Inner City Families* (1975)?

124. What African American received the 1975 Newberry Medal—an annual award for the best children's or young-adult's book based on content—for her book entitled *M.C. Higgins, the Great*?

125. Who was raised in Detroit, Michigan, and later became a community activist and wife of Malcolm X?

126. Who grew up in Harlem and later received rave reviews when he starred in the movies *The Empire Strikes Back* and *Return of the Jedi*?

127. Who attended Nicholtown Elementary School and Sterling High School in Greenville, South Carolina, and later founded PUSH (People United to Save Humanity)?

128. Who wrote his first novel when he was 13 years old, wrote eight novels while attending high school, and wrote the novel *The Jewels of Aptor*?

129. Who attended Power Memorial High School in New York City and later had a distinguished basketball career with UCLA, the Milwaukee Bucks, and the Los Angeles Lakers?

130. Who attended East High School in Nashville, Tennessee, starred in the movie *The Color Purple*, and has her own TV talk show?

131. As an adolescent, Dinah Washington toured churches singing and playing the piano, and was noted for what song? She was born Ruth Lee Jones in 1924, in Tuscaloosa, Alabama. Her parents were Alice Williams and Ollie Jones. While she was a young girl, her family moved to Chicago, Illinois. She was a pianist at her church and later studied in Walter Dyett's music program at Du Sable High School. Washington performed in clubs as Dinah Washington and sang in the gospel choir as Ruth Jones. She

Figure 37—Dinah Washington. Copyright © U.S. Postal Service. Reproduced with permission of the U.S. Postal Service.

joined Lionel Hampton's band in the 1940s. Some of her hits included "Evil Gal Blues" (1943), "Cold, Cold Heart" (1946), "Baby Get Loss" (1949), "Trouble in Mind" (1952), "Unforgettable" (1959), "This Bitter Earth" (1960), "September in the Rain" (1960), "Rockin' Good Way" (1960) recorded with Brook Benton, and "Where Are You" (1962). She was referred to as the "Queen of the Blues" and the "Queen of Jukeboxes." She married seven times and her last husband was Dick "Night Train" Lane. Washington died on December 14, 1963 in Detroit, Michigan.

132. Who attended Jordan High School in Los Angeles, California, and won the women's 100-meter run and 200-meter dash in the 1988 Olympics?

133. What song is a ballad about two African American lovers?

134. Who revered her grandmother, Louvenia Watson, with whom she lived during her sophomore and junior years of high school and who taught her responsibility to African American people, and later became a noted poet?

135. Louretta Hawkins is the main character in what novel by Kristin Hunter?

136. What Broadway play was a take-off on the *Wizard of Oz*?

137. What young-adult book by Joyce Hansen reflects on the experiences of an African American soldier who survived the Fort Pillow massacre during the Civil War?

138. What movie includes Morgan Freeman, Robert Guillaume, and Beverly Todd, and is about a high school principal, Joe Clark?

Answers — 1 — Adolescence

1. Boston, Massachusetts

2. Prince Whipple (1750–1796)

3. Oliver Cromwell (1752–1852)

4. Salem Poor (c.1747–c.1780)

5. Battle of Savannah, Georgia (July 22, 1779)

6. Madame Bernard Couvent (1757–1837)

7. Africa

8. Richard Allen (1760–1831)

9. Charles Bowles (1761–1843)

10. Josiah Henson (1789–1883)

11. Abraham (1790–1870)

12. George Moses Horton (c.1797–1883)

13. Eleven

14. Patrick Henry Reason (1817–1856)

15. Frederick Douglass (1817–1895)

16. Freedom

17. Hiram Revels (1822–1901)

18. Peter H. Clark (1829–1925)

19. Louis Moreau Gottschalk (1829–1869)

20. Joseph Henry Hudlun, Sr. (1839–1871)

21. Anna Hudlun (1840–1914)

22. Blanche Kelso Bruce (1841–1898)

23. Edmonia Lewis (1845–1911)

24. John R. Lynch (1847–1939)

25. Julia Hooks (1852–1942)

26. Anna J. Cooper (1858–1964)

27. Booker T. Washington (1856–1915)

28. William D. Crum (1859–1912)

29. Madam C.J. Walker (1867–1919)

30. Nettie Langston Napier (1861–1938)

31. *Memphis Free Speech and Headlight*, later changed to *Free Speech*

32. Margaret Murray Washington (1863–1953)

33. Nora Antonia Gordon (1866–1901)

34. Scott Joplin (c.1867–1917)

35. John Hope (1868–1936)

36. Atlanta, Georgia

37. Sutton Griggs (1872–1933)

38. William C. Handy (1873–1958)

39. Charles Clinton Spaulding (1874–1952)

40. Mary McLeod Bethune (1875–1955)

41. Robert Russa Moton (1876–1940)

42. Garrett A. Morgan (1877–1963)

43. Bill "Bojangles" Robinson (1878–1949)

44. James R. Europe (1881–1919)

45. Ernest E. Just (1883–1941)

46. Mamie Smith (1883–1946)

47. Charlotte Hawkins Brown (1883–1961)

48. Rosalie "Rose" McClendon (1884–1936)

49. Oscar Micheaux (1884–1951)

50. John Henry Lloyd (1884–1965)

51. Elijah McCoy (c.1844–1929)

52. Huddie Ledbetter (1885–1949), whose nickname was Leadbelly because of his toughness

53. Lelia Walker (1886–1954)

54. Alain L. Locke (1886–1954)

55. Florence Price (1888–1953)

56. Horace Pippin (1888–1946)

57. Dr. Louis T. Wright (1891–1952)

58. Frederick McKinley Jones (1893–1961)

59. Lloyd A. Hall (1894–1971)

60. Bessie Smith (1894–1937)

61. Catherine A. Latimer (c.1895–1948)

62. Zora Neale Hurston (1891–1960)

63. Ethel Waters (1896–1977)

64. Gertrude Malissa "Ma" Rainey (1896–1939), who was born Gertrude Malissa Nix Pridgett

65. William G. Still (1895–1978)

66. Marian Anderson (1897–1993)

67. Paul Robeson (1898–1976)

68. Modjeska Simkins (1899–1992)

69. May Miller (1899–1995)

70. Selma Hortense Burke (1900–1995)

71. Sterling Brown (1901–1989)

72. A. Philip Randolph (1889–1979)

73. Richmond Barthé (1901–1989)

74. Louis Armstrong (1901–1971)

75. Roy Wilkins (1901–1981)

76. Allison Davis (1902–1983)

77. Count Basie (1904–1984)

78. Ralph Bunche (1904–1971)

79. Frederick O'Neal (1905–1992)

80. Satchel Paige (1906–1982)

81. Richard Wright (1908–1960)

82. Josephine Baker (1906–1975)

83. Lionel Hampton (1908–2002)

84. Katherine Dunham (1909–)

85. National Association for the Advancement of Colored People (NAACP)

86. Delilah L. Beasley (1872–1934)

87. Sonny Terry (1911–1986)

88. Ethel L. Payne (1911–1991)

89. Dorothy I. Height (1912–)

90. Benjamin O. Davis, Jr. (1912–2002)

91. Juanita Mitchell (1913–1992)

92. Mahalia Jackson (1911–1972)

93. Joe Louis (1914–1981)

94. Josh White (1914–1969)

95. Ella Fitzgerald (1917–1996)

96. John Hope Franklin (1915–)

97. Dr. Daniel A. Collins (1916–)

98. Thelonious Monk (1917–1982)

99. Jacob Lawrence (1917–2000)

100. Rufus Thomas (1917–2001)

101. Juanita K. Stout (1919–)

102. Charlie Parker (1920–1955)

103. Whitney Moore Young (1921–1971)

104. Dorothy Dandridge (1922–1965)

105. Pinkie Gordon Lane (1923–)

106. Shirley Anita Chisholm (1924–2005)

107. Patricia Roberts Harris (1924–1985), President Jimmy Carter's Secretary of Health, Education and Welfare

108. Sarah Vaughan (1924–1990)

109. Samella Sanders Lewis (1924–)

110. James Baldwin (1924–1987)

111. Malcolm X (1925–1965)

112. Leontyne Price (1927–)

113. Althea Gibson (1927–)

114. Otis Redding (1941–1967)

115. Coretta Scott King (1927–)

116. Norma Merrick Sklarek (1928–)

117. Dr. Martin Luther King, Jr. (1929–1968)

118. Kristin Hunter Lattany (1931–)

119. Dick Gregory (1932–)

120. Roberto Clemente (1934–1972)

121. Camille Billops (1933–)

122. Hank Aaron (1934–)

123. Margaret M. Lawrence (1914–)

124. Virginia Hamilton (1936–2002)

125. Betty Shabazz (1936–1997)

126. Billy Dee Williams (1937–)

127. Jesse Jackson (1941–)

128. Samuel R. Delany (1942–)

129. Kareem Abdul-Jabbar (1947–)

130. Oprah Winfrey (1954–)

131. "What a Difference a Day Makes" (1959)

132. Florence Griffith-Joyner (1959–1998)

133. "Frankie and Johnny"

134. Nikki Giovanni (1943–)

135. *Soul Brothers and Sister Lou* (1968)

136. *The Wiz* (1978)

137. *Which Way Freedom* (1986)

138. *Lean on Me* (1989)

2 —Art

1. Phillis Wheatley dedicated a poem to what young African American painter after seeing his works?

2. A painting by what artist is entitled *San Juan Nepomuceno*?

3. Who is the best-known African American portrait painter of the nineteenth century?

4. *Portrait of a Cleric* by Joshua Johnston is the only known painting which shows the qualities of what subject?

5. Who was born in slavery in Puerto Rico and later became a well-known painter in Puerto Rico?

6. John James Audubon (1785–1851), whose mother was Haitian, in 1900 became a member of the Hall of Fame for Great Americans located in New York City, and is known for what drawings?

7. Whose work concentrated on New Orleans architecture and portraits of its leaders and people?

8. Engravings and lithographs of Granville Sharp, James Williams, and DeWitt Clinton are the works of what African American artist?

Figure 38—Joshua Johnston's *Portrait of a Cleric*, oil on canvas, Museum Purchase, Hamlin Fund, Bowdoin College Museum of Art, Brunswick, Maine.

9. Whose best-known work is a bust of John Young Mason, now housed at the Virginia Historical Society?

10. What African American was a stonemason before becoming a sculptor, went to Europe, and settled in Rome, Italy, where he remained until his death in 1859?

11. Who worked as a Daguerreotype photographer in Hartford, Connecticut, from 1844 to 1853, and in Liberia from 1853 to 1875?

12. In the South, who constructed many of the early wrought-iron balconies, doors, grilles, fences and lamp standards, which were skills in metallurgy brought with them from Africa?

13. Who was noted for his versatility as a landscapist, figure painter, portrait artist, and painter of murals?

14.

Figure 39—Robert Scott Duncanson's *Mountain Pool*. Oil on canvas, 11¼ x 20 in. (28.3 x 50.6 cm.), National Museum of American Art, Smithsonian Institution. Gift of Dr. Richard Frates.

Robert Scott Duncanson's *Mountain Pool* expresses the view of people in harmony with what environment?

15. In 1848, Robert Scott Duncanson was commissioned to paint a series of wall decorations and murals for Nicholas Longworth's mansion, which later became what museum? He was born in 1821 in Seneca County, New York. His mother was a free woman of African American ancestry and his father was Scottish Canadian. He spent his youth in Canada and later moved close to Cincinnati, Ohio. The Freedmen's Aid Society of Ohio raised funds to send Duncanson to Glasgow, Scotland to study art in 1839 and he returned in 1842. He was known for his landscape paintings as well as his portraits and murals. Nicholas Longworth was an abolitionist patron of Duncanson. Duncanson painted 8 large wall murals at the Longworth home. While he painted, he traveled to such places as: Detroit, Michigan, New England, North Carolina, Pennsylvania, Canada, and Scotland. He died in 1872.

Figure 40—Robert S. Duncanson's *Mural*, c.1848–1950. Oil on plaster, 109 x 91 in. The Taft Museum of Art. Bequest of Mr. and Mrs. Charles Phelps Taft, 1932.237.

16.

Figure 41—Robert Scott Duncanson's *Romantic Landscape*, ca. 1871. Oil on canvas, 7-1/8 x 19 in., National Museum of American Art, Smithsonian Institution. Gift of Carroll Greene, Jr.

Although Robert Scott Duncanson's *Romantic Landscape* shows his talent, what is unique about this painting?

17. What landscape painter founded the Provi dence Art Club of Providence, Rhode Island? He was born in 1828 in St. Andrews, New Brunswick, Canada and was orphaned at age 16. In 1848, he traveled to Boston, where he became a barber and a member of New England society. Later, he met and married Christina Carteaux, a successful businesswoman. Christina operated a number of hair salon shops which catered to the elite. Because of his wife's business success, Bannister was able to pursue art as a profession. He attended Lowell Institute, which was established in the will of John Lowell, Jr. and administered by a male descendent trustee of his grandfather, John Lowell. Bannister was influenced by the French Barbizon style of painting, which depicts a deep love of religion, social purpose, and the country or rural life. Many of his ear-

Figure 42—Edward M. Bannister. Courtesy of the Providence Art Club.

lier works are lost and are only known from writings. In 1871, Bannister moved to Providence, Rhode Island and was one of the founding members of the Providence Art Club. He was one of the first African American artists to receive national recognition and received an award for the painting *Under the Oaks* at the Philadelphia Centennial Exposition in 1876. He is one of the few artists who did not travel to Europe to study art. Some of his notable works included: *Driving Home the Cows* (1881), *Approaching Storm* (1895), *Newspaper Boy* (1869), *Under the Oaks* (1875), *Landscape with a Boat* (1898), *Oak Trees, Newport Scene, Landscape* and *Train*. He died in 1901.

18.

Figure 43—Edward M. Bannister's *Sunset*, 1883. Oil on canvas, 16-1/8 x 24 in. (40.9 x 61 cm.), National Museum of American Art, Smithsonian Institution. Gift of William G. Miller.

Edward M. Bannister's *Sunset* emphasizes what effects on the Rhode Island landscape?

19. In Edward Mitchell Bannister's *News paper Boy*, what is the racial identity of the newspaper boy? *Newspaper Boy* was completed in 1860.

Figure 44—Edward Mitchell Bannister's *Newspaper Boy*. Oil on canvas, 30-1/8 x 25 in. (76.6 x 63.7 cm.), National Museum of American Art, Smithsonian Institution. Gift of Frederick Weingeroff.

20. Born in Port-au-Prince, Haiti, what African American photographer was active during the 1850s? African American J.P. Ball of Cincinnati, Ohio produced daguerreotypes during the same period. In addition, Augustus Washington, who lived in Hartford, Connecticut, produced many daguerreotypes before he moved to Liberia in 1853. Augustus Washington attended Oneida Institute in Whitesboro, New York, for 1-1/2 years and starting in 1841, attended the Kimbell Union Academy in Meridian, New Hampshire, for two years. He also attended Dartmouth College, where he was the only African American student. Washington used photography to pay his college expenses; however, in 1844 he quit college and moved to New Haven, Connecticut, where he became a teacher at the North African School, an African American school. In 1846, he opened his own studio in Hartford and later he moved to Liberia and prospered. He died in 1875.

21. Who was America's first African American woman artist to be recognized as a sculptor? Her works are notable examples of neoclassical sculpture. Her exact birth date is not clear—one account puts it in 1840 and another in 1845, but Lewis claimed she was born in 1854. Historians are not sure if she was born in New York, Ohio, or New Jersey. She had a brother whose name was Sunrise. Her father was African American and her mother was Chippewa Indian, and she was orphaned at an early age. She attended Oberlin College and changed her name from Wildfire to Mary Edmonia Lewis, but she signed her works Edmonia Lewis, and the "Mary" was dropped. While attending Oberlin College, she was accused of poisoning two White students and was beaten by a White mob. She was acquitted, but forced to leave the college, and she moved to Boston. The Story family were her patrons and encouraged her to pursue a career in sculpture. Some

Figure 45—Edmonia Lewis. Library of the Boston Athenaeum.

of her noted works include: *Bust of Colonel Robert Gould Shaw* (1864), *Hagar* (1869), *Hygieia* (1874), *Bust of John Brown* (1876), *Old Arrow Maker* (1872) and *Poor Cupid*.

22. In *Old Arrow Maker* by Edmonia Lewis, the Indian is making arrows, but what is his daughter making? After being educated in Boston, Lewis pursued her sculpturing career in Rome. While there, she created the sculpture *Cleopatra*, which she brought to the United States for a tour in 1870. *Cleopatra* became a gravestone for a horse at a racetrack, then a golf course, part of a munitions factory, and then part of a U.S. bulk mail services facility before it was discovered. In the 1980s the statue was found and restored, and is said to be at the National Museum of American Art. Other noted sculptures by Lewis included: *Forever Free* (1867; now at Howard University), *The Freed Woman and Her Child, The Marriage of Hiawatha* (c.1868), *Copy of Michelangelo's Moses, Young Octavian, Awake* (1874), *Asleep* (1874), *Henry Wadsworth Longfellow* (1869)

Figure 46—Edmonia Lewis's *Old Arrow Maker*, 1872. Marble, 21½ x 13-5/8 x 13-3/8 in., National Museum of American Art, Smithsonian Institution.

and *The Death of Cleopatra* (1875). The name of the sculpture *Forever Free* was taken from the language of the Emancipation Proclamation, issued by President Abraham Lincoln on January 1, 1863. This statue was dedicated to the abolitionist William Lloyd Garrison. The exact date and place of death for Lewis are unknown.

23. *Hagar* by Edmonia Lewis depicts the Egyptian maidservant of Sarah who struggled to survive what environment?

24. Who created a bust of Henry Wadsworth Longfellow for the Harvard University Library?

25. Who created a bust of Colonel Robert Gould Shaw, the commander of the African American 54th Massachusetts regiment during the Civil War?

26. Who was known for his painting of early California and Nevada towns? He was born on February 24, 1841, in Pennsylvania. His parents were free African Americans. He went to California in the 1850s and worked as an artist and lithographer in San Francisco. He also established a commercial drafting business. He later sold the business and moved to Canada, which was more racially tolerant. He died in 1918.

Figure 47—Edmonia Lewis's *Hagar*, 1875. Marble, 52-5/8 x 15¼ x 17 in., National Museum of American Art, Smithsonian Institution. Gift, Delta Sigma Theta Sorority.

27. Henry O. Tanner painted *The Banjo Lesson* while teaching at what university in Atlanta?

28. The noted painter Henry O. Tanner abandoned African American subject matter and left America in 1891 for what city, to concentrate on religious themes? With the exception of visits to his family in 1893 and 1896, Tanner did not return to the United States. He made a trip to North Africa in 1908 and to the Holy Land. His *Sand Dunes at Sunset, Atlantic City* is the first painting acquired for the art collection of the White House in Washington, D.C. The painting was acquired in 1996. His painting *The Resurrection of Lazarus* (1897) so impressed Rodman Wanamaker that he funded both of Tanner's trips to the Holy Land. The painting was later purchased by the French government for exhibition and became part of the art collection of the Louvre. Tanner painted *The Banjo*

Figure 48—Henry O. Tanner. Schomburg Center for Research in Black Culture, New York Public Library.

Lesson (1893; now in the Hampton Institute collection) while on a visit to the United States. In 1894, he painted *The Thankful Poor* (1894; now in the private collection of Bill Cosby). Tanner was also well-known for the paintings *Daniel in the Lion's Den* (1895) and *Two Disciples at the Tomb* (c. 1905). In 1923, Tanner received the Legion d'Honneur, France's highest civilian award. Tanner died in 1937 in Paris, France.

29.

Figure 49—Henry Ossawa Tanner's *Daniel in the Lion's Den*. Los Angeles County Museum of Art, Mr. & Mrs. William Preston Harrison Collection.

What award did Henry O. Tanner receive in 1895 for the painting *Daniel in the Lion's Den*? The painting was exhibited at the Paris Salon Exhibition of 1895

30. *The Two Disciples at the Tomb* by Henry O. Tanner was awarded what prize by the Art Institute of Chicago? The painting depicts the disciple John (far right) and the disciple Peter at the tomb of Christ on Easter Sunday, as they discover that Christ is no longer in the tomb. Both disciples have the look of amazement and there is a reflection lighting John's face. A sense of spirituality was conveyed by the light illuminating from the tomb. The event is covered in the four gospels, Matthew, Mark, Luke and John. Henry O. Tanner created the painting about 1905. The Art Institute of Chicago purchased the painting in 1906. This painting is considered an exceptional painting by Henry O. Tanner.

Figure 50—Henry Ossawa Tanner (1859–1937), *The Two Disciples at the Tomb*. Oil on canvas, 129.5 x 105.7 cm, Robert A. Waller Fund, 1906.300 © 1992, The Art Institute of Chicago. All Rights Reserved.

31.

Figure 51—Henry Ossawa Tanner's *Lions in the Desert*, c.1897–1900. Oil on plywood, National Museum of American Art, Smithsonian Institution. Gift of Mr. and Mrs. Norman B. Robbins.

The setting for Henry O. Tanner's *Lions in the Desert* is probably the area around what city?

32.

Figure 52—Henry Ossawa Tanner's *Annunciation*, 1898. Oil on canvas, Philadelphia Museum of Art, W.P. Wilstach Collection.

The Annunciation by Henry O. Tanner was the first work by Tanner to become what type of acquisition by an American museum?

33.

Figure 53—Henry Ossawa Tanner's *Flight into Egypt*, c.1899. Oil on canvas, 19-3/4 x 25 in. © The Detroit Institute of Arts, Founders Society Purchase, African Art Gallery Committee Fund.

The two favored themes of Henry O. Tanner were the Good Shepherd and what event?

34.

Figure 54—Henry O. Tanner's *Nicodemus*, 1899. Oil on canvas. Courtesy of the Pennsylvania Academy of the Fine Arts, Philadelphia, Joseph E. Temple Fund.

What award did the painting *Nicodemus* by Henry O. Tanner receive?

35.

Figure 55—Henry Ossawa Tanner's *Abraham's Oak*, 1905. Oil on canvas, 21-5/8 x 28-5/8 in. National Museum of American Art, Smithsonian Institution. Gift of Mr. and Mrs. Norman Robbins.

The influence of what school of painting is evident in Henry O. Tanner's *Abraham's Oak*?

36. Whom did Henry O. Tanner use as a model for Mary in the painting *Christ and His Mother Studying the Scriptures*? In 1899, Tanner married Jessie Olssen, an American White opera singer from San Francisco, California, whom he had met in Paris. Both families approved the marriage. Their only child was born in New York in 1903. After settling in Paris, Tanner divided his time between a farm near Etaples, Normandy and Paris. In 1900, Tanner's *Daniel an the Lion's Den* also received a silver medal at the Universal Exposition in Paris. And the next year, the painting received a silver medal at the Pan American Exhibition held in Buffalo, New York. He was the first African American elected a full member of the National Academy of Design. His son's name was Jesse. Jesse was the model for Jesus and Jessie was the model for Mary. During World War I, Tanner worked for the American Red Cross and painted African American soldiers.

Figure 56—Henry Ossawa Tanner's *Christ and His Mother Studying the Scriptures*, c.1909. Oil on canvas. Dallas Museum of Art, Deaccession Funds © Dallas Museum of Art. All Rights Reserved.

37.

Figure 57—Henry Ossawa Tanner's *Sunlight, Tangiers*, c.1910. Oil on cardboard. Milwaukee Art Museum. Gift of Mr. Walter I. Frank, P. Richard Eells Photography.

Henry O. Tanner painted *Sunlight, Tangiers* on his visit to what country?

38.

Figure 58—Henry Ossawa Tanner's *The Disciples on the Sea*, c.1910. Oil on canvas. Toledo Museum of Art. Gift of Frank W. Gunsaulus.

Henry O. Tanner's *The Disciples on the Sea* shows the influence of his father, Benjamin T. Tanner. What was his father's occupation?

39.

Figure 59—Henry Ossawa Tanner's *The Good Shepherd*, c.1914. Oil on canvas, 20-1/8" x 24-1/8". New Orleans Museum of Art, Museum Purchase.

How many versions of Henry O. Tanner's *The Good Shepherd* are there?

40.   Completed in 1917, Henry O. Tanner's *Portrait of Booker T. Washington* was considered what type of tribute to Washington? Booker T. Washington died in 1915 in Tuskegee, Alabama. At the time of his death, White Americans considered Washington the leader of African Americans, and presidents consulted with him on federal appointments of African Americans. Some African Americans such as W.E.B. Du Bois did not agree with Washington's position that African Americans should ignore the right to vote and concentrate on obtaining a skill. In 1899, Booker T. Washington traveled to Paris and met Henry O. Tanner. After the meeting, Washington wrote an article that helped establish Tanner as a talented artist in America in such cities as New York, Chicago, Boston, Philadelphia, Washington, and other major cities. The painting was a tribute to him.

Figure 60—*Portrait of Booker T. Washington* by Henry O. Tanner, photo. Courtesy State Historical Society of Iowa.

41. The painting *The Good Shepherd* (1920) is probably based on what Bible passage?

42. Who was a protégé of Henry O. Tanner, whose works some consider superior to Henry O. Tanner?

Figure 61—Henry Ossawa Tanner's *The Good Shepherd*, 1920. Oil on canvas. Collection of the Newark Museum. Gift of Mr. and Mrs. Henry H. Wehrhane, 1929 © The Newark Museum.

43. What famous African American sculptor was also a noted ceramicist? He was born on April 4, 1874, in Lexington, Kentucky. His mother died when he was two years old. At age 9, when he was touring a museum with his father, he asked why there were no busts of his hero Frederick Douglass in the museum? His father told him there were no trained Negro sculptors to make the busts. Hathaway said he would make busts of famous African Americans and put them where people could see them. He died on March 12, 1967.

44. Some of what African American's works include sculptures of Frederick Douglass, Booker T. Washington, Paul Dunbar, the Booker T. Washington commemorative coin and the George Washington Carver commemorative coin? This artist taught ceramics at Tuskegee Institute from 1937 to 1947.

45. Although the painting *Langston Hughes* denotes the talent of Winold Reiss, what is the title of the book Reiss authored with Frank B. Liberman? Reiss was born in Germany in 1886 and left Munich for New York City in 1913. He encouraged Aaron Douglas to paint murals and themes about African American culture. Some of his works included *Harlem at Night* (1924), *Harlem Girl* (c.1925), *Floyd Middle Rider* (1948), and *Nobody Has Pity on Me or Burton Bearchild* (1948). He painted portraits of American Indians in Montana in 1919, and painted Mexican peasants. His goal was to paint or record people who were not European. When the Great Northern Railroad hired him, he returned to Montana, set up a studio at a Glacier National Park hotel, and painted Indians, getting paid for something he had always wanted to do. He died in 1953.

Figure 62—*Langston Hughes* by Winold Reiss, c.1925. Pastel on artist board, 30-1/16 x 21-5/8 in. National Portrait Gallery, Smithsonian Institution, Washington, D.C., Art Resource.

46. Who began drawing at age 83 and first exhibited his work six years later? He was born a slave in 1856 near Benton, Alabama. In 1939, he was homeless and no one knows why he started to draw, as there were no artistic aspirations in his background. Charles

Shannon, a local artist in Montgomery, Alabama, saw his work, became his friend, and encouraged him to draw. Charles was impressed with his knowledge of geometric figures and his drawings.

47.

Figure 63—Bill Traylor's *Pig with Corkscrew Tail*, c.1939–1942. Tempera and pencil on paperboard, 12 x 18 in., National Museum of Art, Smithsonian Institution. Gift of Chuck and Jan Rosenak.

Bill Traylor's *Pig with Corkscrew Tail* illustrates which abstract view?

48. The sculpture entitled *Water Boy* is made of what substance? The artist, Meta Vaux Warrick Fuller, was born in 1877 in Philadelphia, Pennsylvania. She grew up in Philadelphia and received a scholarship to study at the Pennsylvania School of Industrial Art. Afterwards, she studied art in Paris, France and eventually she became a prolific sculptor. In 1899, while in Paris, she met Henry O. Tanner and August Saint-Gaudens. In 1900 at the Paris Exposition, she met W.E.B. Du Bois, who encouraged her to sculpt African Americans. She was asked to help repair a diorama from Washington, D.C. Colored High School, sent to Paris for the exposition. This diorama traced the history of African American education since the Civil War. She accepted a federal commission to create a diorama of the history of African Americans

Figure 64—Meta Vaux Warrick Fuller's *Water Boy*. Courtesy of National Archives.

from 1619 to the 1900s for the Jamestown Tercentennial (1907). *Water Boy*, produced in 1910, shows a young African American boy struggling to carry a heavy jug of water.

49. Who is noted for the sculptures *Richard B. Harrison* (circa 1935), *The Wretched* (1903). and *The Talking Skill* (1937)? While studying art in Paris, Fuller was tutored by Auguste Rodin. After her return from Paris, 16 years of her work was lost in a warehouse fire. Undaunted, Fuller became one of the most prolific sculptors in America. In 1913, she sculpted the *Emancipation Group* to celebrate the 50th anniversary of the Emancipation Proclamation. The following year, she created her famous bronze sculpture *Ethiopia Awakening*, of an ancient Egyptian queen awakening from a mummy cocoon, representing the African American awakening from bondage into life without fear.

Figure 65—Meta Vaux Warrick Fuller. Schomburg Center for Research in Black Culture, New York Public Library.

50. *The Awakening of Ethiopia* by Meta Vaux Warrick Fuller was created for what event?

51. Who was a master Harlem Renaissance printmaker?

52. Who was an outstanding wood carver from Columbus, Ohio? He was born in Mississippi on March 5, 1892. At about age 7, he began carving after his father gave him a pocket knife. He became a barber in Baldwyn, Mississippi and continued carving. He married Zetta Palm and lived in Baldwyn. About a year later, his son Willie was born, but Zetta died shortly afterwards, and Pierce moved to Danville, Illinois, where he met Cornelia Houeston from Columbus, Ohio. When Cornelia returned to Columbus, Pierce missed her and traveled to Columbus. They were later married. Pierce became a barber and resumed his carving In 1982, Pierce was awarded a National Heritage Fellowship by the National Endowment of the Arts. He died on May 7, 1984.

Figure 66—*The Awakening of Ethiopia* by Meta Vaux Warrick Fuller, c.1914. Schomburg Center for Research in Black Culture, New York Public Library. Photograph by Lee White.

53. What painter from Hartford, Connecticut was known for his paintings of fruit and flowers, and had the patronage of Mark Twain (Samuel Clemens)?

54. What painter is noted for his *John Henry* series of paintings? He was born Peyton Cole Hedgeman on January 15, 1890 in Widewater, Virginia. The *John Henry* series consisted of twelve paintings. It took the artist ten years to complete the paintings, from 1944 through 1954.

55. Palmer Hayden is well-known for his painting *The Janitor Who Paints*. What was his occupation when he won the Harmon Foundation Award in 1926 for his painting of the Portland, Maine water-front? According to the artist, this painting is not an autobiographical painting, but rather a tribute to a friend Cloyd L. Boykin. No one ever called Cloyd a painter, only a janitor. The painter in *The Janitor who Paints* is right-handed, whereas Hayden is left-handed. Hayden died on February 18, 1973.

Figure 67—Palmer Hayden's *The Janitor Who Paints*, c.1937. Oil on canvas, 39-1/8 x 32-7/8 in. National Museum of American Art, Smithsonian Institution. Gift of the Harmon Foundation.

56. Who was the first African American sculptor to gain acceptance into the National Association of Women Printers and Sculptors? She was born in 1892, in Green Cove Springs, Florida. Her father was a minister and did not support her artistic ambitions, but she was motivated to pursue sculpture after winning an award at a county fair in West Palm Beach, Florida. In the early 1920s, she married James Savage. She moved to New York City, where she studied sculpture at Cooper Union, in 1921. In 1923, Savage was involved in a scandal with the French government, which had invited 100 American women to study art in Paris; she was refused because of her race. Savage publicized the incident and was invited to study in Paris by Herman Atkins McNeil, a member of the selection committee.

57. What award did Augusta Savage receive for the sculpture *Gamin*, of a young boy of Harlem, which made it possible for her to study in France? The artist used her nephew as a model for the sculpture *Gamin*. In Harlem, she became successful as an artist and teacher. Most of her sculptures reflected some aspect of African American culture. Savage studied in Paris, France from 1929 through 1931. The Great Depression brought art sales to a virtual halt. Upon her return to New York City, Savage opened her own art school in Harlem. In 1937, she became the director of the Harlem Community Art Center. In the late 1930s, she was commissioned to create the sculpture *Lift Every Voice and Sing*. Unfortunately, this piece was lost or destroyed. Savage died in 1962.

Figure 68—*Gamin* by Augusta Savage, c.1930. Painted plaster, 9 x 5-5/8 x 4¼ in. National Museum of American Art, Smithsonian Institution. Gift of Olya and Ben Margolin.

58. In 1939, whose symbolic sculpture piece *Lift Every Voice and Sing* was shown at the New York World's Fair Community Arts Building?

59. Who developed a series of mural panels entitled *The Art of the Negro*, for Atlanta University?

60. Who was commissioned in 1939 by Talladega College to create *The Amistad Murals*, an episodic depiction of a slave revolt?

Figure 69—Augusta Savage.
Courtesy of National Archives.

61. Who teamed up with Charles Alston to work on the Golden State Mutual Life Insurance Company murals in California, which presented the contribution of African Americans to the history and development of California?

62.

Figure 70—Hale Aspacio Woodruff's *Georgia Landscape*, c.1934–1935. Oil on canvas, 21-1/8 x 25-5/8 in. National Museum of American Art, Smithsonian Institution. Gift of Alfred T. Morris. Jr.

Although Hale Woodruff's *Georgia Landscape* shows his talent, many of his works exhibit what painting style?

63. As shown in his *Poor Man's Cotton*, Hale Woodruff was widely known as what type of painter? Woodruff was born in 1900 in Cairo, Illinois and lived in Nashville where he was a cartoonist for his school paper. In 1923, at Herron Art Institute, a friend gave him Carl Einstein's book *Afrikaniche Plastik (African Sculpture)*, leading him to study African art. A Harmon Foundation Award and the sale of his works allowed him to study in Europe (*Card Players* [1928–1929] is influenced by Picasso and Cézanne). In 1931 he came to the U.S. to teach at Clark Atlanta University, started an exhibition of African American art, and painted murals at Talladega College and Clark Atlanta University. He worked for New York University 1946–1968 and died in 1980.

Figure 71—Hale A. Woodruff's *Poor Man's Cotton*, 1944. Collection of the Newark Museum, Purchase 1944, Sophronia Anderson Bequest Fund. Photograph © The Newark Museum.

64. What painter was gratified by candid depictions of African Americans? One of his paintings is entitled *Black Belt*. He was born in 1891 in New Orleans, studied at the Art Institute of Chicago from 1914–1918, and was known for the various skin tones of African Americans in his paintings. He used light in his paintings, and some of his subjects appeared to be in a hurry.

65. In Sargent Johnson's *Forever Free* (1933), a weary mother cradles her children to give them strength and support for their battle in what existence? Johnson was born in 1877 in Boston, of Swedish and African American/Cherokee Indian parents. His aunt, sculptress May Howard Jackson, had a profound effect on Johnson. Johnson moved to San Francisco in 1915, married Pearl Lawson, and gained notoriety from the San Francisco Art Association exhibition in 1925. He received awards for *Pearl* (1933), *Chester* (1935), and *Forever Free* (1938). In 1940, Johnson worked for the Federal Arts Project, and in 1942 he completed a large frieze in San Francisco. In 1944 and 1949, he received the Abraham Rosenberg Scholarship, and traveled to study African art from 1944 through 1965. He died on October 10, 1967.

Figure 72—Sargent Johnson's *Forever Free*. Lacquered cloth over wood, 36 x 11½ x 9½ in. San Francisco Museum of Modern Art. Gift of Mrs. E.D. Lederman, 52.4695.

66. Who is the author of the classic *Modern Negro Art* (1943), the first comprehensive history of African American art? This educator, painter, and historian, put African American art in the category of American art history and is referred to as the "father of African American art history."

67. *Colonial Soldier* shows the skill of James Porter as a painter, but in what other field of art was he known? He grew up in Washington, D.C., graduated from Howard University, and earned a master's degree in history of art at New York University in 1937. Porter is noted for his portraits of well-known African Americans. After World War II, he received Rockefeller grants to study African American art in other countries. He died in 1970.

Figure 73—James A. Porter's *Colonial Soldier*, 1937. Oil on canvas, 18¼ x 14-1/8 in. (46.3 x 35.8 cm.). National Museum of American Art, Smithsonian Institution. Museum Purchase.

68. What African American from Nashville, born c.1874, was a prolific sculptor in limestone? Some regard his work as primitive. In 1931 he was a stonemason's helper. Sidney Hirsch brought his works to the Board of the Museum of Modern Art. In the 1930s, *Harper's Bazaar* could not print a story about him because he was African American. Edmondson died in 1951.

69.

Figure 74—Horace Pippin's *Domino Players*, 1943. Oil on composition board, 12-3/4 x 22 in. The Phillips Collection, Washington, D.C.

Horace Pippin received the Croix de Guerre, the highest French honor, during World War I. His painting entitled *Domino Players*, illustrates that he is what type of painter?

70. *Brothers* is an example of Malvin Gray Johnson's work as an artist. What characteristic is associated with him?

71. Who photographed subjects so her husband, Edwin Harleston (1882–1931), could work from them to create portraits? She was born in 1891, became a photographer, and with her husband Edwin, opened a studio in Charleston, South Carolina. The studio featured her photographs and Edwin's paintings. Edwin joined the NAACP and later became the president of the Charleston branch. He also assisted Aaron Douglas in the painting of the mural at Fisk University, which depicts Black history. Elise Forrest Harleston died in 1970.

Figure 75—Malvin Gray Johnson's *Brothers*. Oil on canvas, 38 x 30-1/8 in. National Museum of American Art, Smithsonian Institution. Gift of the Harmon Foundation.

72.

Figure 76—Allan Rohan Crite's *Shadow and Sunlight*, 1941. Oil on board, 25¼ x 39 in. (64.2 x 99.1 cm.). National Museum of American Art, Smithsonian Institution.

Although *Shadow and Sunlight* by Allan Rohan Crite, is an excellent example of his work, what type of events is he known for painting?

73. One of what painter's works is entitled *Southern Gate* (1942–1943)? He was born January 10, 1916, in Richmond, Virginia. His parents were Ophelia and John Cortor. He took art classes at the Art Institute of Chicago.

74. One of William H. Johnson's early paintings, *Self-Portrait*, illustrates the influence of his teacher, Charles W. Hawthorne, at what art institution? He was born in Florence, South Carolina in 1901. His father was Caucasian and did not support Johnson or his mother. After winning the Harmon Award, Johnson studied painting in Europe. While there, he met Holca Krake, whom he married in 1930; she died of cancer in 1943. From 1946 until his death in 1970, Johnson was in a mental institution. In 1956, the Harmon Foundation acquired all of Johnson's works, but in 1967, the Foundation closed its doors and transferred the artwork to the National Museum of American Art, which later became the Smithsonian American Art Museum, but Johnson did not receive recognition for his work until after his death. Some of Johnson's paintings include: *Girl in a Red Dress* (c.1936), *Chain Gang*, *Flowers*, *Ferry Boat Trip*, and *Street Life—Harlem*.

Figure 77—William H. Johnson's *Self-Portrait*, c.1923–1926. Oil on canvas, 29-3/4 x 23-3/4 in. National Museum of American Art, Smithsonian Institution. Gift of the Harmon Foundation.

75. What approach does William H. Johnson use to portray *Man in a Vest*? Johnson began painting in a style referred to as primitive. This style is characterized by the use of bright and contrasting colors with two-dimensional figures and shapes. In 1938, Johnson and his wife moved to New York City, and traveled back and forth to Europe to visit relatives. After his wife's death in 1944, Johnson turned to religious themes, such as *David and Goliath* (1944), *Lamentations* (1944), and *Swing Low Sweet Chariot* (1944). In 1945, he painted a "Fighters of Freedom" series, which included Frederick Douglass, John Brown, Abraham Lincoln, and George Washington Carver. He also did a "Woman Builders" series, which included Harriet Tubman, Mary McCleod Bethune, and Jane Edna Hunter. Other paintings by Johnson include: *Mom and Dad*, *Booker T. Washington, Moon over Harlem*, *Café, Still Life, Portrait of a Boy, I Baptise Thee*, and *Jacobia Hotel*.

Figure 78—William H. Johnson's *Man in a Vest*, c.1938. Oil on burlap, 30 x 24 in. National Museum of American Art, Smithsonian Institution. Gift of the Harmon Foundation.

76.

Figure 79—William H. Johnson's *Going to Church*, c.1940–1941. Oil on burlap, 38-1/8 x 45½ in. National Museum of American Art, Smithsonian Institution. Gift of the Harmon Foundation.

In William H. Johnson's *Going to Church*, what is the dominating characteristic?

77. William H. Johnson, creator of *Swing Low Sweet Chariot* (c.1944), was inspired by what form of African American culture? Some of Johnson's works were lost in a fire that destroyed most of his possessions. The paintings stand out for their use of contrasting colors. Johnson was at one time a landscape painter, and was considered an expressionist painter. Other paintings by Johnson included: *Mom Alice, Doug, Abraham Lincoln* (c.1945), *Adam and Eve* (c.1944), *African Woman—Study in Tunis* (1932), *Ahlgaarden* (1933), and *A View Down Akersgate, Oslo* (c.1935). Johnson died April 13, 1970.

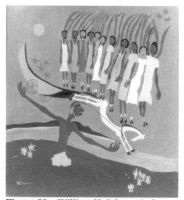

Figure 80—William H. Johnson's *Swing Low Sweet Chariot*, c.1944. Oil on paperboard, 28-5/8 x 26½ in. (72.6 x 67.2 cm.). National Museum of American Art, Smithsonian Institution, 1983.95.52.

78.

Figure 81—William H. Johnson's *Lamentation (or) Descent From the Cross*, c.1944. Oil on fiberboard. National Museum of American Art, Smithsonian Institution. Gift of the Harmon Foundation.

William H. Johnson's *Lamentation (or) Descent From the Cross* is based on the death of Christ and the lamenting by whom?

79. Laura Wheeler Waring, known for such portraits as the *Portrait of Alma Thomas*, shows what distinctive type of influence? (Alma Thomas was a noted African American painter) Waring was born in Hartford, Connecticut in 1887. Her parents were Mary and Reverend Robert Wheeler. While directing the music and art department at Cheyney State College, she met her husband, Walter E. Waring, who was from Lincoln University (Pennsylvania). While at Cheyney, she made several trips to Europe, to further her education and to exhibit her works. Waring is known for her painting of famous African Americans, but because she avoided publicity, not much is known about her.

Figure 82—Laura Wheeler Waring's *Portrait of Alma Thomas*, c.1945. Oil on canvas, 30 x 25-1/8 in. National Museum of American Art, Smithsonian Institution.

80.

Figure 83—Lois Mailou Jones's *Jardin Du Luxembourg*, c.1948. Oil on canvas. National Museum of American Art, Smithsonian Institution. Gift of Gladys P. Payne in honor of Alice P. Moore.

What artist has a distinctive style which is evident in *Jardin Du Luxembourg*, a style influenced by Paul Cézanne (1839–1906)?

81. Who became noted for his painting entitled *The Brown Bomber*, depicting the boxing victory of Joe Louis over Max Schmeling?

82. What African American painter is called the "father of African American art"? He was born in Kansas and was influenced by Henry Tanner. He studied fine arts, graduated from Teachers College of Columbia University, and painted the mural at Fisk University. Douglas and his wife met Henry O. Tanner in Paris. He settled in New York City, became president of the Harlem Artist Guild, and worked with the Works Progress Association (WPA).

83. A notable work of what African American artist is entitled *Murals in the Cullen Branch of the New York City Public Library*?

Figure 84—Aaron Douglas. Fisk University Library's Special Collections.

84. A notable painting by what artist is entitled *Illustrations in Books by Cullen*?

85. Who painted the murals at the Fisk University Library depicting the history of African Americans?

86. *Sojourner Truth and Booker T. Washington*, by Charles White, illustrates what about the artist? White was born on April 2, 1918 in Chicago, Illinois. At age 7, he knew he could draw. He attended the Art Institute of Chicago and later taught at the South Side Community Art Center of Chicago from 1939 to 1941. In 1941, he married Elizabeth Catlett. In 1944, he established the Committee for the Negro in Arts in New York City and he taught at the Otis Art Institute in Los Angeles, California from 1965 until 1979. He was the second African American to be elected a full member of the National Academy of Design. Some of his works include: *Frederick Douglass* (1951), *Goodnight Irene* (1952), *Awaken from Unknowing* (1961), *Homage to Langston Hughes* (1971), and *John Henry* (1975). White is known for historical African American figures and paintings depicting the African American community. He died in 1971.

Figure 85—Charles W. White's *Sojourner Truth and Booker T. Washington*, 1943. Collection of the Newark Museum. Purchase 1944 Sophornia Anderson Bequest Fund. Photograph © The Newark Museum.

87. Richmond Barthé's first love was painting, but his fame came from what type of artwork?

88. Whose bust of Henry O. Tanner and Pierre Dominique Toussaint-L'Ouverture brought him fame?

89. Whose works include 60 panels entitled *The Negro Migration Northward in World War* (1941)? This artist was the 1970 Spingarn Medal recipient (the Spingarn Medal award is presented annually by the National Association for the Advancement of Colored People to an African American for outstanding achievement). He was born in Atlantic City, New Jersey in 1917. Later his family moved to Easton, Pennsylvania. He moved to New York City after his parents separated. Some of his noted works include: *Pool Parlor* (1942), *The Street* (1957), *Café Comedian* (1957), *Street to Mbari* (1964), *Toussaint L'Ouverture* (1937–38), *Frederick Douglass* (1938–1939), *Harriet Tubman* (1939–1940), *The Migration of the Negro* (1941–1941), *John Brown* (1941–1942), *The Library* (1960), *Over the Line* (1967),

Figure 86—*Richmond Barthé* by Betsy Graves Reyneau (1888–1964), 1946. Oil on canvas, 62½ x 34½ in. National Portrait Gallery, Smithsonian Institution, Washington, D.C.

The Pool Game (1970), and *Builders* (1980). This series of paintings told the story of many African Americans migrating from the rural South to the cities of the North around the time of World War I. He died on June 9, 2000.

90. What are the African Americans in *The Migration of the Negro, Panel No. 59* doing? The series consisted of 60 panels. Lawrence's narrative for *The Migration of the Negro, Panel No. 59* was as follows: "In the North the African American had freedom to vote."

91. Whose works include 40 panels entitled *The Life of Harriet Tubman* (1940)? He considered himself an artist as well as an educator. *The Life of Harriet Tubman* panels depict the life of Harriet Tubman in her quest to lead slaves to freedom via the Underground Railroad. The narrative for *The Life of Harriet Tubman, Panel 4* was as follows: "On a hot summer day about 1820, a group of slave children were tumbling in the sandy soil in the state of Maryland—and among them was one, Harriet Tubman, Dorchester County, Maryland." Lawrence researched each series thoroughly before he started on the paintings. He also selected the colors and the narratives to tell the story for the entire series before he started the work.

Figure 87—Jacob Lawrence's *The Migration of the Negro, Panel No. 59*, 1940–1941. 11½ x 17½ in. The Phillips Collection, Washington, D.C.

92. Whose works include 41 panels entitled *The Life of Toussaint-L'Ouverture* (1937)? Lawrence was inspired by his teacher, Charles Seifert, who taught African American history at the 135th Street public library. As a result of Seifert's lectures, Lawrence became very interested in the historical struggle of the African American people. His paintings tell a story of a particular struggle, life, event, or dignity. He was 21 years old when he completed the panels depicting the successful rebellion of Haitian slaves. In 1941 he married Gwendolyn Knight and in 1970 they moved to Seattle, Washington, where Lawrence became an art professor at the University of Washington. Lawrence's narrative for *The Life of Toussaint L'Ouverture, Panel No. 21* was as follows: "statesman and military genius, esteemed by the Spaniards, feared by the English, dreaded by the French, hated by the planters, and revered by the Blacks." Lawrence also had a George Washington Bush series.

Figure 88—Jacob Lawrence. Schomburg Center for Research in Black Culture, New York Public Library.

93.

Figure 89—Jacob Lawrence's *The Library*, 1960. Tempera on fiberboard, 24 x 29-7/8 in. (60.9 x 75.8 cm.). National Museum of American Art, Smithsonian Institution. Gift of S.D. Johnson & Son, Inc.

The Library by Jacob Lawrence, as well as many of his other paintings, depicts events in the lives of whom?

94. Whose murals depicting the history of medicine adorn the facade of Harlem Hospital in New York City?

95. The murals of what painter have established his reputation and ensured his fame as an African American artist of importance?

96. In *Family*, by Charles H. Alston, the subjects have a sense of what type of worthiness? He was born on November 28, 1907, in Charlotte, North Carolina. His father, Henry Alston, was an Episcopal minister and died when Charles was 3 years old. In 1914, his mother moved to New York City. He received his bachelor's and master's degree from Columbia University and became the first African American supervisor in the Works Progress Administration (WPA) directing New York's Federal Arts Project. He directed the artist who painted the murals in the Harlem Hospital. His best-known paintings were *The Family* and *Walking at the Whitney Museum*. He died on April 27, 1977.

Figure 90—Charles H. Alston's *Family*, 1955. Oil on canvas. Collection of Whitney Museum of American Art, New York. Purchased with funds from the Artists and Students Assistance Fund.

97.

Figure 91—Romare Bearden's *After Church*. Courtesy of National Archives.

Although *After Church* by Romare Bearden illustrates his talent, what type of style is associated with him?

98. Who is one of the best-known African American collagists in the world? He was born in Charlotte, North Carolina in 1911. His family moved to Pittsburgh and then to Harlem in New York City, and he graduated from New York University. He served in the Army from 1942–1945 and in 1954 he married Nanette Rohan. Some of his works include: *Mysteries* (1964), *The Street* (1964), and *The Return of the Prodigal Son* (1967). Bearden died in 1988.

99. The American flag is a recurring theme in what African American's early works?

Figure 92—Romare Bearden. Reproduced from the Collections of the Library of Congress.

100. Who painted the portraits of Louis Armstrong, Ethel Waters, and Duke Ellington, and gained national recognition when *Life* magazine did an article on him in 1938? He was born in Knoxville, Tennessee in 1901. He met and painted many noted African Americans during the Harlem Renaissance. Later, he moved to Paris, France and was known as the "dean of African American artists living in Europe." He died in Paris in 1979.

101. *Man of Sorrows* by Marion Perkins, displays a face that is in what condition?

102. Langston Hughes worked with what African American photographer to create the book *Sweet Flypaper of Life* (1955)?

103. Portraits and life in Harlem are the principal subjects of whose photographs?

104. What African American photographer gained notoriety as a photographer for *Life* magazine, and received the 1972 Spingarn Medal Award?

105. One of what artist's works is entitled *Black Queen*?

Figure 93—Marion Perkins (1908–1961), *Man of Sorrows*, 1950. Grey marble. Pauline Palmer Purchase Prize, 1951.129 © 1992 Art Institute of Chicago.

106. Who painted the mural entitled *Negro Women in American Life and Education* on the Blue Triangle Branch of the Young Women's Christian Association (YWCA) in Houston, Texas?

107. Although *The Cradle* by John Biggers, illustrates his talent for African composition and design, he derived much of his subject matter from the contribution made by African Americans to the development of what country?

108. What African American artist is renowned for the portrayal of children in his paintings and illustrations?

109. What painter and sculptor created the prize-winning sculpture *Phoenix* (1965)?

Figure 94—John Thomas Biggers's *The Cradle*, c.1950. Museum of Fine Arts, Houston, 25th Annual Houston Artists Exhibition. Museum Purchase Prize, 1950.

110. Who is considered by many to be the foremost African American abstract artist?

111.

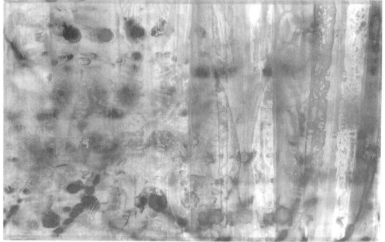

Figure 95—Sam Gilliam's *April 4*, 1969. Acrylic on canvas, 110 x 179-3/4 in. (179.4 x 256.0 cm.). National Museum of American Art, Smithsonian Institution.

What event is associated with Sam Gilliam's *April 4*?

112. What painter produces hanging canvases which are laced with pure color pigments?

113. What North Carolina painter's works, one of which is entitled *Visions of Angels*, were influenced by her dreams? She was born Minnie Eva Jones in 1892, in Long Creek, North Carolina and was raised by her grandmother. At 16, she met and married Julius Caesar Evans, who was 19, but she claimed she was 18 on the marriage license. Evans began drawing when she was about 43. Nina Howells Star discovered her and organized her exhibits from 1962–1984. Evans died in 1987.

114. What was used to create the painting *The Eclipse, March 1970* by Alma Thomas, as well as many of her other works?

115. What African American photographer specialized in portraits and landscapes?

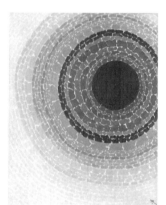

116. Some subjects of what noted painter and engraver show the effects of their struggle with erosion? She was born in New Haven, Connecticut in 1928 and studied art at the Whitney School of Fine Arts in New York City.

Figure 96—Alma Woodsey Thomas's *The Eclipse, March 1970*, 1970. Acrylic on canvas, 62 x 49-3/4 in. (57.5 x 126.5 cm.). National Museum of American Art, Smithsonian Institution. Gift of Alma W. Thomas.

117. The Center for Research in Black Culture in New York City is named in honor of what individual? He was born in 1874 in Puerto Rico. His parents were a German-born merchant and an African American midwife from the Virgin Islands. He came to New York City in 1891, worked various jobs, and attended night school. He joined a Mason group founded by Puerto Rican and Cuban expatriates, became master of the lodge, and renamed the lodge in honor of Prince Hall, the first African American Mason. He collected material related to Black history, met John Edward Bruce in 1911, and joined Bruce's Men's Sunday Club. He and Bruce established the Negro Society for Historical Research. He worked tirelessly to acquire

Figure 97—Arthur P. Schomburg. Schomburg Center for Research in Black Culture, New York Public Library.

works by people of African descent from all over the world. In 1914, he was president of the American Negro Academy and in 1922, curator at Fisk University and the New York Library. He met and formed friendships with noted African Americans such as W.E.B. Du Bois, Marcus Garvey, Charles Spurgeon Johnson, Alexander Crummell, Carter G. Woodson, Alain Locke and others. He died in 1938.

118.

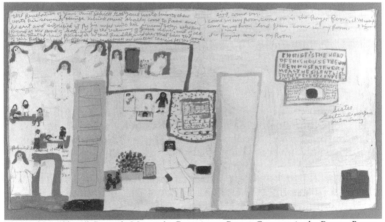

Figure 98—"Sister" Gertrude Morgan's *Come in my Room, Come on in the Prayer Room*, c.1970. Tempera, acrylic, ballpoint pen, pencil on paper. National Museum of American Art.

In *Come in my Room, Come on in the Prayer Room* by "Sister" Gertrude Morgan, what is included in this creation as well as many of her other creations?

119. *Alex Haley, Harriet Tubman, Malcolm X, A. Philip Randolph,* and *Marcus Garvey* are among works by what sculptor?

120. *Singing Head* by Elizabeth Catlett Mora exhibits what influence, which is evident in most of her works? Mora was born in 1915, in Washington, D.C. In 1937, she graduated from Howard University's School of Art with honors. In 1940, she earned her M.F.A. from the University of Iowa. In 1941, she studied ceramics at the Art Institute of Chicago, and taught at Dillard and Hampton universities. In 1942 and 1943, she studied lithography in New York and studied sculpture with Ossip Zadkine. In 1946, she received a Julius Rosenwald Fellowship and produced *I Am a Negro Woman*, a series of paintings, prints, and sculptures. In 1947 she married Francisco Mora and studied wood carving with José Ruiz in Mexico. In 1949, she became the first female teacher at the School of Fine Arts at the National Autonomous University of Mexico, and chaired the Department of Sculpture. She retired in 1976 and moved to Mexico,

Figure 99—Elizabeth Catlett Mora's *Singing Head*, 1980. Marble, 16 x 19½ x 12 in. National Museum of American Art, Smithsonian Institution, 1989.52.

where she continued to work. In 2005, Mora received the Legends and Legacy Award from the Art Institute of Chicago. Some of her works include: *I Have Reservations* (1946), *Sharecropper* (1957 cut into a linoleum block; printed 1970), *Negro Women* (c.1960), *Civil Rights Congress* (1949), *Dancing* (1966), *Bread* (1968), *Homage to My Young Black Sisters* (1968), *Malcolm X Speaks for Us* (1969), *Target* (1970), *Survivor* (1978), *Latch Key Child* (1988), *Three Women of America* (1990), *To Marry* (1992), *A Second Generation* (1992), *Blues Player* (1995), *Elvira* (1997), and *Black Girl* (2004).

121. Who founded the Howard University Art Department? He was born in Clio, South Carolina in 1887. He studied art at Syracuse University, Columbia University, and Harvard University. He was chair of the art department at Howard University from 1931–1952.

122. What Kentucky native painted African American scenes from daily life? He was born in 1899 in Mayfield, Kentucky. He attended Kentucky Normal and Industrial Institute (later Kentucky State University) and graduated from the Art Institute of Chicago in 1923. In 1944, he earned a Guggenheim Fellowship. His paintings include: *Funeral Procession* (c.1950s), *Lumberjacks* (1944–45), and *Two Women with Lanterns* (c.1950). *The Funeral Procession* was displayed on the set of "The Cosby Show" during the 1980s.

123. Which Smithsonian museums are noted for African American culture?

124. What African American museum is located in Dallas, Texas?

Answers — 2 — Art

1. Scipio Moorhead (c.1773)

2. José Campeche (1751–1809)

3. Joshua Johnston (1765–1830)

4. African Americans

5. Pio Casimiro Bacener (1840–1900)

6. "The Birds of America"

7. Jules Lion (1810–1866)

8. Patrick Henry Reason (1817–1856)

9. Eugéne Warburg (1825–1859)

10. Eugéne Warburg (1825–1859)

11. Augustus Washington (1820–1875)

12. African Americans

13. Robert Scott Duncanson (1821–1872)

14. A Wilderness Oasis

15. Taft Museum of Art

16. The small size of the canvas

17. Edward M. Bannister (1828–1901)

18. Atmospheric

19. Indeterminable

20. Francis Grice (18?–18?)

21. Edmonia Lewis (1845–1911)

22. Moccasins

23. The wilderness

24. Edmonia Lewis (1845–1911)

25. Edmonia Lewis (1845–1911)

26. Grafton Tyler Brown (1841–1918)

27. Clark University

28. Paris, France

29. Salon Award, an honorable mention

30. Harris Prize

31. Jerusalem

32. Purchased

33. The flight of the Holy Family

34. Lippincott Prize, 1900

35. Impressionism

36. Photographs of his wife, Jessie M. Olssen Tanner, and son

37. Morocco

38. A bishop in the African Methodist Church

39. Many

40. A memorial; Booker T. Washington died in 1915.

41. Twenty-third Psalm

42. William Harper (1873–1910)

43. Isaac Hathaway (1874–1967)

44. Isaac Hathaway (1874–1967)

45. *Blackfeet Indians*

46.	Bill Traylor (1856–1947)	72.	Social
47.	Abstract view of a pig	73.	Eldzier Cortor (1916–)
48.	Bronze	74.	National Academy of Design
49.	Meta Warrick Fuller (1877–1968)	75.	Distortion
50.	The New York State Centennial	76.	Contrasting stripes
51.	Dox Thrash (1893–1965)	77.	The Negro spiritual
52.	Elijah Pierce (1892–1984)	78.	The Three Marys
53.	Charles Ethan Porter (1847–1923)	79.	Impressionistic
54.	Palmer C. Hayden (1890–1973)	80.	Lois Mailou Jones (1905–1998)
55.	Janitor	81.	Robert Riggs (1896–1970)
56.	Augusta Savage (1892–1962)	82.	Aaron Douglas (1898–1979)
57.	A scholarship from the Julius Rosenwald Fund	83.	Aaron Douglas (1898–1979)
		84.	Aaron Douglas (1898–1979)
58.	Augusta Savage (1892–1962)	85.	Aaron Douglas (1898–1979)
59.	Hale Woodruff (1900–1980)	86.	Forcefulness
60.	Hale Woodruff (1900–1980)	87.	Sculptures
61.	Hale Woodruff (1900–1980)	88.	Richmond Barthé (1901–1989)
62.	Expressionism	89.	Jacob Lawrence (1917–2000)
63.	Mural painter	90.	Voting
64.	Archibald Motley (1891–1981)	91.	Jacob Lawrence (1917–2000)
65.	Life	92.	Jacob Lawrence (1917–2000)
66.	James A. Porter (1905–1970)	93.	African Americans
67.	An art historian	94.	Charles Alston (1907–1977)
68.	William Edmondson (c.1874–1951)	95.	Charles Alston (1907–1977)
69.	Primitive	96.	Dignity
70.	Versatility	97.	Collagist
71.	Elise Forrest Harleston (1891–1970)	98.	Romare Bearden (1911–1988)
		99.	David Hammonds (1943–)

100. Beauford Delaney (1901–1979)

101. Unshaven

102. Roy DeCarava (1919–)

103. James Van Der Zee (1896–1983)

104. Gordon Parks (1912–)

105. Margaret Burroughs (1917–)

106. John Biggers (1924–2001)

107. United States

108. Ernest Crichlow (1914–)

109. Geraldine McCullough (1922–)

110. Ronald Joseph (1910–1992)

111. The death of Martin Luther King, Jr.

112. Sam Gilliam (1933–)

113. Minnie Evans (1892–1987)

114. A small paintbrush

115. Billie Louise Barbour Davis (1906–1955)

116. Norma Morgan (1928–)

117. The Schomburg Center for Research in Black Culture, New York Public Library, founded by Arthur P. Schomburg (1874–1938)

118. Her writings

119. Tina Allen (1955–)

120. An African

121. James V. Herring (1887–1969)

122. Ellis Wilson (1899–1977)

123. The Anacostia Museum and the National African American Museum

124. African American Museum

3 — Business and Professional Associations

1.   Who signed on in 1781, at 15 years of age, as a powder boy aboard the American ship *Royal Louis*, commanded by Steven Decatur, Sr.? He later became a wealthy African American in early America, deriving part of his wealth from a sail-making business?

2.   Some African Americans owned slaves prior to the Civil War. Marie Therese Moteyor, also referred to as Marie Therese Coincoin (1742–1816), owned slaves on the Yucca Plantation (Melrose) in what state?

3.   In 1810, who arrived in the Hawaiian Kingdom from Schenectady, New York, and received a land grant from the kingdom? He later opened a bowling alley, bar room, and boarding house, and established a place for the recuperation of seasick individuals. He also maintained a farm with cows, and was a blacksmith.

4.   Along with Samuel E. Cornish (1795–1858), who founded the first African American newspaper in 1827?

5.   What establishment in Milton, North Carolina, was the workshop of Tom Day (1801–1861), who was born of free parents, and was one of the great African American artisans and furniture makers of the Deep South prior to the Civil War?

6.   Who was the Haitian-born barber to Abraham Lincoln, and a real estate owner in Springfield, Illinois?

7.   Who was a well-known barber, builder, diarist, and businessman in Natchez, Mississippi prior to the Civil War?

8.   Who became president of the Capital City Savings Bank in Little Rock, Arkansas, and a partner in the Little Rock Electric Light Company?

9.   In 1850, who was the director of the Philadelphia Building and Loan Association, an early African American mortgage company?

10.   In 1854, who established a foundry near Ripley, Ohio, named the Ripley Foundry and Machine Company? His father was a wealthy White man and his mother a slave who worked very hard to purchase his freedom. He worked to free many slaves from bondage, independent of the church. The Ripley town mentioned in the novel *Uncle Tom's Cabin*, by Harriet Beecher Stowe, refers to this town and the assistance to slaves provided by the minister, John Rankin, and the businessman, John P. Parker. The Parker house, which is located in Ripley, Ohio has been restored and offers tours on the weekends.

11.

Figure 100—Barney L. Ford. Denver Public Library, Western History Department.

In 1863, who owned hotels in Denver, Colorado and Cheyenne, Wyoming?

12. What was the name of the African American bank established by Congress on March 3, 1865, to assist newly freed African Americans and African American soldiers?

13. Who was the owner of the Chesapeake Marine Railway and Dry Dock Company of Baltimore, which was established in 1868?

14. In 1870, the board of trustees of the Freedman's Bank, who were all White former abolitionists, changed the charter of the bank to allow speculation into what financial products?

15. In 1871, who was a well-known hotel owner in Washington, D.C.?

16. In 1872, Elijah McCoy developed the lubricating device that led to the mass production of what product?

17. After the board of trustees resigned, who became president of the Freedman's Bank in 1873? Despite his efforts, it was too late to save the bank, which closed on June 2, 1874.

18. In 1880, what former lieutenant-governor of Louisiana was president of the Cosmopolitan Life Insurance Company?

19. Prior to his election, what was the occupation of Joseph Rainey (1832–1887), the first African American from South Carolina elected to the U.S. House of Representatives?

20. Who is the founder of the *Afro-American Newspaper* in Baltimore, Maryland?

21. Who was the owner of the Berry Hotel in Athens, Ohio, which was established in 1893 and was the first hotel to put a Bible in every room? As a hotel owner, he also put a closet in every room in his hotel. He was also a trustee of Wilberforce University. He was born on December 10, in 1854, and died in 1931.

22. What is the name of the association of African American doctors established in 1895?

23. In 1897, who extracted $30,000 worth of gold from the Klondike gold fields and later left the state of Alaska?

24. What is the name of the oldest African American insurance company, which was organized in 1898, opened for business in 1899, and is noted for the triumvirate of Dr. Aaron McDuffie Moore (physician), John Merrick (barber), and Charles Clinton Spaulding (manager)?

25. Who was the first president of the North Carolina Mutual Life Insurance Company?

26. What organization was founded in 1900 by Booker T. Washington?

27. In 1901, who opened the Auto Transportation and Sales Company in New York City?

28. In 1903, what African American woman founded the successful Saint Luke Penny Savings Bank in Richmond, Virginia (which later became the Consolidated Bank and Trust), and became the first woman to establish and head a bank?

29. On November 5, 1903, who was one of the organizers of the One-Cent Savings Bank and Trust Company of Nashville (which became the Citizens Savings Bank and Trust Company in 1920), and also served as its first president? He was born a slave in 1855 in Texas and was given the family name of his owner. After the Civil War, he changed his name to Richard Henry Boyd and became a minister, and in 1896, he moved to Nashville to establish a publishing company for the Baptist church. Boyd was involved in the founding and growth of Bishop College, Roger Williams University and The Baptist Training in Nashville, Tennessee. He wrote numerous books and helped organize a Nashville newspaper.

Figure 101—Maggie Lena Walker. Courtesy of the Virginia Historical Society.

30. What well-known entrepreneur established the Atlanta Life Insurance Company on September 3, 1905?

31. What African American newspaper was founded in Chicago in 1905 by Robert S. Abbott (1870–1940)?

32. What African American architectural firm headquartered in Washington, D.C., was established in 1905, and is still in business today? Buildings designed and built by this company include the Carnegie Library at Fisk University in Nashville (1908), the Tennessee State University Memorial Library in Nashville (1927), the Universal Life Insurance Company Building in Memphis (1929), and the 99th Pursuit Squadron Air Base in Tuskegee, Alabama (1942).

Figure 102—Alonzo Herndon. Schomburg Center for Research in Black Culture, New York Public Library.

33. Who started selling her cosmetic products in 1905 in Denver, Colorado, opened an office in Pittsburgh in 1908, and in 1910 moved both offices to Indianapolis, Indiana, where a plant was constructed to manufacture her cosmetics?

34. Who established the Solvent Savings and Trust Company in Memphis in 1906, became the first millionaire in Memphis as a result of buying and selling real estate, and has a park on Beale Street named in his honor?

35. In Chicago, who was known as a realtor and owner of the Binga State Bank, which was established in 1908?

Figure 103—Madam C.J. Walker. Walker Collection of A'Lelia Perry Bundles.

36. Who founded the *Amsterdam News* of New York City on December 4, 1909?

37. Who became editor of the *Pittsburgh Courier* newspaper in 1910?

38. What organization was founded in New York City on September 29, 1910 to help African Americans moving from rural areas to find jobs and housing and adjust to urban life? This interracial organization maintains a chairman of the board who is White, and the chief executive who is Black.

39. What employee of the U.S. Department of Reclamation arrived on the island of Oahu in Hawaii in 1915, worked for the company Castle and Cook as the superintendent of the docks, and later helped organize the civil service system of the Hawaiian government?

40. In 1917, who founded Poro College for beauty culture in St. Louis, Missouri, and developed and manufactured several bath and toilet preparations?

41. In 1919, who founded the Liberty Life Insurance Company, located in Chicago, Illinois, which later became the Supreme Life Insurance Company of America?

42. Who was the first African American member of the Real Estate Board of New York City in the 1920s?

43. In addition to doctors and pharmacists, who were some of the principal financial backers of the old Negro professional baseball teams (1920–1948)?

Figure 104—Annie M. Turbo Malone. Missouri Historical Society.

44. In 1922, Carl Murphy became the editor of what newspaper?

45. Who was a well-known pharmacist in Toledo, Ohio, from 1922 to 1945?

46. What well-known practicing physician in Memphis, Tennessee founded Universal Life Insurance Company in 1923?

47. What is the name of the association of African American funeral directors established in 1924?

48. What is the name of the association of African American attorneys established in 1925?

49. In 1925, who organized the Douglass National Bank and the Victory Life Insurance Company in Chicago, Illinois, established the *Chicago Bee*, and was the recipient of the 1927 Spingarn Medal? He was born a slave in Monroe, Louisiana in 1865 and his family moved to Kansas, where he attended school and obtained a law degree from Washburn College in Topeka, Kansas. He later moved to Chicago. The

Figure 105—Dr. J.E. (Joseph Edison) Walker. Mississippi Valley Collection Libraries, University of Memphis, Memphis, Tennessee.

Chicago Bee was a successful newspaper. The Douglass National Bank became insolvent in 1932 during the Great Depression, and the board of directors of Victory Life Insurance Company voted to remove him as the president because he was also the owner of the Douglass National Bank. The ouster probably saved Victory Life Insurance Company from insolvency.

50.   In what year did Norman O. Houston, William Nickerson, Jr., and George A. Beaver found Golden State Mutual Life Insurance Company? Houston later served as the company's president.

51.   Who formulated Murray Hair Pomade and, along with his wife Lilli, founded Murray Cosmetics in 1926?

52.   In 1929, the Liberty Life Insurance Company of Chicago, Illinois, merged with the African American-owned Northeastern Life Insurance Company of Newark, New Jersey, and African American-owned Supreme Life and Casualty Company of Columbus, Ohio. This created a new company named the Supreme Liberty Life Insurance Company, located in Chicago. Who became the president of the new company?

Figure 106—Norman O. Houston. UCLA.

53.   Who first opened a hotel in 1929, and by the early 1950s had become one of the largest landowners in Anchorage, Alaska?

54.   Who became president of the Brotherhood of Sleeping Car Porters in 1929, later fought against racial discrimination in the defense industry and federal offices, and received the 1942 Spingarn Medal and the Presidential Medal of Freedom in 1964?

55.   Who was a well-known entrepreneur at the North Carolina Mutual Life Insurance Company? He was born on August 4, 1874, in Columbus County, North Carolina. He completed high school in Durham, North Carolina in 1898, and managed a grocery store in 1899. Later he worked part-time and then full-time for North Carolina Mutual and Provident Association. In 1919, when the company changed its name to North Carolina Mutual Life Insurance Company, he was promoted to treasurer of the company. In 1923, he became president of the company and held the position until his death in 1952. He also supported education for African Americans and served as trustee for Shaw University and Howard University.

Figure 107—Charles Clinton Spaulding. North Carolina Mutual Life Insurance Company.

56. What architect, who designed many homes in California including many for movie stars, was the recipient of the 1953 Spingarn Medal? He was born in 1894, exhibited a talent for drawing at an early age and later pursued architecture. After he graduated from the University of Southern California he joined a residential architectural firm, became a licensed architect in 1921, and started his own firm in 1922. Some of his commercial designs include Saks Fifth Avenue building, Beverly Hills; Golden State Mutual Life Insurance building; St. Jude Hospital in Memphis; First Methodist Church and Second Baptist Church, Los Angeles; and Palm Springs Tennis Club. He designed homes for movie stars, including Anthony Quinn, Zsa Zsa Gabor, Lucille Ball, Frank Sinatra, Lon Chaney, Desi Arnaz, and Zasu Pitts. He de-

Figure 108—Paul R. Williams. Courtesy, Bancroft Library, University of California, Berkley.

signed around 3,000 projects and wrote two books, *New Homes for Today* and *The Small Home of Tomorrow*. Williams died in 1980.

57. What architect was noted in the late 1920s and 1930s for his designs of the Philadelphia Museum of Art and Duke University? He was born in 1881 in Philadelphia, attended the Institute for Colored Youth and the Pennsylvania Museum and School of Industrial Art, and earned a B.S. from the University of Pennsylvania in 1902. He was the first African American to receive a degree in architecture at the University of Pennsylvania. He worked for the architectural firm Horace Trumbaur and Associates, became the chief designer at the firm, and worked on the design of the Widener Library at Harvard University and the Free Library of Philadelphia. He died in 1950.

58. Who organized the United Transport Service Employees, who were sometimes referred to as "redcaps," during the 1930s? He became president of the International Transport Service Employee Union.

59. What African American from Birmingham, Alabama, founded the Booker T. Washington Insurance Company (1932), the Booker T. Washington Business College (1939), and the Citizens Federal Savings and Loan Association (1957)?

60. Who founded the Fuller Products Company of Chicago, Illinois, which produced hair care products, cosmetics, and clothes, in 1935? He was born in Quachita Parish, Louisiana in 1905 and moved to Chicago in 1920. The

Figure 109—A.G. Gaston. Reproduced from the Collections of the Library of Congress.

Fuller products were sold door-to-door and were quite successful. The company also published two newspapers, the *Pittsburgh Courier* and the *New York Age*. After a speech in 1963 about African American self help, both the African American community and the White community boycotted his products in protest, and his company filed for bankruptcy in 1969. He died in 1988.

61.   Who founded Johnson Publishing Company in 1942 when the *Negro Digest* was first published? He was born in Arkansas City, Arkansas in 1918. He founded his own publishing business and launched *Ebony* magazine in 1945. His autobiography is entitled *Succeeding Against the Odds*, and he received the 1966 Spingarn Medal and the Presidential Medal of Freedom in 1996. He received the Black Journalists' Lifetime Achievement Award in 1987, and died in 2005.

62.   What successful African American magazine was established in 1945? This was the first magazine in the country to show all facets of African American life and used African American models to sell products. There were positive images of African Americans in business, entertainment, law, sports, science, literature and the military.

Figure 110—John H. Johnson. Chicago Historical Society.

63.   Who is a well-known entrepreneur at Universal Life Insurance Company? He was born in 1909 and his father was Joseph E. Walker, a medical doctor, who in 1923 was one of the founders of Universal Life Insurance Company in Memphis. In 1946, Dr. Walker and his son, A. Maceo Walker, established Tri-State Bank in Memphis. In 1952, his son became president and chairman of Universal Life Insurance Company. He retired in 1983, and his daughter Patricia Walker Shaw became president of Universal Life Insurance Company. Patricia served until her death in 1985. A. Maceo Walker died in 1994.

64.   What is the name of the magazine, founded by the Johnson Publishing Company, that was discontinued in 1951? The idea for the magazine was developed as Johnson worked at Supreme Insurance Company, collecting articles to keep up awareness of African American interest. In 1970, the name was changed to *Black World*. The advertising for *Black World* was for products produced

Figure 111—A. Maceo Walker. Mississippi Valley Collection Libraries, University of Memphis, Memphis, Tennessee.

by John H. Johnson. There was little advertising revenue to sustain the magazine and it ceased publication in 1976.

65. Who began manufacturing hair care products in 1954, and later founded Johnson Products Company, Incorporated?

66. Who began in the recording industry as a song writer, producer, and publisher, and in 1959 started his own record label, Tamla, which merged in 1961 with his other label, Motown, in Detroit, Michigan?

67. What was Harlem's first African American-chartered, African American-run commercial bank, founded in 1963 and lasting until 1990? Jackie Robinson, who wanted African Americans to share in economic prosperity, was one of the founders.

Figure 112—George Johnson. Chicago Historical Society.

68. In 1966, who became the first African American member of the Federal Reserve Board?

69. What is the name of the African American association of social workers established in 1968?

70. What is the name of the African American association of psychologists established in 1968?

71. What is the name of the association of African American accountants established in 1969?

72. Who was the first African American to purchase a seat on the New York Stock Exchange in 1970?

73. What is the name of the African American fire fighters' association established in 1970?

74. What is the name of the African American educational organization established in 1970?

75. Who founded *Black Enterprise Magazine* in 1970, published the book *How to Succeed in Business Without Being White* in 1997, and was the recipient of the 1999 Spingarn Medal?

76. What is the name of the African American anthropologists' organization established in 1970?

77. What is the name of the association of African American MBAs established in 1970?

78. Who founded the Pro-Line Corporation, which manufactures ethnic health and beauty aids, in 1970?

79. Who resigned as U.S. ambassador to Sweden to become the first African American director of the New York Stock Exchange in 1972?

80. What is the name of the association of African American policemen established in 1972?

81. Who founded the magazine *Encore* in 1972 and in 1984 was the publisher of *Five Fifteen*, a newspaper with the subtitle "The First Black Woman's Newspaper"?

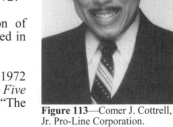

Figure 113—Comer J. Cottrell, Jr. Pro-Line Corporation.

82. What is the name of the association of African American nurses established in 1972?

83. What was the name of the African American organization of chemists established in 1972?

84. Who became president of Supreme Life Insurance Company of America in 1973?

85. What is the name of the African American criminal justice association established in 1974?

86. What African American cardiologists' association was established in 1974?

87. What is the name of the association of African American data processing associates established in 1975?

88. What association of African American journalists was established in 1975?

89. What is the name of the association of African American dentists established in 1976?

90. What is the name of the African American organization of physicists established in 1977?

91. Who was the first African American to serve on the board of directors of the General Motors Corporation? He was the recipient of the 1971 Spingarn Medal and the Presidential Medal of Freedom in 1991.

92. What St. Lucia-born British economist received the Nobel Prize in economics in 1979?

93. Who founded the Black Entertainment Television network in 1980?

94. Who founded her own beauty products company in 1985?

95. What is the name of an African American telecommunications organization established in 1990?

96. What company ceded its operations in 1991 to the United Insurance Company of America?

97. Who were the founders of FUBU in 1992?

98. Who became the first African American U.S. Secretary of Commerce in 1993?

99. What is the name of a major African American bank in the city of Chicago, Illinois?

100. What is the name of an African American bank in Washington, D.C.?

101. What is the name of an African American bank in Baltimore, Maryland?

102. What is the name of an African American bank in Milwaukee, Wisconsin?

103. What is the name of the African American culinary organization established in 1993?

104. What is the name of an African American bank in Atlanta, Georgia?

105. What is the name of an African American bank in Detroit, Michigan?

106. What is the name of an African American savings and loan in New York City?

107. What is the name of an African American insurance company in Brownsville, Tennessee?

108. What is the name of an African American newspaper in Louisville, Kentucky?

109. What is the name of an African American-owned bank in Memphis, Tennessee?

110. What is the name of an African American savings and loan in Birmingham, Alabama?

111. What is the name of an African American insurance company in Monroe, Louisiana?

112. What is the name of an African American bank in Kansas City, Kansas?

113. What is the name of the oldest African American savings and loan?

114. Who became the first African American CEO (Chief Executive Officer) of Symantec Corporation in 1999, after a 28-year career with IBM?

115. What is the name of an African American business magazine?

116. What is the name of an African American savings and loan in Los Angeles, California?

117. What is the name of an African American savings and loan in New Orleans, Louisiana?

118. What is the name of the oldest African American bank?

119. What is the name of an African American bank in Nashville, Tennessee?

120. What is the name of an African American bank in Durham, North Carolina?

121. What is the name of an African American bank in Newark, New Jersey?

122. Viacom acquired what company's holdings in the year 2000 for $2.5 billion in stock, and assumed $500 million in debt?

123. What is the name of an African American insurance company in Los Angeles, California?

124. What is the name of an African American insurance company in Birmingham, Alabama?

125. What is the name of an association of African American engineers?

126. What is the name of an association of African American real estate brokers?

127. What is the name of an African American-owned bank in the city of Philadelphia, Pennsylvania?

128. The Southeast Fort Worth Federal Credit Union of Fort Worth, Texas, was established by whom?

129. The lack of what commodity is the major reason for the very small number of African American businesses in proportion to its population?

130. In order for African Americans to obtain economic parity, they must patronize what type of business?

131. What is one of the largest African American majority-owned corporations in America?

132. Who was a prominent labor union leader in Miami, Florida and has a center named in his honor?

133. In 2001, who was the first African American CEO of a blue-chip company listed on the Dow Jones?

134. What is the name of an African American bank in Boston, Massachusetts?

135. In January of 2003, the *Tri-State Defender Newspaper* of Memphis, Tennessee, the *New Pittsburgh Courier*, the *Chicago Defender*, and the *Michigan Chronicle* of Detroit, Michigan, were all purchased by what company?

Figure 114—Kenneth I. Chenault. Courtesy of American Express.

Answers — 3 — Business and Professional Associations

1. James Forten (1766–1842)

2. Louisiana (near Melrose)

3. Anthony D. Allen (1775–1835)

4. John B. Russwurm (1799–1851), *Freedman's Journal*

5. Yellow Tavern

6. William Florville (c.1806–c.1868)

7. William T. Johnson (1809–1851)

8. Mifflin Gibbs (1823–1915)

9. Robert Mara Adger (1837–1910)

10. John P. Parker (1827–1900)

11. Barney L. Ford (1824–1902)

12. Freedman's Bank

13. Isaac Myers (1835–1891)

14. Stocks, real estate, bonds, and unsecured loans

15. James Wormley (1819–1884)

16. Cigarettes

17. Frederick Douglass (1817–1895)

18. Caesar C. Antoine (1836–1921)

19. Barber

20. John Henry Murphy (1840–1922)

21. Edwin C. Berry (1854–1931)

22. National Medical Association

23. St. John Atherton, originally from the state of Georgia

24. North Carolina Mutual Life Insurance Company, Durham, North Carolina

25. Dr. Aaron McDuffie Moore (?–?), uncle of Charles Clinton Spaulding

26. National Negro Business League

27. William McDonald Felton (?–?)

28. Maggie Lena Walker (1867–1934)

29. Richard Henry Boyd (1855–1912)

30. Alonzo Herndon (1858–1927)

31. *Chicago Defender*

32. McKissack and McKissack, founded in Nashville by Moses McKissack, III (1879–1952). The first Moses McKissack (?–1865) was a slave from the Ashanti tribe, located in West Africa, whose owner was a William McKissack of Tennessee. Moses McKissack became a noted builder.

33. Madam C.J. (Charles Joseph) Walker (1867–1919)

34. Robert Church, Sr. (1839–1912)

35. Jesse Binga (1865–1950)

36. James H. Anderson (?–?)

37. Robert L. Vann (1887–1940)

38. The National Urban League

39. Nolle Smith (1888–1982)

40. Annie M. Turbo Malone (1869–1957)

41. Frank L. Gillespie (1876–1925)

42. John E. Nail (1883–1947)

43. African American funeral businesses

44. *Afro American Newspaper*

45. Ella P. Stewart (1893–1987)

46. Dr. J.E. Walker (1880–1958)

47. National Funeral Directors & Morticians Association

48. National Bar Association

49. Anthony Overton (1865–1946)

50. 1925

51. Charles D. Murray, Sr. (?–?)

52. Harry H. Pace (1884–1943), former president of Northeastern Life Insurance Company

53. Zula Swanson (?–1973)

54. A. Philip Randolph (1889–1979)

55. Charles Clinton Spaulding (1874–1952) who became president of the North Carolina Mutual Life Insurance Company after the death of Dr. Aaron McDuffie Moore

56. Paul R. Williams (1894–1980)

57. Julian Abele (1881–1950)

58. Willard Townsend (1895–1957)

59. Arthur G. Gaston (1892–1996)

60. Samuel B. Fuller (1905–1988)

61. John H. Johnson (1918–2005)

62. *Ebony* magazine

63. A. Maceo Walker (1909–1994)

64. *Negro Digest*

65. George E. Johnson (1927–)

66. Barry Gordy, Jr. (1929–)

67. Freedom National Bank

68. Andrew F. Brimmer (1926– 1966)

69. National Association of Black Social Workers

70. Association of Black Psychologists

71. National Association of Black Accountants (NABA)

72. Joseph L. Searles, III, 1970 (?–?)

73. International Association of Professional Fire Fighters

74. National Alliance of Black Educators

75. Earl G. Graves, Sr. (1935–)

76. Association of Black Anthropologists

77. The National Black MBA Association

78. Comer J. Cottrell, Jr. (1931–). Pro-Line Corporation was acquired by Alberto Culver Corporation in 2000.

79. Jerome Heartwell Holland (1916–1985)

80. National Black Police Association

81. Ida E. Lewis (1935–)

82. National Black Nurses Association

83. National Organization for the Professional Advancement of Black Chemists and Chemical Engineers

84. Ray Irby (?–?)

85. National Association of Blacks in Criminal Justice

86. Association of Black Cardiologists

87. Black Data Processing Associates

88. National Association of Black Journalists

89. National Dental Association

90. National Society of Black Physicists

91. Reverend Leon Sullivan (1922–2001)

92. Arthur Lewis (1915–1990)

93. Robert L. Johnson (1946–)

94. Naomi Sims (1949–), Naomi Sims Beauty Products

95. National Association of Black Telecommunications Professionals

96. Supreme Life Insurance Company

97. Daymond John, J. Alexander Martin, Carl Brown, and Keith Perrin

98. Ronald H. Brown (1941–1996)

99. Seaway National Bank or Highland Community Bank or Illinois Service Federal S & L

100. Industrial Bank of Washington or Independence Federal Savings Bank

101. The Harbor Bank of Maryland

102. Legacy Bank

103. Black Culinary Alliance

104. Citizens Trust Bank of Atlanta or Capital City Bancshares, Inc.

105. First Independence National Bank of Detroit

106. The Carver Federal Savings Bank

107. Golden Circle Insurance Company

108. *Louisville Defender*

109. Tri-State Bank

110. The Citizens Federal Savings and Loan

111. Reliable Life Insurance Company

112. Douglass Bank

113. Berean Savings Association, 1888, Philadelphia, Pennsylvania

114. John W. Thompson (1949–)

115. *Black Enterprise* magazine

116. Broadway Federal Savings and Loan Association

117. Liberty Bank and Trust Company

118. Consolidated Bank and Trust Company, Richmond, Virginia

119. Citizens Savings Bank and Trust Company

120. Mechanics and Farmers Bank

121. City National Bank of New Jersey

122. Black Entertainment Television

123. Golden State Mutual Life Insurance Company

124. The Booker T. Washington Insurance Company or the Protective Industrial Insurance Co. of Alabama, Inc.

125. The National Action Council for Minorities in Engineering, Inc.

126. National Association of Independent Real Estate Brokers

127. United Bank of Philadelphia

128. African Americans

129. Money

130. African American

131. TLC Beatrice International Holdings, Inc., New York, New York

132. Joseph Caleb (c.1939– 1972)

133. Kenneth I. Chenault (1951–), Chairman and Chief Executive Officer, American Express, 2001

134. In 2003, the Boston Bank of Commerce changed its name to OneSource. The bank included the acquisitions of the Peoples Bank of Commerce and Founders National Bank, both of Los Angeles, California, and Peoples National Bank of Commerce, Miami, Florida.

135. Real Times, Inc.

4 — Children

1. Whose name means "Ethiopian" in Greek, and was known for his fables and children's stories?

2. Who spent his youth in Framingham, Massachusetts, and later became the first African American to die in the American Revolution during the Boston Massacre, which occurred on March 5, 1779?

3. As a youth, what African American scientist attended an integrated private school, later drew the plans for the city of Washington, D.C., from memory after the French architect departed, and accurately predicted a solar eclipse?

Figure 115—Benjamin Banneker. Copyright © U.S. Postal Service. Reproduced with permission of the U.S. Postal Service.

4. Who was born a slave, became the plaintiff in an historic civil rights suit in which she claimed the Bill of Rights and the new Massachusetts Constitution meant she was free, and won the case that ended slavery in the state of Massachusetts? Her mother worked in the 1700s as a slave for Pieter Hogeboom in Claverack, New York. She was born around 1742 and her sister Lizzie was born about a year later. She was sometimes referred to as "Mumbet." After Pieter Hogeboom died, the children were inherited by his daughter Hannah, married to John Ashley, in Berkshire County, Massachusetts. Mumbet's husband was killed in the Revolutionary War. One day Hannah Ashley became enraged and attempted to strike Mumbet's sister Lizzie with a heated kitchen shovel. Mumbet moved between Hannah and Lizzie and was struck, and the blow left a scar on her arm. Outraged by her mistress's behavior, Mumbet left and consulted a lawyer, Theodore Sedgwick, who agreed to represent her. He filed a writ of *replevin*—a motion to recover property, in this case—with the Berkshire County Court on behalf on Mumbet and another of Ashley's slaves, Brom. The property Mumbet and Brom were asserting that they had been deprived of was their own persons: the plaintiffs claimed they were being held in bondage illegally. The claim was based on the Bill of Rights of the U.S. Constitution, which stated that "All men were created equal." Colonel Ashley contended that Mumbet and Brom were servants for life and that he had clear title to his property. The jury ruled that Mumbet and Brom were not Ashley's servants and ordered Ashley to also pay court costs. After the trial Mumbet changed her last name to "Freeman" and refused Colonel Ashley's plea to return to the Ashley home. She worked for the Theodore Sedgwick household and never remarried.

5. Who was born a slave in Framingham, Massachusetts, spent his youth there, and later became noted for his heroics in the Battle of Bunker Hill when the Americans were ordered to surrender by British Major John Pitcairn? This painting of the Battle of Bunker Hill by John Trumbull is on display at Yale University. The stamp (see Figure 116) was first issued on October 18, 1968, in New Haven, Connecticut. Salem was born a slave, around 1756, but little is known about his childhood and there is uncertainty as to his actual birth year. He was sold by his original owner, Jeremiah Belknap, to Lawson Buckminister, who allowed him to enlist in the Continental Army. In exchange for enlisting and serving, he received his freedom. Salem served in Captain Drury's company during the Battle of Bunker Hill, and served for the entire Revolutionary War. He died in the poorhouse in Framingham, Massachusetts, in 1816. Later, the city of Framingham established a monument in his honor.

Figure 116—Lieutenant Thomas Grosvenor and his attendant, Peter Salem. Copyright © U.S. Postal Service. Reproduced with permission of the U.S. Postal Service.

6. Who saved the life of Colonel William Washington at the Battle of Cowpens (South Carolina, January 17, 1781), during the Revolutionary War? He grew up as a slave. The Continental Army was led by Brigadier General Daniel Morgan and the British were led by Lt. Colonel Banastre Tarleton, sometimes referred to as "The Butcher" because he was known for killing prisoners. Prior to the battle, Major General Nathaniel Greene decided that he needed to

Figure 117—William Ball. Copyright © U.S. Postal Service. Reproduced with permission of the U.S. Postal Service.

increase the army's effectiveness. He divided his force into two groups, one commanded by Brigadier General Daniel Morgan and the other by Greene himself. Morgan's force was considered a mobile force. The British Lt. General Charles Cornwallis recognized Greene's strategy and divided his force into two groups, sending Tarleton after Morgan. After several weeks, Morgan fought Tarleton at Cowpens. Believing that the British would expect his militia to retreat, Morgan ordered the militia commanded by Andrew Picken to withdraw as planned. The British became disorganized and their lines separated, allowing the Americans to defeat them in a counterattack. In a postcard first issued on January 17, 1981 (see Figure 117), William Ball is on the horse on the right, firing his revolver to save a relative of George Washington. In 1845, William Ranney painted the *Battle of Cowpens*, based on John Marshall's biography of George Washington. The painting is hung in the South Carolina State House. Ball is sometimes referred to as the bugler in the painting.

7. What African American, who spent his youth in Haiti, founded the city of Chicago?

8. Who was born a slave and worked as a hairdresser, supported the family that owned him, and when he was freed, founded an orphanage for children and helped the sick?

9. Who grew up in Massachusetts and was a leading participant in Shays's Rebellion, a protest of high land taxes that took place in Massachusetts in the winter of 1786–1787?

10. Who grew up a slave, later became a guide, interpreter, and negotiator with Indians, and explored the Upper Missouri River region?

11. Who became deeply religious at an early age and in 1843, left New York City to become a well-known abolitionist?

12. Who spent his youth in St. Louis, Missouri, and later became a mountain man and war chief of the Crow Indians?

13. What African American was the drummer boy during the Battle of New Orleans? His drums are preserved in the state of Louisiana, Office of State Museum, in Baton Rouge.

14. Who was raised in Caroline County, Maryland, and later became the first wife of Frederick Douglass and an activist in anti-slavery societies?

15. Who grew up as a slave in Kent County, Maryland, and later became a clergyman, abolitionist, editor, minister to Liberia and advocate of the production of cotton in Africa to break the South's monopoly on cotton production?

16. Who was taught the trade of tailoring as a youth and later became a prosperous tailoring merchant in Chicago, Illinois, fighting for African American equality from 1845 to 1879? He was born free in 1817 in North Carolina and taught himself to read and write. He later moved to Chicago and became part of the Underground Railroad.

Figure 118—Jean Baptiste Pointe Du Sable. Copyright © U.S. Postal Service. Reproduced with permission of the U.S. Postal Service.

Figure 119—Jim Beckwourth. Copyright © U.S. Postal Service. Reproduced with permission of the U.S. Postal Service.

17. Frederick Douglass (1817–1895), who became a great orator and abolitionist in the nineteenth century, was born a slave in Tuckahoe, Maryland, and spent his youth as a houseboy in what city?

18. What leader of the Underground Railroad received many whippings as a young slave because she was thought to be unintelligent?

19. What famous doctor became an apprentice shoemaker at age 11, and as an adolescent, operated a barber shop in Wisconsin? He later became a well-known surgeon at Provident Hospital in Chicago, Illinois.

Figure 120—Frederick Douglass. Copyright © U.S. Postal Service. Reproduced with permission of the U.S. Postal Service.

20. Who was born in 1828 in St. Andrews, New Brunswick, Canada, spent his youth there, and later became a noted landscape painter in Providence, Rhode Island?

21. Who was born of free parents and later wrote the book, *A Voice from Harper's Ferry*, which is the only eyewitness account of the raid?

22. Who spent his youth as a slave in Beaufort, South Carolina, and later captured the *CSS* (Confederate States Ship) *Planter*?

23. What African American folklore hero was based on an actual person born in 1844, who won a contest with a machine by driving railroad spikes with a large hammer, but died afterwards?

24. Who attended the Institution for the Education of Colored Youth in Washington, D.C., and later became the first African American woman attorney?

25. Who grew up in Mercer County, Virginia, and became the second wife of Booker T. Washington and cofounder of Tuskegee Institute?

Figure 121—John Henry. Copyright © U.S. Postal Service. Reproduced with permission of the U.S. Postal Service.

26. Who was born and grew up in Davidson County, Tennessee, and later became a cowboy known as Deadwood Dick, whose nickname was bestowed by a crowd after he won several roping and shooting contests in Deadwood, South Dakota?

27. Jan Earnst Matzeliger (1852–1899) developed a machine that mass-produced shoes. In what country did he spend his youth? He was born in Parariibo, Surinam in 1852 and his native language was Dutch. He began working in his father's machine shop at age 10. His father was his mentor and taught him the shoe trade. He also worked for several years as a sailor on a merchant ship and later settled in Philadelphia, Pennsylvania. After hearing about the rapid expansion of the shoe industry in Massachusetts, he traveled to Lynn, Massachusetts, where he began working at a shoe factory. It took Matzeliger about five years to develop the lasting machine and in 1882, he filed a patent for it. His invention allowed manufacturers to attach the top of the shoe to the sole, increasing shoe production at a cheaper price. He taught oil painting and Sunday school and worked on new inventions. He died of tuberculosis on August 24, 1899 in Lynn, Massachusetts, but left a lasting legacy. Matzeliger left the bulk of his wealth to the North Congregational Church of Lynn, Massachusetts, one of the few churches in the area to accept African Americans. In 1984, Lynn, Massachusetts named a bridge in his honor.

Figure 122—Jan Matzeliger. Copyright © U.S. Postal Service. Reproduced with permission of the U.S. Postal Service.

28. Who, as a child, worked in a salt mine in Malden, West Virginia, and in 1940 became the first African American educator honored with a U.S. postage stamp? He was born in 1856 in Franklin County, Virginia to an African American slave woman and an unknown White man. He attended Hampton Institute and in 1881, founded Tuskegee Normal and Industrial Institute, which emphasized industrial education and learning a trade. Under Washington's leadership, the school became one of the best of its type. In 1882, Washington married Fannie N. Smith, who died in 1884. In 1885, he married his second wife, Olivia A. Davidson. The couple had two sons, Booker T. Washington, Jr. and Ernest Davidson Washington.

Figure 123—Booker T. Washington. Copyright © U.S. Postal Service. Reproduced with permission of the U.S. Postal Service.

Olivia died in 1889 and in 1893, Washington married Margaret James Murray. In an 1895 speech at the Cotton States Exposition in Atlanta, Washington urged African Americans to forget about the right to vote and urged them to obtain a skill, though some African American leaders did not agree with him. The year of Washington's death, 1915, marked the beginning of the great migration of African Americans from the South to the North.

29. What son of a minister began his education at the Randolph Street School in Philadelphia, Pennsylvania, and became a well-known African American painter? He was born in Pittsburgh in 1859. His father discouraged his interest in art by apprenticing him into the milling trade, but the work made Tanner ill. He resumed painting during his recuperation. In 1880, he enrolled at the Pennsylvania Academy of Fine Arts and was influenced by Thomas Eakins. He became one of America's great painters, and died in 1937.

Figure 124—Henry O. Tanner. Copyright © U.S. Postal Service. Reproduced with permission of the U.S. Postal Service.

30. What famous scientist could sew, knit, make candles, make soap, cook, and make quilts, and had a great talent for making plants grow, all by the age of 10?

31. Who grew up in New York City and later became an editor and founder of the White Rose Home, located on 136th Street in Harlem?

32. Who grew up in Charlotte, North Carolina, taught in Covington, Tennessee, and later became known for a volume of poems entitled *Morning Glories*?

Figure 125—George Washington Carver. Copyright © U.S. Postal Service. Reproduced with permission of the U.S. Postal Service.

33. Who grew up on a farm in southeast Tennessee and became the first African American woman to graduate from Meharry Medical College, and the first Meharry graduate to serve as a missionary to Africa?

34. Who was born on August 8, 1886, in Charles County Maryland and spent his youth in Georgetown, Maryland, later accompanying Commander Peary on an expedition to the North Pole?

35. What elementary school student in Great Barrington, Massachusetts became aware of a difference when a child refused to exchange a card with him, and he never forgot it?

Figure 126—Matthew Henson. Copyright © U.S. Postal Service. Reproduced with the permission of the U.S. Postal Service.

36.   Who was robbed of his inheritance at the age of 9, and later became a well-known educator and the first president of Atlanta University?

37.   Who grew up in Kansas and later became a pharmacist, community activist and civil rights leader in Washington, D.C., for more than 60 years?

38.   Who grew up in Williamson County, Texas, became a well-known cowboy, and was the first African American cowboy elected to the Cowboy Hall of Fame?

39.   Who grew up in Boston, Massachusetts, became the wife of William Monroe Trotter and co-editor of the Boston *Guardian*, and was often referred to as "Deenie" by her friends?

40.   Who spent her childhood in Beaufort, South Carolina, opened a home for unwed mothers in 1941, and practiced medicine in Washington, D.C., for more than 40 years? She was born on September 8, 1872 to William J. Whipper, a municipal court judge, and Frances Rollin Whipper, a physician. She was educated in Washington, D.C. and attended Howard University Medical School, where she graduated in 1893.

Figure 127—Bill Pickett. Copyright © U.S. Postal Service. Reproduced with permission of the U.S. Postal Service.

41.   Paul Laurence Dunbar (1872–1906), who became a famous poet, spent his youth in what city? He was born in Dayton, Ohio on June 27, 1872. His parents were Joshua and Matilda Dunbar. His mother was a former slave from Kentucky and his father was a former slave who served with the 55th Massachusetts Infantry Regiment and the 5th Massachusetts Calvary Regiment. Dunbar attended public school in Dayton and graduated from Dayton's Central High School in 1891. His first job was elevator operator at a Dayton hotel. He wrote poetry on the job when there was not much to do and was known as the "elevator poet." He published his first poetry, *Oak and Ivy*, in 1893. He used his church's press to print the book and sold copies at the World's Columbian Exposition. As a result of exposition he acquired patrons, one of whom was Frederick Douglass. Dunbar died on February 6, 1906.

Figure 128—Paul Laurence Dunbar. Copyright © U.S. Postal Service. Reproduced with permission of the U.S. Postal Service.

42. What well-known African American historian was born on December 19, 1875, in New Canton, Virginia, spent his youth there, and worked in the coal mines?

Carter G. Woodson

Black Heritage USA 20c

Figure 129—Carter G. Woodson. Copyright © U.S. Postal Service. Reproduced with permission of the U.S. Postal Service.

43. Who grew up in Richmond, Virginia, became a teacher, and helped implement the ideas of Anna T. Jeanes—a Philadelphia, Pennsylvania Quaker who wanted to improve rural education for African Americans—by devoting full-time to the supervision of other teachers?

44. What well-known educator never forgot being told, as a child at a soda fountain along with his mother, they could no longer be served there?

45. Who grew up in Tazewell, Virginia, then moved to Cleveland, Ohio, became involved in the community, and became president of the Organization of Negro Women?

46. Mary McLeod Bethune (1875–1955), the fifteenth of seventeen children, started working in the cotton fields of South Carolina at the age of 5, and started school at what age? She was born in Maysville, South Carolina in 1875 to Patsy and Samuel McLeod, former slaves. She attended the Maysville Presbyterian Mission School, graduated from the Scotia Seminary School, and studied at the Moody Bible Institute in Chicago to become a missionary, but was rejected because she was African American. She returned to the South and married Albert Bethune. Mary Bethune founded Daytona Normal and Industrial Institute for Negro Girls (now Bethune-Cookman College) in 1904, served as its president 1904–1942 and 1946–1947, and died in 1955.

Mary McLeod Bethune

Black Heritage USA 22

Figure 130—Mary McLeod Bethune. Copyright © U.S. Postal Service. Reproduced with permission of the U.S. Postal Service.

47. What artist was born in 1877 in Philadelphia, Pennsylvania, spent her youth there, and was educated at the School of Industrial Art, the Pennsylvania Academy, and the Academie Colarossi in Paris, France? One of her works is entitled *The Wretched.*

48. Who attended school in Washington, D.C., and founded the National Training School for Women and Girls? Born in 1879, she studied domestic science and business, received an honorary M.A. degree from Eckstein-Norton University in 1907, and was denied a teaching position by the District of Columbia Board of Education. She convinced the National Baptist Convention and Women's Convention to endorse her school, which opened in 1909.

49. Who grew up in Washington, D.C., was inspired by African American soldiers assigned to Washington, D.C. after the Indian Wars, and later became America's first African American General?

50. Who grew up in Nashville, Tennessee, attended Fisk University, and in 1916 founded a hospital in Nashville to care for sick and injured African Americans?

51. Who grew up in Farmville, Virginia, attended Virginia State College in Petersburg, Virginia (which following the Civil War also contained a high school for African Americans), and became the first African American woman president of Tillotson College (now known as Huston-Tillotson College) in Austin, Texas?

Figure 131—Benjamin O. Davis, Sr. Copyright © U.S. Postal Service. Reproduced with permission of the U.S. Postal Service.

52. Who was raised in Charleston, South Carolina and studied medicine at Harvard University, but became an outstanding painter? One of his paintings is entitled *Portrait of Dr. Ware* (Edmund A. Ware, former president of Atlanta University).

53. What famous composer was the last of ten children and the only one to live beyond 2 months of age?

54. Who was born in Charleston, South Carolina, in 1883, spent his youth there, and later became a biologist noted for his research in eggs?

55. Who grew up in Memphis, Tennessee, taught American History and English at Booker T. Washington High School, wrote many songs (one of which is entitled "Something Within"), and was active in the Central Baptist Church, Inc. and the Tabernacle Baptist Church, Inc.?

Figure 132—Eubie Blake. Copyright © U.S. Postal Service. Reproduced with permission of the U.S. Postal Service.

56. Whose father died when she was 9 months old, mother died when she was six years old, and was later one of the founders of the Alpha Kappa Alpha sorority at Howard University?

57. Who spent her youth in St. Louis, inherited her mother's cosmetics business, and became a noted entrepreneur and patron of the Harlem Renaissance?

58. Who spent her youth near Natchitoches, Louisiana, and later became a noted folk artist?

59. Who spent her youth in Pittsburgh, Pennsylvania, increased membership in the NAACP in Pittsburgh, and became an honorary member of the Delta Sigma Theta Sorority?

60. Who spent his youth on a farm in Jamaica and was later known for such works as *Banjo* and *Harlem Shadow*?

61. What artist at age 7, would have to stay after school because at the end of a word such as dog, stove, or the like, he would draw a picture of the object?

62. Who was raised in the Storyville area of the city of New Orleans, and later claimed to have invented jazz? He was born on October 20, 1890, in New Orleans. At age 12, he was playing piano in Storyville. In 1925, he recorded the "King Porter Stump," and he recorded "Red Hot Peppers" in Chicago 1926–1928. In 1938, Alan Lomax, of the Library of Congress, conducted a series of recorded interviews with Morton regarding early jazz. The interviews lasted about 8 hours. These recorded interviews were released in 1948 and re-released in 1957. Morton's works were well received and well written. He died on July 10, 1941.

Figure 133—Jelly Roll Morton. Copyright © U.S. Postal Service. Reproduced with permission of the U.S. Postal Service.

63. Who was born in Atlanta, Texas, on January 26, 1892, and became the first African American woman airplane pilot to be licensed in France? She was the tenth of thirteen children. When she was two years old, her parents moved to Waxahachie, Texas; when she was nine, her father left the family. Her father was three-quarters American Indian and was frustrated by racial discrimination, and he felt he could do better in Oklahoma. She picked cotton as a youngster. After completing the 8th grade, she worked in the laundry business, attended college in Langston, Oklahoma for one semester, then went back to Texas. She left Texas for Chicago in 1915; in Chicago, she became a manicurist and met Robert S. Abbott, publisher of the *Chicago Defender*. Abbott encouraged her to pursue her dream as a pilot and became a supporter and patron.

Figure 134—Bessie Coleman. Copyright © U.S. Postal Service. Reproduced with permission of the U.S. Postal Service.

64. Who was born in New Brunswick, New Jersey in 1894, studied classical music and ragtime as a child, and later became a celebrated jazz musician? He was a noted jazz pianist and a significant person in the transition from ragtime to jazz. Some of his compositions include: *Yamecraw: A Negro Rhapsody* (1928), *Harlem Symphony* (1932), and *De Organizer* (c.1940).

Figure 135—James P. Johnson. Copyright © U.S. Postal Service. Reproduced with permission of the U.S. Postal Service.

65. Who attended grammar school in Newburyport, Massachusetts, became a community and civil rights activist in Boston, Massachusetts, and was sometimes referred to as the "First Lady of Roxbury"?

66. Who grew up in Washington, D.C., and New York City, became a stage performer, and is known for the song "Little Blackbird Lookin' for a Bluebird"?

67. Who was born in 1897 in Yazoo City, Mississippi, educated at Columbia University and the University of Chicago, worked at the Chicago Library, and wrote the books *We Build Together* (1948), *Christmas "Gif": An Anthology of Christmas Poems, Songs and Stories Written by and about Negroes* (1963), and *They Showed the Way: Forty American Negro Leaders* (1964)?

68. What painter, considered the father of African American art, was born in Topeka, Kansas, and as a young child was inspired by African American cultural heritage?

69. Who spent her youth in Washington, D.C., and later became the first African American woman to receive a Ph.D.?

70. Who was so flamboyant in his appearance in grammar school that his schoolmates called him "Duke"? He was born in 1899 in Washington, D.C. His parents were James Edward Ellington and Daisy Kennedy Ellington. He took piano lessons when he was about 7 and worked at the Washington Senators baseball games. After meeting Harvey Brook, he decided to become a piano player. Some of his compositions include: the *New Orleans Suite*, the *Newport Jazz Festival* suite (1966), and the *Sacred Music* suite (1966). He also appeared in movies and wrote music for movies as *Black and Tan Fantasy* (1929) and *Paris Blues* (1961). He received honorary doctorates from Yale and Howard Universities.

Figure 136—Duke Ellington. Copyright © U.S. Postal Service. Reproduced with permission of the U.S. Postal Service.

71. While attending elementary school Percy Julian (1899–1975)—who later became a renowned chemist—came in waving his arithmetic paper with a grade of 80. His father told him he should not be satisfied until he made 100. In what city did this happen? He was born in 1899 in Montgomery, Alabama. He graduated from DePauw University in 1920 and became a chemistry instructor at Fisk University. In 1923, he received a fellowship to Harvard and finished his master's degree in chemistry. He earned his Ph.D. in chemistry from the University of Vienna in 1931. He developed synthetic cortisone, a product from the soy bean, and held chemical patents on over 100 items. He died in 1975.

Figure 137—Percy Lavon Julian. Copyright © U.S. Postal Service. Reproduced with permission of the U.S. Postal Service.

72. Who grew up in Darlington, South Carolina, became a nurse and a writer, one of whose novels is entitled *Don't Walk on My Dreams* (1961)? She was born in 1902 in Darlington, South Carolina, the oldest of fourteen children. Her parents were Nancy and Sylvester Greene. She attended Benedict College and Vorhees College. She later became a noted author. Some of her books included: *After the Storm* (1945), *The Dawn Appears* (1914), and her unpublished autobiography, *To Paw With Love*. She died in 1993.

73. What well-known poet and writer was introduced to books and poetical recitation in Topeka, Kansas, at the age of 5, by his grandmother? He later attended Central High School in Cleveland, Ohio, and was influenced by his English teacher, Ethel Weimer. His autobiography is entitled *The Big Sea* (1940).

74. What writer and poet was greatly influenced as a young child by his Uncle Buddy's pride in African American culture?

75. Who spent her youth in Pasadena, California, and later as an actress played the suffering but understanding mother of a beautiful and rebellious daughter, in the movie *Imitation of Life*? She was born on March 8, 1902, in Cincinnati, Ohio but spent her teen years in California. She was not obese and had to gain weight for her roles. She did not have a southern accent, and had to develop one. She played Delilah Johnson in the film *Imitation of Life*. She appeared in other films such as *The Jackie Robinson Story* and *Belle Star*.

Figure 138—Langston Hughes. Copyright © U.S. Postal Service. Reproduced with permission of the U.S. Postal Service.

76. Who was born and raised in Oklahoma City, Oklahoma, later becoming a noted jazz musician?

77. Who, as a youth, was given by his grandmother the book *The Animal Kingdom, Illustrated* by S.G. Goodrich, which he treasured, and which started his interest in anatomy?

78. What Nobel Peace Prize recipient moved with his parents to Albuquerque, New Mexico, when he was a child, due to poor health?

Figure 139—Jimmy Rushing. Copyright © U.S. Postal Service. Reproduced with permission of the U.S. Postal Service.

79. Dr. Charles Drew (1904–1950) lived in an area known as Foggy Bottom, and attended Stevens Elementary in what city? He attended Amherst College on an athletic scholarship, graduated from Amherst in 1926, then directed the sports programs and taught at Morgan State College in Baltimore until 1928, when he entered McGill University. He was elected to Alpha Phi Omega, an honorary medical society. In 1933, he graduated from McGill with a medical degree and a Master of Surgery, and graduated in 1940 from Columbia University with a Doctor of Science degree. His dissertation detailed how blood plasma could be saved over long periods, unlike whole blood. In 1977, the American Red Cross named their Washington, D.C. headquarters in his honor.

Figure 140—Dr. Charles R. Drew. Copyright © U.S. Postal Service. Reproduced with permission of the U.S. Postal Service.

80. Who was born in St. Louis, Missouri, in 1904, received a saxophone at the age of 9, and later became a noted jazz tenor saxophonist?

81. What singer and dancer born in St. Louis, Missouri began working at age 8 in order to help support her family? She was born Freda Josephine McDonald on June 3, 1906. Her parents were Carrie McDonald and Eddie Carson. She worked as a domestic worker and babysitter, and never depended on a man for support. She married Willie Baker in

Figure 141—Coleman Hawkins. Copyright © U.S. Postal Service. Reproduced with permission of the U.S. Postal Service.

1921, and even though she remarried two more times after Baker, she decided to keep his last name.

82.   Who was born in Norwood, Massachusetts, and was employed by the Urban League in Springfield, Massachusetts and the New York City Urban League for over 50 years?

83.   Who was born in Baltimore, Maryland, on July 2, 1908, and spent his youth there, where he developed an appreciation for the U.S. Constitution? In 1967 he became the first African American appointed to the U.S. Supreme Court. He attended Lincoln University in Chester, Pennsylvania and applied to the University of Maryland Law School, but was rejected because he was African American. He then applied to Howard University Law School and was accepted. In his first major case, he sued the University of Maryland to admit an African American. The African American was Donald Gaines Murray, who graduated from Amherst University. Marshall won the case. He was also instrumental in winning *Brown v. Board of Education, Topeka, Kansas.* In 1954, Marshall was appointed to the U.S. Court of Appeals by President John F. Kennedy. On June 13, 1967, President Lyndon B. Johnson appointed Marshall to the U.S. Supreme Court.

Figure 142—Thurgood Marshall. Copyright © U.S. Postal Service. Reproduced with permission of the U.S. Postal Service.

84.   Who was born in Helena, Arkansas, in 1907, and became a well-known gospel singer? Her parents were Anna Winston and William Martin and she was one of six children. At the age of 6, she took piano lessons from her brother's wife. Her family moved to Cairo, Illinois and then to Chicago. In the 1930s she formed a quartet that included Theodore Fry. She left Fry in 1935 and formed a group which she called the Roberta Martin Singers. In the 1940s she added other singers and founded a publishing company. Her first composition was "Try Jesus, He Satisfies" (1943). Before her death in 1969, she had composed over one hundred songs with Fay Brown.

Figure 143—Roberta Martin. Copyright © U.S. Postal Service. Reproduced with permission of the U.S. Postal Service.

85. Who was born in West Point, Mississippi June 10, 1910, during his youth sang in the church choir, and later became a noted blues singer? Charlie Patton taught him the Delta Blues style of playing the guitar at age 18. His family moved to Arkansas in 1933 and his brother-in-law, Sonny Boy Williams, taught him to play harmonica. He played in juke joints with Robert Johnson and Sonny Boy Williams. In 1948, he had a radio show on KWEM in West Memphis, Arkansas. Some of his recordings include "Smokestack Lightnin'" (1956), "Wang Dang Doodle" and "Back Door Man" (1960), and "Little Red Rooster" (1961).

Figure 144—Howlin' Wolf (Chester Burnett). Copyright © U.S. Postal Service. Reproduced with permission of the U.S. Postal Service.

86. Who was born in Hazelhurst, Mississippi, in 1911, lived in Memphis, Tennessee, and Robinsonville, Mississippi, during his youth and later became a noted blues musician? His parents were Noah Johnson and Julia Dodds. His first instrument was the harmonica, and he became interested in the guitar in the 1920s. He married Virginia Travis in 1929; she died in childbirth in 1930. Many consider "Sweet Home Chicago" (1937) one of his best songs. Johnson died August 16, 1938.

Figure 145—Robert Johnson. Copyright © U.S. Postal Service. Reproduced with permission of the U.S. Postal Service.

87. Who grew up in Buena Vista, Georgia, and later became one of the greatest hitters in the Negro Leagues, hitting almost 800 home runs in his 17 years as a player?

88. Who grew up in Hattiesburg, Mississippi, later worked for equal rights, founded the New York City Urban League Guild in 1942, and worked as a community activist for nearly 40 years?

89. Who grew up in Clarksburg, Virginia, and later became a noted librarian? Her dissertation for her Ph.D. in librarianship was *The Problems of Negro High School Libraries in Selected Southern Cities* (University of Chicago, 1943).

Figure 146—Josh Gibson. Copyright © U.S. Postal Service. Reproduced with permission of the U.S. Postal Service.

90. What Cleveland, Ohio youth, who was urged to run track because he had pneumonia four times over a three-year period and because running track would help develop his lungs, attended Ohio State University and won four gold medals at the 1936 Olympics in Berlin, Germany? His given name was James Cleveland Owens and he went by the initials "J.C." His teacher thought it was Jesse, and people began to associate that name with him.

Figure 147—Jesse Owens. Copyright © U.S. Postal Service. Reproduced with permission of the U.S. Postal Service.

91. What jazz great spent his youth in Pittsburgh, Pennsylvania, and was later known as "The Great Mr. B"?

92. Who was born in Cotton Plant, Arkansas, spent her youth there and in Chicago, Illinois, and later became a well-known gospel singer? She was born on March 20, 1915 to Katie Bell Nubin, a singing evangelist. She could play the guitar at age 6. She signed with Decca in 1938 and recorded "Rock Me" and "This Train." Two of her popular records in 1942 were "Shout Sister Shout" and "That's All." In 1970, she had a stroke that impaired her speech, but it did not impair her singing. Tharpe died on October 9, 1973.

Figure 148—Sister Rosetta (Tharpe). Copyright © U.S. Postal Service. Reproduced with permission of the U.S. Postal Service.

93. Who was born on April 7, 1915 in Philadelphia, Pennsylvania, spent her youth there, and later became a well-known jazz singer who usually wore a white gardenia in her hair? Her parents were Sadie Fagan and Clarence Holiday. Her mother was 13 years old when Billie was born., and her father was 15. Her parents married when Billie was three, but soon divorced. At age 17, she began to sing in Harlem clubs and in 1934, she performed at the Apollo Theater. Her notable songs include "God Bless the Child," "I Love You Porgy," and "Fine and Mellow."

Figure 149—Billie Holiday. Copyright © U.S. Postal Service. Reproduced with permission of the U.S. Postal Service.

94. Who was born McKinley Morganfield in Rolling Fork, Mississippi in 1915, and was given the nickname "Muddy Waters" by his grandmother because he played in mud puddles?

95. What civil rights leader was the youngest of twenty children of poor sharecropping parents, and as a child worked in the cotton fields of Mississippi?

Figure 150—Muddy Waters. Copyright © U.S. Postal Service. Reproduced with permission of the U.S. Postal Service.

96. What husband and wife acting team grew up in Waycross, Georgia, and Cleveland, Ohio, respectively, met while they both appeared in the movie *Jeb*, and appeared together in movies and on television?

97. Who grew up in Montgomery, Alabama, attended Spelman College, and later became ambassador to the United Republic of Cameroon (1977 to 1980) and ambassador to the Republic of Equatorial Guinea (1979 to 1980)?

98. Who was born in Cairo, Georgia in 1919, spent his youth in Pasadena, California, and later became the first African American to play major league professional baseball? He was born Jack Roosevelt Robinson. His parents were Mallie and Jerry Robinson and he was one of five children. His father left the family when Jackie was an infant. Around 1932, Mallie moved to Pasadena with her family to start a new life. Mallie washed and ironed clothes for people and was also on welfare. Carl Anderson, a neighborhood mechanic, advised Jackie as he grew up. At Muir Technical High School, Jackie lettered in baseball, football, basketball, and track. From 1939 to 1941 he attended UCLA but left in his third year to help support his family. He was later drafted into the Army and wanted to become an officer, but was denied. He asked assistance from Joe Louis, who was stationed at his base. With Louis's help he attended Officer Candidate School and became an officer. He was discharged in 1945 and Branch Rick signed him with the Dodgers' farm team, the Montreal Royals, of the International League. In 1947, he was called up to play in the major leagues for the Brooklyn Dodgers.

Figure 151—Jackie Robinson. Copyright © U.S. Postal Service. Reproduced with permission of the U.S. Postal Service.

99. Who spent his youth in Montgomery, Alabama, and Chicago, Illinois, and became a well-known singer and pianist? He was born Nathaniel Adams Coles in 1919. His mother taught him to play piano and by age 12, he was an accomplished pianist. In 1938, he put together a group to play at Sewanee Inn in Los Angeles. The owner named the group the King Cole Trio and Cole, the leader, became known as Nat "King" Cole. He recorded for Capitol Records and sold over 50 million records. He was also known for the movies *St. Louis Blues*, in which he played W.C. Handy, and *The Nat King Cole Story*.

Figure 152—Nat "King" Cole. Copyright © U.S. Postal Service. Reproduced with permission of the U.S. Postal Service.

100. Who began playing the piano at the age of 3 but never learned to read music, began appearing at the age of 7 on a radio station in Pittsburgh, Pennsylvania, and later became a noted jazz artist?

101. Who grew up in Detroit, Michigan, becoming a noted physician, educator and co-editor with A. F. Coner-Edwards of *Black Families in Crisis: The Middle Class*? In 1947, she earned her medical degree from the Howard University College of Medicine.

Figure 153—Erroll Garner. Copyright © U.S. Postal Service. Reproduced with permission of the U.S. Postal Service.

102. What well-known jazz musician, whose early musical influence was his church, was raised in Watts, California? He was born in 1922 and received a trombone when he was 7. In 1934, he began playing bass and became a noted band leader, composer, and bassist. In the 1950s he founded his own publishing and recording companies, and played with leading jazz musicians Miles Davis, Duke Ellington, Charlie Parker, Bud Powell, and Art Tatum. He wrote his first composition, "Half-Mast Inhibition," at age 17, but did not record it until 20 years later. He died in 1979 in Cuernavaca, Mexico, of Lou Gehrig's disease, Amyotrophic Lateral Sclerosis (ALS).

Figure 154—Charles Mingus. Copyright © U.S. Postal Service. Reproduced with permission of the U.S. Postal Service.

103. Who began singing at age 5 and later was referred to as the "Queen of the Moaners," when she became a noted gospel singer? She was born in 1924 in Philadelphia, Pennsylvania. Her mother was Gertrude Mae Murphy. At age 10, Clara was a member of the Ward Trio with her mother and her sister Willa. She received national recognition after appearing at the 1943 National Baptist Convention. The group was known for such songs as "Packin' Up" and "How I Got Over."

Figure 155—Clara Ward. Copyright © U.S. Postal Service. Reproduced with permission of the U.S. Postal Service.

104. Who grew up in High Point, North Carolina, and later became a noted jazz musician?

105. Who was born in 1927 in North, South Carolina, was orphaned at the age of 6, became a noted actress and member of the Katherine Dunham Dance Company? Her first movie was *Casbah* (1948), and she made other movies, including *St. Louis Blues* (1958). She portrayed Catwoman in the TV series *Batman* and was the voice of Yzma in *The Emperor's New Groove* (2000).

Figure 156—John Coltrane. Copyright © U.S. Postal Service. Reproduced with permission of the U.S. Postal Service.

106. What African American civil rights leader's first name was changed from "Michael" to "Martin" when he was about 6 years old?

107. What baseball player from Alabama was introduced to the pepper game, which consisted of fielding balls hit by his father from about 15 feet away, when he was 10 years old? He was born May 6, 1931, in Westfield, Alabama. He attended high school in Fairfield, Alabama and joined the Birmingham Black Barons after high school. As a professional baseball player he was known as the "Say Hey Kid." In 1950, he was signed by the New York Giants. He played for the farm teams at Trenton and Minneapolis and was called up to the major leagues by the New York Giants in 1951. The Giants won the pennant that year.

Figure 157—Martin Luther King, Jr. Copyright © U.S. Postal Service. Reproduced with permission of the U.S. Postal Service.

108. Who was born in Durham, North Carolina in 1932, sang in the church choir, and later became a pop singer, counting among his recordings, *Lover Please* (1962)? He founded a successful gospel music group, the Mount Lebanon Singers. He joined Billy Ward and the Dominoes as the lead singer, and was later replaced by Jackie Wilson. Atlantic Records built a group around him—Clyde McPhatter and the Drifters. In 1962, Ray Stevens was recording "Ahab, the Arab" when he noticed McPhatter in the studio. He changed the words of his song, naming his camel in honor of Clyde. Clyde died in 1972.

Figure 158—Clyde McPhatter. Copyright © U.S. Postal Service. Reproduced with permission of the U.S. Postal Service.

109. Who was born in Rogers, Texas in 1931, and later became a well-known dance choreographer?

110. What famous basketball player, who lived in Monroe, Louisiana, always wanted a train set when he was young, but his parents could not afford it?

Figure 159—Alvin Ailey. Copyright © U.S. Postal Service. Reproduced with permission of the U.S. Postal Service.

111. What singer and actress won a Metropolitan Opera scholarship at the age of 10?

112. What music conductor began studying piano and percussion at the age of 10?

113. Who grew up in Houston, Texas, and became a teacher and playwright known for the play *Black Girl*?

114. What country music singer, born in the small town of Sledge, Mississippi, began working in the cotton fields at age 5?

115. Who, as a youth, was interested in things that flew, and later became the first African American in space?

116. Who grew up in Eatonton, Georgia, at the age of 8 lost the sight in her right eye after she was shot by her older brother with a BB gun, and later wrote the novel *The Color Purple* (1983)?

117. Who grew up in Washington, D.C., attended the University of Maryland, became an entrepreneur and supporter of African American colleges, and was noted for philanthropic activities?

118. Who, in her youth, was interested in anthropology and archaeology, and later became the first African American woman in space?

119. What is the title of the children's book by the famous African American artist Jacob Lawrence?

120. *The Black Troubadour: Langston Hughes* (1970) received the Coretta Scott King Award in what year?

121. Who is the author of the children's books *Rosa Parks* (1973), *Paul Robeson* (1975), *Grandmama's Joy* (1980), and *Grandpa's Face* (1988)?

122. *Let the Circle Be Unbroken* (1981) by Mildred D. Taylor received the Coretta Scott King Award for Text in what year?

123. Who takes the little girl on a trip in the children's book *Just Us Women* (1982) by Jeannette Caines?

124. Who received the 1984 Coretta Scott King Award for Illustration, for the book *My Mama Needs Me*, with text by Mildred Pitts Walter?

125. The children's book *Stevie* (1986), by John Steptoe, is about sibling rivalry and is narrated by whom?

126. Who is the author of the children's books *Stevie* (1986), *Mufaro's Beautiful Daughters* (1987), and *The Story of Jumping Mouse* (1989)?

127. Who are Manyara and Nyasha?

128. *The Friendship* (1987) by Mildred D. Taylor received the Coretta Scott King Award for Text in what year?

129. Who did Mirandy dance with in the children's book, *Mirandy and Brother Wind* (1988)?

130. In the children's book *The Baby Leopard* (1990) by Linda and Clay Goss, the baby leopard got his spots because he played with what?

131. What award did Mildred D. Taylor receive for the children's book *The Road to Memphis* (1990)?

132. Who is the author of the children's book *Ma Dear's Apron* (1997)?

133. *Bud, Not Buddy* (2000) by Christopher Paul Curtain received the Coretta Scott King Award for Text in what year?

134. *Miracle's Boys* (2001) by Jacqueline Woodson received the Coretta Scott King Award for Text in what year?

135. *Land* (2001) by Mildred D. Taylor received the Coretta Scott King Award for Text in what year?

136. *Bronx Masquerade* (2002) by Nikki Grimes received the Coretta Scott King Award for Text for what year?

Answers — 4 — Children

1. Aesop (6th century BCE)

2. Crispus Attucks (c.1723–1779)

3. Benjamin Banneker (1731–1806)

4. Elizabeth Freeman (c.1742–1829)

5. Peter Salem (c.1756–1816)

6. William Ball (?–?)

7. Jean Baptiste Pointe Du Sable (c.1745–1818)

8. Pierre Toussaint (1766–1853)

9. Moses Sash (1755–?)

10. Edward Rose (c.1786–1834)

11. Sojourner Truth (1797–1883)

12. James P. Beckwourth (1798–c.1867)

13. Jordan B. Noble (c.1800–1880)

14. Anna Murray Douglass (1813–1882)

15. Henry H. Garnet (1815–1882)

16. John Jones (1817–1879)

17. Baltimore, Maryland

18. Harriet Tubman (1820–1913)

19. Daniel Hale Williams (1856–1931)

20. Edward M. Bannister (1828–1901)

21. Osborne Perry Anderson (1830–1872), Canadian

22. Robert Smalls (1839–1915)

23. John Henry (c.1844–c.1887)

24. Charlotte E. Ray (1850–1911)

25. Olivia Davidson Washington (1854–1889)

26. Nat Love (1854–1921)

27. Surinam

28. Booker T. Washington (1856–1915)

29. Henry O. Tanner (1859–1937)

30. George Washington Carver (1864–1943)

31. Victoria Earle Matthews (1861–1907)

32. Josephine D. Heard (1861–c.1921)

33. Georgia E.L. Patton (1864–1900)

34. Matthew Henson (1866–1955)

35. W.E.B. Du Bois (1868–1963)

36. John Hope (1868–1936)

37. Amanda Gray Hilyer (1870–1957)

38. Bill Pickett (1870–1932)

39. Geraldine "Deenie" Pindell Trotter (1872–1918)

40. Dr. Ionia Rollin Whipper (1872–1953)

41. Dayton, Ohio

42. Dr. Carter G. Woodson (1875–1950)

43. Virginia Randolph (1874–1958)

44. Charles Spurgeon Johnson (1893–1956)

45. Lethia C. Fleming (1876–1963)

46. Eleven

47. Meta Vaux Warrick Fuller (1877–1968)

48. Nannie Helen Burroughs (1879–1961)

49. Benjamin O. Davis, Sr. (1877–1970)

50. Millie E. Hale (1881–1930) founded the Millie E. Hale Hospital and Training School

51. Mary E. Branch (1881–1944)

52. Edwin Harleston (1882–1931)

53. James Hubert "Eubie" Blake (1883–1983)

54. Dr. Ernest E. Just (1883–1941)

55. Lucie Campbell Williams (1885–1962)

56. Lucy Diggs Slowe (1885–1937)

57. A'Lelia Walker (1885–1931)

58. Clementine Hunter (1886–1988)

59. Daisy Lampkin (c.1884–1965)

60. Claude McKay (1889–1948)

61. Horace Pippin (1888–1946)

62. Ferdinand "Jelly Roll" Morton (1890–1941). There were several versions of the origin of the nickname, "Jelly Roll."

63. Bessie Coleman (1892–1926)

64. James P. Johnson (1894–1955)

65. Melnea Cass (1896–1978)

66. Florence Mills (1896–1927)

67. Charlemae Hill Rollins (1897–1979)

68. Aaron Douglas (1898–1979)

69. Sadie T.M. Alexander (1898–1989)

70. Duke Ellington (1899–1974)

71. Montgomery, Alabama

72. Annie Greene Nelson (1902–1993)

73. Langston Hughes (1902–1967)

74. Arna Bontemps (1902–1973)

75. Louise Beavers (1902–1962)

76. Jimmy Rushing (1902–1972)

77. W. Montague Cobb (1903–1990)

78. Ralph Bunche (1904–1971)

79. Washington, D.C.

80. Coleman Hawkins (1904–1969)

81. Josephine Baker (1906–1975)

82. Ann Tanneyhill (1906–2001)

83. Thurgood Marshall (1908–1993)

84. Roberta Martin (1907–1969)

85. Chester Arthur Burnett (1910–1976). His nickname was "Howlin' Wolf."

86. Robert Johnson (1911–1938)

87. Josh Gibson (1911–1947)

88. Mollie Moon (1912–1990)

89. Virginia Lacy Jones (1912–1984)

90. Jesse Owens (1913–1980)

91. Billy Eckstine (1914–1993)

92. Sister Rosetta Tharpe (1915–1973)

93. Billie Holiday (1915–1959)

94. McKinley Morganfield (1915–1983)

95. Fannie Lou Hamer (1917–1977)

96. Ossie Davis (1917–2005) and Ruby Dee (1924–)

97. Mabel Murphy Smythe-Haithe (1918–)

98. Jackie Robinson (1919–1972)

99. Nat "King" Cole (1919–1965)

100. Erroll Garner (1921–1977)

101. Jeanne Spurlock (1921–1999)

102. Charles Mingus (1922–1979)

103. Clara M. Ward (1924–1973)

104. John Coltrane (1926–1967)

105. Eartha Kitt (1927–)

106. Martin Luther King, Jr. (1929–1968)

107. Willie Mays (1931–)

108. Clyde McPhatter (1932–1972)

109. Alvin Ailey (1931–1989)

110. Bill Russell (1934–)

111. Diahann Caroll (1935–)

112. James Depriest (1936–)

113. Jennie E. Franklin (1937–)

114. Charley Pride (1938–)

115. Guion Bluford, Jr. (1942–)

116. Alice Walker (1944–)

117. Camille Cosby (1945–)

118. Dr. Mae C. Jemison (1956–)

119. *Harriet and the Promised Land* (1968)

120. 1971

121. Eloise Greenfield (1929–)

122. 1982

123. Aunt Martha

124. Pat Cummings (1950–)

125. Robert

126. John Steptoe (1950–1989)

127. Mufaro's two daughters in *Mufaro's Beautiful Daughters*

128. 1988

129. Ezel

130. Fire

131. Coretta Scott King Award

132. Pat Cummings (1950–)

133. 2000

134. 2001

135. 2002

136. 2003

5 — Education

1. Who established a school for African Americans in Philadelphia, Pennsylvania, in 1795, and in 1804 founded the Society of Free People of Colour for Promoting the Instruction and School Education of Children of African Descent?

2. In 1798, what prominent African American established, in his Boston home, a school for African Americans?

3. Who was one of three former slaves, who in 1807 founded the first school for African Americans in Washington, D.C.? The school was located in the vicinity of 3rd and D Streets, Southeast (SE).

4. Who founded a day school in Baltimore, Maryland, that taught people of color from about 1830 to 1869?

5. Whose estate led to the 1837 founding of the educational entity that became Cheyney University?

6. In 1849, who was the first African American to hold a professorship at a predominantly White college?

7. What African American woman arrived in Los Angeles in 1850 as a slave, petitioned the court for her freedom and obtained it, and with other African Americans, established the First African Methodist Episcopal Church in 1872? As a nurse and midwife she helped deliver babies of all races and also donated land to schools.

Figure 160—Biddy Mason. Courtesy of the Natural History Museum, Los Angeles County Museum of Natural History, Seaver Center for Western Research

8. What African American abolitionist organized schools in San Francisco, Oakland, Sacramento and Stockton, California, and sometimes served as a temporary teacher until a teacher could be located?

9. What African American teacher and journalist was known for helping fugitive slaves living in Canada, from 1852 to 1854?

10. Who was the leader of Miner Teachers' College, District of Columbia, for 37 years?

11. What college was established in 1854 by John Miller Dickey and his wife, Sara Emlen Cresson, in Chester County, Pennsylvania? Its first name was Ashmun Institute; in 1866 the college was renamed to its current name.

12.   What Kentucky college was established in 1855 to educate African Americans and Caucasians at the same time?

13.   Wilberforce University was founded in 1856; in whose honor was it named?

14.   What college began in 1862 in Camp Shiloh and moved to Memphis, Tennessee, in 1863? In 1870, after receiving a donation of $20,000 from Dr. Francis J. LeMoyne, a doctor and abolitionist from Pennsylvania, the American Missionary Association constructed two buildings. In 1968, the college merged with Owen College, which was established in 1950 by the Tennessee Baptist Missionary and Educational Convention, and named in honor of S.A. Owen, a well-known religious and civic citizen.

15.   Who married Francis J. Grimké and maintained a diary while teaching former African American slaves of Port Royal, South Carolina—the Gullah or Geechee Sea Islanders—from October 27, 1862 through the last of May in 1864?

16.   In 1863, who became the first African American president of Wilberforce University?

17.   The majority of African American colleges were established after what historical event?

18.   Many African American colleges were established by what two entities?

19.   In 1866, what college was founded in Jefferson City, Missouri, by former Union soldiers of the 62nd U.S. Colored Infantry? These soldiers were located at Fort McIntosh, Texas, but were composed primarily of soldiers from the state of Missouri.

20.   What university was established in Nashville, Tennessee in 1866 by the American Missionary Association to educate African Americans?

21.   In 1873, who graduated from Atlanta University and later helped found the Haines Normal and Industrial Institute, located in Augusta, Georgia, which closed in 1949?

22.   Rust College was established in 1866, and named in whose honor?

23.   In 1867, Morgan State University was founded; how did it get its name?

24.   In 1867, Augusta Institute was established by Reverend William Jefferson White in Augusta, Georgia. The institute was later moved to Atlanta, Georgia and became Morehouse College, named in whose honor?

25.   Howard University was established in 1867 by an act of Congress and named in whose honor?

26. Scotia Seminary was established in 1867 by which North Carolina religious group?

27. What 1867 amendment was adopted to the U.S. Constitution and provided education as a right for African Americans?

28. Who opened an industrial school for Colored youth near Savannah, Georgia, in 1868?

29. Who became the first African American principal in the New York public school system?

30. Who served as Republican Texas state senator from 1870 to 1872, campaigned for education, protection for African Americans, prison reform, and tenant-farming reform, and attempted to establish a congressional district in Texas for African Americans? He voted (along with all African American members of the Texas legislature) for the bill that later enabled the establishment of Texas A&M University and Prairie View A&M University?

31. Who was the first African American to graduate from Harvard? This 1870 graduate became a professor of mental and moral philosophy at the University of South Carolina in 1873.

32. In 1871, the land of the defunct Oakland College in Lorman, Mississippi, was purchased by the state of Mississippi to establish what college for African Americans? This college was named after the 1871 governor of Mississippi, James L. Alcorn (1816–1894).

33. What representative of the state of Mississippi resigned his seat in the U.S. Senate on March 3, 1871, to become president of Alcorn State University in Lorman, Mississippi?

34. Where was Booker T. Washington educated?

35. What college was established in 1875 in Knoxville, Tennessee, by the United Presbyterian Church of North America? In the early days, education among African Americans was such that, until around 1931, the education offered by practically all the colleges ranged from first grade through high school. The structure of segregated schooling forced it to be shared with colleges.

Figure 161—Hiram Revels. U.S. Senate.

36. Established in 1875, Stillman College was named in whose honor?

37. In 1876, who became the first African American to obtain a Ph.D. from an American college?

38.   Meharry Medical College was established in 1876 in Nashville, Tennessee, and was named in whose honor?

39.   In 1876, who sponsored a bill in the Texas legislature that created Prairie View Normal College, later known as Prairie View A&M University? How did this school get its name?

40.   What college was founded by the American Baptist Home Mission Society in 1877 in Natchez, Mississippi, and moved to Jackson, Mississippi, in 1882? The state of Mississippi began supporting the college in 1940.

41.   Livingstone College in Salisbury, North Carolina, was established in 1879 by what religious organization?

42.   Spelman College was established in 1881 by Sophia B. Packard and Harriet E. Giles, and later renamed in whose honor?

43.   In 1881, Tuskegee Institute was established. How did it get its name?

44.   What college was founded in Jackson, Tennessee, by the Colored Methodist Episcopal (CME) Church (now Christian Methodist Episcopal [CME] Church) in 1882? In whose honor was the college named?

45.   Texas College, Paine College, Miles College, and Lane College were all founded by what religious organization?

46.   Atlanta University (now Clark Atlanta University), Fisk University, Talladega College, and Tougaloo College were established by what association?

47.   Morehouse College, Virginia Union University, Shaw University, and Benedict College were supported by what society?

48.   Allen University, Campbell College, Daniel Payne College, Edward Waters College, Kittrell College, Morris Brown College, Paul Quinn College, Payne Theological Seminary, Shorter College, Turner Theological Seminary, and Wilberforce University were established by what religious organization? The African Methodist Episcopal Church came into existence as a result of the Methodist Church, founded by John Wesley. Wesley, an Anglican, started a movement within the Church of England to improve the spiritual life of the Church. The movement spread to the English colonies. John Wesley ordained Dr. Thomas Coke and sent him to the colonies to organize the Church. Dr. Coke arranged a general meeting of the Church in Baltimore, Maryland in December 1784. Richard Allen, founder of the African Episcopal Methodist Church, was present at the conference. The African Episcopal Methodist denomination was established in Philadelphia, Pennsylvania in 1816. Richard Allen became the first bishop at a General Conference in Philadelphia, Pennsylvania, on April 10, 1816.

49. George Washington Carver was traded for a racehorse when he was an infant, attended Simpson College in 1887, and transferred to Iowa Agricultural College (now Iowa State University) in 1891. He received a B.S. degree in 1894 and an M.S. degree in 1896, and later taught at what colleges?

50. What college for African Americans was founded in Tallahassee, Florida, in 1887, by the state of Florida?

51. Who petitioned the Texas legislature in 1887 to establish a school in Texas for hearing-impaired and blind African American youth?

52. Where was Ida B. Wells-Barnett educated?

Figure 162—George Washington Carver. Reproduced from the Collections of the Library of Congress.

53. What college for African Americans was established in 1891 in Dover, Delaware, by the state of Delaware?

54. Whose speech, heard while John Hope attended Brown University (1890–1894), inspired Hope to become an educator?

55. What college, established in 1895 by the state of West Virginia to train African American teachers to educate children of African American coal miners, was initially known as Bluefield Colored Institute?

56. What are the names of the universities where W.E.B. Du Bois taught?

57. Fort Valley State College, Georgia was founded in 1895, and became a major educational institution under whose leadership from 1904 to 1938? Its founder received the 1930 Spingarn Medal. He was born in 1866 in Sparta, Georgia to Henry Alexander Hunt, Sr. and Mariah Hunt. He earned his B.A. from Atlanta University in 1890. In 1904, he became the second principal of Fort Valley High and Industrial School, changed the curriculum from liberal arts to industrial education, and increased enrollment. He died in 1938.

58. What 1896 court case legalized "Separate But Equal"?

59. In 1896, who became the first African American to receive a Ph.D. in history from Harvard University, and was the recipient of the 1920 Spingarn Medal?

60. In 1897, who founded the Denmark Industrial School, located in Denmark, South Carolina, which later became Voorhees College? She graduated from Tuskegee Institute and was influenced by Booker T. Washington. She wanted to develop a school similar to Tuskegee Institute in South Carolina. When a wealthy industrialist, Ralph Vorhees, donated 380 acres to the school in 1902, she honored the benefactor by changing the school's name to Vorhees Industrial School.

61. Who founded the American Negro Academy, which encouraged scholarly publications on African American culture and history, in 1897? He was born in 1819 in New York City, attended the Noyes Academy in Canaan, New Hampshire and the Oneida Institute in Whitesboro, New York. In 1844, he became an Episcopal minister and traveled to Cambridge, England, where he attended Queen's College. He earned his bachelor's degree in 1853. He returned to the United States in 1873 after 16 years in Liberia, and established St. Luke's Episcopal Church in Washington, D.C. He retired from the ministry in 1894 and taught at Howard University from 1895–1897. He died in 1898, about a year after he established the American Negro Academy.

Figure 163—Alexander Crummell. Moorland Spingarn Research Center, Howard University.

62. The Colored Industrial and Agricultural School was established in 1901 as a private industrial school; its name was changed in 1946 to what? In 1974, the name was changed to Grambling State University. The university is located in north central Louisiana. From the 1970s to the present, the university has prospered.

63. What is the title of Booker T. Washington's autobiography, written in 1901? He was born on April 5, 1856, in Hales Ford, Virginia. His mother's name was Jane and his biological father was said to be James Burroughs, their master. His mother later married Washington Ferguson. He had two brothers, John and an adopted brother, James, and a sister, Amanda.

64. Who founded the Teacher Training and Industrial Institute in Athens, Georgia in 1902, and organized land clubs to purchase land for African Americans? She was born on February 1, 1873, in the city of Athens, Georgia. Her parents were Alfred and Louise Terrell Jackson. She attended public school in Athens, and attended the Normal Department of Atlanta University from 1890 to 1894. She attended Harvard in 1904, the University of

Figure 164—Booker T. Washington. Reproduced from the Collections of the Library of Congress.

Chicago in 1909, and the University of Pennsylvania in 1915, and married Samuel Harris. Her major book was *Race Relations*, which was published in 1925. The purpose of the book was to promote better race relations and feelings among the races. She also sought expression from a diverse group of people. She was an early multiculturalist.

65. Who founded the all woman's college, Palmer Memorial Institute, in Sedalia, North Carolina in 1902?

66. Who founded Utica College, which is now the Utica campus of the Hinds Community College of Jackson, Mississippi, in 1903?

67. Who founded the Franklin Normal and Industrial Institute, located in Franklin, Virginia, in 1904?

68. What college was established in 1904 as Daytona Normal and Industrial Institute for Negro Girls, by Mary McLeod Bethune?

Figure 165—Charlotte Hawkins Brown. State of North Carolina, Department of Cultural Resources.

69. What college was established in 1905 by Bishop Elias Cottrell in Holly Springs, Mississippi, and lasted until 1982?

70. Miles College was established in 1905, and was named in whose honor?

71. Who was a recognized teacher and community activist in the early 1900s, who later founded the Dorchester Home for elderly women in Lynchburg, Virginia?

72. Who established a hospital for African Americans at her college in the early 1900s, and was the recipient of the 1935 Spingarn Medal?

73. Who became the first African American president of Morehouse College in 1906, in 1929 became the first African American president of Atlanta University (now Clark Atlanta University), and was the recipient of the 1936 Spingarn Medal?

74. What fund was founded in 1907 to improve the quality of instruction in rural American schools, named in honor of a wealthy Quaker philanthropist?

Figure 166—Mary McCleod Bethune. Reproduced from the Collections of the Library of Congress.

75. Who established the National Training School for Women and Girls in Washington, D.C. in 1909, and advocated racial pride and heritage?

76. In 1910, what college was founded in Durham, North Carolina, by James E. Shepard, to educate African Americans?

77. What college opened in Nashville, Tennessee in 1912, as a land-grant college by the state of Tennessee?

78. What African American educator and writer taught philosophy at Howard University from 1912 to 1953, and was the first African American Rhodes Scholar?

79. Who was associated with Cheyney State College from 1913 to 1951, and increased the college's prominence?

80. Who taught German at Howard University from 1913 to 1918, was on the National Board of Directors of the NAACP for 36 years, and was the recipient of the 1955 Spingarn Medal?

81. What fund was established in 1913 to provide grants for African American school construction, and was named in honor of a wealthy business man?

82. What term did W.E.B. Du Bois use to refer to African American leaders?

83. Who wanted Booker T. Washington to build a medical center at Tuskegee?

84. The disagreement among Booker T. Washington and other African American educators centered around Booker T. Washington's encouragement of African Americans to forget about the right to what?

85. What colleges did Paul Robeson attend?

86. What descendant of an African chief was born in Amelia County, Virginia, worked for racial goodwill, and in 1915, succeeded Booker T. Washington at Tuskegee? His autobiography is entitled *Finding a Way Out*, and he was the recipient of the 1932 Spingarn Medal. He was born in 1867 to Emily Brown and Booker Moton. He enrolled in Hampton Institute, but failed the entrance exam. He worked at the Hampton Institute saw mill during the day and attended school at night. He passed the entrance exam and graduated from Hampton Institute in 1890. He worked at Hampton Institute for 25 years and became the principal of Tuskegee Institute after Booker T. Washington's death. Moton retired in 1932 after working 19 years at Tuskegee Institute.

Figure 167—Robert Russa Moton. Schomburg Center for Research in Black Culture, New York Public Library.

87. What school was established to train African American officers in World War I?

88. In 1923 this university's name was changed to Johnson C. Smith University; what was the prior name? The university is affiliated with the Presbyterian Church of the United States and became a coeducational institution in 1932.

89. Who was an assistant to Carter G. Woodson (1875–1950), wrote many African American articles, and was the recipient of the 1926 Spingarn Medal? He was born in 1897 in Washington, D.C. In 1917 he graduated Phi Beta Kappa from Williams College. He enlisted in the military and fought in World War I, advancing from private to lieutenant in the African American 372d Infantry, and was wounded during combat. From 1919–1924, he lived in Paris, France, where he saw the international scope of the "race problem." He returned to the United States to fight racism and taught at Virginia Union University (1925–1931) and Atlanta University (1933–1938). In 1929, he earned his M.A. from Williams College and earned his Ph.D. from Harvard in 1930. In 1932–1933, he was an assistant to Carter G. Woodson at

Figure 168—Rayford W. Logan. Schomburg Center for Research in Black Culture, New York Public Library.

the Association for the Study of Negro Life and History. In 1941, Logan published *The Diplomatic Relations of the United States and Haiti, 1776–1891*, and Haiti awarded him the Order of Honor and Merit. He was chair of the Department of History at Howard University and editor of the *Journal of Negro History*, and died in 1982.

90. Who became the first African American president of Howard University in 1926, and was the recipient of the 1929 Spingarn Medal? Wyatt Mordecai Johnson was born in 1890, in Paris, Tennessee to Wyatt and Carolyn Johnson. He graduated from Atlanta Baptist College (later Morehouse College) in 1911. He graduated from Harvard University Divinity School in 1922 and received his Doctor of Divinity degree in 1928 from Gammon Theological Seminary. While president of Howard University, he doubled teachers' salaries. He attracted top African Americans in various fields, such as Dr. Charles Drew (medicine), and Rayford W. Logan and John Hope Franklin (history). Howard Thurman was brought in to develop a religious program. Johnson sought congressional appropriations for the university,

Figure 169—Mordecai Johnson. Schomburg Center for Research in Black Culture, New York Public Library.

and raised academic standards and admission requirements.

91. Where did Dr. Charles Drew attend college?

92. Who was the dean of the college at Tuskegee Institute from 1927 to 1936, and the recipient of the 1934 Spingarn Medal?

93. Dr. Ralph Bunche (1904–1971) taught at what universities?

94. What magazine was a popular source about African American education from 1932 to 1997?

95. What institution published the *Journal of Negro Education*? The *Journal of Negro Education* was founded in 1932 and was published from 1932 until 1971. The purpose of the journal was to identify and discuss problems in education relating to African Americans. The three missions of the journal were as follows: 1) to collect and disseminate facts on African American education, 2) present discussion on proposals relating to African American education, and 3) sponsor investigations of issues relating to African American education.

Figure 170—Dr. Ralph Bunche. Reproduced from the Collections of the Library of Congress.

96. Who was the dean of the Howard Law School from 1932 to 1935, brought full accreditation to the school, and was the recipient of the 1950 Spingarn Medal?

97. Who was the head of the Howard University's sociology department from 1934 to 1959?

98. Who taught history at Shaw University (1935–1939), Dillard University (1939–1953), and Morgan State University (1953–1974)?

99. What college was part of the Houston Independent School District in 1935, and in 1947 was established by the Texas legislature as an institution for the education of African Americans?

Figure 171—Charles Hamilton Houston. Schomburg Center for Research in Black Culture, New York Public Library.

100. In 1939, the U.S. Supreme Court ruled that the Law School at the University of Missouri must build a law school for African Americans equal to the existing law school, or admit what African American student to the University of Missouri Law School? In 2001, the University of Missouri, Columbia campus, renamed its Black Culture Center in honor of Lloyd Gaines. A scholarship is also offered in his honor by the University of Missouri, Columbia.

101. Who was on the faculty of Howard University for 30 years and authored the book entitled *Quest for Equality from Civil War to Civil Rights*?

102. Who was president of Fort Valley State College (1939–1945), the first African American president (1945–1957) of Lincoln University (Oxford, Pennsylvania), which was established in 1854, and the father of Julian Bond?

103. Who was dean of the Howard University School of Law from 1939 to 1946, and the first African American to become a judge in the U.S. Circuit of Appeals?

104. What educator titled his autobiography *Born to Rebel*, served as president of Morehouse College from 1940 to 1967, and was the recipient of the 1982 Spingarn Medal?

105. Who said that one of his greatest honors was teaching and advising the Morehouse College student, the late Dr. Martin Luther King, Jr.?

106. What was the name of the college used to train African American pilots in World War II?

107. Who was the first African American hired as a professor at a prestigious university, in 1941?

108. Who challenged the testing of African American children?

109. Who founded the United Negro College Fund in 1944, and was the recipient of the Presidential Medal of Freedom in 1987 and the 1988 Spingarn Medal? He was born on October 10, 1901. In 1923, he received a doctorate in veterinary medicine and in 1927, a Master of Science degree, both from Iowa State College. He also receive a Ph.D. from Cornell University in 1932. He joined Tuskegee in 1928, headed the veterinary division, and was Director of the School of Agriculture. He became president of Tuskegee and served from 1935 to 1953. The

Figure 172—Dr. Allison Davis. University of Chicago.

purpose of the United Negro College Fund is to assist historically Black universities and colleges through programs and scholarships. By the time of his death in 1988, the fund had assisted 42 colleges and universities.

110.

Figure 173—Booker T. Washington Memorial Commemorative Coin. Courtesy U.S. Mint.

Who was the first African American honored by the issuance of a commemorative U.S. half dollar in 1946? These coins were issued from 1946 through 1951.

111. Who became the first African American president of Fisk University in 1947, and founded *Opportunity*, the Urban League's journal?

112. Who became the second African American educator to appear on a U.S. postage stamp (in 1947), and a member of the Hall of Fame for Great Americans in 1973?

113. How did Dr. Charles Drew meet his demise in 1950?

Figure 174—Charles Spurgeon Johnson. Fisk University Library's Special Collections.

114. What college was started in 1950 in Itta Bena, Mississippi by the Mississippi legislature as Mississippi Vocational College? Its purpose was to educate rural and elementary teachers, and to provide vocational education to African Americans. The university is located in Leflore County. In 1964, the name was changed from Mississippi Vocational College to Mississippi Valley State College. In 1974, the name was changed to Mississippi Valley State University. The university is located on 450 acres.

115.

Figure 175—George Washington Carver–Booker T. Washington Commemorative Coin. Courtesy U.S. Mint.

What two African Americans were honored in 1951 by the issuance of a commemorative U.S. half dollar? These coins were issued from 1951 through 1954.

116. In the 1954 case of *Brown v. Board of Education of Topeka, Kansas*, which resulted in the desegregation of public schools, what was Brown's first name?

117. What African American educator and psychologist is known for his studies on school segregation and its effects on students, and was the recipient of the 1961 Spingarn Medal?

118. President Eisenhower deputized the Arkansas National Guard in 1957 and dispatched federal troops from the 101st Airborne Division of the U.S. Army to Little Rock Central High School to protect whom, while they were attempting to integrate the school?

119. Who was mentor to the nine African Americans attempting to attend the all-White Little Rock Central High School? All ten were recipients of the 1958 Spingarn Medal.

120. Who taught the first civil rights course in an American law school and was president of Howard University from 1960 to 1969?

121. In 1962, who was escorted by federal marshals and became the first African American to integrate the University of Mississippi?

122. In 1963, the governor of Alabama stood in the entrance when what two African American students attempted to register escorted by U.S. Marshals?

123. Who founded of the Harlem School for the Arts in 1964?

124. Who was president of Jackson State University from 1967 to 1984?

125. Who boycotted classes in 1968 to show support for the striking sanitation workers and Martin Luther King, Jr.?

126. In 1968, who became the first African American president of the National Education Association (NEA)?

127. Who was Superintendent of Public Education for the state of California from 1970 to 1982, and was the recipient of the 1973 Spingarn Medal?

Figure 176—Dr. John A. Peoples, Jr. Jackson State University.

128. Who founded the Westside Preparatory School, located in Chicago, Illinois, in 1975?

129. What became the new name of Tuskegee Institute in 1985?

130. What African American woman educator was honored in 1985 by her appearance on a U.S. postage stamp?

131. When was the *Brown v. Board of Education of Topeka, Kansas* case reopened?

132. What Hunter College anthropologist became the first African American president of Spelman College (a women's college), in 1987?

133. What African American college located in Dallas, Texas closed in 1988, and what college later reopened on that site?

Answers — 5 — Education

1. Richard Allen (1760–1831)

2. Prince Hall (c.1735?–1807)

3. George Bell (?–?)

4. Mary Ann Prout, also known as "Aunt Mary Prout" (1801–1884)

5. Richard Humphreys, a Quaker (1750–1832)

6. Charles L. Reason (1818–1893), New York Central College in McGrawville (Cortland County), New York

7. Biddy Mason (1818–1891) is now remembered in Los Angeles with the memorial "Biddy Mason's Place: A Passage of Time"

8. Jeremiah Burke Sanderson (1821–1875)

9. Mary Ann Shadd Carey (1823–1893), born in Wilmington, Delaware. She later returned to the United States and obtained a law degree from Howard University in 1870, becoming the first female African American to receive a law degree

10. Lucy Ellen Moten (1851–1933). The College was founded by Myrtilla Miner (1815–1864) in 1851 to educate African American women. In 1955 the Miner Teachers' College merged with the Wilson Teachers' College, forming the District of Columbia Teachers' College. In 1977 the District of Columbia Teachers' College, the Federal City College, and the Washington Technical Institute merged, creating the University of the District of Columbia.

11. Lincoln University, Pennsylvania

12. Berea College, Berea, Kentucky

13. It was named for the eighteenth-century British abolitionist William Wilberforce (1759–1833).

14. LeMoyne-Owen College

15. Charlotte L. Forten Grimké (1837–1914)

16. Daniel A. Payne (1811–1893), 1863 to 1876

17. Civil War

18. Religious organizations or the states

19. Lincoln University, Missouri

20. Fisk University. It was named for General Clinton B. Fisk (1828–1890), assistant commissioner of the Freedman's Bureau for Tennessee and Kentucky.

21. Lucy Laney (1854–1933)

22. It was named for Richland S. Rust (1815–?), secretary of the Freedmen's Aid Society. Richland S. Rust was also the first president of Wilberforce University. The original name of the institution was Shaw University. Later the name was changed to Rust University and then to Rust College.

23. It was named for Dr. Lyttleton F. Morgan (1759–1833), a trustee and benefactor.

24. Henry L. Morehouse (?–1913), the secretary of the Atlanta Baptist Home Mission

25. Civil War General Oliver Otis Howard (1830–1909), who was also commissioner of the Freedman's Bureau. General Howard served as president from 1869 to 1873.

26. Presbyterians

27. Fourteenth Amendment to the U.S. Constitution, adopted in 1867.

28. Ellen Craft (c.1826–c.1897) and William Craft (1824–1900)

29. Sarah J. Garnet (1831–1911), 1870

30. Matthew Gaines (1840–1900)

31. Richard Theodore Greener (1844–1922)

32. Alcorn State University

33. Hiram Revels (1822–1901)

34. Hampton Institute, 1872–1875

35. Knoxville College

36. It was named for Charles A. Stillman (1819–1895), a Presbyterian minister.

37. Edward Bouchet (1852–1918), Yale University

38. It was named for the five Meharry brothers, who had supported the medical school in the 1870s.

39. William H. Holland (1841–1907). The original settlement of Alta Vista was changed to Prairie View when it became the site for the African American school. It was the former plantation home of Colonel Jack Kirby.

40. Jackson State University

41. African Methodist Episcopal Zion Church

42. In 1884 the name was changed from Atlanta Baptist Female Seminary to Spelman, to honor Mrs. Laura Spelman Rockefeller and her parents, whose names were Harvey Buel Spelman and Lucy Henry Spelman, activists in the anti-slavery movement.

43. It was named for Tuskegee, Alabama, which was named for a Creek town Taskigi, a nearby Native American Indian village. Some contend that Taskigi is a derivation of the Creek word for warrior.

44. Lane College, Bishop Isaac Lane (1834–1937)

45. Christian Methodist Episcopal (CME) Church

46. American Missionary Association

47. American Baptist Home Mission Society

48. African Methodist Episcopal (AME) Church

49. Iowa State University and Tuskegee Institute

50. Originally called the State Normal College for Colored Students, the name was later changed to Florida A&M University.

51. William H. Holland (1841–1907)

52. Rust College, Holly Springs, Mississippi

53. Originally named the State College for Colored Students, the name was later changed to Delaware State University

54. John M. Langston (1829–1897)

55. Bluefield State College

56. Wilberforce University (1894–1896), University of Pennsylvania (1896–1900), and Atlanta University (1901–1914)

57. Henry Alexander Hunt (1866–1938), received the Spingarn Award in 1930

58. *Plessy v. Furgeson*, 1896

59. W.E.B. Du Bois (1868–1963)

60. Elizabeth "Lizzie" Wright (1872–1906)

61. Alexander Crummell (1819–1898)

62. Grambling College. The city of Grambling, Louisiana, was named for P.G. Grambling (?–?).

63. *Up from Slavery* (1901)

64. Judia C. Jackson Harris (1873–19?)

65. Charlotte Hawkins Brown (1883–1961)

66. William H. Holtzclaw (?–1943)

67. Della Irving Hayden (1851–1924)

68. Bethune College, which merged with Cookman College in 1923 to become Bethune-Cookman College

69. Mississippi Industrial College

70. It was named for Bishop William H. Miles (?–?).

71. Amelia Perry Pride (1858–1932)

72. Mary McLeod Bethune (1875–1955)

73. John Hope (1868–1936), a Phi Beta Kappa

74. Anna T. Jeanes (1822–1907) Fund

75. Nannie Helen Burroughs (1879–1961). In 1964, The school was renamed the Nannie Burroughs School.

76. North Carolina Central College

77. Tennessee State University

78. Alain L. Locke (1886–1954)

79. Leslie Pinckney Hill (1880–1960)

80. Carl Murphy (1889–1967)

81. Julius Rosenwald (1862–1932) Fund

82. "Talented Tenth"

83. Daniel Hale Williams (1856–1931)

84. Vote

85. Rutgers College (1915–1919)— now Rutgers University—and Columbia (1920–1923), receiving a law degree

86. Robert Russa Moton (1867–1940)

87. Fort Des Moines, Iowa

88. Biddle Memorial Institute (1870–1883) and Biddle University (1883–1923)

89. Rayford W. Logan (1897–1982)

90. Mordecai Johnson (1890–1976)

91. Bachelor of Arts from Amherst College in Massachusetts in 1926, Medical Doctorate (M.D.) and Master of Surgery (C.M.) from McGill University, located in Montreal, Quebec, in 1933, Doctor of Science in Medicine from Columbia Presbyterian in 1940

92. William Taylor Burell Williams (?–?)

93. Howard University, Chairman of the Political Science Department

(1928–1950), taught at Harvard, 1951 through 1952

94. *Journal of Negro Education*

95. Howard University

96. Charles Hamilton Houston (1895–1950)

97. E. Franklin Frazier (1894–1962)

98. Benjamin A. Quarles (1904–1996)

99. Texas Southern University

100. Lloyd Gaines of St. Louis, Missouri. The case was *Gaines v. Canada, Registrar of the University of Missouri, et al.*

101. Charles Harris Wesley (1891–1987)

102. Dr. Horace Mann Bond (1904–1972), who wrote *Education of the Negro in the American Social Order* (1934), *Negro Education in Alabama: A Study in Cotton and Steel* (1939), *A Study of Factors Involved in the Identification and Encouragement of Unusual Academic Talent Among Underprivileged Populations* (1967), and *Education for Freedom: A History of Lincoln University, Pennsylvania* (1976)

103. William H. Hastie (1904–1976)

104. Benjamin E. Mays (1894–1984)

105. Dr. Benjamin E. Mays (1894–1984), president of Morehouse from 1940 through 1967

106. Tuskegee Institute

107. Allison Davis (1902–1983), University of Chicago, 1941

108. Horace Mann Bond (1904–1972)

109. Frederick D. Patterson (1901–1988)

110. Booker T. Washington (1856–1915)

111. Charles Spurgeon Johnson (1893–1956)

112. George Washington Carver (1864–1943)

113. Dr. Drew died as the result of an automobile accident in 1950 near Burlington, North Carolina, on his way to a medical conference at Tuskegee Institute.

In the days of segregation, Whites were admitted to White hospitals and African Americans were admitted to African American hospitals. Unfortunately, the closest hospital to Dr. Drew was a White hospital and Dr. Drew did not receive the medical treatment needed to save his life.

The separate facilities was made the law of the country by the 1896 Supreme Court ruling of *Plessy v. Furgeson* which endorsed separate facilities.

This meant separate cemeteries, medical facilities, housing, educational institutions (from kindergarten through college), riding sections in buses, trains and planes, separate groups in the armed forces, separate sections in concerts, theaters, separate water fountains and the like. The 1954 Supreme Court case *Brown v. the Board of Education of Topeka, Kansas* overturned the *Plessy v. Ferguson* case.

114. Mississippi Valley State University

115. Booker T. Washington and George Washington Carver

116. Linda, as in Linda Brown

117. Kenneth B. Clark (1914–)

118. Nine African American students

119. Daisy Bates (1914–1999)

120. James M. Nabrit, Jr. (1900–1997)

121. James Meredith (1933–)

122. Two African Americans, Vivian Malone (?–) and James Hood (?–)

123. Dorothy Maynor (1910–1996)

124. Dr. John A. Peoples, Jr. (?–)

125. African American students of the Memphis City Schools

126. Elizabeth Duncan Koontz (1919–1989)

127. Wilson C. Riles (1917–1999)

128. Marva Collins (1936–)

129. Tuskegee University

130. Mary McLeod Bethune (1875–1955)

131. 1986

132. Johnetta Cole (1936–), president from 1987 through 1997

133. Bishop College, Paul Quinn College

6 — Entertainment

1. Who was a great nineteenth-century Shakespearean actor?

2. Who was born in slavery, raised in freedom in Philadelphia, Pennsylvania, by a Quaker, and later became an acclaimed vocalist, referred to as the "Black Swan" in the 1850s? This artist sang before Queen Victoria in England in 1854.

3. What blind slave, who was a talented pianist, had many concerts in the United States and in Europe, winning fame for himself and profit for his owner, Colonel Bethune?

4. What college group was famous for singing spirituals after the Civil War, and how did the group get its name?

5. Who was the composer of the song "Carry Me Back to Old Virginny" (1873), which was the state song of the Commonwealth of Virginia until it was retired in 1997?

6. Who was known as the "greatest female ballad singer"?

7. What British composer of African descent achieved fame with the premiere of his "Hiawatha's Wedding Feast" (1898)?

8. Who is the composer of "Charleston Rag" (1899), "Classic Rag" (1914), "Love Will Find a Way" (with Noble Sissle) (1921), and "You Were Meant for Me" (1922), and was recipient of the Presidential Medal of Freedom in 1981? He was born in Baltimore, Maryland on February 7, 1883 or 1887. Other compositions include "I'm Just Wild About Harry," "Bandana Days," and "Memories of You." In 1998 a high school was built in his honor in Silver Spring, Maryland. The name of the high school is the James Hubert Blake High School.

Figure 177—James "Eubie" Blake. Schomburg Center for Research in Black Culture, New York Public Library.

9. What is the name of Scott Joplin's (c.1867–1917) classic ragtime composition, which was produced in 1899?

10. What composer pioneered the introduction of African American spirituals to the concert stage in the early 1900s? One of his songs was "Deep River" (1917), and he was the recipient of the 1917 Spingarn Medal. He graduated from high school in 1887 in Erie, Pennsylvania. In 1892, he entered the National Conservatory Music School in New York City, and taught there from 1896 to 1898. One of Burleigh's objectives was to document the Negro spirituals developed in the South prior to the Civil War. The songs had not been written down and the authors were not known, but they were a part of the cultural heritage of the southern African

Figure 178—Scott Joplin. Fisk University.

Americans. Burleigh published art songs such as "Jean" (1903), *Saracen Songs* (1914), *Five Songs of Laurence Hope* (1915), and "Ethiopia Saluting the Colors" (1915). Other songs attributed to Burleigh are "Swing Low, Sweet Chariot" (1917), "Go Down Moses" (1917), "By an' By" (1917), "Nobody Knows de Trouble I've Seen" (1928), "Weepin' Mary" (1928), and "Wade in de Water" (1928). He died on September 12, 1949.

11. Who was considered the "Father of the Blues," taught music at the Alabama A&M College in Normal, Alabama in 1900, and left because the college emphasized music he considered inferior? Two of his compositions were "Memphis Blues" (1912) and "St. Louis Blues" (1914), and some of his books include *Blues: An Anthology* (1926), *Negro Authors and Composers of the United States* (1935), *Father of the Blues* (1941), and *Unsung Americans Sung* (1944)?

12. Who claimed to have invented jazz in 1902? He was the composer of "Big Foot Ham" (1924) and "Honky Tonk Music" (1938). His birth name was Ferdinand Joseph La Menthe, or La Mothe or Lemott.

Figure 179—W.C. Handy. Mississippi Valley Collection Libraries. University of Memphis, Memphis, Tennessee.

Researchers have debated the spelling of his last name. Other compositions by Morton include "Black Bottom Stomp," "Muddy Water Blues," and "The Pearls." He died on July 10, 1941.

13. Who was noted for playing the lead in Eugene O'Neill's play *The Emperor Jones* during the 1920s, and was the recipient of the 1921 Spingarn Medal? He was born in 1878 in Richmond, Virginia. He worked as a print shop apprentice before launching a career in the theater. In 1914, he appeared in the play *The Girl at the Fort*. In 1907, Gilpin joined one of the first African American theater companies, the Pekin Company of Chicago. He was a founding member of the Anita Bush Players of New York City (later changed to the Lafayette Players). In 1919, he debuted in the role of the former slave Curtis in John Drinkwater's play *Abraham Lincoln*. In 1920, Gilpin played Buster Jones in *The Emperor Jones*, the first play on Broadway in which an African American played the lead role. Paul Robeson played the lead when the play toured in London. Gilpin contributed funds to the Karamu

Figure 180—Charles Gilpin. Reproduced from the Collections of the Library of Congress.

Playhouse of Cleveland, Ohio. The Karamu Players were renamed the Gilpin Players to honor Gilpin. In 1926, Gilpin played the lead role in the movie version of *Ten Nights in the Barroom*. About 1929, Gilpin lost his voice, and he died in 1930, at age 52.

14. What blues musician, known as Leadbelly, was noted for the songs "On Top of Old Smokey" and "Irene, Good Night"?

15. Who is known as the first African American opera singer? She was born Lillian Evans in 1890 and graduated from the Howard University School of Music in 1917. The name Evanti is a combination of her maiden name and her husband's last name. Evanti performed in the Casino Theater in Nice, France (1925), the Triannon Lyrique in Paris (1926), and Town Hall in Washington, D.C. (1932).

Figure 181—Huddie Ledbetter. Reproduced from the Collections of the Library of Congress.

16. What famous African American lyric tenor was famous for his recital of classical songs and African American melodies, and was received the 1924 Spingarn Medal?

17. What comedienne was known as "Moms"? She was born Loretta Mary Aiken in Brevard, North Carolina but later changed her name because her brother was embarrassed by her entry into show business. When she was 11, her father died as the result of a fire truck explosion. Later, her mother died after being struck by a mail truck. She referred to her audience as children, and they called her "Moms."

18. Who is known for the recording "Carolina Shout" (1921), and for writing the Broadway musical *Runnin' Wild* (1923), which included the recording "The Charleston"? He was born in 1894 in New Brunswick, New Jersey. He was considered the "father of the stride piano" (a contest in which piano players competed against each other with an increasingly difficult level of piano renditions. Some of Johnson's songs include "Keep Off the Grass" (1921), "The Harlem Strut" (1921), "Old Fashioned Love" (1923), and "Jingles" (1930).

Figure 182—James P. Johnson. Schomburg Center for Research in Black Culture, New York Public Library.

19. What singer, called the "Empress of the Blues," recorded "Gulf Coast Blues" (1923) and "Down Hearted Blues" (1923)? She died as the result of an automobile accident near Clarksdale, Mississippi in 1937, and an observance is held every year in her home town of Chattanooga, Tennessee.

20. In the 1920s, who was referred to as the "Uncrowned Queen of the Blues"? She was born Ida Prater in Toccoa, Georgia on February 25, 1896. She was raised in Cedartown, Georgia, and left the town in her teens. She married Adler Cox and kept his last name, even though she remarried twice after he died in World War I. She had a daughter, Helen, with her second husband, Eugene Williams. Her third husband was Jesse Crump, who played the piano in some of her recordings and became her musical director. Some of Cox's notable songs include: "Coffin Blues," "Mississippi River Blues," "Death Letter Blues," "Kentucky Man Blues," "Rambling Blues," and "Wild Women Don't Have the Blues." Cox died in Knoxville, Tennessee on November 10, 1967.

Figure 183—Bessie Smith. Schomburg Center for Research in Black Culture, New York Public Library.

21. Who became famous as a music hall star in Paris during the 1920s, and adopted and taught children of all races? She starred in the movies *Zou-Zou* and *Princess Tam-Tam* in the 1930s, entertained the French troops during World War II, and worked for the French Resistance. She was the first American woman to be accorded French military honor during her funeral, and was buried in the country of Monaco. She was a performer in the Broadway show *Shuffle Along* and also stared in *Chocolate Dandies*. In 1925, she went to Paris, France and performed at the Folies Bergere in 1926 and 1927. The French were more accepting of her as an African American; as a result, Baker chose to remain in Paris. She worked for the French Red Cross during World War II and in 1946, she was accorded the Croix de Guerre and the Medal of the Resistance. In 1961, President Charles de Gaulle of France awarded Baker the Legion d'Honneur for her services during World War II.

Figure 184—Josephine Baker. Schomburg Center for Research in Black Culture, New York Public Library.

22. Who gave style to the big bands with his light touch on the piano, and received the Presidential Medal of Freedom posthumously in 1985?

23. What blues song is said to be the first blues classic song?

24. Who was nicknamed "Papa Joe," and is noted for his Creole Jazz Band in Chicago, Illinois during the 1920s?

25. What blues artist recorded "Matchbox Blues" during the 1920s? He was born in Couchman, Texas in 1897. It was not known if he was born blind or could partially see. In 1917, he moved to Dallas, Texas, where he sometimes sang with Huddie Ledbetter. Some of his many songs include "Long Lonesome Blues" (1926), "Black Snake Moan" (1927), "Blind Lemon's Penitentiary Blues" (1928), and "Pneumonia Blues" (1929).

Figure 185—Count Basie. Reproduced from the Collections of the Library of Congress.

26. Who went to New York City to study chemistry, but became one of the great band leaders and arrangers of the 1920s, 1930s, and 1940s?

27. The play *Shuffle Along* (1921) was written by whom?

28.   Among this artist's many recordings were
        "Down Home Blues" (1921), "Oh Daddy"
        (1921); among her films were *Gift of Gab*
        (1934), *Rufus Jones for President* (1934),
        Cabin in the Sky (1942), *Tales of
        Manhattan* (1942), *Cairo* (1942), *Pinky*
        (1943), *The Member of the Wedding*
        (1952), and *The Sound and the Fury*
        (1959). A play in which she appeared was
        entitled *As Thousands Cheer* (1933). Irving
        Berlin wrote three songs for this artist to
        sing in the play. Her autobiographies were
        His Eye Is on the Sparrow (1958), and *To
        Me It's Wonderful* (1972).

Figure 186—Ethel Waters.
Courtesy of the Academy of
Motion Picture Arts and Sciences.

29.   Who is the noted blues singer who wrote
        the song "Down Hearted Blues" in 1922?
        In 1921, Hunter moved to New York City.
        From the 1920s to the 1930s, she performed
        in clubs, made recordings and traveled the vaudeville route frequented by
        African Americans. Some of her other compositions include "Tain't No-
        body's Biz-ness If I Do" (1923) and "If You Want to Keep Your Daddy
        Home" (1923). In the year 1956, Hunter changed careers after her mother
        died. She became a nurse in New York City after telling the hospital she was
        12 years younger than her age. She only recorded her signature song "Down
        Hearted Blues" during the entire time she worked as a nurse. Hunter con-
        tinued as a nurse until she was asked to retire in 1977. She was thought to be
        at the mandatory retirement age of 70, but she was actually 82. From 1977
        until her death in 1984, she pursued her singing career. She performed at
        nightclubs and TV talk shows. She recorded new albums and re-released
        some of her previous recordings.

30.   Who is an early comedian whose last and
        perhaps best show was *Under the Bamboo
        Tree* (1922)?

31.   Who is the first jazzman to achieve fame on
        the clarinet and soprano saxophone? He was
        born in 1897 in New Orleans and his love of
        music is attributed to his grandfather's influ-
        ence. He became an accomplished clarinet
        player and was often the featured player in a
        band. While playing in Europe in the 1920s,
        he purchased a soprano saxophone, which be-
        came his instrument of choice. Bechet was a
        traveling player from the 1920s to the 1950s,
        playing in New York City, London, Paris,
        and Berlin, and finally settled in Paris. Some
        of Bechet's compositions are highlighted in
        the *Clarence Williams Blue Five* (1924), and

Figure 187—Sidney Bechet.
Copyright © William P. Gottlieb,
1979.

as a trumpeter in the band New Orleans Feetwarmers (1941). His audio autobiography is entitled *Treat it Gentle*. He died in 1959.

32. Who grew up in Memphis, Tennessee, became a noted jazz musician, and became the wife of Louis Armstrong in 1924?

33. What world-renowned contralto from Philadelphia, Pennsylvania sang in Europe (1925–1935) before returning to the United States, performed on the steps of the Lincoln Memorial on April 9, 1939, and was the recipient of the 1939 Spingarn Medal and the Presidential Medal of Freedom in 1963? Her autobiography is entitled *My Lord, What a Morning* (1956).

Figure 188— Marian Anderson. Schomburg Center for Research in Black Culture, New York Public Library.

34. Who was born Lionel Canegata in 1907, changed his name in 1926, and is best known for his work in the Broadway version of *Native Son* (1940s)—in which he played Bigger Thomas—and for his performance in the film *Cry, the Beloved Country* (1951)?

35. As a member of the cast of *Showboat* in 1927, who created the role of Joe and sang "Old Man River"? He was born in Waco, Texas in 1897 to Jessie Cobb and Henry Bledsoe. He graduated from Bishop College in 1918. Later he attended Virginia Union University and Columbia University. Films by Bledsoe include *Safari, Santa Fe Trail, Western Union*, and *Drums of the Congo*.

36. "Basin Street Blues," "Tiger Rag," and "Muskat Ramble" are associated with what jazz musician? He was known for his trumpet playing and singing. He joined Joe Oliver's Creole Jazz Band in 1922 and in 1924, he played with the Fletcher Henderson Orchestra in New York City. He returned to New Orleans and King Oliver's Creole Jazz Band in 1931. Two of his notable recordings are "Hello Dolly" (1968) and "What a Wonderful World" (1970). He also has many film credits. The airport in New Orleans is named in his honor.

37. Who received the Harvard University Prize in 1928 for the best composition for *Don't Be Weary Traveler*?

Figure 189—Louis Armstrong. Mississippi Valley Collection Libraries, University of Memphis, Memphis, Tennessee.

38. What artist recorded "Avalon My Home Town" (1928)? He was born in 1893 in Carroll County Mississippi. Although a talented musician, he did not pursue a musical career.

39.

Figure 190—Left to right: Gabriel Washington, drums; Al Wynn, trombone; Dave Nelson, trumpet: Ma Rainey; Ed Pollock, alto sax; and Thomas A. Dorsey, piano. Schomburg Center for Research in Black Culture, New York Public Library.

What artist recorded the blues song "C.C. Rider" (1928)? She was born Gertrude Pridgett on April 26, 1886 in Columbus, Georgia. Her parents were Ella and Thomas Pridgett. In 1904, she married William "Pa" Rainey; they became known as "Ma"and "Pa" Rainey. She performed for about 25 years before she received a recording contract with Paramount Records. She released many recordings, including "Bo Weevil Blues" and "Jelly Bean Blues." Rainey was referred to as the "Mother of the Blues." She retired in Columbus, Georgia, and died there in 1939.

40. Who is dubbed the "First Lady of Jazz"? One of her compositions is entitled "Froggy Bottom" (1929). She was born in 1910, in Atlanta, Georgia and lived in Pittsburgh as a child. In 1927, she married John Williams and began touring as a music arranger, composer, and pianist. Her celebrated work as a composer was *Zodiac Suites* (1946). Other recordings include "Night Life" (1930), an album *Black Christ of the Andes* (1963), "Mary Lou's Mass" (1969), and "History of Jazz" (1977). She taught at Duke University from 1977 until her death in 1981. In 1983, the Mary Lou Williams Center for Black Culture was established in her honor.

Figure 191—Mary Lou Williams. Copyright © William P. Gottlieb, 1979.

41. Two of what artist's compositions were "Ain't Misbehavin'" (1929) and "Honeysuckle Rose" (1941)? He was born in New York City in 1904 and became a composer and jazz pianist. James P. Johnson taught him how to play jazz piano. He died in 1943, in Kansas City, Missouri. Two of the songs attributed to him are "Squeeze Me" (1919) and "I've Got a Feeling I'm Falling" (1929).

42. Two of Duke Ellington's hits include "Mood Indigo" and "It Don't Mean a Thing (If It Ain't Got That Swing)" (1932). He was the recipient of the 1959 Spingarn Medal and the 1969 Presidential Medal of Freedom. What phrase has been used to refer to Duke Ellington (1899–1974)? He moved to New York City in 1923 and focused on musical arrangement and harmony. He signed an exclusive agreement to perform at the Cotton Club (at this time, the Cotton Club did not admit African Americans as patrons). A few of Ellington's many songs include "Sophisticated Lady" (1933), "Solitude" (1934), "Black and Tan Fantasy" (1938), and "Take the A Train" (1940–1943). A few of his symphonic suites include *Symphony in Black* (1935), *Creole Rhapsody* (1932), *Black, Brown, and Beige* (1943), *Liberian Suite* (1947), *Harlem* (1951), *Night Creatures* (1955), *Festival Suite* (1956), *Such Sweet Thunder* (1957), a tribute to Shakespeare—*Suite Thursday* (1960), a tribute to John Steinbeck, and *Far East Suite* (1966).

Figure 192—Edward "Duke" Ellington. Reproduced from the Collections of the Library of Congress.

43. Who is noted for being an outstanding athlete at Rutgers (1915–1918), attended Columbia Law School (1919–1923), and fought for civil rights on the international stage? During 1933, he donated his earnings from the play *All God's Chillun* to Jewish refugees fleeing Nazi Germany. He appeared in the movies *Body and Soul* (1924) and *Jerico* (1937). He was the recipient of the 1945 Spingarn Medal. His autobiography was entitled *Here I Stand* (1958). He was recognized posthumously in 1978 for his campaign against racism, and he was posthumously inducted into the College Football Hall of Fame in 1995.

Figure 193—Paul Robeson. Courtesy of National Archives.

44. Who gained national prominence portraying "De Lawd" in the play *Green Pastures* (1930–1931), and received the Spingarn Medal in 1931? He was born on September 28, 1864. After seeing a performance of Shakespeare's *Richard III*, his mother named him Richard. Harrison moved to Detroit, where he studied drama at the Detroit School of Dramatic Art. In 1922 he convinced the president of North Carolina A&T, James Dudly, to offer drama courses. He taught and performed in plays until his death on March 14, 1935.

45. Whose famous musical compositions include *Africa* (1930), the *Afro-American Symphony* (1931), and *Symphony No. 2 in G-Minor* (1937)?

46. Who is known for the recording, "My Blue Heaven" (1930s)?

47. Who is known as "The Father of Gospel Music"? Thomas Dorsey's (see Figure 190) composition, "Precious Lord" (1932), was recorded by Mahalia Jackson, Tennessee Ernie Ford, and Elvis Presley. Dorsey was the first African American elected to the Nashville Songwriters International Hall of Fame, and wrote over 1,000 songs. He died in 1993.

Figure 194—William G. Still. Reproduced from the Collections of the Library of Congress.

48. Who was born in Toledo, Ohio in 1909, and is considered one of the great jazz pianists? His signature song was "Tea for Two" (1933). After losing most of his sight by age 4, he studied piano at the Toledo School of Music and was self-taught by listening to records and radio. Tatum later organized a trio consisting of himself (piano), Ting Grimes (drums), and Slam Steward (bass). The group successfully toured the United States.

49. Who had his cartoon illustrations in every issue of *Esquire Magazine* from 1933 to 1958? Two of his most popular characters were *Cutie* and *Sultan*.

50. What movie is about a young woman's conflict with her mother because she was an African American?

51. Compositions by what composer include "Lady with a Fan" (1934) and "That Man's Here Again" (1937)?

52. Who was known as the "King of Tap Dancers," and danced with Shirley Temple in the movie *The Little Colonel* (1935)? He was born in 1878 in Richmond, Virginia and was raised by his grandmother after his parents died. His original name was Luther but he and his younger brother Bill exchanged names (his brother later changed his name from Luther to Percy). Robinson began dancing at age 6 and joined a traveling vaudeville group at age 14. Because of segregation, he danced exclusively for African American audiences until he was about 50. His first theatre exposure was in the play *Blackbirds* (1928), which was pro-

Figure 195—Bill "Bojangles" Robinson. Reproduced from the Collections of the Library of Congress.

duced for a White audience. Movies by Robinson included *In Old Kentucky* (1935), *One Mile from Heaven* (1937), *Rebecca of Sunnybrook Farm* (1938), *Up the River* (1938), and *Stormy Weather* (1943). When he died in New York City in 1949, schools were closed and thousands paid their respects.

53. Who was born Rosetta Nubin in Cotton Plant, Arkansas, and in 1938, as a gospel singer, recorded a song written by Thomas Dorsey, "Hide Me in Thy Bosom"? In 1938, she signed a recording contract with Decca Records and became an overnight sensation with the recording of the Dorsey songs "This Train" and "Rock Me." Other recordings included "Down by the Riverside," "End of My Journey," "Precious Lord," and "Beams of Heaven." Tharpe teamed with Sammy Price to produce the song "Strange Things Happening Every Day" (1944). In 1946, she collaborated with Madam Marie Knight to produce the noted "Up Above My Head." Tharpe's gospel audience was not happy with her singing pop music, but Tharpe continued to tour until she suffered a stroke in 1970. She died in 1973, in Philadelphia, Pennsylvania.

Figure 196—Sister Rosetta Tharpe. Schomburg Center for Research in Black Culture, New York Public Library.

54. Who achieved success from her first song, "A Tisket, a Tasket" (1938), and was the recipient of the Presidential Medal of Freedom in 1992? She was born on April 25, 1917, in Newport News, Virginia to Temperance and William Fitzgerald. In 1934, she was chosen to appear at the Apollo Theater. She planned to dance until she saw the Edwards Sisters dance, and she made a last-second change, singing Hoagy Carmichael's "Judy." The audience demanded an encore. Fitzgerald sold over 40 million albums and received 13 Grammy awards. She sang for over 50 years.

Figure 197—Ella Fitzgerald. Courtesy of the Academy of Motion Picture Arts and Sciences.

55. What actor is best known for his work with Jack Benny? He was born September 18, 1905 in Oakland, California. In 1936, he was invited to appear on the Jack Benny radio show to play the role of Rochester van Jones, a Pullman porter. The scheduled on-show performance turned into a permanent character on both the radio and the TV shows. A few of his film credits include *Man About Town* (1939), *Gone with the Wind* (1939), *You Can't Cheat an Honest Man*

(1939), *Buck Benny Rides Again* (1940), *Birth of the Blues* (1941), *Cabin in the Sky* (1943), *Calling All Kids* (1943), and *Stormy Weather* (1943).

56. Who was the first African American to win an Academy Award (sometimes referred to as an Oscar) for her portrayal of Mammy in the movie *Gone with the Wind* (1939)? This actress also appeared in other movies, including *Alice Adams* (1935), *The Little Colonel* (1935), *Showboat* (1936), *Quick Money* (1937), *Since You Went Away* (1944), and *Song of the South* (1946). After she died, this actress was the first African American to be buried in the Rosedale Cemetery of Los Angeles.

Figure 198—Hattie McDaniel (left) with Fay Bainter. Courtesy of the Academy of Motion Picture Arts and Sciences.

57. Who was dubbed "Lady Day" and was known for the song about racism entitled "Strange Fruit" (1939)? She was discovered by John Hammon in 1933, in the Harlem club Monette's. Her hit song "Strange Fruit" was banned by many radio stations. The flip side of the recording, "Fine and Mellow," was also very popular. Both sides of the recording were played on juke boxes, which the radio stations could not control. Her songs include "God Bless the Child" (1941), "Crazy He Calls Me," "Lover Man," and "Them There Eyes." Holiday also made songs for which she never received royalties.

Figure 199—Billie Holiday. University of Mississippi, Delta Blues Museum.

58. A recording by what group from Indianapolis, Indiana, is entitled "If I Didn't Care" (1939)?

59. What musical instrument is Dizzy Gillespie noted for playing?

60. Who was noted for the jazz recording "Body and Soul" (1940)? He was born on November 21, 1904, in St. Joseph, Missouri. The name Coleman was his mother Cordelia's maiden name. Coleman began playing the saxophone at age 9. He attended high school in Chicago and in Topeka, Kansas, then attended Washburn College in Topeka for about two years. His nickname was "Hawk." He played in the Fletcher Henderson band in New York, where his music matured, and he developed the jazz ballad. In 1934, he left New York to tour and play in Europe. He returned to the United States in 1939 and released his major work, "Body and Soul." In the early 1940s, Haw-

Figure 200—Coleman Hawkins.
Copyright © William P. Gottlieb, 1979.

kins recorded bebop with Max Roach and Dizzy Gillespie. He toured with Norman Granz's "Jazz at the Philharmonic" concerts until 1967. He died on April 20, 1969, in Chicago.

61. Who was nicknamed "Bird" and recorded "Confessing the Blues" (1941)? As a teen, he developed a morphine addiction while he was in the hospital after an automobile accident. The addiction followed Parker for the rest of his life and probably caused his death. In 1945, Parker had his own band and also collaborated with Dizzy Gillespie.

62. Who was noted for playing the butler in the movie *The Invisible Ghost* (1941)? He was born in 1889 in Baltimore, Maryland. In 1911, he received a degree from Dickinson School of Law in Pennsylvania. Muse wrote plays, sketches, and songs, and was a member of the all-African American Lincoln Players. Some of his movie credits include: *Tales of Manhattan* (1942), *Tough as They Come* (1942), *Heaven Can Wait* (1943),

Figure 201—Charlie Parker.
Reproduced from the Collections of the Library of Congress.

Johnny Come Lately (1943), *Jam Session* (1944), *Boston Blackie's Rendezvous* (1945), *Two Smart People* (1946), *The Peanut Man* (1947), *An Act of Murder* (1948), *Apache Drums* (1951), *Porgy and Bess* (1959), *Buck and the Preacher* (1972), *Car Wash* (1976), and *The Black Stallion* (1979). Muse supported the TV series *Amos n' Andy* and was inducted into the Black Filmmakers Hall of Fame in 1973. He died in Perris, California in 1979.

63. Dizzy Gillespie and Charlie Parker are co-founders of what type of jazz which existed from around 1942 to 1950?

64. What jazz musician is known for the recordings "Night in Tunisia" (1942),
"Groovin' High" (1945), "Salt Peanuts"
(1945), "Shaw Nuff" (1945), and "Man-
teca" (1946)? He was born on October
21, 1917, in Cheraw, South Carolina.
His parents were James and Lattie Gillespie and he was the youngest of nine
children. He initially played the trombone, but his arms were too short for the
instrument so he switched to the trumpet. After hearing Roy Eldridge play on
the radio, he wanted to play the trumpet
like Eldridge. He received a scholarship
to attend Laurinburg Institute in North
Carolina but dropped out after two
years. His family moved to Philadelphia
in 1935, where he played in a local band
and acquired the nickname "Dizzy" be-

Figure 202—Dizzy Gillespie.
Reproduced from the Collections of the
Library of Congress.

cause of his antics on stage. Gillespie was noted for playing a trumpet whose
bell was bent at a 45-degree right angle, rather than the traditional straight
bell. The trumpet was originally bent because of an accident, but the con-
striction caused by the bending changed the tone of the instrument, which
Gillespie very much liked. Gillespie was also known for his distending
cheeks or pouches while playing the trumpet.

65. What blues artist recorded "The Jinx Blues" (1942)?

66. In 1987, the University of Idaho School of
Music was named in honor of what jazz artist who recorded "Flying Home" in 1942?
He was born in 1908 in Louisville, Kentucky. His father was killed in World War I
and his mother moved to Birmingham, Alabama, then to Chicago. He took drum lessons and sold newspapers to join the *Chicago Defender* Newsboys Band, where he
played bass drum and snare drum. After high
school, he went to Los Angeles and played
drum in several bands. In 1930, Louis Armstrong asked him to play the vibraphone in
Eubie Blake's "Memories of You," which
became a hit. In 1936, Benny Goodman invited Hampton to play in an interracial band
with Gene Krupa, Teddy Wilson, and himself. The band was known as the Benny
Goodman Quartet and was the first interra-

Figure 203—Lionel Hampton.
Copyright © William P. Gottlieb,
1979.

cial band to tour nationally. Later Hampton formed his own band and continued to perform. The proudest moment of his life was the 1987 dedication of
the Lionel Hampton School of Music at the University of Idaho.

67. Which artist's most popular hits include "Blues in the Night" (1941) and "Stormy Weather" (1943)? Among her movies were *The Duke is Tops* (1938), *Thousands Cheer* (1943), *Spring Fever* (1943), *Stormy Weather* (1943), *Broadway Rhythm* (1944), *Ziegfeld Follies* (1946), *'Till the Clouds Roll By* (1946), *Duchess of Idaho* (1950), *Death of a Gunfighter* (1969), and the movie *The Wiz* (1978)? She is also the recipient of the 1983 Spingarn Medal. She was born Lena Calhoun Horne on June 30, 1917, in Brooklyn, New York. Around 1924, Lena went to live in New York City with her mother. At age 16, she began working at the Cotton Club. In 1940, she toured with Charlie Barbett's band, which launched her career. In many of her movies, her scenes were edited out and not shown in southern theaters. Horne referred to her roles in movies as "window dressing," because she refused to "pass as a Latin" with her fair complexion. Horne starred in the famous African American musical, *Cabin in the Sky* (1943) and in the Broadway play *Jamaica*, in 1957. One of her proudest accomplishments was receiving an honorary doctorate from Howard University in 1980.

Figure 204—*Lena Horne*, oil on canvas, 51 x 31 in., by Edward Biberman. National Portrait Gallery, Smithsonian Institution, Washington, D.C./Art Resource, New York.

68. What artist's popular songs included "Straighten Up and Fly Right" (1944), "I Love You for Sentimental Reasons" (1946), "The Christmas Song," which starts out with "Chestnuts roasting on an open fire..." (1947), and "Mona Lisa" (1950)? He also portrayed W.C. Handy in the movie *St. Louis Blues* (1958) and Professor Sam The Shade in the movie *Cat Ballou* (1965). In his early career, he was known as a piano player. He later formed the King Cole Trio, consisting of Wesley Prince on bass, Oscar Moore on electric guitar, and himself. The band changed members and continued during the 1930s–1940s. In the 1950s, Cole became a solo artist. He also had his own television show in 1957 and 1958. Some of his notable songs include: "It's Only a Paper Moon" (1945), "Nature Boy" (1948), "Too Young" (1951), "Unforgettable" (1952), "Pretend" (1953), "Answer Me, My Love" (1954), "Darling, Je Vous Aime Beaucoup" (1955), "Looking Back" (1958), "Ramblin Rose" (1962), and "Those Lazy, Hazy, Crazy Days of Summer" (1963).

Figure 205—Nat King Cole. Courtesy of the Academy of Motion Picture Arts and Sciences.

69.   A song by what blues folk singer is entitled "One Meat Ball" (1944)? He was born Joshua Daniel White in Greenville, South Carolina on February 11, 1915. His parents were Daisy Elizabeth Humphrey and Dennis White. He quit school to work and between the ages of 7 and 16 he guided blind singers. He led such singers as Blind Lemon Jefferson, Blind John Henry Arnold, Blind Joe Taggart, Blind Blake, and others. Later he recorded secular blues music under the name Pinewood Tom. He recorded his spiritual music under the name Josh White, "The Singing Christian." Due to an injury to his hand, he could not play the guitar and did not perform between 1936 and 1940. In 1941, he recorded the song "Southern Exposure." Someone sent a copy of the song to president Franklin Delano Roosevelt, who invited White to the

Figure 206—Josh White. Copyright © William P. Gottlieb, 1979.

White House, because he knew what the song was about and wanted to meet the singer. Josh put on a concert on for President Roosevelt and had a private talk with him. White complained about the "walking tax" he and other African Americans had to pay to use the streets in his home town of Greenville, South Carolina. He died on September 5, 1969 in Manhasset, New York.

70.   Whose songs included "Prisoner of Love" (1945), "Everything I Love Is Yours" (1947), and "That Old Black Magic"? He was born William Clarence Eckstein on July 8, 1914, in Pittsburgh, Pennsylvania. He started singing at an early age, and also played sports. After completing high school, he spent a year at Howard University, but decided to pursue a music career when he won an amateur music contest. He changed his name to Eckstine because club owners thought his name was too Jewish. At one time he was known as "Billy X. Stine," and later, "Billy Eckstine," and his nickname was "Mr. B." Some of his noted songs include: "A Cottage for Sale" (1945),

Figure 207—Billy Eckstine. Copyright © William P. Gottlieb, 1979.

"Blue Moon" (1947), "Caravan" (1949), and "My Foolish Heart" (1950). In 1957, he recorded the song "Passing Strangers" with Sarah Vaughan. "Something More" (1981) was also successful. He died in Pittsburgh on March 8, 1993.

71. Who made her stage debut in the Broadway play *St. Louis Woman* (1946)? She was born on March 29, 1918, in Newport News, Virginia. Her parents were Reverend Joseph James Bailey and Ella Mae Bailey. She sang in church and later left high school in Philadelphia for a career in singing and dancing. Memorable roles by Bailey include Frankie in *Carmen Jones*; Maria in *Porgy and Bess*; and Aunt Hagar in *St. Louis Blues*. She hosted her own television show in 1971 and was awarded the Presidential Medal of Freedom in 1988.

Figure 208—Pearl Bailey. Courtesy of the Academy of Motion Picture Arts and Sciences.

72. A recording by what blues singer is entitled "Call It Stormy Monday (But Tuesday's Just as Bad)" (1947)?

73. What blues harmonica player recorded "City Blues" (1949)?

74. Who, along with the gospel group the Ward Singers, recorded the song "Surely God Is Able" (1949)? She moved gospel music from the church into nightclubs. Clara and her group, the Ward Singers, dressed in colorful outfits, sparkling jewelry, and wigs. The group concentrated on the most popular gospel music in order to achieve commercial success. Later, Clara and her group performed in Vietnam and in Europe. They were also the first group to perform at the Newport Jazz Festival. Clara died on January 16, 1973.

Figure 209—Clara Ward. Reproduced from the Collections of the Library of Congress.

75. What jazz pianist is noted for his recording of "Un Poco Loco" (1951)?

76. Who is known for the 1952 recording "Moaning at Midnight"?

77. Who was known for the songs "Dust My Broom" (1951), "Hawaiian Boogie" (1952), and "The Sky Is Crying" (1959)? He was born on January 27, 1918, in Richland, Mississippi. He was given his last name by his stepfather, Joe Willie James. He served in the army from 1943 to 1945. When he recorded "Dust My Broom," he was led to believe it was a rehearsal. Once he found out otherwise, he refused to record a B-side to the record, so another artist was used for the B-side. The record was released without his approval. James died on May 24, 1963, as a result of a heart condition. He was only 45 years old.

78. What artist is famous for the songs entitled "Danny Boy" (1952) and "Lonely Teardrops" (1957)? He was born Jack Leroy Wilson on June 9, 1934, in Detroit, Michigan. His parents were Eliza Mae and Jack Wilson, and he was their only son. His father was at times unemployed and his mother was influential on his life. He suffered a massive heart attack on September 29, 1975, while performing in Cherry Hill, New Jersey, and was in a coma until his death on January 21, 1984.

Figure 210—Jackie Wilson. MichaelOchsArchives.com

79. Clyde McPhatter was a member of what group, one of whose songs was entitled "Honey Love" (1954)? The original members who signed with Atlantic Records, were McPhatter, Bill Pinkney, and Andrew and Gerhart Thrasher. Subsequent members were Ben E. King, Rudy Lewis, Johnny Moore, and Charlie Thomas. McPhatter was born in 1932 in Durham, North Carolina. McPhatter became a member of the Drifters in 1953. Some of his hits include: "Sixty Minute Man" (1951), "Have Mercy Baby" (1952), "Money Honey" (1953), "Way I Feel" (1953), "White Christmas" (1954), "Lucille" (1954), "Whatcha Gonna Do" (1955),"Treasure of Love" (1956), "Seven Days" (1956), "Long Lonely Nights" (1957), "Lover's Question" (1958), "Little Bitty Pretty One" (1962), "Everybody's Somebody's Fool" (1965), and "Crying Won't Help You Now" (1965). He starred in the movie *Mister Rock and Roll* (1957), and died in 1972 at age 39.

80. One of what gospel singer's best-known albums is *He's Got the Whole World in His Hand* (1954)? In her early career, Jackson sang with the Johnson Brothers until they went their separate ways in the mid-1930s, when she launched her own career. After signing a contract with Apollo Records, she became well-known for her recordings. Some of her recordings

Figure 211—Mahalia Jackson. Schomburg Center for Research in Black Culture, New York Public Library.

included "Move Up a Little Higher" (1948), "Silent Night," and "I Can Put My Trust in Jesus." "Move Up a Little Higher" sold over 8 million copies. She died on January 13, 1972, in Chicago.

81. Who is the blues singer, whose home town is Pontotoc, Mississippi, and who recorded the songs "Hoochie Coochie Man" (1954) and "Got My Mo Jo Working" (1957)? He was born McKinley A. Morganfield on April 4, 1915, in Mississippi, near Rolling Fork. In 1943, he left Mississippi for Chicago. Later his uncle gave him an electric guitar. He made many records in Chicago. Chicago renamed a section of 43rd Street in his honor. He died in Westmart, Illinois on April 30, 1983.

Figure 212—Muddy Waters or McKinley Morganfield. Reproduced from the Collections of the Library of Congress.

82. A song by what singer is entitled "School Days" (1955)?

83. "Only You" (1955) and "The Great Pretender" (1955) are two of the many songs by what group? The original members of the group were Tony Williams, Herb Reed, David Lynch, and Alex Hodge.

84. What group recorded the song "Earth Angel" in 1955? The original members were Cleveland Duncan, Bruce Tate, Dexter Tisby, and Curtis Williams.

85. What singer was born in McComb, Mississippi, and counts among his noted songs "Bo Diddley" (1955) and "I'm A Man" (1955)? Most of the signs carried by the striking 1968 Memphis sanitation workers were entitled "I'm a Man."

86. Who was born Richard Wayne Penniman, and recorded "Lucille" (1955) and "Long Tall Sally" (1956)?

87. What group recorded the songs entitled "Oh What a Night" (1956) and "Stay in My Corner" (1969)? The members of the group are Verne Allison, Charles Barksdale, Johnnie Carter, Marvin Junior, and Michael McGill.

88. A song by what singer is entitled "Fever" (1956)?

89. The instrumental entitled "Honky Tonk" (1956) was recorded by what artist?

90. Who was the first African American to become a permanent member of the New York Ballet Company in 1955, and founded the Dance Theater of Harlem in 1969?

91. What artist recorded the song entitled "It's Not for Me to Say" (1956)?

92. "Let the Good Times Roll" (1956) is a song by what duo?

93. What artist recorded the song entitled "Blueberry Hill" (1956)? He was born on February 28, 1928, in New Orleans, Louisiana. His first major success was the 1955 recording, "Ain't That a Shame." Other notable songs include: "That Fat Man" (1949), "Blueberry Hill" (1956), "I'm in Love Again" (1956), "I'm Walking" (1957), "Bo Weevil" (1957), "Blue Monday" (1957), "Walking To New Orleans" (1960), and "Let the Four Winds Blow" (1961).

Figure 213—Antoine "Fats" Domino. MichaelOchsArchives.com.

94. The song "Since I Met You Baby" (1956) was recorded by whom? His other songs include: "I Almost Lost My Mind" (1949), "It's a Sin" (1950), "Empty Arms" (1957), and "City Lights" (1959).

95. What jazz artist is well-known for his recording "Brilliant Corners" (1956)?

96. Who, in the later 1950s, founded a dance group that won international fame, and was the recipient of the 1976 Spingarn Medal?

97. A song by what group is entitled "Dedicated to the One I Love" (1957)? The original members were Doris Coley, Addie "Micki" Harris, Beverly Lee, and Shirley Owens.

Figure 214—Thelonious Monk. Copyright © William P. Gottlieb, 1979.

98. What jazz trumpeter born in Mobile, Alabama was known for the album *The Big Challenge* (1957)?

99. Who recorded the song entitled "C.C. Rider" in 1957?

100. A song by what group is entitled "Charlie Brown" (1958)? In 1958, the members of the group were Carl Gardner (born in Tyler, Texas), Billy Guy, Will "Dub" Jones, and Cornell Gunter. Other members of the group, at various times, included Ronnie Bright, Earl Carroll, Sonny Forriest, Carl Gardner, Jr., Vernon Harrell, Leon Hughes, Adolph Jacobs, J.W. Lance, Alvin Morse, Jimmy Norman, Bobby Nunn, and Thomas Palmer. Saxophonist King Curtis sometimes accompanied the group as well.

101. What group recorded the song entitled "Get a Job" (1958)?

102. The song "Rockin' Robin" (1958) was recorded by what artist?

103. What artist recorded the song entitled "Jim Dandy" (1959)?

104. What artist recorded the 1959 song, "Stagolee"?

105. The song "I Only Have Eyes for You" (1959) was recorded by what group? In 1959, the members of the group were Jake Carey, Zeke Carey, Tommy Hunt, Terry Johnson, Nate Nelson, and Paul Wilson.

106. Who recorded the song entitled "Kansas City" in 1959?

107. Who was a 1959 Tony Award winner for his role in the Broadway play *The Great White Hope*, and starred in the movie *Field of Dreams* (1989)? He was born in 1931 and started acting to help with his stuttering. He earned his B.A. degree from the University of Michigan. His voice is linked to Darth Vader in *Star Wars* and King Mufasa in *The Lion King*.

108. Who is known for the songs "Everybody Loves to Cha Cha Cha" (1959), "Chain Gang" (1960), "Bring It on Home to Me" (1962), "Having a Party" (1962), "A Change Is Gonna Come" (1963), and "Another Saturday Night" (1963)? He was born in Clarksdale, Mississippi in 1931 and later moved to Chicago. Some of Cooke's songs included: "Wind Your Love for Me" (1957), "Only Sixteen" (1957), "You Send Me" (1957), "Cupid" (1960), and "Twistin' the Night Away" (1962). He died in 1964, at age 33.

Figure 216—Sam Cooke. Photographer, James J. Kriegsmann.

109. What group recorded the song "Let's Go, Let's Go, Let's Go" (1960)?

110. Who was born Ruth Lee Jones, and later teamed with Brook Benton on the song "Baby, You Got What It Takes" (1960)?

111. What artist recorded the song "The Twist" in 1960?

112. Who is considered the "Crown Prince of Gospel music"? One of his songs is entitled "The Love of God" (1960)?

113. Who played Cat Woman in the 1960s TV series "Batman"?

114. What artist recorded the song "Money" in 1960?

Figure 215—Dinah Washington. Schomburg Center for Research in Black Culture, New York Public Library.

115. Who was referred to as "the world's greatest entertainer," starred in the movie *Ocean's Eleven* (1960), and was the recipient of the 1968 Spingarn Medal?

116. Whose blues songs were entitled "Big Boss Man" (1960) and "Bright Lights, Big City" (1961)? He was born Mathis James Reed on September 6, 1925, in Leland, Mississippi.

117. What comedian had a running part in the television series "Car 54, Where Are You?" (1961)?

118. What artist recorded the song entitled "I Know (You Don't Love Me No More)" (1961)?

119. The song entitled "Please, Mr. Postman" (1961) was recorded by what group? The original members were Katherine Anderson, Juanita Cowart, Georgia Dobbins, Gladys Horton, and Georgeanna Tillman.

Figure 217—Jimmy Reed. University of Mississippi, Delta Blues Museum.

120. What artists recorded the songs "Stand by Me" (1961) and "Spanish Harlem" (1961)?

121. A record by what artist is entitled "Gee Whiz" (1961)?

122. What singer recorded the song entitled "Mother-in-Law" (1961)?

123. A song by what artist is entitled "Tossin' and Turnin'" (1961)?

124. The song "Sweet Home Chicago" (1961) was recorded by what blues singer?

125. What blues singer recorded the song "I Pity the Fool" (1961)?

126. What artist recorded the song called "Raindrops" (1961)?

Figure 218—Carla Thomas with her father Rufus Thomas. Special Collections, University of Memphis Libraries.

127. What artist recorded the song "Cry to Me" in 1961?

128. What premier tenor saxophone stylist once lived in Copenhagen, Denmark (1962–1977)? Two of his albums were *Sophisticated Giant* (1977) and *Manhattan Symphonie* (1978), and he was nominated for an Academy Award for his portrayal of Dale Turner in the movie *Round Midnight* (1986).

129. What female artist's popular songs include "Let It Be" (1962) and "Just Jesus and Me" (1966)?

130. Whose songs include "Stubborn Kind of Fellow" (1962) and "Sexual Healing" (1982)?

131. The song "The Loco-Motion" was recorded in 1962 by what artist?

132. Which artist recorded the song entitled "Any Day Now" (1962)?

133. Who has been referred to as the "Matriarch of Black Dance," appeared in the Broadway musical "Banboche" in 1962, and established a Performing Arts Training Center in East St. Louis, Illinois in 1967?

134. A recording by what group is entitled "Green Onions" (1962)?

135. What artist recorded the records "Walking the Dog" (1963) and "Blues Thang" (1996)?

136. The songs "Heatwave" (1963), "Dancing in the Street" (1964), "Jimmy Mack" (1967), and "Honey Child" (1967) were recorded by what group? The members of the group were Rosalind Ashford, Annette Beard, and Martha Reeves.

Figure 219—Katherine Dunham. Schomburg Center for Research in Black Culture, New York Public Library.

137. Who won the Academy Award for best actor for his performance in the movie *Lilies of the Field* (1963)? He was born in 1927 in Miami, Florida and has dual citizenship in the United States and the Bahamas. Some of his many movie credits include: *Cry, the Beloved Country* (1951), *The Defiant Ones* (1958), *A Raisin in the Sun* (1961), *A Patch of Blue* (1965), *In the Heat of the Night* (1967), *Guess Who's Coming to Dinner* (1967), *To Sir, With Love* (1967), *They Call Me Mister Tibbs!* (1970), and *Uptown Saturday Night* (1974).

138. What group, whose lead singer was Curtis Mayfield (1942–1999), recorded "It's All Right" (1963) and "We're a Winner" (1968)? Jerry "The Iceman" Butler, known for the recording "Only the Strong Survive" (1969), left the group in 1958. In 1963, the other members of the group were Fred Cash and Samuel Gooden.

Figure 220—Sydney Poitier (left) with Ann Bancroft. Courtesy of the Academy of Motion Picture Arts and Sciences.

139. Two songs by what artist are entitled "I Can't Stop Loving You" (1962) and "Busted" (1963)? He was born in 1930, in Albany, Georgia and was blind at age 7. He attended the Florida School for the Deaf and Blind in St. Augustine, Florida. He became a star at the 1959 Newport Jazz Festival. His hits include: "I Got a Woman" (1955), "What I Say" (1959), "Georgia on My Mind" (1960), "Ruby" (1961), "Hit the Road Jack" (1961), "Born to Lose" (1962), "Crying Time" (1966), and "Seven Spanish Angels" with Willie Nelson (1984). He received twelve Grammy awards, and received an honorary doctorate from Wilberforce University in 1999. He died in 2004.

Figure 221—Ray Charles. Special Collections, University of Memphis Libraries.

140. What duo recorded the song entitled "Mockingbird" in 1963?

141. The song entitled "Cry Baby" (1963) was recorded by what group?

142. A song by what artist is entitled "My Guy" (1964)?

143. A song by what group is entitled "Don't Have to Shop Around" (1964)?

144. What group recorded the song entitled "Who's That Lady" (1964), and an album entitled *Body Kiss* (2003)? The original members of the group were O'Kelly, Ronald, Rudolph, and Vernon Isley.

145. Who played a role in the transition of jazz from hard bop to softer, more subtle jazz? He recorded "Four and More" (1964), and the albums *On the Corner* (1972) and *Black Beauty— Miles Davis at Filmore West* (1997). He was born in 1926 in Alton, Illinois. In 1944, while Billy Eckstine visited East St. Louis, Illinois, Davis stood in for him for about two weeks and played trumpet with Dizzy Gillespie and Charles Parker. In 1945, Davis went to New York City to study at the Julliard School of Music, but his objective was to rejoin the band. He played in several jazz bands, and later formed his own band. Some of his albums included: *Birth of the Cool* (1957), *Miles Ahead* (1957) with Gil

Figure 222—Miles Davis (top) and Howard McGhee (bottom). Copyright © William P. Gottlieb, 1979.

Evans, *Milestones* (1958), *Kind of Blue* (1959) with his band and Bill Evans, and *A Tribute to Jack Johnson* (1971). Davis died in 1991.

146. An album by what jazz artist is entitled *A Love Supreme* (1964)? He was born in 1926 in Hamlet, North Carolina and grew up in High Point, North Carolina. He began playing the clarinet and then switched to the alto saxophone. In 1955 through 1957, his acclaim grew as a member of the Miles Davis quintet, which included Red Garland, Paul Chambers, and Philly Joe Jones. Some of his notable works include "Blue Train" (1957), "Impressions" (1963), and "Transition" (1965). He also played with Thelonious Monk and later formed his own band. He died at age 40 in 1967, in Long Island, New York. Coltrane had a significant influence on jazz, even after his death. His son Ravi followed in his footsteps and became a saxophonist.

Figure 223—John Coltrane. Schomburg Center for Research in Black Culture, New York Public Library.

147. What group recorded the song "The Tracks of My Tears" (1965)? Originally the group was called the Matadors and included - Pete Moore, Smokey Robinson, Claudette and Bobby Rogers, and Ronnie White. Because of Claudette, they changed the name to the Miracles. The group's hits include: "Shop Around" (1960), "You Really Got a Hold on Me" (1962), "Mickey's Monkey" (1963), "Going to a Go-Go" (1965), "My Girl Has Gone" (1965), "Ooh Baby Baby" (1965,

Figure 224—Smokey Robinson and the Miracles. Left to right: Warren "Pete" Moore, Bobbie Rogers, William "Smokey" Robinson, and Ronnie White. MichaelOchsArchives.com.

"I Second That Emotion" (1967), and "Tears of a Clown" (1970).

148. A song by what artist is entitled "We're Gonna Make It" (1965)?

149. What group recorded the songs "I Can't Help Myself (Sugar Pie, Honeybunch)" (1965) and "Reach Out and I'll Be There" (1966)? In 1965, the members of the group were Renaldo "Obie" Benson, Abdul "Duke" Fakir, Lawrence Payton, and Levi Stubs.

150. A song by what group is entitled "Stop! In the Name of Love" (1965)? The Supremes performed as a group from 1959 to 1969. Other recordings by the Supremes included: "Where Did Our Love Go" (1964), "Baby Love" (1964), "Come See About Me" (1964), "Back in My Arms Again" (1965), "I Hear a Symphony" (1966), "You Can't Hurry Love" (1966), "You Keep Me Hangin' On" (1966), "Love is Here and Now You're Gone" (1967), "The Happening" (1967), "Love Child" (1968), and "Some Day We Will Be Together" (1969).

Figure 225—The Supremes. Diana Ross (top), Mary Wilson (left), Florence Ballard (right). MichaelOchsArchives.com.

151. The record "In the Midnight Hour" (1965) was recorded by what artist? His other songs include: "Mustang Sally" (1966), "Land of 1000 Dances" (1966), "634-5789" (1966), "Funky Broadway" (1967), "Engine Number 9" (1970), "Don't Knock My Love—Pt. 1" (1971), and "Fire and Water" (1972).

152. Which of the world's leading lyric sopranos was inspired by Marian Anderson and was the recipient of the 1965 Spingarn Medal? She was born Mary Violet Leontine Price on February 10, 1927, in Laurel, Mississippi. Her parents were Kate and James Price. In 1937, she attended the Oak Park Vocational High School and in 1944, studied at the College of Educational and Industrial Arts in Wilberforce, Ohio. According to her brother, after taking a French course, she spelled her name Leontyne. In 1948, she attended the Julliard School of Music in New York City. In June 1952, she made her debut in Dallas, Texas, playing the role of Bess in George Gershwin's *Porgy and Bess*. For the next two years she toured the world with the play. In 1955, she made her television debut as Floria Tosca in Puccini's

Figure 226—Leontyne Price. Schomburg Center for Research in Black Culture, New York Public Library.

Tosca. In 1957, she performed at the San Francisco Opera House in Poulenc's *Dialogues of the Carmelites*. In 1958, she made her European debut in *Aida* at the Vienna Staatsoper. That same year, she debuted in London in *Aida* at Covent Gardens. In 1960, she performed *Aida* at the Teatro alla Scala, the world's most famous opera house, which is in Milan, Italy. One of her greatest performances was in 1961 at the Metropolitan Opera in New York City, in the role of Leonora in Verdi's *Il Trovatore*. Between 1961 and 1969 she performed at the Metropolitan Opera many times. She received 15 Grammy awards for her recordings.

153. The song "My Girl" (1965) was recorded by what group?

154. What group is noted for the recording "Shotgun" (1965)?

155. Who is known as the "Godfather of Soul," and recorded "Papa's Got a Brand New Bag" (1965)?

156. What artist recorded the song "Rescue Me" (1965)?

Figure 227—The Temptations. Left to right: Eddie Kendricks, Paul Williams, Otis Williams, Melvin Franklin, David Ruffin. MichaelOchsArchives.com.

157. An instrumental by what artist is entitled "Mercy, Mercy, Mercy" (1966)?

158. What artist recorded the instrumental entitled "Wade in the Water" (1966)?

159. Who recorded the song entitled "Knock on Wood" in 1966?

160. The song "When a Man Loves a Woman" (1966) was recorded by whom?

161. A song by what artist is entitled "What Becomes of the Brokenhearted" (1966)?

162. Which artist recorded the song entitled "But It's Alright" in 1966?

163. A recording by what jazz artist is entitled "Goin' Out of My Head" (1966)? He was a noted jazz guitarist, and one of his albums was *Smokin' at the Half Note* (1965).

164. What duo, referred to as "Double Dynamite," recorded the songs "You Got Me Hummin'" (1966), "Soul Man" (1967), "I Thank You" (1968), and "Hold On! I'm Comin'" (1968)?

165. Who grew up in New York City, was a writer, composer, and concert pianist, and died tragically in a helicopter crash in Vietnam in May, 1967, on her way to perform for the troops?

Figure 228—Sam (left) and Dave. Special Collections, University of Memphis Libraries.

166. What was the title of the final popular song by Otis Redding (1941–1967)?

167. Which artist recorded the song entitled "Tell It Like It Is" in 1967?

168. An album released in 1967 by The Experienced and what artist, is entitled *Are You Experienced*?

169. What artists recorded the songs "Nine Pound Steel" (1967), "The Choking Kind" (1969), and "Get Down Get Down (Get Down on the Floor)" (1975)?

170. A song by what group is entitled "Up, Up and Away" (1967)? In 1967, the members of the group were Billy Davis, Jr., Florence LaRue, Marilyn McCoo, Lamonte McLemore, and Ron Towson.

Figure 229—Otis Redding. Special Collections, University of Memphis Libraries.

171. What group recorded "Soul Finger" in 1967? The original members, who signed with STAX Records, were James Alexander, Ben Cauley, Ronnie Caldwell, Carl Cunningham, Phalin Jones, and Jimmy King. In 1967, Ronnie Caldwell, Carl Cunningham, Phalin Jones, Jimmy King, and Otis Redding died when their airplane crashed into Lake Monona in Madison, Wisconsin.

172. What singer is known as the "Queen of Soul," and counts among her many songs, "I Never Loved a Man (The Way I Love You)" (1967)? She was born in Memphis, Tennessee in 1942. Her songs include: "Respect" (1967), "Do Right Woman—Do Right Man" (1967), "(You Make Me Feel Like) A Natural Woman" (1967), "See Saw" (1968), "Chain of Fools" (1968), "Ain't No Way" (1968), "Think" (1968), "I Say a Little Prayer" (1968), "The House That Jack Built" (1968), "You Send Me" (1968), "Share Your Love with Me" (1969), "Call Me" (1970), "Don't Play That Song (You Lied)" (1970), "Rock Steady" (1971), "Bridge Over Troubled Water" (1971), "Spanish Harlem" (1971), "Master of Eyes" (1973), "Ain't Nothing Like the Real

Figure 230—Aretha Franklin. Mississippi Valley Collection Libraries, University of Memphis, Memphis, Tennessee.

Thing" (1974), and "Freeway of Love" (1985). She received 15 Grammy awards. Her movie credits include: *The Pelican Brief* (1993), *Forest Gump* (1994), *Waiting to Exhale* (1995), *Bound* (1996), *The First Wives Club* (1996), and *Two Weeks Notice* (2002).

173. What blues singer was known as "Mr. Five by Five," and recorded the album entitled *Every Day I Have the Blues* (1967)?

174. A song by what artist is entitled "Do You Know the Way to San Jose" (1968)?

175. What singer was born Joseph Arrington, Jr., in Rogers, Texas, and recorded the song entitled "Skinny Legs and All" (1968)?

176. Who is known for the recording "Little Green Apples" (1968)?

Figure 231—Jimmy Rushing. Copyright © William P. Gottlieb, 1979.

177. Who is known for the songs entitled "Slip Away" (1968) and "Patches" (1970)?

178. What artist recorded for over four decades, including songs such as "Who's Making Love" (1968), "I Believe in You (You Believe in Me)" (1973), "Cheaper to Keep Her" (1973), and "Disco Lady" (1976)?

179. What comedian ran for president of the United States in 1968?

180. What artist recorded the album entitled *Soul Serenade* (1968)?

181. Some of the songs of what artist are "Tell Mama" (1968), "Good Rockin' Mama" (1981), and the album *Mystery Lady* (1994)?

Figure 232—Johnnie Taylor. MichaelOchsArchives.com.

182. What actor was known for playing Barney Collier on the TV series "Mission: Impossible" during the 1960s and 1970s?

183. A song by what group is entitled "Everyday People" (1969)?

184. Who is referred to as the "High Priestess of Soul," and recorded the song entitled "To Be Young, Gifted and Black" (1969)?

185. What group recorded the song entitled "Tighten Up" in 1969?

186. Who was the director of the movies *Watermelon Man* (1969) and *Sweetback* (1971)?

187. Two songs by what artist are entitled "By the Time I Get to Phoenix" (1969) and "Shaft" (1971)? He was born in 1942, in Covington, Tennessee and was raised by his grandparents. He received an Academy Award for Best Music, Original Song, for his "Theme from Shaft" (1970). *Hot Buttered Soul* (1969), *The Isaac Hayes Movement* (1970), *To Be Continued* (1970), and *Black Moses* (1971) were all hit albums. One song on *Hot Buttered Soul*, "By the Time I Get to Phoenix," was a classic. Some of Hayes' television credits included: *The Rockford Files*, *The A-Team*, *The Hughleys*, *Girlfriends*, *Stargate SG-1*, and *The Bernie Mack Show*.

Figure 233—Isaac Hayes. Special Collections, University of Memphis Libraries.

188. Who had his own TV show from 1970 through 1974? He was born Clerow Wilson in 1933, in Jersey City, New Jersey. He served in the U.S. Air Force from 1949 to 1954. His other television credits include: *Rowan & Martin's Laugh-in* (1968), *Jack Benny's First Farewell Special* (1973), *Clerow Wilson's Great Escape* (1974), and *The Cheap Detective* (1980). Some of his movies include: *Uptown Saturday Night* (1974), *Skatetown USA* (1975), and *The Fish That Saved Pittsburgh* (1979). He died November 25, 1998.

189. What music figure grew up in New York City, worked in Europe as a music conductor, and returned to America in 1970 after 21 years abroad, to conduct the New York Philharmonic in Central Park? He was born in New York City in 1915, graduated from the Julliard School of Music in 1936, and later graduated from Columbia University. In 1941, he became the first African American to conduct the New York Philharmonic. He went to Europe in 1949, as a result of an invitation from the French National Radio Orchestra. He conducted the Swedish Goteberg Symphony (1953–1960), and the Frankfort Radio Symphony Orchestra (1961–1970). From 1964 to 1967, he was the principal conductor of Australia's Sydney Orchestra. He spoke several languages. Dixon died in 1976, in Switzerland.

Figure 234—Dean Dixon. Schomburg Center for Research in Black Culture, New York Public Library.

190. What blues singer recorded the song entitled "The Thrill Is Gone" (1970)? Some of King's notable songs are: "Sweet Sixteen" (1960), "Woke Up This Morning" (1960), "Don't Answer the Door" (1966), "Paying the Cost to Be the Boss" (1968), "Nobody Loves Me But My Mother" (1971), "Never Make Your Move Too Soon" (1977), and "Better Not Look Down" (1979).

191. A song by what artist is entitled "A Rainy Night in Georgia" (1970)?

192. The song "Highway Blues" was recorded in 1971 by what blues singer?

Figure 235—B.B. King. MichaelOchsArchives.com.

193. What group recorded the song entitled "Have You Seen Her" in 1971? The original members of the group were Clarence Johnson, Creadel "Red" Jones, Robert Lester, Eugene Record, and Marshall Thompson.

194. A song by what duo is entitled "Proud Mary" (1971)?

195. What artist recorded the song entitled "Clean Up Woman" (1971)?

196. Songs by what group include "I'll Be There" (1971) and "The Love You Save" (1971)? The members of the group were Jackie, Jermaine, Marlon, Michael, and Tito Jackson.

197. Which artist recorded the following songs: "Tired of Being Alone" (1971), "Let's Stay Together" (1972), and "I'm Still in Love with You" (1972)? He was born in Forest City, Arkansas in 1946. At about age 10, his family moved to Grand Rapids, Michigan. He signed with Willie Mitchell in 1969 and the rest is history. Some of his many hits include: "Back Up Train" (1967), "Let's Stay Together" (1972), "Look What You Done for Me" (1972), "Call Me" (1973), "Here I Am (Come and Take Me)" (1973), "Livin' for You" (1973), "L-O-V-E (Love)" (1975), and "Put a Little Love in Your Heart" (1988).

Figure 236—Al Green. MichaelOchsArchives.com.

198. Who started out as a baseball player, but became a successful African American country music performer? One of his records was "Kiss an Angel Good Morning" (1971).

199. What jazz musician taught himself to play music but never learned to read music, and later composed the ballad "Misty," for the movie *Play Misty for Me* (1971)? He was born in 1921, in Pittsburgh, began playing piano at age 3, and by age 11 was playing on river boats. In the 1940s, he went to New York City and was a background player on Charlie Parker's *Cool Blues* in 1947. *Concert by the Sea* (1955) is one of Garner's most notable albums. Some of his musical compositions include: "Mambo Garner" (1954), "Misty" (1954, originally produced in the early 1950s), "Solitaire" (1955), "Just Blues" (1958), "Paris Bound" (1958), "Nervous Waltz" (1967), "You Turn Me Around" (1970), and "Nightwind" (1974). He died in 1977, in Los Angeles.

Figure 237—Erroll Garner. Reproduced from the Collections of the Library of Congress.

200. A song by what group is entitled "I'll Take You There" (1972)?

201. What artist recorded the song "Drift Away" in 1972?

202. Which artist recorded the song entitled "I Can See Clearly Now" (1972)?

203. What actor was known for playing Fred Sanford on the TV series "Sanford and Son" during the 1970s?

Figure 238—The Staple Singers (Cleotha Staples (left), Roebuck "Pops" Staples (center) and Mavis Staples (right)). Special Collections, University of Memphis Libraries.

204. What artist is noted for the song "(If Loving You is Wrong) I Don't Want to Be Right" (1972), which was written by Homer Banks, Carl Hampton, and Raymond Jackson?

205. What comedian grew up in Peoria, Illinois, made several movies including *Up Town Saturday Night* (1972), *Silver Streak* (1976), *Car Wash* (1977), and *The Wiz* (1978), and recorded the album *Is It Something I Said*?

206. What artist recorded "Cumbia and Jazz Fusion" and authored his autobiography, entitled *Beneath the Underdog* (1972)?

207. A song by what artist is entitled "The First Time Ever I Saw Your Face" (1972)?

208. Which artist recorded the song "Lean on Me" in 1972?

209. What actor is noted for calypso music, and appeared in the movies *Buck and the Preacher* (1972) and *Uptown Saturday Night* (1974)?

210. A song by what group is entitled "Midnight Train to Georgia" (1973)?

211. Who recorded the song entitled "You Are the Sunshine of My Life" (1973)?

212. What group recorded the album *That's the Way of the World* (1974), which included songs such as "Shining Star" and "Reasons"? The members of the group in 1974 were Philip Bailey, Larry Dunn, Johnny Graham, Ralph Johnson, Al McKay, Andrew Woolfolk, Fred White, Maurice White, and Verdine White. Maurice White, the primary creator of the group, is from Memphis, Tennessee.

213. An album by what artist is entitled *Can't Get Enough* (1974)?

214. The TV series, "Good Times," started in 1974 and lasted how many years?

215. The TV series, "The Jeffersons," made its debut in 1975 and lasted how many years?

216. What Jamaican-born artist, whose group was called the Wailers, recorded the album entitled *Exodus* (1977)?

217. What group recorded the song entitled "Back in Love Again" in 1977?

218. Which duo recorded the song entitled "Strawberry Letter 23" (1977)?

219. An album by what artist is entitled *When You Hear Lou, You've Heard It All* (1977)?

220. The song entitled "Three Times a Lady" was recorded in 1978 by what group?

221. What group recorded the song entitled "Shout" in 1978?

222. The album *Fantastic Voyage* (1980) was recorded by what group?

Figure 239—Lou Rawls. MichaelOchsArchives.com.

223. The song "Celebration" was recorded in 1980 by what group? The original members were Robert "Kool" Bell, Ronald Bell, George Brown, Robert Mickens, Charles Smith, and Dennis Thomas. Subsequent members were James Taylor and Earl Toon.

224. Which artist recorded the song entitled "Turn Out the Lights" in 1980?

225. What is the name of a Broadway play based on the Supremes?

226. Who was the male star of the Broadway play *Sophisticated Ladies* (1981), and appeared in the movie *Bojangles* (2001)? He was born on February 14, 1946, in New York City. He began tap dancing with his older brother Maurice at the early age of 3. When he was 5, he and his brother Maurice performed at the Apollo Theater in New York City. His father joined the duo and they were known as "Hines, Hines, and Dad." In 1992, he earned a Tony Award for his portrayal of "Jelly Roll" Morton in the Broadway musical *Jelly's Last Jam*. He performed in other Broadway plays, including *Eubie* (1979) and *Comin' Uptown* (1980). Some of his movies include: *Running Scared* (1981), *Wolfen* (1981), *History of the World: Part 1* (1981), *Deal of the Century* (1983), *The Cotton Club* (1984), *The Muppets Take Manhattan* (1984), *White Nights* (1985), *Off Limits* (1987), *Tap* (1989), *Renaissance Man* (1994), and *Waiting to Exhale* (1995). He earned an Emmy for the PBS special, *Gregory Hines: Tap Dance in America*. He died August 9, 2003.

227. What group recorded the song entitled "Slow Hand" in 1981? The members of the group were Anita, Bonnie, June, and Ruth Pointer.

228. What group recorded the song "You Dropped the Bomb on Me" (1982)? The original members were Charlie Wilson, Robert Wilson, and Ronnie Wilson.

229. A song by this artist is entitled "Superfreak" (1981).

230. What blues singer was known for the song "Down Home Blues" (1982)? He was born Arzell Hill on September 30, 1935, in Naples, Texas. He fashioned his initials after B.B. King. In 1984, Hill received the Blues Vocalist of the Year award from the Blues Foundation in Memphis, Tennessee. Albums by Hill include; *Lot of Soul* (1967), *Brand New Z.Z. Hill* (1971), *Dues Paid in Full* (1972), *The Best Thing That's Ever Happened to Me* (1972), *Keep on Loving You* (1975), *Let's Make a Deal* (1978), *The Mark of Z.Z. Hill* (1979), *Z.Z. Hill—Malco* (1981), *The Rhythm and Blues* (1982), *Down Home* (1982), *I'm a Blues Man* (1983), and *Bluesmaster* (1984).

Figure 240—Z.Z. Hill. University of Mississippi, Delta Blues Museum.

231. Who received an Academy Award as best supporting actor for his portrayal of Drill Sergeant Emit Foley in the movie, *An Officer and a Gentleman* (1982)? He was born in 1936, in Brooklyn, New York. Gossett made his acting debut in the Broadway play *Take a Giant Step* (1953). He received an Emmy for the role of Fiddler in Alex Haley's 1977 TV miniseries *Roots* (1977). His movies include: *The Deep* (1977), *Don't Look Back: The Story of Leroy "Satchel" Paige* (1981), *Sadat* (1983), *Enemy Mine* (1985), *Firewalker* (1986), *Diggstown* (1993), *Y2K* (1999), *The Highwayman* (2000), and *Widow* (2005). Gossett received a Golden Globe Award for HBO's *The Josephine Baker Story* (1991). Two of his TV miniseries were *Return to Lonesome Dove* (1993) and *Story of a People* (1993).

Figure 241—Louis Gossett, Jr. Courtesy of the Academy of Motion Picture Arts and Sciences.

232. Who received a Grammy Award in 1982 for her album *Gershwin Live!*?

233. What artist recorded the 1983 song "Billie Jean"?

234. Who starred in the movies *Beverly Hills Cop* (1984) and *Daddy Day Care* (2003)?

235. Which blues artist recorded the song entitled "I'm a Phone Booth Baby" in 1984?

236. The song "Ghostbusters" was recorded by what artist in 1984?

Figure 242—Sarah Vaughan. Copyright © William P. Gottlieb, 1979.

237. Who was known as Clifford Huxtable on the television show "The Cosby Show" (1984–1992), and along with his wife, Camille, donated funds to Spelman College? He was the recipient of the 1985 Spingarn Medal and the Presidential Medal of Freedom in 2002.

238. A song by what artist is entitled "What's Love Got to Do with It?" (1984)?

239. Who started her TV show in 1985, was inducted into the TV Hall of Fame in 1994, and was the recipient of the 2000 Spingarn Medal?

240. Who starred in these movies: *The Color Purple* (1985), *Lethal Weapon* (1987), *Lethal Weapon 2* (1989), *Lethal Weapon 3* (1992), *Angels in the Outfield* (1994), and *Lethal Weapon 4* (1998)?

241. A song by what artist is entitled "The Greatest Love of All" (1986)?

242. Which group recorded the song entitled "Word Up" in 1986?

243. Which artist recorded an album entitled *Rapture* (1986)?

244. The song "Lean on Me" (1987) was recorded by what group? The original members of the group were Denzil Foster, Jay King, Thomas McElroy, Samuelle Pratter, and Valerie Watson.

245. An album by what artist is entitled *Back on the Block* (1989)?

246. What artists recorded the song entitled "Wild Thing" (1989)?

247. *Do the Right Thing* (1989), *Jungle Fever* (1991), and *Malcolm X* (1992), are three of the many movies by what director? He was born in Atlanta, Georgia on March 20, 1957. His mother gave him the nickname "Spike" because of his toughness. His film making career began in 1986 with his independently produced film *She's Gotta Have It*. Some of Lee's other films include *Mo' Better Blues* (1990) and *Summer of Sam* (1999).

248. Who was a leading dancer with the Alvin Ailey American Dance Theater for 15 years, and in 1989 began to manage the theater, succeeding Alvin Ailey?

249. What male actor starred in the movies *Glory* (1989) and *Mo' Better Blues* (1990), and received the Academy Award as best supporting actor for the movie *Glory*? In 2001, he received the Academy Award as best actor for the movie *Training Day* (2001). He was born in 1954, in Mount Vernon, New York. After high school, he entered Fordham University. He planned to become a journalist, but became interested in acting. He later attended the American Conservatory Theater in San Francisco. His first movie was *Carbon Copy* in 1981. He also performed on the medical television series *St. Elsewhere*. His movies include: *Cry Freedom* (1987), *The Mighty Quinn* (1989), *Malcolm X* (1992), *The Pelican Brief* (1993), *Philadelphia* (1993), *Devil in a Blue Dress* (1995), *Crimson Tide* (1995), *Courage Under Fire* (1996), *The Hurricane* (1999), *The Bone Collector* (1999), *Antwone Fisher* (2002), and *The Manchurian Candidate* (2004).

Figure 243—Denzel Washington. Courtesy of the Academy of Motion Picture Arts and Sciences.

250. Which group recorded the song "The Blues" in 1990? The original members were Timothy Christian, Dwayne Wiggins, and Raphael Wiggins.

251. What artist recorded the song "U Can't Touch This" (1990)?

252. Who received an Academy Award as best supporting actress for her role in the movie, *Ghost* (1990)?

253. An album by what artist is entitled *2pacalypse Now* (1991)?

254. What father and daughter duo recorded the song entitled "Unforgettable" in 1991?

255. Which group recorded the 1991 song "It's So Hard to Say Goodbye to Yesterday"? The original members were Michael Mc-Cary, Nathan and Wanya Morris, and Shawn Stockman.

Figure 244—Whoopi Goldberg. Courtesy of the Academy of Motion Picture Arts and Sciences.

256. After the passing of William Grant Still, what composer was referred to as "Dean of Afro-American Composers"? An opera by this composer is entitled *Frederick Douglass* (1991).

257. Which group recorded the song entitled "Tennessee" in 1992? The members of the group were Dan Ajile, Arnae, Kwesi Asuo, Rasha Don, Montsho Eshe, Dionne Farris, Foley, D.J. Headliner, Baba Oje, Speech, Nadirah Shakoor, and Aerle Taree.

258. The songs "Dreamlover" (1993) and "Shake It Off" (2005), were recorded by what artist?

259. What artist recorded the song entitled "That's the Way Love Goes" (1993)?

260. Whose first album was entitled *Age Ain't Nothing but a Number* (1994)?

261. An album by what artist is entitled *Ready to Die* (1994)?

262. Who starred in the movies *Bad Boys* (1995), *Big Momma's House* (2001), and *Bad Boys II* (2003)?

263. Who received the 1996 Academy Award as best supporting actor for his role in the movie *Jerry Maguire*, and starred in the movie *The Fighting Temptations* (2003) with Beyoncé Knowles?

264. Who starred in the TV series "The Steve Harvey Show" (1996–2002), as vice-principal Steve Hightower?

265. The album *Men in Black* (1997), is by which artist and actor?

266. An album by what group is entitled *Who Let the Dogs Out* (2000)? The members of the group are Rick Carey, Omerit Hield, Marvin Prosper, Herschel Smith, and Isaiah Taylor.

267. Who received the 2001 Grammy Award for the Best New Artist?

268. Who received the 2001 Academy Award as best actress for the movie *Monster's Ball*?

269. Who received the Grammy Award for best jazz instrumental album, individual or group, for the album *This Is What I Do*?

270. Who is the lead singer for the group Destiny's Child? Her 2003 solo record is entitled *Dangerously in Love*.

271. An album by what artist is entitled *Dance with My Father* (2003)?

272. Who starred in the movie *Bringing Down the House* (2003) as Charlene Morton?

273. A song by this artist is entitled "Burn" (2004).

274. Who won the 2004 National Association of Broadcasters' Marconi Award for network/syndicated personality of the year? He was inducted into the Radio Hall of Fame in 1998 and is the founder of Reach Media, parent company of BlackAmericaWeb.com. He also established a foundation in his name, which assists teachers and students attending historically black colleges and universities, and received the "Best DJ of the Year" Award from *Impact Magazine* so many times the award was renamed in his honor. His daily commute between Dallas and Chicago earned him the nickname, "The Fly Jock."

Figure 245—Destiny's Child. Left to right: Kelly Rowland, Beyoncé Knowles, and Michelle Williams. Sue Schneider/ MichaelOchsArchives.com.

275. What actor, who was born Eric Bishop in Terrell, Texas, received the 2005 Academy Award for best actor, for his portrayal of Ray Charles in the movie *Ray* (2004)?

276. What actor was born in Memphis, Tennessee, and in 2005 received his first Academy Award for best supporting actor, for his portrayal of Eddie Scrap-Iron Dupris in the movie *Million Dollar Baby* (2004)? He was born on June 1, 1937. He attended Los Angeles Community College and served several years as a mechanic in the U.S. Air Force. Some of his movies include: *Driving Miss Daisy* (1989), *Glory* (1989), *Robin Hood: Prince of Thieves* (1991), *Unforgiven* (1992), *Shawshank Redemption* (1994), *Chain Reaction* (1996), *Amistad* (1997), *Deep Impact* (1998), *Along Came a Spider* (2001), *Dreamcatcher* (2003), and *Bruce Almighty* (2003).

Answers — 6 — Entertainment

1. Ira Aldridge (1807–1867)

2. Elizabeth Taylor Greenfield (c.1819–1876)

3. "Blind Tom" Bethune or Thomas Wiggins (1849–1908)

4. Fisk Jubilee Singers (1871–1926). The group was named by George L. White (?–?), the Fisk University musical director. The name is in honor of "jubilee," which refers to the Old Testament, where each fiftieth Pentacost (a Judaic festival celebrating the visiting of the Holy Spirit with the Apostles) is followed by a "year of jubilee" in which, according to Hebrew law, all slaves are set free.

5. James Bland (1854–1911)

6. Flora Batson Berger (1864–1906)

7. Samuel Coleridge-Taylor (1875–1912)

8. James Hubert "Eubie" Blake (1883–1983)

9. "Maple Leaf Rag" (1899)

10. Harry T. Burleigh (1866–1949)

11. W.C. Handy (1873–1958)

12. Ferdinand "Jelly Roll" Morton (1890–1941)

13. Charles Gilpin (1878–1930)

14. Huddie Ledbetter (1885–1949)

15. Lillian Evanti (1890–1967)

16. Roland Hayes (1887–1977)

17. Jackie "Moms" Mabley (1894–1975)

18. James P. Johnson (1894–1955)

19. Bessie Smith (1894–1937)

20. Ida Cox (1896–1967)

21. Josephine Baker (1906–1975)

22. Count Basie (1904–1984)

23. "Joe Turner"

24. Joe "King" Oliver (1885–1938)

25. Blind Lemon Jefferson (1897–1929)

26. Fletcher Henderson (1897–1952)

27. Nobel Sissel (1889–1975) and Eubie Blake (1883–1983)

28. Ethel Waters (1896–1977)

29. Alberta Hunter (1895–1984)

30. Bert Williams (1874–1922)

31. Sidney Bechet (1897–1959)

32. Lillian "Lil" Hardin Armstrong (1898–1971)

33. Marian Anderson (1897–1993)

34. Canada Lee (1907–1952)

35. Julius Bledsoe (1897–1943)

36. Louis Armstrong (1901–1971)

37. Robert Nathaniel Dett (1882–1943)

38. Mississippi John Hurt (1893–1966)

39. Ma Rainey (1886–1939)

40. Mary Lou Williams (1910–1981)

41. Thomas "Fats" Waller (1904–1943)

42. "King of Swing"

43. Paul Robeson (1898–1976)

44. Richard B. Harrison (1864–1935)

45. William G. Still (1895–1978)

46. Robert Johnson (1911–1938)

47. Thomas Dorsey (1899–1993)

48. Arthur "Art" Tatum (1909–1956)

49. E. Simms Campbell (1908–1971)

50. *Imitation of Life* (1934)

51. Cab Calloway (1907–1994)

52. Bill "Bojangles" Robinson (1878–1949)

53. Sister Rosetta Tharpe (1915–1973)

54. Ella Fitzgerald (1917–1996)

55. Eddie "Rochester" Anderson (1905–1977)

56. Hattie McDaniel (1895–1952), *Gone with the Wind*, 1940

57. Billie Holiday (1915–1959)

58. Ink Spots, original members: Jerry Daniels, Charles Fuqua, Orville "Hoppy" Jones, and Deek Watson

59. Trumpet

60. Coleman Hawkins (1904–1969)

61. Charlie Parker (1920–1955)

62. Clarence Muse (1889–1979)

63. Bebop, which is music for listening, rather than dancing

64. Dizzy Gillespie (1917–1993)

65. Son House (1902–1988)

66. Lionel Hampton (1908–2002)

67. Lena Horne (1917–)

68. Nat "King" Cole (1919–1965)

69. Josh White (1915–1969)

70. Billy Eckstine (1914–1993)

71. Pearl Bailey (1918–1990)

72. T-Bone Walker (1910–1975), born Aaron Thibeaux Walker

73. Sonny Terry (1911–1986)

74. Clara Ward (1924–1973); Clara Ward Singers, Clara Ward, Willarene Ward, Henrietta Waddy, and Marion Williams

75. Earl "Bud" Powell (1924–1966)

76. Chester Arthur Burnett (1910–1976), also known as "Howlin' Wolf"

77. Elmore James (1918–1963)

78. Jackie Wilson (1934–1984)

79. Drifters

80. Mahalia Jackson (1911–1972)

81. McKinley Morganfield, or Muddy Waters (1915–1983)

82. Chuck Berry (1926–)

83. Platters

84. Penguins

85. Bo Diddley (1928–)

86. Little Richard (1932–)

87. The Dells

88. "Little" Willie John, born William Edgar John (1937–1966)

89. Bill Doggett, born William Ballard Doggett (1916–1996)

90. Arthur Mitchell (1934–)

91. Johnny Mathis (1935–)

92. Shirley and Lee: Shirley Goodman (1936–) and Leonard Lee (1936–1976)

93. Antoine "Fats" Domino (1928–)

94. Ivory Joe Hunter (1914–1974)

95. Thelonious Monk (1917–1982)

96. Alvin Ailey (1931–1989)

97. Shirelles

98. Charles Melvin "Cootie" Williams (1908–1985)

99. Chuck Willis (1928–1958)

100. Coasters

101. Silhouettes: Earl Beal (1924–2001), Raymond Edwards (1922–), Bill Horton (1929–1995), and Rich Lewis (1933–)

102. Bobby Day (born Robert Byrd) (1932–1990)

103. LaVern Baker (1929–1997)

104. Lloyd Price (1933–)

105. Flamingoes

106. Wilbert Harrison (1929–1994)

107. James Earl Jones (1931–)

108. Sam Cooke (1931–1964)

109. Hank Ballard (1936–2003) and the Midnighters

110. Dinah Washington (1924–1963)

111. Chubby Checker, born Ernest Evans (1941–)

112. Reverend James Cleveland (1932–1991)

113. Eartha Kitt (1927–)

114. Barrett Strong (1941–)

115. Sammy Davis, Jr. (1925–1990)

116. Jimmy Reed (1925–1976)

117. Nipsey Russell (1934–)

118. Barbara George (1942–)

119. Marvelettes

120. Ben E. King (1938–)

121. Carla Thomas (1942–)

122. Ernie K-Doe, born Ernest Kadoe, Jr. (1936–2001)

123. Bobby Lewis (1933–)

124. Junior Parker, born Herman Parker, Jr. (1932–1971)

125. Bobby "Blue" Bland, born Robert Calvin Bland (1930–)

126. Dee Clark, born Delectus Clark (1938–1990)

127. Solomon Burke (1936–)

128. Dexter Gordon (1923–1990)

129. Roberta Martin (1907–1969)

130. Marvin Gaye (1939–1984)

131. Little Eva, born Eva Narcissus Boyd (1943–2003)

132. Chuck Jackson (1937–)

133. Katherine Dunham (1909–)

134. Booker T. (Jones) (1944–) and the MGs (Memphis Group)

135. Rufus Thomas (1917–2001)

136. Martha and the Vandellas

137. Sydney Poitier (1927–)

138. Impressions

139. Ray Charles (1930–2004)

140. Charles (1939–) and Inez Foxx (1942–) (brother and sister)

141. Garnet Mimms and the Enchanters

142. Mary Wells (1943–1992)

143. Mad Lads, original members: William Brown, Julius Green, Robert Phillips, and John Gary Williams

144. Isley Brothers

145. Miles Davis (1926–1991)

146. John Coltrane (1926–1967)

147. Smokey Robinson and the Miracles

148. "Little" Milton Campbell, Jr. (1934–2005)

149. Four Tops

150. Supremes

151. Wilson Pickett (1941–2006)

152. Leontyne Price (1927–)

153. The Temptations

154. Junior Walker (1931–1995) and The All Stars

155. James Brown (1933–)

156. Fontella Bass (1940–)

157. Julian "Cannonball" Adderley (1928–1975). "Cannonball," his nickname, is a corruption of the word cannibal, because of his appetite.

158. Ramsey Lewis Trio

159. Eddie Floyd (1935–)

160. Percy Sledge (1941–)

161. Jimmy Ruffin (1939–?), older brother of David Ruffin (1941–1991) of the Temptations

162. J.J. Jackson (1941–)

163. Wes Montgomery (1925–1968)

164. Sam and Dave: Sam Moore (1935–) and Dave Prater (1937–1988)

165. Philippa Schuyler (1931–1967)

166. "(Sittin' on) The Dock of the Bay" (1967)

167. Aaron Neville (1941–)

168. Jimi Hendrix (1942–1970)

169. Joe Simon (1943–)

170. 5th Dimension

171. Bar-Kays

172. Aretha Franklin (1942–)

173. Jimmy Rushing (1902–1972)

174. Dionne Warwick (1940–)

175. Joe Tex (1933–1982)

176. O.C. Smith (1931–2001)

177. Clarence Carter (1936–)

178. Johnnie Taylor (1938–2000)

179. Dick Gregory (1932–)

180. Willie Mitchell (1928–)

181. Etta James, who was born Jamsetta Hawkins (1938–)

182. Greg Morris (1935–1996)

183. Sly and the Family Stone, or Arrested Development

184. Nina Simone (1933–2003)

185. Archie Bell and The Drells

186. Melvin Van Peebles (1932–)

187. Isaac Hayes (1942–)

188. Flip (or Clerow) Wilson (1933–1998)

189. Dean Dixon (1915–1976)

190. B.B. King, born Riley B. King (1925–). B.B. stands for "Beale Street Blues Boy."

191. Brook Benton (1931–1988)

192. John Lee Hooker (1917–2001)

193. Chi-Lites

194. Ike (1931–) and Tina (1939–) Turner

195. Betty Wright (1953–)

196. Jackson 5

197. Al Green (1946–)

198. Charley Pride (1938–)

199. Erroll Garner (1921–1977)

200. Staple Singers

201. Dobie Gray (1940–)

202. Johnny Nash (1940–)

203. John Elroy Sanford (1922–1991), also known as Redd Foxx

204. Luther Ingram (1944–)

205. Richard Pryor (1940–2005)

206. Charles Mingus (1922–1979)

207. Roberta Flack (1937–)

208. Bill Withers (1938–)

209. Harry Belafonte (1927–)

210. Gladys Knight and the Pips

211. Stevie Wonder (1950–)

212. Earth, Wind & Fire

213. Barry White (1944–2003)

214. 6 years

215. 10 years

216. Bob Marley (1945–1981)

217. LTD

218. Brothers Johnson

219. Lou Rawls (1935–2006)

220. Commodores, original members: William King, Ronald LaPread, Thomas McLary, Walter Orange, Lionel Ritchie, and Milan Williams

221. Otis Day and the Knights

222. Lakeside

223. Kool & The Gang

224. Teddy Pendergrass (1950–)

225. *Dream Girls* (1981)

226. Gregory Hines (1946–2003)

227. Pointer Sisters

228. Gap Band

229. Rick James (1948–2004)

230. Z.Z. Hill (1935–1984)

231. Louis Gossett, Jr. (1936–)

232. Sarah Vaughan (1924–1990)

233. Michael Jackson

234. Eddie Murphy (1961–)

235. Albert King (1923–1992)

236. Ray Parker, Jr. (1954–)

237. Bill Cosby (1937–)

238. Tina Turner (1939–)

239. Oprah Winfrey (1954–)

240. Danny Glover (1946–)

241. Whitney Houston (1963–)

242. Cameo

243. Anita Baker (1958–)

244. Club Nouveau

245. Quincy Jones (1933–)

246. Tone Loc, born Anthony Terrell Smith (1966–)

247. Spike Lee (1957–)

248. Judith Jamison (1943–)

249. Denzel Washington (1954–)

250. Tony! Toni! Tone!

251. M.C. Hammer, born Stanley Kirk Burrell (1962–)

252. Whoopi Goldberg (1950–)

253. Tupac Shakur (1971–1996)

254. Nat and Natalie Cole

255. Boyz II Men

256. Ulysses Kay (1917–1995)

257. Arrested Development

258. Mariah Carey (1970–)

259. Janet Jackson (1966–)

260. Aaliyah Haughton (1979–2001)

261. Christopher Wallace (1972–1997), also known as Biggie Smalls. His nickname was "The Notorious Big."

262. Martin Lawrence (1965–)

263. Cuba Gooding, Jr. (1968–)

264. Steve Harvey (1956–)

265. Will Smith (1968–)

266. Baja Men

267. Alicia Keys (1981–)

268. Halle Berry (1966–)

269. Sonny Rollins (1930–)

270. Beyoncé Knowles (1981–)

271. Luther Vandross (1951–2005)

272. Queen Latifah (1970–)

273. Usher Raymond (1978–)

274. Tom Joyner, Sr. (1949–)

275. Jamie Foxx (1967–)

276. Morgan Freeman (1937–)

7 — Geography

1. What pilot or navigator of Christopher Columbus's ship the *Niña*, was of African descent?

2. Who accompanied the Spanish conquistadors such as Hernando Cortez in Mexico, Francisco Pizarro in Peru, Ponce de Leon in Florida, Cabeza de Vaca in the American Southwest, and Christopher Columbus?

3. What conquistador of African descent accompanied Vasco Nuñez de Balboa as he discovered the Pacific Ocean in 1513?

4. In the 1500s, what European of African descent (far right) explored Florida, Texas, Mexico, Arizona, and New Mexico, and was later killed by the Zuni Indians?

5. In the early 1500s, what conquistador of African descent accompanied Ponce de Leon in Puerto Rico and Florida, and accompanied Hernando Cortez in Mexico? He was the first to plant wheat in Mexico.

Figure 246—Estivanico (Stephen) Dorantes (extreme right). Arizona State Library, mural by Jay Datus.

6. Hernando Cortez gave California its name to honor whom?

7. Dedicated to the first African American Baptist missionary, the Reverend George Lisle (c.1742–?) Monument at First Bryant Baptist Church is located in what city?

8. Where was Phillis Wheatley born in 1753?

9. The Revolutionary War site of the Battle of Rhode Island (August 29, 1778), where an all-African American unit fought, is located in what Rhode Island city?

10. Manual Camero was one of twelve men who founded what city in southern California in 1781? Camero was one of the first elected *regidores* or town councilmen.

11. Jean Baptiste Pointe Du Sable was the first resident in 1789 of what city?

12. Jean Baptiste Pointe Du Sable was arrested by the British as a spy for America and sent to what Michigan island?

13. Thomas Pierre Motoyer deeded the Yucca Plantation to Marie Therese Coincoin (1742–1816), a former slave (freed in 1778) who became a wealthy businesswoman and owner of slaves. Marie Therese eventually freed her fourteen children from bondage. In what Louisiana city is this plantation located?

14. Some African Americans, loyal to the British during the American Revolutionary War, settled in Canada. Many left in 1792 and established what country in Africa?

15. In what New Hampshire town was a fund for the church and school set up by Amos Fortune in 1801? In 1947, the residents started the Amos Fortune Forum in his honor.

16. What African American helped explore the mid-western United States with Lewis and Clark from 1803 to 1806?

17. Fort Negro, which was destroyed in 1816 by Andrew Jackson, was located in what state?

18. Who was one of the founders of Olympia, Washington, and aided early settlers during the lean times? He was born near Philadelphia, Pennsylvania

Figure 247—*York*, 1908. Watercolor, by Charles M. Russell. Courtesy of Montana Historical Society. Gift of the Artist, 109.01.01.

around 1779, and was an only child. His father and mother cared for a shipping merchant, Mr. Stevenson, and his wife. When the Stevensons died, their estate was left to Bush's father and mother, who passed the fortune on to their son, George Washington Bush.

19. What community existed from 1825 to 1857 on Manhattan Island in New York City, and was acquired by the state of New York for Central Park?

20. What African American, killed in 1836 at the Battle of the Alamo in what city, is referred to on a plaque in the Alamo as "John _____, A Negro Slave"?

21. Who was an early settler of Superior City, Wisconsin during the 1840s and 1850s? His mother was an Ojibway Indian. At an early age, Bonga was sent to a missionary school for education. He later quit and joined the fur trade business. After becoming successful, he married an Ojibway Indian and became an interpreter. In 1937, Bonga was an interpreter for the Ojibway Indians when they signed a treaty with the U.S. government. He later became a clerk at a fur company and traveled extensively in Minnesota and Wisconsin. He also served as a guide and interpreter for the artist Eastman Johnson.

Figure 248—Stephen Bonga. From the Collection of the Minnesota Historical Society.

22. Who discovered a pass in the Sierra Nevada Mountains of western California in 1850 while working as a scout for General Freemont? He was born a slave in 1798 in Frederick, Virginia. His father was White and his mother was an African American slave. His father later freed him from slavery. His first job was an apprentice blacksmith in St. Louis. Later, he went to New Orleans and signed as a fur trapper with General Ashly and they traveled to the Rocky Mountains. After trapping for a while, he opened a trading post with the Blackfeet Indians. He was subsequently captured by the Crow Indians. He became chief of the Crows and had traveled to California, where he discovered the pass later named in his honor. The Beckwourth Pass is near Reno, Nevada, just inside the California state line. Just west of the pass, Beckwourth established a trading post. The Beckwourth Trail travels north and west roughly along the route of Highway 395. The trail winds along Grizzly Creek through the towns along the creek and ends at Bidwell's Bar, which is now covered by Lake Oroville.

23. Who was an early western fur trader and mountain man, who wrote about his adventures? During 1854 and 1855, he dictated his autobiography to Thomas D. Bonner, who edited the narrative *The Life of James P. Beckwourth, Mountaineer, Scout, and Pioneer, and Chief of the Crow Nation of Indians*. The book was published in 1856 by Harper and Brothers and was very successful. A British edition was published in 1856, followed by a second edition in 1858, and in 1860 a French edition was published. Originally, historians dismissed the book, but later found out that many of the events referenced in the book actually happened, although some may have been exaggerated. Some dates and names were not exact because of Beckwourth's memory, but once the dates were corroborated, the accounts were considered accurate.

Figure 249—James P. Beckwourth. Courtesy of the Colorado Historical Society.

24. Who was a leading citizen and early pioneer of Central City, Colorado from about 1860 to about 1880?

25. Fortress Monroe (now Fort Monroe), a refuge for African Americans who wanted to join the Union forces during the Civil War, was located in which state?

26. During the Civil War, President Lincoln attempted to compensate slave owners in the District of Columbia (emancipated compensation), and to colonize African Americans on an island of what country?

Figure 250—Aunt Clara Brown. Courtesy of the Colorado Historical Society.

27. Where did the Civil War battle of Fort Wagner (July 18, 1863), in which the 54th Massachusetts infantry participated, take place?

28. A Civil War battlefield memorial, located in what Florida city, marks the site where the 54th Massachusetts rescued unseasoned soldiers of the 8th U.S. Colored Troops on February 20, 1864?

29. Jenkins Ferry State Park, near the site of a Civil War battle fought by the 2nd Kansas Colored Troops on April 30, 1864, is located near what Arkansas town?

30. What Civil War national battlefield site in Mississippi was noted for the valor of the 59th U.S. Colored Troops on June 10, 1864?

31. In which state do African Americans annually celebrate June 19, also referred to as "Juneteenth," as the day slavery ended in that state in 1865?

32. In what city did Booker T. Washington labor in the salt works from 1865 to 1866?

33. What African American college was founded in 1866 by a group of African American Civil War soldiers?

34. African American George Washington (1817–1905) founded what city in Washington state in 1875?

35. The name of what African American town founded in 1877, was derived from a slave who came over on a slave ship and later purchased his freedom?

Figure 251—George Washington. Oregon Historical Society, Portland, Oregon.

36. African American Isaiah Thornton Montgomery (1847–1924), founded what Mississippi town in 1886, as a haven for African Americans? He was born in Mississippi on the Hurricane Plantation, owned by Joseph Davis, the older brother of Jefferson Davis. His parents, who were both from Virginia, had two sons, William Thornton and Isaiah Thornton Montgomery. At the start of the Civil War, he joined the river boat forces of Union Admiral David Porter and was at Vicksburg when the Confederates surrendered to General Grant on July 4, 1863. After the Civil War, Montgomery and his father Benjamin opened a family store. In 1867, Joseph Davis sold the plantation to Benjamin Montgomery and his two sons. In 1872, Montgomery established and became mayor of the town of Mound Bayou, named after a large Native American mound located in the center of the town. In 1902, he

Figure 252—Isaiah T. Montgomery. Courtesy of Mississippi Department of Archives and History.

accepted a federal appointment as the receiver of public funds for Mississippi but the following year a special federal agent accused Montgomery of wrongdoing in regard to bank deposits. The charges were unfounded, but Montgomery was forced to resign. President Theodore Roosevelt made a trip to Mound Bayou as a public gesture, after the resignation.

37. On October 22, 1890, Edward P. McCabe (1850–1923), founded what Oklahoma city and named it in honor of a Howard University educator? He was born on October 10, 1850, in Troy, New York. He advocated the migration of African Americans to Kansas, hoping to create a state with an African American majority to free African Americans from the White domination prevalent throughout the South. His failure to become elected to a third term as Kansas state auditor led him to consider the Oklahoma Territory as a possible African American majority state. He served as deputy auditor of the Oklahoma Territory from 1897 to 1907 and died in 1923 in Chicago, Illinois.

Figure 253—Edward McCabe. Kansas State Historical Society, Topeka, Kansas.

38. William G. Still, an African American composer who spent his youth in Little Rock, Arkansas, was born in 1895 in what city?

39. Mary Church Terrell, the woman who achieved national prominence in 1896 as the first president of the National Association of Colored Women, made her home in what city?

40. In 1908, what California town was founded and named after an African American
administrator, educator, and minister?
The city was later changed to the Allensworth State Historical Park. He was born
a slave in 1842, in Louisville, Kentucky
to Phyllis and Levi Allensworth. At the
age of 20, he escaped from slavery. In the
Civil War, he served as a civilian nurse
during the Nashville campaign. He later
joined the Navy, serving on an Ohio
gunboat, and after the Civil War, became
a Baptist minister in 1871. In 1886, President Grover Cleveland appointed him
chaplain for the 24th Infantry. At the time
of the Spanish-American War, Allensworth was a lieutenant colonel, the highest ranking African American in the
Army at that time.

Figure 254—Allen Allensworth
(1842–1914). Courtesy of the
Bancroft Library, University of
California, Berkeley.

41. Who explored the North Pole with
Robert Peary and was the first American
to raise the American flag at the North
Pole on April 6, 1909? He was born on
in 1866 in Maryland and lost both his
parents while he was young. As a teenager, he found a job as a sailor and was
an experienced sailor by the time he was
an adult. One day between jobs on the
sea, while working in a store in Washington, D.C., Robert Peary came in
looking for a servant to take with him to
map Nicaragua for a possible government canal. The store owner recommended Henson and he was hired. Peary was
so impressed with Henson on the trip to
Nicaragua that he made him his assistant. Peary later wanted to reach the
North Pole and took Henson with him.

Figure 255—Matthew Henson.
Reproduced from the Collections of the
Library of Congress.

The first four attempts were failures but on the fifth attempt, they reached the
North Pole.

42. Francis Ellen Watkins Harper (1825–1911), social activist, made her home
in what city? Harper was born September 24, 1825, in Baltimore, Maryland,
to free parents. Her mother died when she was three year old and she was
raised by her relatives. She was educated by her uncle, Reverend William
Watkins. In 1845, she published *Forest Leaves*. In 1860, she married Fenton
Harper. She published a novel, *Lola Leroy*, in 1892. She was a writer,
activist, and supporter of women's suffrage, antislavery.

43. Engineered and built in 1914 by African American Archie A. Alexander, former governor of the Virgin Islands, the Tidal Basin Bridge is located in what city? He was born on May 14, 1888, in Ottumwa, Iowa. His parents were Price and Mary Hamilton Alexander. In 1899, his parents moved to an area just outside Des Moines, Iowa. He studied engineering at the University of Iowa and graduated in 1912. He worked for the Marsh Engineering Company for two years and then formed his own company, which was called Alexander and Repass. Because of his participation in politics, he was appointed governor of the Virgin Islands, which had been purchased from Denmark by the United States in 1917. He was appointed governor of the Virgin Islands in 1954 and was governor for 16 months before he was forced to resign. Alexander died in Des Moines, Iowa, on January 4, 1958. After the death of his wife in 1975, a trust fund in Alexander's will created engineering scholarships at the University of Iowa and Tuskegee University.

Figure 256—Archie Alexander. Office of the Governor, Virgin Islands.

44. What city, located on the Mississippi River, has a park and monument to Tom Lee (1910–1952)? This monument honored Lee for his valor in using his boat to save 32 lives, when the steamer *M.E. Norman* sank twenty miles south of this city on May 8, 1925. On that day, the 113-foot-long steamboat carried 72 passengers on a trip to see the river and have a picnic. The passengers were attending a convention in Memphis. A strong current caught the steamboat and caused it to capsize in the river. Lee, who could not swim, witnessed the tragedy and raced to the overturned ship in his 28-foot motorboat, rescuing 32 survivors. Twenty-three people from the boat drowned. Tom Lee Park is a mile and a half along the banks of the Mississippi River. A monument dedicated to Tom Lee is located in the park, near Front Street. Some of the annual events held at the park include: the Barbecue Contest, the Memphis in May Festival, the Sunset Symphony concert, and the Jazz Festival.

Figure 257—Tom Lee. Mississippi Valley Collection Libraries, University of Memphis, Memphis Tennessee.

45. Although Bill Pickett (1870–1932) is buried in Ponca City, Oklahoma, his family was from what city in Texas?

46. What city is the birthplace of W.C. Handy?

47. The Mary McLeod Bethune Memorial is located in what city?

48. Where is North Carolina A&T State University located?

Figure 258—Bill Pickett (second from left). National Cowboy Hall of Fame and Western Heritage Center, Oklahoma City.

49. In what city is the Schomburg Center for Research in Black Culture located?

50. Where is the Frederick Douglass Monument located?

51. In what city are Beale Street, W.C. Handy Park, and the National Civil Rights Museum located?

52. Philander Smith College is located in what city?

53. In what city is W.E.B. Du Bois buried?

54. What city is home to the Delta Blues Museum?

55. In what city is Huston-Tillotson College located?

56. Auburn Avenue and Ebenezer Baptist Church, once pastored by Dr. Martin Luther King, Jr., are located in what city?

57. Where is Bethune-Cookman College located?

58. Poison Spring State Park is located near what Arkansas town?

59. What city is located on the Cuyahoga River and has a well-known Euclid Avenue?

60. Roxbury is a section of what city?

61. Where is Lane College located?

62. Where is Fisk University located?

63. The Black Revolutionary War Patriots' Memorial is located in what city?

64. The Paul Cuffee farm is located in what Massachusetts town?

65. Where is Sojourner Truth buried?

66. Where was Mary Allen Junior College located?

67. Where is Stillman College located?

68. Where is Voorhees College located?

69. What African American-established town in Oklahoma was visited by Booker T. Washington?

70. Liberty City is part of what city?

71. Where is Mississippi Valley State University located?

72. Where are Tuskegee University and the George Washington Carver Museum located?

73. Provident Hospital and Ida B. Wells-Barnett's home are located in what city?

74. Where is Morgan State University located?

75. What was the name of the Montgomery, Alabama church where Dr. Martin Luther King, Jr. organized the city bus boycott?

76. Where is Port Royal located?

77. Where is Port Chicago located?

78. What famous street in Chicago is sometimes referred to as the "Harlem of Chicago"?

79. South Street is a well-known street in what city?

80. Where are James Baldwin and Richard Wright buried?

81. What college located in Norfolk, Virginia was once a division of Virginia State College (now known as Virginia State University)?

82. Uncle Tom's cabin is located in what Maryland city?

83. Harriet Tubman established the Harriet Tubman Home for the Aged in what city?

84.   *Voice and Viewpoint News* was an African American newspaper in what city?

85.   Where is Norbert Rillieux buried?

86.   Where is W.C. Handy buried?

87.   In what city was Elijah McCoy an apprentice?

88.   The residential section in uptown Harlem is known as what?

89.   Daniel Hale Williams' home was located in what city?

90.   Housed in the Phillips Gallery, thirty panels of the 60-panel study of African American migration by Jacob Lawrence are located in what city?

91.   Where is Hiram Revels buried?

92.   Where is Miles College located?

93.   What city is the birthplace of Martin Luther King, Jr., and the home of Morris Brown College?

94.   The home of James H. Dillard, the Caucasian in whose honor Dillard University was named, is located in what city?

95.   The *Monitor* was an African American newspaper in what city?

96.   Where is Kentucky State University located?

97.   The African American abolitionist David Walker (1785–1830) and African American writer William Monroe Trotter (1872–1934) made their homes in what city?

98.   Carter G. Woodson's home was in what city?

99.   The Apollo Theater and Louis Armstrong's home are located in what city?

100. What Missouri town is the site of the Carver National Monument, which commemorates the birthplace of the African American scientist George Washington Carver?

101. Scott Joplin's home was in what city?

102. Garrett Morgan made his home in what city?

103. The home of Richmond Barthé, African American sculptor, and the Regal Theater are located in what city?

104. The early Oklahoma towns of Clearview, Summit, Taft, and Wellston were founded by whom?

105. Where is Daniel Payne College located?

106. Where is Wiley College located?

107. Where is Coahoma Community College located?

108. Where is the burial place of blues singer Bessie Smith, who was inducted into the National Women's Hall of Fame in 1984?

109. Where is Allen University located?

110. Where is Alabama State University located?

111. Where is Talladega College located?

112. Where is Florida A&M University located?

113. Where is Tougaloo College located?

114. In which city in Mississippi did Oprah Winfrey spend her childhood?

115. In what city did Arsenio Hall spend his youth?

116. Where is Southern University located?

117. Where is Texas College located?

118. Where is North Carolina Central University located?

119. Where is Virginia State University located?

120. Where is South Carolina State University located?

121. What states in Mexico have a significant Black population?

122. Harvey Gantt became the first African American mayor of what city?

123. Wellington Webb was the first African American elected mayor of what city?

Figure 259—Harvey Gantt. Chapel Hill, North Carolina, Mayor's Office.

Answers — 7 — Geography

1. Pedro Alonzo Nino (1470–c.1524)

2. Europeans of African descent

3. Nuflo de Olano (?–?)

4. Estivanico, Esteban or Stephen Dorantes (c.1500–1539)

5. Juan Garrido (c.1478–c.1538)

6. Queen Califa, mythical African Amazon queen who helped in the Battle between the city of Constantinople and the Turks

7. Savannah, Georgia

8. The country of Senegal in Africa

9. Portsmouth, Rhode Island

10. Los Angeles, California

11. Chicago, Illinois

12. Mackinac Island

13. Melrose, Louisiana

14. Sierra Leone

15. Jaffrey, New Hampshire

16. York Clark (1779–1832)

17. Florida

18. George Washington Bush (1779–1863)

19. Seneca Village

20. John Du Sauge (?–1836), San Antonio, Texas

21. Stephen Bonga (?–1884)

22. James Beckwourth (1798–c.1867)

23. James Beckwourth (1798–c.1867)

24. Aunt Clara Brown (1803–1885)

25. Virginia

26. Haiti, the island of Ile à Vache

27. Morris Island, South Carolina

28. Olustee, Florida

29. Sheridan, Arkansas

30. Battle of Brices Crossroads, near Tupelo, Mississippi

31. Texas

32. Malden, West Virginia

33. Lincoln College, Jefferson City, Missouri

34. Centralia, Washington

35. Nicodemus, Kansas

36. Mound Bayou, Mississippi

37. Langston, Oklahoma

38. Woodville, Mississippi

39. Washington, D.C.

40. Allensworth, California

41. Matthew Henson (1866–1955)

42. Philadelphia, Pennsylvania

43. Washington, D.C.

44. Memphis, Tennessee

45. Taylor, Texas

46. Florence, Alabama

47. Washington, D.C.

48. Greensboro, North Carolina

49. New York City

50. Rochester, New York

51. Memphis, Tennessee

52. Little Rock, Arkansas

53. Accra, Ghana

54. Clarksdale, Mississippi

55. Austin, Texas

56. Atlanta, Georgia

57. Daytona Beach, Florida

58. Camden, Arkansas

59. Cleveland, Ohio

60. Boston, Massachusetts

61. Jackson, Tennessee

62. Nashville, Tennessee

63. Washington, D.C.

64. Westport, Massachusetts

65. Battle Creek, Michigan

66. Crockett, Texas

67. Tuscaloosa, Alabama

68. Denmark, South Carolina

69. Boley, Oklahoma

70. Miami, Florida

71. Itta Bena, Mississippi

72. Tuskegee, Alabama

73. Chicago, Illinois

74. Baltimore, Maryland

75. Dexter Avenue Baptist Church

76. South Carolina

77. San Francisco Bay area

78. South Parkway, now Martin Luther King Drive

79. Philadelphia, Pennsylvania

80. Paris, France

81. Norfolk State University

82. Rockville, Maryland

83. Auburn, New York

84. San Diego, California

85. Paris, France

86. New York, New York

87. Edinburgh, Scotland

88. Sugar Hill

89. Chicago, Illinois

90. Washington, D.C.

91. Holly Springs, Mississippi

92. Birmingham, Alabama

93. Atlanta, Georgia

94. New Orleans, Louisiana

95. East St. Louis, Illinois

96. Frankfort, Kentucky

97. Boston, Massachusetts

98. Washington, D.C.

99. New York, New York

100. Diamond, Missouri

101. St. Louis, Missouri

102. Cleveland, Ohio

103. Chicago, Illinois

104. African Americans

105. Birmingham, Alabama

106. Marshall, Texas

107. Clarksdale, Mississippi

108. Mount Lawn Cemetery, Philadelphia, Pennsylvania

109. Columbia, South Carolina

110. Montgomery, Alabama

111. Talladega, Alabama

112. Tallahassee, Florida

113. Tougaloo, Mississippi

114. Kosciusko, Mississippi

115. Cleveland, Ohio

116. Baton Rouge, Louisiana

117. Tyler, Texas

118. Durham, North Carolina

119. Petersburg, Virginia

120. Orangeburg, South Carolina

121. Costa Chica areas of Guerrero and Oaxaca and Veracruz

122. Charlotte, North Carolina

123. Denver, Colorado

8 — History and Civil Rights

1.   What culture was the "Mother Culture" for Aztec and Mayan Indians?

2.   The writing and language of the Olmec (1200 BCE–600 AD), ancient people of Mexico, appear to be similar to the language and writing of what people?

3.   In 1570, who led a slave revolt on sugar plantations in the Mexican state of Veracruz (there is also a city with the same name), and later secured autonomy and peace with the Mexican government?

4.   What was a powerful incentive for slaves in Mexico to marry Indian women?

5.   The Republic of Palmares, located in Brazil, existed from 1595–1696 as a haven for escaped slaves. Who was the last leader of Palmares, who chose to jump to his death rather than surrender?

6.   Who was the leader of the Stono slave rebellion in South Carolina in 1739?

7.   Who developed a cure for rattlesnake bite and was given his freedom by the South Carolina General Assembly in the 1700s?

8.   Who was the only African American to die in the Boston Massacre (March 5, 1770), which started the American Revolution? The other four patriots to die were James Caldwell, Patrick Carr, Samuel Gray, and Samuel Maverick. The British soldiers were led by Captain Thomas Preston.

9.   Prior to 1776, what were the only ways slaves could secure their freedom?

10.   Which states prohibited slavery by their state constitutions?

11.   The Ordinance of 1787 for the Northwest Territory prohibited slavery in which states?

Figure 260—Crispus Attucks. Schomburg Center for Research in Black Culture, New York Public Library.

12.   Who founded the first African American Masonic organization in 1787? Researchers are not in agreement as to his place of birth.

13.   Which states prohibited slavery by legislative acts?

14. Sojourner Truth, who was born Isabella Baumfree in 1797 in Ulster County, originally only spoke Dutch and was a slave in which state?

15. Who planned a slave revolt in Virginia in 1800, but postponed the attack due to floods?

16. How did Lower Canada (Quebec and Canada East) force the end of slavery?

17. Who was the leader of independent Baptist churches in the United States, established the African Baptist Church in Boston in 1805, and helped found the Abyssinian Baptist Church of New York City in 1809?

18. Who founded the African Methodist Episcopal Church in 1816?

Figure 261—Sojourner Truth. Reproduced from the Collections of the Library of Congress.

19. Who led a slave revolt on the island of Barbados in 1816, and died in battle at Bayley's?

20. How did Upper Canada (Ontario and Canada West) force the end of slavery?

21. Which states were admitted to the union as free states via compromises?

22. Harriet Tubman (1820–1913) was awarded the Silver Medal by Queen Victoria in 1897. What was her original name?

23. Who was a famous fur trapper and Indian interpreter in Minnesota from the 1820s through the 1870s?

24. Who was said to have planned a slave insurrection in South Carolina and was captured in June 1822 in Charleston, South Carolina?

25. As a descendant of African slaves brought to Mexico during colonial times, what Mexican president abolished slavery in Mexico in 1829, was the first president of African descent, and has a state named in his honor? He was born August 10, 1782, in Tixtla, Guerrero, and was killed on February 14, 1831.

Figure 262—George Bonga. From the Collection of the Minnesota Historical Society.

26. Starting August 13, 1831, who led the most successful slave revolt?

27. Who was the Mexican governor of African descent, for the area the Mexicans referred to as Alta California? He governed in 1832, and from March to July 1845 when California was part of Mexico. He was the last Mexican governor.

28. Who was the African prince who, in 1839, led a successful revolt aboard the slave ship *Amistad*, and returned to Africa? He was born in Sierra Leone and was captured by Spanish slave traders in 1839. He was taken to Cuba and sold to José Ruiz, who hired Ramon Ferrer to take his ship, the *Amistad*, to Cuba. On July 2, 1839 the slaves killed Ferrer, took possession of the ship, and ordered the navigator to return to Africa, but the ship was intercepted by the *USS Washington* off Long Island. The Spanish demanded the ship be returned to Cuba, but President Martin Van Buren wanted the

Figure 263—Pio Pico. Seaver Center for Western History Research, National History Museum of Los Angeles County.

mutineers tried for murder. In the first trial, the judge ruled that while slavery was legal in Cuba, the slaves had been kidnapped in violation of Spanish law. The U.S. government appealed the decision, and the case went to the Supreme Court, with former President John Quincy Adams representing the Africans. That court set the Africans free. The ship was sent back to Cuba and the Africans gave anti-slavery speeches to pay for their return to Africa.

29. Although many of the Northern states had abolished slavery, according to the 1840 census, slavery remained. In the 1860 census, slavery still existed in what state?

30. What African American of early California opened San Francisco's first hotel in 1844, and owned 35,000 acres of land in the San Francisco area from a Mexican land grant? He has a street named after him in downtown San Francisco.

31. African Americans founded what country in Africa in 1847? Liberia began as a colony established in 1820 by the American Colonization Society (ACS). The objective of the ACS was to repatriate slaves back to Africa. The colony declared independence in 1847 and in 1848, a constitution was ratified and the first elections were held. The first president of the country was Joseph Jenkins Roberts, who emigrated from Virginia. The United States recognized the country in 1862. After the Civil War, repatriation to Liberia was minimal.

Figure 264—William A. Leidesdorff. California Section, California State Library.

32. In 1850, William Lloyd Still (1821–1902) was a chronicler of the Underground Railroad, and encountered what escapee from Alabama? Still was born in New Jersey in 1821 and spent his youth working on his father's farm. In 1847, he became a clerk in the Pennsylvania Anti-slavery Society. After escaping from slavery, his parents changed their name from Steel to Still, to conceal their identity. In 1850, he met a slave who described his parents and realized he was talking to his older brother, Peter. In 1872, Still published a book called *The Underground Railroad*, which gave accounts of the struggle and success of the network.

Figure 265—William Lloyd Still. Reproduced from the Collections of the Library of Congress.

33. Who was the well-known Pony Express rider who carried the mail from Stockton, California to the gold mines?

34. Whose fame as a stagecoach driver led to Monroe Meadows in Yosemite National Park, located in east central California, being named after him?

35. Who worked in 1854 to help fugitive slaves from her home in Windsor, Ontario, and was a recruiter for the Union Army during the Civil War?

36. In 1855, who became the second president of Mexico to be of African descent?

37. In 1855 and 1881, Frederick Douglass wrote his own autobiographies entitled what?

Figure 266—George Monroe. California Section, California State Library.

38. On March 6, 1857, whom did the Supreme Court rule still a slave, although he had lived in Missouri for years? The significance of the Supreme Court ruling was that slaves or free African Americans could not become citizens and could not sue the government, and the federal government did not have the authority to restrict slavery in the territories. The North was outraged and the South was very happy, and the decision probably put the country on the road to the Civil War.

39. How many African Americans were with John Brown at Harpers Ferry, Virginia, on October 16, 1859?

40. Which state entered the Union as a free state just prior to the start of the Civil War? Which states entered the Union during the Civil War?

41. Who led over 300 slaves to their freedom via the Underground Railroad, never losing a passenger, and served as a spy for the Union Army during the Civil War?

Figure 267—Harriet Tubman. Reproduced from the Collections of the Library of Congress.

42. Who fought for civil rights in California during and after the Civil War? She was born a slave between 1814 and 1817 near Augusta, Georgia and was the illegitimate daughter of a son of a Virginia governor. She grew up in Nantucket, Massachusetts. She arrived in San Francisco around 1852. Initially, she used two identities: "Mrs. Ellen Smith," a White owner of a boarding house, and "Mrs. Pleasants," to help African Americans. She was sometimes referred to as the "Black City Hall." In 1858, she went to Canada and donated $30,000 to John Brown. She did not declare her race until after the Emancipation Proclamation in 1863. She died in 1904 in San Francisco.

43. What noted abolitionist and statesman helped organize all-African American units during the Civil War?

44. When was slavery abolished in the District of Columbia and the remaining western territories?

45. What is the relationship between Missouri, Maryland, Tennessee, Kentucky, parts of Louisiana, parts of Virginia, and the Emancipation Proclamation issued January 1, 1863?

Figure 268—Frederick Douglass. Moorland Spingarn Research Center, Howard University.

46. Who led a group of Missouri slaves to St. Paul, Minnesota, and founded the Pilgrim Rest Baptist Church?

47. What made slavery illegal in the United States in 1865?

48. What was the purpose of the Civil Rights Act of 1866?

49. Who was a noted preacher at funerals, and in 1867, became the pastor of the Sixth Zion Baptist Church in Richmond, Virginia?

50. Who was elected in 1868 to the highest elective office held by an African American in Louisiana, by becoming the lieutenant governor of that state?

51. In 1869, who became the first African American elected to the U.S. House of Representatives from the state of South Carolina, as a Republican, to the 41st Congress? He was born a slave in South Carolina in 1832. His father Edward was a very successful barber, which allowed him to purchase his family's freedom not long after his son Joseph's birth. Rainey was drafted to help build Confederate fortifications in Charleston and to work as a laborer on ships. He and his wife escaped to St. Georges, Bermuda, where they remained until the war ended. Rainey joined the South Carolina Republican Party and was later appointed to complete the term of B. Franklin Whitmore, who had been expelled from Congress for corruption. Rainey was the first African American to serve in the U.S. House of Representatives and was re-elected to Congress four times. After leaving Congress, Rainey was appointed an internal revenue agent of South Carolina. He died in 1887, in Georgetown, South Carolina.

Figure 269—Joseph H. Rainey. Reproduced from the Collections of the Library of Congress.

52. In 1869, who became the first African American elected to the U.S. House of Representatives from the state of Georgia as a Republican to the 41st Congress? Andrew Young served from 1973 to 1977; John Lewis served from 1987 to the present; Sanford D. Bishop, Jr. served from 1993 to the present; and Cynthia McKinney served from 1993 to the present. He was born in Knoxville, Tennessee in 1836. He was self-educated and later became a merchant and tailor in Macon, Georgia before being elected to represent the state of Georgia in the House of Representatives. He died in Macon, Georgia in 1901.

Figure 270—Jefferson Franklin Long. Reproduced from the Collections of the Library of Congress.

53.

Figure 271—Group picture of the 41st and 42nd Congress African Americans. Top: Robert C. DeLarge, M.C. of South Carolina (left), Jefferson F. Long, M.C. of Georgia. Bottom (left to right): U.S. Senator Hiram R. Revels, of Mississippi, Benjamin S. Turner, M.C. of Alabama, Josiah T. Walls, M.C. of Florida, Joseph H. Rainey, M.C. of South Carolina, R. Brown Elliot, M.C. of South Carolina. Reproduced from the Collections of the Library of Congress.

Who was appointed by the Mississippi legislature on February 25, 1870—to fill the unexpired U.S. Senate term of Jefferson Davis—becoming the first African American senator as a Republican in the 41st Congress? He was born in 1822 in Fayetteville, North Carolina. His parents were free and of African American and Croatan or Lumbee Indian heritage. Revels was educated by the Quakers in Liberty, Indiana. He also attended school in Ohio, and attended Knox College, and became an ordained African Methodist minister in 1845. Revels resigned his seat in the U.S. Senate to become president of Alcorn College.

54.   In 1869, who was appointed minister to Haiti, the first African American to represent the United States? He was born in Connecticut in 1833, was educated in Connecticut, and was a teacher in Philadelphia for 14 years. He was the minister to Haiti from 1869 to 1879 and was the first African American appointed to a diplomatic position. He also served as the Haitian Consul in New York City, and died in 1908.

55.   In 1870, what amendment to the U.S. Constitution established the right to vote for male African Americans?

56.   From what state were the following African
       Americans elected to the U.S. House of
       Representatives? Joseph H. Rainey (1832–
       1887) was the first, and served from 1870 to
       1879; Robert C. DeLarge (1842–1874)
       served from 1871 to 1873; Robert B. Elliott
       (1842–1884) served from 1871 to 1874;
       Alonzo J. Ransier (1834–1882) served from
       1873 to 1875; Richard H. Cain (1825–1887)
       served from 1873 to 1875 and from 1877 to
       1879; Robert Smalls (1839–1915), who cap-
       tured the *CSS Planter*, served from 1875 to
       1879; Thomas E. Miller (1849–1938) served
       from 1890 to 1891; George W. Murray
       (1853–1926) served from 1893 to 1895 and
       from 1896 to 1897; and Jim Clyburn served
       from 1993 to the present. Smalls captured
       the *CSS Planter* on May 13, 1862, in Char-
       leston, South Carolina, while the White

Figure 272—Robert Smalls.
Reproduced from the Collections
of the Library of Congress.

officers slept. Smalls and the crew of 12 slaves raised the Confederate flag
and sailed the ship past other Confederate ships out to sea. Once at sea, he
raised the flag of truce and delivered the ship to the Union fleet. Later,
Smalls and the crew were honored by President Lincoln in Washington, D.C.
Smalls was given command of the *Planter* as a Union ship and was made a
captain in the U.S. Navy, a post he held throughout the war. He served in the
U.S. House of Representatives as a Republican.

57.   The following African Americans were
       elected to the U.S. House of Representatives
       from what state? Benjamin S. Turner (1825–
       1894) was the first African American elected
       from this state, from 1871 to 1873; James T.
       Rapier (1837–1883) from 1873 to 1875,
       Jeremiah Haralson (1846–1916) from 1875 to
       1877; Earl Hilliard from 1993 to 2002; and
       Arthur Davis, from 2003 to the present.
       Benjamin Sterling Turner was born a slave in
       1825 in Halifax County, North Carolina. He
       was taken to Alabama at age 5 and secretly
       educated. In 1867, he was elected tax collec-
       tor of Dallas County in Alabama. In 1869, he
       was elected to the city council of Selma,
       Alabama. He was elected to the House of
       Representatives from the state of Alabama in
       1871 and was the first African American
       elected to the House of Representatives from
       Alabama. He died on March 21, 1894.

Figure 273—Benjamin S.
Turner. Reproduced from the
Collections of the Library of
Congress.

58. What U.S. congressman served the second district of South Carolina from 1871 to 1873, and was noted for supporting the Fourteenth Amendment to the U.S. Constitution? This amendment granted citizenship to African Americans and abolished the 3/5 clause which counted African Americans as three-fifths of a person. He was born on March 15, 1842, in Aiken, South Carolina and became a farmer after he finished high school. He was a member of the South Carolina legislature from 1868 to 1870. Later he was elected State Land Commissioner. In 1871, he was elected as a Republican to the U.S. House of Representatives, where he served until January 24, 1873. He died on February 14, 1874, in Charleston, South Carolina.

Figure 274—Robert C. DeLarge. Reproduced from the Collections of the Library of Congress.

59. Serving from 1871 to 1873, who was the first African American from Florida to be elected to the U.S. House of Representatives? Carrie P. Meek served from 1993 to 2003; Alcee Hastings and Corrine Brown served from 1993 to the present. He was born a slave near Winchester, Virginia in 1842. During the Civil War, he was conscripted into the Confederate Army as a servant. After being captured by the Union Army, he was sent to Harrisburg, Pennsylvania to be educated, and he enlisted in Company F of the 3rd U.S. Colored Infantry in 1863. He later became a sergeant, and was discharged in Florida in 1865. He became a farmer, served in the Florida legislature from 1868 to 1869 and the Florida Senate in 1870. He became mayor of Gainesville early in 1870,

Figure 275—Josiah T. Walls. Reproduced from the Collections of the Library of Congress.

and was elected to the U.S. House of Representatives as a Republican. His seat was challenged by Democrats, and he was unseated after two months. He was elected again in 1872, but was not seated because of alleged voter intimidation. He died on May 15, 1905.

60. What African American was elected U.S. Senator and U.S. Representative from the state of Louisiana in 1873, but was rejected by both the Senate and the House of Representatives because the election was disputed? He was born free in 1837. Pinchback's mother had been a slave but was freed prior to his birth and married her former master, his father. His family moved to Mississippi but his father died in 1848, and the paternal relatives disinherited his mother. She took the children and fled to Ohio. In 1860, Pinchback married Nina Hawthorne, from Memphis. He moved to New Orleans and joined the Louisiana National Guard Corps d'Afrique. He later resigned because he was passed over for a promotion. When the Civil War ended in 1865, he moved to Alabama, where he saw occupying Union soldiers dress up as Confederate soldiers at night, to frighten African Americans. Pinchback believed the Union soldiers held the same view toward African Americans as the Confederates or Southern Whites. He eventually returned to New Orleans, and later moved to New York City and then to Washington, D.C. He died in 1921.

Figure 276—Pinckney B. S. Pinchback. Reproduced from the Collections of the Library of Congress.

61. Who was the first African American elected to the U.S. House of Representatives from the state of Mississippi, serving from 1873 to 1877 and from 1877 to 1879? Mike Espy served from 1987 to 1993, and Bennie Thompson served from 1993 to the present. John Lynch was born in 1847, in Concordia Parrish, Louisiana. His father Patrick was an Irish plantation manager and his mother was a slave. Before Patrick died, he had planned to free Lynch and his mother, but the friend who was suppose to execute the plan betrayed them. Lynch remained a slave until he was freed by the Union Army. He worked as a cook in the army and after the war, became a photographer in Natchez, Mississippi. He became active in politics, serving in the Mississippi legislature, and was elected to the U.S. House of Representatives. In 1912, he moved to Chicago and published a book, *The Facts of Reconstruction* (1913). He died in 1939, in Chicago.

Figure 277—John R. Lynch. Courtesy of Mississippi Department of Archives and History, Archives & Library Division, Special Collections Section.

62. What Reconstruction congressman's biography is entitled *Reminiscences of an Active Life* (1970), and is written by John Hope Franklin?

63. Who was South Carolina's first African American lieutenant governor? This person represented the second congressional district of South Carolina from 1873 to 1875, and strongly supported the Civil Rights Act of 1875. This act granted to African Americans equal accommodations without discrimination in public places, and was declared unconstitutional by the U.S. Supreme Court in 1883. He was born free on January 3, 1834, in Charleston, South Carolina. He became a shipping clerk at age 16, for a shipping house in Charleston. After the Civil War, he became associate editor of the *South Carolina Leader* newspaper. He was a member of the South Carolina state legislature from 1868 through 1870. Also in 1868, he was chosen to be chairman of the Republican Party in the state of South Carolina. After leaving the U.S. Congress, he served as an Internal Revenue Service collector from 1875 through 1877. He died on August 17, 1882.

Figure 278—Alonzo J. Ransier. Reproduced from the Collections of the Library of Congress.

64. Who became the first African American lawyer in the state of North Carolina in 1873, and later was a representative of the state of North Carolina in the U.S. Congress? He was born in New York City on February 24, 1844. His father was an Irish seaman and his mother was an African American from the West Indies. He attended Howard University and became an attorney in North Carolina in 1873. O'Hara was elected to the U.S. House of Representatives as a Republican in 1883 and served in the 48th Congress.

65. Who was the first African American from Louisiana elected to the U.S. House of Representatives in 1874, and served from 1875 to 1877? William Jefferson served from 1991 to the present, and Cleo Fields served from 1993 to 1996. He was born Charles Edward Nash on May 23, 1844, in Opelousas, Louisiana. He attended school in New Orleans and became a bricklayer. Later he joined the Union Army but lost part of his right leg at Fort Blakely, Alabama. Afterwards, he received a Republican appointment as inspector at a New Orleans custom house and later was elected to the U.S. House of Representatives. Unlike other African American congressmen, he did not receive any challenges to his election, possibly due to his military record. After his terms in the U.S. House of Representatives, he returned to his craft as a bricklayer.

Figure 279—James E. O'Hara. T.O. Fuller, *Pictorial History of the American Negro.*

66. The following African Americans were elected to the U.S. House of Representatives from what state? John A. Hyman (1840–1891) was the first African American elected from this state and served from 1875 to 1877; James E. O'Hara (1844–1905) served from 1883 to 1887; Henry P. Cheatham (1857–1935) served from 1889 to 1893; George W. White (1852–1918) served from 1897 to 1901; and Melvin L. Watt served from 1993 to the present. He was born John Adams Hyman, a slave, on July 23, 1840, near the town of Warrenton in Warren County, North Carolina. In 1861, he was sold to an owner in Alabama. When the Civil War ended, he returned to Warren County. In 1868, he was elected to the North Carolina state senate and served until 1874. In 1874, he became the first African American from North Carolina elected to serve in the U.S. House of Representatives.

Figure 280—John A. Hyman. State of North Carolina, Department of Cultural Resources.

tatives. He was unsuccessful in his attempt to win re-election in 1876, and returned to farming. Later he moved to Washington, D.C. and was employed by the Department of Agriculture. He died in 1891, in Washington, D.C.

67. What African American Republican served as a U.S. senator from Mississippi, from 1875 to 1881? He was born Blanche Kelso Bruce in Farmville, Virginia on March 1, 1841. He was the son of an African American slave and a White plantation owner and was the youngest of 11 children. In 1850, he was taken to Missouri to learn printing. He escaped in 1861 to Kansas, where he organized an African American school in Lawrence, Kansas. In 1864, he returned to Missouri and established the first school for African Americans. He worked as a steamboat porter in 1868 and settled in Tallahatchie County, where he was appointed an election official. He then moved to Bolivar County where he became sheriff and tax collector, and served on the Mississippi Levee Board.

Figure 281—Blanche K. Bruce. U.S. Senate.

In 1874, the Mississippi legislature elected Bruce to the U.S. Senate. Bruce served from 1875 to 1881. At the swearing-in service for the newly elected senator from Mississippi, James Alcorn refused to present Bruce to be sworn in, and Roscoe Conkling, senator from New York, made the presentation. Bruce supported reconciliation of the races, opposed the Chinese Exclusion Act of 1878, and worked with Mississippi senator Lucius Q.C. Lamar to get government aid for railroads, better navigation on the Mississippi River, and other projects for the state of Mississippi. He moved to Washington, D.C. after he left the Senate, and died on March 17, 1898.

68. Who organized a successful movement of African American settlers from the South to Kansas, in 1879? He was born a slave in 1809 in Nashville. After 37 years of bondage, he escaped slavery and moved to Detroit, where he helped African Americans escape slavery. After the Civil War, he helped African Americans move from the South to Kansas. Singleton viewed Kansas as Canaan and he was "Black Moses." Those who went to Kansas were called "Exodusters"; Singleton was the "father of the Exodus." By 1879, over 50,000 African Americans had migrated to Kansas, Missouri, Indiana, and Illinois. Thousands more were turned back by Whites patrolling roads and rivers. Singleton was so successful he was called in 1880 to testify before Congress. He established the United Colored Links to help African Americans acquire their own factories, but learned that he needed

Figure 283—Benjamin "Pap" Singleton. Kansas State Historical Society, Topeka, Kansas.

money to do this. He established the Chief League to encourage African Americans to migrate back to their ancestral homes, and formed the Trans-Atlantic Society to help them move. He died in 1892 in St. Louis.

69. Who wrote the books *The History of the Negro Race in America 1619–1880* (1882), and *A History of Negro Troops in the War of Rebellion, 1861–1865* (1888), and later examined European treatment of Africans in the Belgian Congo?

70. Who became the first African American Roman Catholic priest in Quincy, Illinois on July 18, 1886, and later was a priest in Chicago, Illinois? One of the first Catholic saints of African descent was St. Maurice, leader of the Theban Legion, in 286 AD. The legion consisted of about 6,600 Coptic Christian soldiers stationed in Europe under the command of the Romans. When ordered to kill Christians they refused, and their ranks were decimated by the Romans. Each refusal meant one-tenth of the soldiers of the legion were put to death. The angry emperor ordered the whole legion destroyed. Maurice and the legion died in the small city of Aguanum, Switzerland, which is now called Saint Moritz or Saint Maurice. Diocletian was emperor at the time of the Theban Legion.

71. Who was elected U.S. congressman representing the second district of the state of North Carolina in 1888 and 1890, and introduced bills to aid African Americans?

Figure 282—Henry P. Cheatham. State of North Carolina, Department of Cultural Resources.

72. Who was the first African American to win elective office in the United States, and was also elected by the state of Virginia to serve in the U.S. House of Representatives from 1890 to 1891? Robert C. "Bobby" Scott has served in this position from 1993 to the present. Langston was born in 1829 in Louisa County, Virginia. His father was Ralph Quarles, a wealthy White planter, and his mother was Lucy Langston, an emancipated slave of African and Indian ancestry. By age 5, Langston was an orphan. He graduated from Oberlin College in 1849 and became involved in the anti-slavery movement. In 1855, he was elected clerk of Brownhelm Township. In 1869, he became a law professor at Howard University and held the position until 1877,

Figure 284—John Mercer Langston. Reproduced from the Collections of the Library of Congress.

when he became the minister to Haiti. He returned to the United States in 1885 and became president of Virginia Normal and Collegiate Institute (later Virginia State University). In 1888, he ran as an independent for a seat in the U.S. House of Representatives and became the first African American to represent the state of Virginia in the House. He retired in 1894 and wrote his autobiography, *From the Virginia Plantation to the National Capital*. He died November 15, 1897, in Washington, D.C.

73. Who was elected U.S. Congressman representing the state of South Carolina in 1892, reviewed African American inventors' achievements, and read the accomplishments into the Congressional Record?

74. Ida B. Wells-Barnett, who authored the pamphlet *The Red Record* (1895), was a crusader against what crime? She was born in Holly Springs, Mississippi, in 1862. Later, she moved to Memphis, Tennessee and then to Chicago, Illinois. In 1895, she married attorney Ferdinand Barnett and the couple had four children. In addition to campaigning against lynching, she also fought for women's suffrage or the right of women to vote.

75. Who was a crusading African American from Red Bank, New Jersey, and was a staunch defender and supporter of Booker T. Washington?

76. Who was editor of the Boston *Guardian*, which was established in 1901?

Figure 285—Ida B. Wells-Barnett. Moorland Spingarn Research Center, Howard University.

77. Who is the author of *The Souls of Black Folks* (1903)? He was born in 1868, in Great Barrington, Massachusetts. In his youth, he was always interested in his race. He graduated from Fisk University, Nashville, Tennessee, in 1890 and in 1891, completed his master's degree at Harvard. President Rutherford B. Hayes, who handled the fund to educate African Americans, was quoted in the *Boston Herald* as saying he could not find one African American worthy of studying abroad. Du Bois applied for a grant to the University of Berlin, one of the world's finest institutions of higher learning, and he received a letter from the president claiming he had been misquoted. Du Bois needed one more semester to complete his doctoral work at the University of Berlin, but was denied funding, forcing him to receive his doctorate from

Figure 286—W.E.B. Du Bois. Fisk University Library, Special Collection.

Harvard in 1895. He taught at Wilberforce University and Atlanta University. Du Bois was a critic of Booker T. Washington, who at one time was the most powerful African American in the country. Du Bois objected to Washington asking African Americans to forget about their right to vote while dictating political policy from Tuskegee and consulting with presidents and congressmen on political appointments. Du Bois was invited to Ghana in 1961 by President Nkrumah. In 1963, he and his wife Shirley were refused passports because of the government's concern regarding communism, so Du Bois renounced his U.S. citizenship and became a citizen of Ghana. He died in 1963, in Accra, Ghana, at age 95. The U.S. embassy in Accra, Ghana is named in his honor. Du Bois is French and means "of the woods."

78. A monument was constructed in Columbus, Georgia, to honor what African American who died in 1903 attempting to rescue the Public Services Director, his supervisor?

79. Who published his autobiography in 1907, detailing his adventures as a cowboy? He was born in 1854 in Tennessee. In 1876, he acquired the nickname "Deadwood Dick" after winning roping, wild horseback, and shooting contests in Deadwood, South Dakota.

80. In what year was the National Association for the Advancement of Colored People established?

81. Who was the leader of the social revolution in Mexico in 1910 in Cuautla Valley, and was of African and Indian descent?

Figure 287—Nat Love. Reproduced from the Collections of the Library of Congress.

82. In 1911, who founded the Universal Negro Improvement Association in Jamaica, and led a "Back to Africa" movement in the United States? He was born Marcus Mosiah Garvey, Jr. in 1887, in St. Ann's Bay, Jamaica, the youngest of 11 children. His parents were a mason and a domestic worker. The objective of the Universal Negro Improvement Association was to unite all people of African ancestry into one group. He also launched the Black Star Line to distribute goods and people of African descent in the African global economy. In 1925, Garvey was convicted of mail fraud while soliciting funds for the Black Star Line, and was sentenced to five years in prison. He served half the time, then President Coolidge commuted the rest of his sentence and deported him to Jamaica. He died in 1940.

Figure 288—Marcus Garvey. Schomburg Center for Research in Black Culture, New York Public Library.

83. Who was the six-foot-tall African American cowgirl of notoriety from Cascade, Montana, who died in 1914?

84. Who became president of the Washington, D.C. Branch of the NAACP in 1913, held various positions in the NAACP until 1924, and was the recipient of the 1919 Spingarn Medal?

85. What gold medal award has been given by the National Association for the Advancement of Colored People (NAACP) annually since 1915 (except for 1938), for the greatest or highest achievement by an African American? How did the medal get its name?

Figure 289—Mary Fields. Montana Historical Society, Helena.

86. What community leader and political activist co-founded the Neighborhood Improvement League of Baltimore, Maryland, in 1915?

87. Who was president of the National Association of Colored Women's Club from 1916 to 1920, and was the recipient of the 1922 Spingarn Medal?

88. Who was the founder of the Associated Negro Press (ANP) in 1919 in Chicago, Illinois, and was the director for four and a half decades?

89. Who was associated with the Young Men's Christian Association (YMCA) in South Africa during the 1920s and 1930s, later taught African American courses at the City College of New York, and was the recipient of the 1933 Spingarn Medal?

90. What race riot that took place in 1921, was the worst in terms of lives lost?

91. What author of two novels entitled *The Fire and the Flint* (1924) and *Flight* (1926), and *The Negro's Contribution to American Culture* (1927), advocated equality and democracy, and was the recipient of the 1937 Spingarn Medal? He was born in 1893 in Atlanta, Georgia. Despite his blonde hair and blue eyes—indicating that only a fraction of his ancestry was African American—White chose to go through life as an African American. He was executive secretary of the National Advancement for the Advancement of Colored People (NAACP) from 1931 to 1955. The NAACP waged a long campaign against lynching and was against lynching of anyone, regardless of race. White also fought a successful battle against the confirmation of a Herbert Hoover Supreme Court nominee, Judge John J. Parker of North Carolina. Parker was on record as opposing African American voting. White's autobiography was *A Man Called White* (1948).

Figure 290—Walter Francis White. National Portrait Gallery, Smithsonian Institution, Washington, D.C./Art Resource, New York. Bequest of Phyllis Fenner, NPG.82.196.

92. Who did work for the Young Men's Christian Association (YMCA) at home and abroad from 1924 to 1946, and was the recipient of the 1948 Spingarn Medal?

93. Carter G. Woodson, who was the recipient of the 1926 Spingarn Medal, started Negro History Week in 1826. Negro History Week has evolved into what? Black History Month is celebrated in the United Kingdom, Brazil, the United States, and Canada. Woodson was born in 1875 in Virginia. He worked in a coal mine, attended the University of Chicago, where he earned his B.A. in 1907 and his M.A. in 1908, and received his Ph.D. from Harvard in 1912. Woodson concluded that if a race had no recorded history, "its achievements would be forgotten and, in time claimed by other groups." He also noted that many African American achievements were not in history books and hoped that "young African Americans would grow up with a firm knowledge of their ancestors." He died in 1950, in Washington, D.C.

Figure 291—Carter G. Woodson. Schomburg Center for Research in Black Culture, New York Public Library.

94. Dedicated in 1927, a victory monument to honor African Americans of Illinois who served in World War I, was erected near 35th and South Parkway in what city?

95. Oscar De Priest (1871–1951) was the first African American elected to the U.S. House of Representatives from what northern state? He served from 1929 to 1935; Arthur W. Mitchell served from 1935 to 1943; William L. Dawson served from 1943 to 1970; George W. Collins served from 1970 to 1972; Ralph H. Metcalfe served from 1971 to 1978; Curdiss Collins

Figure 292—Oscar De Priest. Reproduced from the Collections of the Library of Congress.

served from 1973 to 1976; Bennett McVey Steward served from 1979 to 1980; Gus Savage served from 1981 to 1992; Harold Washington served from 1981 to 1983; Charles Hayes served from 1983 to 1992; Mel Reynolds served from 1993 to the present; Bobby Rush served from 1993 to the present; Jesse Jackson, Jr. served from 1995 to the present; and Danny K. Davis served from 1997 to the present.

96. What was one of the most noted civil rights trials of the 1930s in the state of Alabama, which established the right of African Americans to serve on juries?

97. What African American from Illinois was elected to the U.S. House of Representatives in 1934?

98. Who chaired an African American delegation in 1935 on a "pilgrimage of friendship" to India, Burma, and Ceylon, sponsored by the YMCA? He discussed nonviolence with Mahatma Gandhi, and in 1953 founded the Church for the Fellowship of All People in San Francisco, California. One of his many books is entitled *Jesus and the Disinherited* (1949).

99. What was the original name of Father Divine, who helped the poor in many cities from the 1930s to the 1960s?

Figure 293—William L. Dawson. Chicago Historical Society.

100. Who was the first president of the National Association of Colored Women? Her autobiography is entitled *A Colored Woman in a White World* (1940). She was born in 1863, in Memphis, Tennessee. Her parents were Robert Church and Louisa Ayers. In 1866, Robert Church was shot in the head and left for dead during a race riot. He recovered and became a successful businessman. Mary attended Oberlin College in Ohio and graduated in 1884. She taught school in Washington, D.C. and Wilberforce, Ohio. In 1892 Tom Moss, a friend of Robert Church, was lynched by a mob of Whites. Robert Church and Frederick Douglass met with President Benjamin Harrison, but Harrison would not make any statements to condemn public lynching. In 1904, Church spoke at the Berlin International Congress of Women. Determined to make a good impression, she gave the speech in German, French and English. Church was a charter member of the National Association of Colored Women. She died in 1954, in Annapolis, Maryland.

Figure 294—Mary Church Terrell. Reproduced from the Collections of the Library of Congress.

101. Who defended the African American sailors court-martialed in Port Chicago, California, argued the school desegregation case *Brown v. Board of Education*, and became the first African American Supreme Court Justice? He was the recipient of the 1946 Spingarn Medal and the Presidential Medal of Freedom in 1999. He was born in Baltimore, Maryland on July 2, 1908. Marshall won 32 of the 35 cases he presented before the U.S. Supreme Court and was the first African American to serve on the Supreme Court. He served from 1967 through 1991. In 1976, the Texas Southern School of Law changed its name to the Thurgood Marshall School of Law in his honor. He died on January 24, 1993.

Figure 295—Thurgood Marshall. Collection of the Supreme Court of the United States.

102. Who established the Congress of Racial Equality (CORE) and became its director in 1942, was the recipient of the Presidential Medal of Freedom in 1998, and later authored the book *Freedom When?* (1965) and *Lay Bare the Heart: An Autobiography* (1985)? He was born in 1920 in Marshall, Texas. Later, he entered Wiley College studying to become a doctor. After earning his bachelor's degree, he decided to become a minister, and graduated from Howard University School of Religion in 1941.

103. Adam Clayton Powell, Jr. (1908–1972) was the first African American elected to the U.S. House of Representatives from what state? He served from 1945 to 1967 and 1969 to 1971. Shirley Chisholm served from 1969 to 1982; Charles B. Rangel served from 1971 to the present; Major Owens served from 1983 to the present; Edolphus Towns served from 1983 to the present; Floyd Flake served from 1987 to 1997; and Gregory Meeks served from 1998 to the present.

Figure 296—Adam Clayton Powell, Jr. Schomburg Center for Research in Black Culture, New York Public Library.

104. From 1946, who served in the NAACP Legal Defense and Education Fund of New York over a period of 20 years, and won 9 out of 10 civil rights cases? In 1966, she became the first African American woman to be appointed a federal judge and was the recipient of the 2003 Spingarn Medal.

105. What civil rights leader is noted for proposing a rent control ordinance, which was voted on by the citizens in 1948, and for her struggle for adequate housing in St. Louis, Missouri during the 1970s, 1980s and 1990s? She is a member of the Washington University Board of Trustees.

106. In 1949, who became the first African American to serve as a U.S. Federal Judge and was the recipient of the 1943 Spingarn Medal?

107. Who became the first African American congressman to head a congressional committee in 1949?

108. In 1950, who became the first African American to receive a Nobel Peace Prize? He also received the 1949 Spingarn Medal and the Presidential Medal of Freedom in 1963.

109. Who was killed in his home in Mims, Florida, in 1951, for his opposition to Florida's treatment of African Americans in the Groveland Case, and was posthumously awarded the 1952 Spingarn Medal?

110. Who used his knowledge of the *Bible* to convert African Americans to Islam from the 1950s through the 1970s and was the leader of the Nation of Islam during the time of Malcolm X?

111. Who was elected the first president of the Anchorage, Alaska branch of the NAACP?

112. Who was referred to as the "Queen Mother" of the civil rights movement?

113. Whose murder in August, 1955 in Money, Mississippi, galvanized the civil rights movement? He was born near Chicago in 1941. His father was killed in World War II. Emmett Till was killed on August 28, 1955, in Money, Mississippi. His mother Mamie brought his body back to Chicago and the body was viewed in an

Figure 297—Emmett Till and his mother Mamie. Reproduced from the Collections of the Library of Congress.

open casket so mourners could see how badly he had been beaten. Mamie died on January 6, 2003.

114. Who was arrested on December 1, 1955, sparking the Montgomery, Alabama bus boycott led by Martin Luther King, Jr., and was the recipient of the 1979 Spingarn Medal and the Presidential Medal of Freedom in 1996? She was born on February 4, 1913, in Tuskegee, Alabama. Her parents were Leona and James McCauley. She grew up on a farm and worked as a seamstress. On December 1, 1955, while riding a bus in Montgomery, Alabama, she refused to give up her seat for Whites, and was arrested. This incident started a boycott of the buses in Montgomery for 381 days. Parks' case ultimately reached the Supreme Court, which ruled that separate services were unconstitutional. The boycott sparked other civil disobedience.

Figure 298—Rosa Parks. Reproduced from the Collections of the Library of Congress.

115. Charles C. Diggs, Jr. was the first African American elected from what state to the U.S. House of Representatives, serving from 1955 to 1980? John Conyers, Jr. served from 1965 to the present; George W. Crockett served from 1980 to 1990; Barbara-Rose Collins served from 1991 to 1996; and Carolyn Cheeks Kilpatrick served from 1997 to the present.

116. Who was the executive director of the NAACP from 1955 to 1977?

117. Who was president of the National Council of Negro Women from 1957 to 1998, director of the Center for Racial Justice from 1965 to 1977, and recipient of the 1993 Spingarn Medal, and the Presidential Medal of Freedom in 1994? She was born on March 24, 1912, in Richmond, Virginia. An outstanding African American social activist and educator, in 1993, she was inducted into the National Women's Hall of Fame. In 2004, she received the Congressional Gold Medal from President George W. Bush.

Figure 299—Roy Wilkins. Reproduced from the Collections of the Library of Congress.

118. Who, along with Bayard Rustin and Martin Luther King, Jr., organized the Southern Christian Leadership Conference in 1957, and later became the president of the Southern Christian Leadership Conference?

119. Who helped nine African American children in their efforts to gain admission to Central High School in Little Rock, Arkansas in 1957, and authored the book entitled *The Long Shadow of Little Rock*?

120. Robert N.C. Nix was the first African American elected from what state to the U.S. House of Representatives, serving from 1958 to 1978? William H. Grey, III served from 1979 to 1991; Lucien Blackwell served from 1991 to 1994; and Chaka Fattah served from 1995 to the present.

Figure 300—Daisy Bates. Arkansas History Commission, State of Arkansas.

121. What African American woman led the civil rights struggle for desegregation of public facilities in Dallas, Texas, and organized youth groups to protest discrimination from the 1960s through the 1980s?

122. Who was one of the founders of the Southern Christian Leadership Conference (SCLC) (1957–1958), the Student Nonviolent Coordinating Committee (SNCC) (1960), and the Mississippi Freedom Democratic Party (MFDP) (1964)?

123. Who established the publication *Muhammed Speaks* in 1961? He was born Malcolm Little on May 19, 1925, in Omaha, Nebraska. His parents were Reverend Earl and Louise Little and Malcolm was one of eight children. His father was a Baptist minister and a fervent supporter of Marcus Garvey and was killed in Lansing, Michigan in 1931. At around age 12, Malcolm was sent to live with the Gohannas family. He dropped out of high school after a teacher discouraged him from aspiring to be a lawyer and told him carpentry would be more realistic. Malcolm committed a burglary and was caught at age 20, and sentenced to 10 years in prison. While in prison he became a Muslim. When he left prison, he changed his surname to X and dedicated himself to the teachings of Elijah Mohammad. In 1964, he left the Muslims and started his own mosque, made the *hajj* to Mecca, and formed the Organization of Afro American Unity. He was killed in New York City on February 21, 1965.

Figure 301—Malcolm X. Schomburg Center for Research in Black Culture, New York Public Library.

124. Whitney M. Young, Jr. was the former executive secretary of what organization from 1961 to 1971? He was the recipient of the 1964 Spingarn Medal and the Presidential Medal of Freedom in 1969? He was born on July 21, 1921, in Lincoln Ridge, Kentucky. His parents were Laura Ray and Whitney Moore Young, Sr. He grew up in Lincoln Ridge and attended Lincoln Institute—his father was president of the institute and his mother taught there. He attended Kentucky State Industrial College and graduated in 1946, and he completed his master's degree at the University of Minnesota in 1947. He began work at the St. Paul Urban League. In 1954, he became the dean of the School of Social Work at Atlanta University. In 1961, he became the executive secretary of the Urban League. Moore authored two books, *To Be Equal* (1964) and *Beyond Racism* (1969). He died in Lagos, Nigeria on March 11, 1971.

Figure 302—Whitney Moore Young. Reproduced from the Collections of the Library of Congress.

125. Who organized the 1963 march on Washington, D.C.?

126. On June 12, 1963, what civil rights leader was killed in Jackson, Mississippi, who was known for his efforts to register voters, and was the recipient of the 1963 Spingarn Medal? On Sunday September 15, 1963, the Sixteenth Avenue Church in Birmingham, Alabama was bombed, killing Addie M. Collins, Denise McNair, Carole Robertson, and Cynthia Wesley.

127. On June 13, 1963, who was appointed head of the Department of Housing and Urban Development (HUD), the first African American to serve at the cabinet level, and was recipient of the 1962 Spingarn Medal?

Figure 303—Medgar Evers. Reproduced from the Collections of the Library of Congress.

128. Augustus F. Hawkins was the first African American elected from which state to the U.S. House of Representatives, serving from 1963 to 1990? Ronald V. Dellums served from 1971 to 1998; Yvonne Brathwaite Burke served from 1972 to 1979; Julian C. Dixon served from 1979 to 2000; Mervyn M. Dymally served from 1981 to 1992; Maxine Waters served from 1991 to the present; Juanita Millender-McDonald served from 1996 to the present; and Barbara Lee served from 1998 to the present.

129. What civil rights activist from Ruleville, Mississippi, was vice chairperson of the Mississippi Freedom Democratic Party (MFDP) in 1964? She was born in 1917, in Montgomery County, Mississippi. Her parents were Ella and Jim Townsend and she was the last of 20 children. The MFDP challenged the seating of the Mississippi Democratic Party in the 1964 Democratic Convention. Although they lost the challenge, the MFDP focused national attention on the exclusion of African Americans from participation in the voting process and fair representation. In 1969, she established the Freedom Farms Corporation to help poor farmers obtain land. She died in 1977 at the Mound Bayou Community Hospital.

Figure 304—Fannie Lou Hamer. Schomburg Center for Research in Black Culture, New York Public Library.

130. What 1964 amendment to the U.S. Constitution eliminated poll taxes? In June 1964, three civil rights workers were killed near Philadelphia, Mississippi—James Chaney, Andrew Goodman, and Michael Schwerner.

131. Who was chairman of the Michigan Civil Rights Commission from 1964 to 1967, and recipient of the 1974 Spingarn Medal?

132. Who was a member of the Southern Christian Leadership Conference (SCLC) from 1965 to 1971, founded People United to Save Humanity (PUSH) in 1971, and ran for president of the United States in 1984 and 1988? He was the recipient of the 1989 Spingarn Medal and the Presidential Medal of Freedom in 2001?

Figure 305—Jesse Jackson. Mississippi Valley Collection Libraries, University of Memphis, Memphis, Tennessee.

133. Who helped found the Student Nonviolent Coordinating Committee, and was elected to the Georgia state legislature in 1965?

134. What festival, which started around 1966, is observed during the week after Christmas and is based on the African agricultural cycle?

135. Who were the founders of the Black Panther Party in 1966? Members Fred Hampton and Mark Clark were killed in 1969, in Chicago, Illinois.

136. Who was elected Manhattan Borough president in 1966, co-founded the Inner City Broadcasting Corporation in 1971, and was the recipient of the 1987 Spingarn Medal?

137. What dentist (also a former Shelby County commissioner) and his wife are noted for their NAACP support, politics, and civil rights activities in Memphis, Tennessee, from the 1960s to the 1990s?

138. In 1967, who became the first African American elected as mayor of New Orleans, Louisiana?

139. In 1967, what African American was elected to the U.S. Senate representing the state of Massachusetts, and was also the recipient of the 1967 Spingarn Medal and the Presidential Medal of Freedom in 1980?

140. Who played a pivotal role in promoting the Civil Rights Act of 1968, and was the recipient of the 1969 Spingarn Medal?

Figure 306—Edward Brooke. U.S. Senate.

141. William L. Clay, Sr. was the first African American elected from which state to the U.S. House of Representatives, serving from 1969 to 2000? Alan Wheat served from 1983 to 1994, and William Clay, Sr. served from 2001 to the present.

142. Louis Stokes was the first African American elected to the U.S. House of Representatives from which state, serving from 1969 to 1998? Stephanie Tubbs Jones served from 1999 to the present.

143. In 1970, who became the first African American mayor of Newark, New Jersey?

144. One of the many slogans of which activist was "Black is Beautiful"? A book authored by him is entitled *Stokely Speaks: Black Power Back to Pan-Africanism* (1971).

145. Walter E. Fauntroy was the first African American to serve as a delegate to the U.S. House of Representatives from which district? He served from 1971 to 1990, and Eleanor Holmes Norton served from 1991 to the present.

146. Parren H. Mitchell was the first African American elected to the U.S. House of Representatives from what state, serving from 1971 to 1986? Kweisi Mfume served in the House of Representatives from 1987 to 1995; Albert Wynn served from 1993 to the present; and Elijah E. Cummings served from 1996 to the present.

147. Who was the first African American woman to run for president of the United States, in 1972? She was born Shirley St. Hill in 1924, in Brooklyn, New York. She grew up with her maternal grandmother in Barbados. In 1934, she returned to Brooklyn and rejoined her parents. She graduated from high school in 1942 and graduated with honors from Brooklyn College in 1946. In 1949, she married Conrad Chisholm. She received her M.A. in elementary education from Columbia University in 1952. Her political career started in 1964 when she was elected to a state assembly seat. She held the seat until 1968, then campaigned for the 12th Congressional District and won, and became the first African American woman in the U.S. House of Representatives. She campaigned for the Democratic nomination for president in 1972 and although George Mc-

Figure 307—Shirley Chisholm. Schomburg Center for Research in Black Culture, New York Public Library.

Govern won the nomination, Chisholm received 151 delegate votes. She held her seat in the House of Representatives until 1982. She received many awards, including one for outstanding work in the field of child welfare. She wrote two autobiographical works, *Unbought and Unbossed* (1970) and *The Good Fight* (1973). Chisholm died in 2005.

148. Who was the first African American member of the Federal Communications Commission, serving from 1972 through 1978, and was the recipient of the 1986 Spingarn Medal?

149. In 1973, who became the first African American mayor of Atlanta, Georgia? He was born Maynard Jackson, Jr. in 1938, in Dallas, Texas. His parents were Irene Dobbs, a college language teacher, and Maynard Jackson, Sr., a Baptist minister. In 1943, the family moved to Atlanta, where his father became pastor of the Friendship Baptist Church. Jackson graduated from Atlanta University in 1956 and received his law degree from North Carolina Central University in 1964. He worked for the National Labor Relations Board in 1965 and afterwards, for the Emory Neighborhood Law Office. From 1969 through 1973, Jackson was a senior partner in the law firm Jackson, Patterson & Parks.

Figure 308—Benjamin Hooks. Mississippi Valley Collection, University of Memphis, Memphis, Tennessee.

He served as mayor of the city of Atlanta from 1972 through 1981 and from 1989 through 1993. He died in Washington, D.C. in 2003.

150. Barbara Jordan (1936–1996) was the first African American elected to the U.S. House of Representatives from which state? She served from 1973 to 1978, and was the recipient of the 1992 Spingarn Medal and the Presidential Medal of Freedom in 1994. Mickey Leland served in the House of Representatives from 1979 to 1989; Craig A. Washington served from 1989 to 1994; Sheila Jackson Lee served from 1995 to the present; and Eddie Bernice Johnson served from 1993 to the present. She was born in 1936, in Houston, Texas, the youngest of three sisters. Her parents were Arlyne and Ben Jordan. She attended Phyllis Wheatley High School, where she was a member of the honor society. She graduated from Texas Southern University in 1956 and Boston University in 1959.

Figure 309—Barbara Jordan. Courtesy of Barbara Jordan.

She was elected to the Texas Senate in 1966, and in 1972, to the U.S. House of Representatives, where she served three terms. Jordan retired from politics in 1979 and became a faculty member of the University of Texas at Austin. She died in 1996, in Austin, Texas.

151. In 1973, who became the first African American elected mayor of Los Angeles, California, and was the recipient of the 1984 Spingarn Medal? He was born on December 27, 1917, in Calvert, Texas. His parents were Crenner and Lee Bradley. Bradley was mayor of Los Angeles from 1973 to 1993. He died on September 29, 1998.

152. The civil rights of children have been one of what woman's principal causes? In 1973, she was founder and president of the Children's Defense Fund, and was recipient of the Presidential Medal of Freedom in 2001.

Figure 310—Tom Bradley. Mayor's Office, City of Los Angeles.

153. In 1974, who was the first African American elected mayor of Detroit, Michigan? He was elected to five terms (1974–1993), and was the recipient of the 1981 Spingarn Medal.

154. Harold Ford, Sr. was the first African American elected to the U.S. House of Representatives from which state, serving from 1975 to 1996? Harold Ford, Jr. served from 1997 to the present.

155. In 1976, who became the first African American to serve as U.S. ambassador to the United Nations, and became the recipient of the 1978 Spingarn Medal and the Presidential Medal of Freedom in 1981?

156. Who became the first African American member of the Daughters of the American Revolution in 1977, after tracing her ancestry to the Revolutionary War soldier William Hood?

Figure 311—Harold Ford, Sr. Special Collections, University of Memphis.

157. Who was appointed in 1977 to the Court of Appeals by President Jimmy Carter, and was the recipient of the 1996 Spingarn Medal and the Presidential Medal of Freedom in 1995?

158. Who led the Urban League as its president from 1977 to 1981, and became the recipient of the 2001 Spingarn Medal?

159. Who was the first African American elected mayor of Birmingham, Alabama, serving from 1979 to 1985? He was born in Livingston, Alabama. He earned his bachelor's degree from Miles College, his master's degree in biology from the University of Detroit, and his doctorates in zoology and biochemistry from the University of Oklahoma.

160. Melvin Evans was the first African American to serve as a delegate to the U.S. House of Representatives from 1979 to 1980, from which location? Victor O. Frazer served from 1995 to 1997, and Donna M. Christensen served from 1999 to the present.

Figure 312—Richard Arrington, Jr. Mayor's Office, City of Birmingham.

161. Katie Hall was the first African American elected from which state to the U.S. House of Representatives, serving from 1982 to 1984? Julia Carson served from 1997 to the present.

162. In 1983, who became the first African American elected mayor of Philadelphia, Pennsylvania? He was born Woodrow Wilson Goode on August 19, 1938 in North Carolina. He earned his B.A. in 1961 from Morgan State University and served in the U.S. Army, where he earned the rank of captain, from 1961 through 1963. In 1968, he earned his Master of Public Administration from the Wharton School of the University of Pennsylvania in Philadelphia.

163. In 1983, who became the first African American to be elected mayor of Chicago? He was born on April 15, 1922, in Chicago, Illinois. His parents were Roy Lee Washington, Sr. and Bertha Jones Washington. Washington attended Du Sable High School. He served in the Army from 1943 to 1946, received his B.A. from Roosevelt College in 1949, and earned his law degree from Northwestern University in 1952. He was an Illinois state representative from 1965 to 1976 and state senator from 1977 to 1980. In 1977, he ran for mayor of Chicago, but did not win. He campaigned for the U.S. House of Representatives to represent the 1st District, and held the seat from 1981 through 1983. Washington was first elected mayor of Chicago in 1983 and won re-election in 1987. He died on November 25, 1987, at his desk in City Hall.

Figure 313—Harold Washington. Chicago Historical Society.

164. Whose birthday is celebrated as a holiday on the third Monday in January—which became a federal holiday in 1986—and was the recipient of the 1957 Spingarn Medal, the 1964 Nobel Peace Prize, and the 1977 Presidential Medal of Freedom (posthumously)? As of 1999, all 50 states officially honored this holiday. President Ronald Reagan signed the bill creating the Martin Luther King holiday into law on November 2, 1983.

Figure 314—Martin Luther King, Jr. Mississippi Valley Collection Libraries, University of Memphis, Memphis, Tennessee.

165. Who was the first African American to be elected mayor of New York City, in 1989? He was born David Norman Dinkins on July 10, 1927, in Trenton, New Jersey. Dinkins graduated from Howard University in 1950 and from Brooklyn Law School in 1956. He established a private law practice, which he maintained until 1975. From 1975 to 1985, he was president of the New York City Board of Elections. In 1985, he became president of the borough of Manhattan and was elected mayor of New York City in 1989. He was mayor from 1990 through 1993; in 1993 he lost the mayoral election, and accepted a professorship at Columbia University.

Figure 315—David Dinkins. Mayor's Office, New York City. Photograph by James Hamilton.

166. What activist authored the book *Women, Culture and Politics* (1989)?

167. What U.S. congressman from Houston, Texas, was killed in an airplane crash near Gambela, Ethiopia on August 7, 1989, while on a mission to feed the hungry? He was born George Thomas Leland on November 27, 1944, in Lubbock, Texas. He attended Texas Southern University in Houston, Texas where he earned his B.S. in pharmacy in 1970. He served in the Texas legislature from 1973 through 1978. He served as congressman for the 18th District of Texas from 1979 until his death in 1989.

168. Donald Payne was the first African American elected to the U.S. House of Representatives from what state, and served from 1989 to the present?

169. In 1990, who became the second African American elected governor of a U.S. state, and also became the 1990 recipient of the Spingarn Medal? Pickney Benton Stewart Pinchback of Louisiana was the first African American to serve as governor, for 30 days, from December 9, 1872 to January 9, 1873. Wilder became the first African American elected mayor of Richmond, Virginia on November 2, 2004.

Figure 316—Lawrence Douglas Wilder. Governor's Office, Commonwealth of Virginia.

170. What museum that highlights the struggle for equality was established in Memphis, Tennessee, in 1991?

171. Whose autobiography is entitled *Delayed Justice for Sale* (1991) and is about Alabama's first African American woman attorney, who fought for justice in Alabama, Indiana, and Alaska?

172. Gary Franks was the first African American elected to the U.S. House of Representatives from which state, serving from 1991 to 1996?

173. Who authored an autobiography entitled *Breaking Barriers* (1991), and is the recipient of the 1997 Spingarn Medal?

174. Who was the second African American appointed to serve on the U.S. Supreme Court, and assumed office October 23, 1991? He was born in Pin Point, Georgia on June 23, 1948. His parents were M.C. and Leola Williams Thomas. His father abandoned the family when Clarence was a toddler. At age 6, Clarence and his younger brother were sent to live with their grandfather in Savannah, Georgia. He received his law degree from Yale University in 1974. In 1975, Thomas was greatly influenced by the book *Race and Economics*, by Thomas Sowell. From 1974 through 1977, Thomas was the Attorney General for Missouri. From 1977 through 1979, he was an attorney for the Monsanto Corporation. From 1979 through 1981, he was an assistant to Senator John Danforth. He was Assistant Secretary of Civil Rights, 1981 to 1982, and chairman of the Equal Employment Opportunity Commission from 1982 through 1990.

Figure 317—Clarence Thomas. Unites States Supreme Court Collection.

175. Who became the first African American elected mayor of Memphis, Tennessee in 1992?

176. Who was the first African American elected to the U.S. House of Representatives representing Dallas, Texas, in 1992? She was born in Waco, Texas in 1935. In 1952, she graduated from high school in Waco. She earned her B.S. in 1967 from Texas Christian University and an M.P.A. from Southern Methodist University in 1976. She was a member of the Texas senate from 1987 to 1993 and from January 3, 1993 to the present, congresswoman representing the 30th District of Texas.

Figure 318—Willie Herenton. Mississippi Valley Collection Libraries, University of Memphis, Memphis, Tennessee.

177. Who was elected to Congress on November 3, 1992 from the state of North Carolina, representing the First Congressional District?

178. In 1992, who became the first African American woman elected to the U.S. Senate?

179. On September 8, 1993, who was appointed the first African American U.S. Surgeon General?

180. Who was the first President of the Republic of South Africa (after all citizens were allowed to vote) from 1994 to 1999, and recipient of the Presidential Medal of Freedom in 2002? Many African Americans identified with Nelson Mandela and the Blacks of South Africa in their struggle against apartheid. He spent 28 years in prison for his beliefs, and was released on February 11, 1990.

Figure 319—Carol Moseley-Braun. Courtesy of Senator's Office.

In 1993, he received the Nobel Peace Prize and is an inspiration to oppressed people.

181. What attorney was noted for his defense of O.J. Simpson?

182. Who is a noted historian and 1995 Spingarn Medal recipient? Some of his books include *The Free Negro in North Carolina, 1790–1860* (1943), *From Slavery to Freedom* (1947), *Color and Race* (1968), and *The Color Line: Legacy for the Twenty-First Century* (1993)?

183. In 1995, who became the first woman to lead the NAACP, and was the recipient of the 1998 Spingarn Medal?

184. Who became the first African American mayor of Dallas, Texas in 1995?

185. J.C. Watts was the first African American elected to the U.S. House of Representatives from what state, and served from 1995 to 2002?

186. Who moved from Charleston, West Virginia in 1996, and established the Potter's House ministry in Dallas, Texas?

187. Who was elected president of the Honolulu, Hawaii branch of the NAACP in 1997?

188. Who became the first African American elected mayor of Houston, Texas in 1997?

189. In 1997, who became the first African American elected mayor of San Francisco, California?

190. Who managed the successful passage on November 19, 2003, of the bill authorizing the creation of the first national museum of African American history and culture, which will be located in Washington, D.C., and was the recipient of the 2002 Spingarn Medal?

191. Who was the first African American elected as Democratic senator from the state of Illinois, on November 2, 2004? He will take office on January 3, 2005.

192. Who was the first cabinet-level National Security Advisor to President George W. Bush, and became the first African American woman to be appointed Secretary of State in 2005?

Answers — 8 — History and Civil Rights

1. Olmec (1200 BCE–600 AD)

2. The Vai of West Africa

3. Gaspar Yanga (c.1542–c.1609)

4. The children by Spanish law will be free.

5. Zumbi (as a result of an interview with a Brazilian), sometimes referred to as Zambi in writings (c.1655–1696)

6. Jemmy (?–1739)

7. Caesar or Cesar (?–?)

8. Crispus Attucks (1723–1770)

9. A gift from the owner or by purchasing their freedom

10. Vermont, 1777; Pennsylvania, 1780; Massachusetts, 1780; Rhode Island, 1784; Connecticut, 1784; New Hampshire, 1784.

11. Ohio, Michigan, Minnesota, Indiana, Illinois, and Wisconsin

12. Prince Hall (c.1735–1807)

13. New York, 1799 and New Jersey, 1804

14. New York

15. Gabriel Prosser (1775–1800)

16. An 1803 court ruling, that any slave who left his owner would not have to return to his owner

17. Thomas Paul (1773–1831)

18. Richard Allen (1760–1831)

19. Bussa (?–1816)

20. 1819, court ruling that citizens of African descent who resided in Canada were free and their rights were protected by law

21. Maine, admitted as a free state and Missouri, admitted as a slave state in 1821. California was admitted as a free state in 1850 in exchange for enhanced fugitive slave laws.

22. Araminta Ross (married John Tubman and changed her name from Araminta to Harriet, which was her mother's name)

23. George Bonga (1802–1880)

24. Denmark Vesey (1767–1822)

25. Vicente Guerrero (1782–1831)

26. Nat Turner (1800–1831)

27. Pio Pico (1801–1894)

28. Joseph Cinque (c.1813–c.1879)

29. New Jersey

30. William A. Leidesdorff (1810–1848)

31. Liberia

32. His brother

33. William Robinson (?–?)

34. George Monroe (?–?)

35. Mary Ann Shadd Carey (1823–1893)

36. Juan Alvarez (1790–1867)

37. *My Bondage and My Freedom* (1855), or *Life and Times of Frederick Douglass* (1881)

38. Dred Scott (1795–1858)

39. Five

40. Kansas, 1861; West Virginia, 1863; and Nevada, 1864

41. Harriet Tubman (1820–1913)

42. Mrs. Mary Ellen Pleasant (c.1814–1904)

43. Frederick Douglass (1817–1895)

44. 1862

45. The Emancipation Proclamation did not apply to these states or parts of the states mentioned.

46. Robert T. Hickman (?–?)

47. The Thirteenth Amendment to the U.S. Constitution, effective December 31, 1865

48. To abolish the Black codes

49. John Jasper (1812–1901)

50. Oscar J. Dunn (18?–1871)

51. Joseph H. Rainey (1832–1887)

52. Jefferson Franklin Long (1836–1901)

53. Hiram Revels (1822–1901)

54. Ebenezer Don Carlos Basset (1833–1908)

55. Fifteenth Amendment to the U.S. Constitution, ratified February 3, 1870

56. South Carolina

57. Alabama

58. Robert C. DeLarge (1842–1874)

59. Josiah T. Walls (1842–1905)

60. Pinckney B.S. Pinchback (1837–1921)

61. John R. Lynch (1847–1939)

62. John R. Lynch (1847–1939)

63. Alonzo J. Ransier (1834–1882)

64. James E. O'Hara (1844–1905)

65. Charles E. Nash (1844–1913)

66. North Carolina

67. Blanche Kelso Bruce (1841–1898)

68. Benjamin "Pap" Singleton (1809–1892)

69. George W. Williams (1849–1891)

70. Father Augustus Tolton (1854–1897)

71. Henry P. Cheatham (1857–1935)

72. John Mercer Langston (1829–1897), elected clerk of Brownhelm Township, Lorain Co., Ohio

73. George Murray (1853–1926)

74. Lynching of African Americans

75. T. Thomas Fortune (1856–1928)

76. William Monroe Trotter (1872–1934)

77. W.E.B. Du Bois (1868–1963)

78. Bragg Smith (?–1903)

79. Nat Love (1854–1921). The book was entitled *The Life and Adventures of Nat Love, Better Known in Cattle Country as "Deadwood Dick," by Himself, a True History of Slavery Days, Life on the Great Cattle Ranges and on the Plains of the "Wild and Woolly" West, Based on Facts, and Personal Experiences of the Author.*

80. 1909

81. Emiliano Zapata (1879–1919)

82. Marcus Garvey (1887–1940)

83. Mary Fields (c.1832–1914)

84. Archibald Grimké (1849–1930)

85. Spingarn Medal. Joel Elias Spingarn (1875–1939), Chairman of the Board of the NAACP in 1914, bequest $20,000 to set up the award in memory of his brother Arthur B. Spingarn and his wife Amy E. Spingarn.

86. Laura Frances Wheatley (18?–19?)

87. Mary B. Talbert (1866–1923)

88. Claude A. Barnett (1889–1967)

89. Max Yergan (1896–1975)

90. Tulsa, Oklahoma, 1921

91. Walter F. White (1893–1955)

92. Channing H. Tobias (1882–1961)

93. Black History Month (February)

94. Chicago, Illinois

95. Illinois

96. Scottsboro Boys of Scottsboro, Alabama (1931–1937)

97. William L. Dawson (1886–1970)

98. Howard Thurman (1900–1981)

99. George Baker (between 1860 and 1880–1965)

100. Mary Church Terrell (1863–1954)

101. Thurgood Marshall (1908–1993)

102. James Farmer (1920–1999)

103. New York

104. Constance Baker Motley (1921–)

105. Margaret Bush Wilson (1919–)

106. William H. Hastie (1904–1976)

107. William L. Dawson (1886–1970)

108. Ralph Bunche (1904–1971)

109. Harry T. Moore (1905–1951)

110. Elijah Muhammad (1897–1975)

111. John Thomas (?–)

112. Septima Clark (1898–1987)

113. Emmett Till (1941–1955)

114. Rosa Parks (1913–2005)

115. Michigan

116. Roy Wilkins (1901–1981)

117. Dr. Dorothy I. Height (1912–)

118. Ralph David Abernathy (1926–1990)

119. Daisy Bates (1914–1999)

120. Pennsylvania

121. Juanita J. Craft (1902–1985)

122. Ella Baker (1903–1986)

123. Malcolm X (1925–1965)

124. Urban League

125. Bayard Rustin (1912–1987)

126. Medgar W. Evers (1925–1963)

127. Robert C. Weaver (1907–)

128. California

129. Fannie Lou Hamer (1917–1977)

130. Twenty-fourth Amendment to the U.S. Constitution, adopted in 1964

131. Damon J. Keith (1922–)

132. Jesse Jackson (1941–)

133. Julian Bond (1940–)

134. Kwanzaa

135. Huey P. Newton (1942–1989) and Bobby Seale (1936–)

136. Percy Ellis Sutton (1920–)

137. Dr. Vasco Smith (1921–) and Maxine Smith (?–)

138. Ernest Morial (1929–)

139. Edward Brooke, III (1919–)

140. Clarence M. Mitchell, Jr. (1911–1984)

141. Missouri

142. Ohio

143. Kenneth Gibson (1932–)

144. Stokely Carmichael (1941–1998)

145. District of Columbia

146. Maryland

147. Shirley Anita St. Hill Chisholm (1924–2005)

148. Benjamin Hooks (1936–)

149. Maynard Jackson (1938–2003)

150. Texas

151. Tom Bradley (1917–1998)

152. Marian Wright Edelman (1939–)

153. Coleman Young (1918–1997)

154. Tennessee

155. Andrew Young (1932–)

156. Karen Farmer (1951–)

157. A. Leon Higginbotham, Jr. (1928–1998)

158. Vernon Jordan (1935–)

159. Richard Arrington, Jr. (1943–)

160. Virgin Islands

161. Indiana

162. W. Wilson Goode (1938–)

163. Harold Washington (1922–1987)

164. Martin Luther King, Jr. (1929–1968)

165. David Dinkins (1927–)

166. Angela Davis (1944–)

167. Mickey Leland (1944–1989)

168. New Jersey

169. Lawrence Douglas Wilder (1931–), Virginia, 1990

170. National Civil Rights Museum

171. M. Ashley Dickerson (1912–)

172. Connecticut

173. Carl T. Rowan (1925–2000)

174. Clarence Thomas (1948–)

175. Dr. Willie Herenton (1940–)

176. Eddie Bernice Johnson (1935–)

177. Eva M. Clayton (1934–)

178. Carol Moseley-Braun (1947–)

179. Dr. Joycelyn Elders (1933–)

180. Nelson Mandela (1918–)

181.   Johnnie Cochran (1937–2005)

182.   Dr. John Hope Franklin (1915–)

183.   Myrlie Evers-Williams (1933–)

184.   Ronald Kirk (1954–)

185.   Oklahoma

186.   Dr. T.D. Jakes (1957–)

187.   Bennie King (?–)

188.   Lee P. Brown (?–)

189.   Willie L. Brown, Jr. (1934–)

190.   U.S. Congressman John Lewis (1940–), Democrat, Georgia

191.   Barack Obama (1961–)

192.   Dr. Condoleezza Rice (1954–)

9 — Literature

1. In the ballad "Bars Fight," who re-created an Indian massacre that occurred in Massachusetts in 1746 during King George's War?

2. Who was a Long Island slave and wrote religious and moral poems? Among the poems were *Evening Thought* (1760), *A Winter Piece* (1783), and *An Address to the Negroes in the State of New York* (1787).

3. Whose book of poems was published in London, England in 1773, due to difficulty locating a publisher in Boston, Massachusetts?

4. Who was kidnapped at age 11 from the province of Benin (located in Nigeria), was sold into slavery, shipped to America, and later wrote an autobiography detailing his accounts as a slave? His autobiography was entitled *Narrative of the Life of Olaudah Equiano or Gustavus Vassa* (1789).

5. What Russian of African descent is considered the greatest Russian poet, and is author of the play *Boris Godunov* (1831)?

Figure 320—Phillis Wheatley. Reproduced from the Collections of the Library of Congress.

6. What Frenchman of African descent is the author of *The Three Musketeers* (1844) and *The Count of Monte Cristo* (1845)?

7. Harriet Beecher Stowe was inspired by whose autobiography, to write the novel *Uncle Tom's Cabin* (1852)?

8. The novel *Clotel, or the President's Daughter* (1853) was written by whom?

9. Who was an escapee from slavery, and later wrote *The Autobiography of a Fugitive Negro* (1855)?

10. Who is the author of *Incidents in the Life of a Slave Girl* (1861), a narrative about a slave girl in Edenton, North Carolina, who formed a relationship with a White man who was not her owner, to protect her children and herself?

11. What is the title of the book compiled by William Lloyd Still that recorded the accounts of escaped slaves using the Underground Railroad?

12. Whose book entitled *House of Bondage* (1890) is a group of seven narratives of former slaves?

13. Who is the author of the book *The Work of the Afro-American Woman* (1894)?

14. Who was the pastor of the Fifteenth Street Presbyterian Church in Washington, D.C., and was known as a teacher and poet?

15. *Lyrics of a Lowly Life* (1896) launched whose career as a poet?

16. Who is the author of *The Conjure Woman* (1899), a collection of short stories, and the novel *The House Behind the Cedars* (1900), and is the recipient of the 1928 Spingarn Medal? He was born in 1858 in Cleveland, Ohio and grew up in Fayetteville, North Carolina. Chesnutt had light skin and easily could have passed for White. But he chose his African American heritage and sought to expose the injustices of slavery and the resulting caste system. In 1880, in a journal entry, he wrote: "The object of my writings would not be so much the elevation of the colored people as the elevation of the Whites, ... for I consider the unjust spirit of caste which is so insidious as to pervade the whole nation, and so powerful as to subject a whole race and all connected to it to scorn and ostracism.... I consider this a barrier to the moral progress of the American people." He returned to

Figure 321—Charles Chesnutt. Courtesy of Moorland Spingard Research Center, Howard University.

Cleveland, where he became a lawyer in 1887. He also worked as a court reporter and established a stenography business in Cleveland. He served on the General Committee of the National Association for the Advancement of Colored People and died in 1932.

17. Who wrote the novel entitled *The Sport of Gods* (1901)? At the age of 17, he published his own newspaper, the *Dayton Tattler*. Dunbar was a friend of Orville and Wilbur Wright his whole life. In 1895, he published *Majors and Minors*, which received a favorable review by William Dean Howells. His next book, *Lyrics of a Lowly Life*, was a combination of his first two books and included an introduction by Howells. In 1897, Dunbar took a job at the Library of Congress but quit the job after six months to concentrate on writing and recitals (he suffered from tuberculosis and needed the rest). In 1903, his condition worsened, and he died in 1906. During Dunbar's lifetime, attention was focused on the fact that Dunbar was of pure African descent, with no White ancestry.

Figure 322—Paul Laurence Dunbar. Reproduced from the Collections of the Library of Congress.

18. Who is the author of a book of poetry entitled *Lyrics of Life and Love* (1904), and the recipient of the 1918 Spingarn Medal?

19. What play by Charles Fuller is about the African American soldiers who were dishonorably discharged on President Theodore Roosevelt's orders in 1906, after a shootout in Brownsville, Texas?

20. Who is the author of the novel *The Quest of the Silver Fleece* (1911), which is about cotton and labor?

21. Who wrote the novel *The Autobiography of an Ex-Colored Man* (1912), became the first African American secretary of the NAACP in 1922, and was the recipient of the 1925 Spingarn Medal?

Figure 323—William Stanley Braithwaite. Reproduced from the Collections of the Library of Congress.

22. Whose best known play is entitled *Rachel* (1916)?

23. Who was a noted poet during the Harlem Renaissance, and published a book of poems entitled *The Heart of a Woman* (1918) as well as *Bronze* (1922), *An Autumn Love Cycle* (1928), and *Share My Mind* (1962)?

24. Who wrote the famous poem "If We Must Die" (1919) after numerous race riots in the United States? The poem, which did not indicate race, was later used by Winston Churchill during the trying times of World War II, to raise British morale.

25. Who was the lyricist for the song "Lift Every Voice and Sing" (c.1920) which at one time was referred to as the "Negro National Anthem"?

26. What poet from Lynchburg, Virginia was noted for her poems during the Harlem Renaissance? Some of her poems were published in *The Book of American Negro Poetry* (1922) by James Weldon Johnson?

27. Who wrote the novel *Cane* (1923)? He was born Nathan Pinchback Toomer in 1894. His parents were Nathan Toomer and Nina Pinchback (the daughter of Pickney B.S. Pinchback). Nathan deserted Nina, and her father would only support her if her son's name was changed. His name was changed to Eugene and later shortened to Jean.

Figure 324—James Weldon Johnson. Reproduced from the Collections of the Library of Congress.

28. Who attended New York University and as a student there, completed a volume of poetry entitled *Color* (1925), and *The Ballad of the Brown Girl* (1927)? He also wrote *Copper Sun* (1927), and later produced a novel entitled *One Way to Heaven*.

29. What poet was born in Joplin, Missouri, and a volume of his poems is entitled *The Weary Blues* (1926)?

30. Who is the author of the book *God's Trombones: Seven Negro Sermons in Verse* (1927)?

Figure 325—Countee Cullen. Moorland Spingarn Research Center, Howard University.

31. Who wrote the plays *Her* (1927), *Foreign Mail* (1927), *The Hunch* (1927), *Fool's Errand* (1927), and *Undertow* (1929)?

32. Who is the author of the novels *Quicksand* (1928) and *Passing* (1929)?

33. Who is the main character in the novel *Quicksand* (1928)?

34. Who is the author of the novel *Home To Harlem* (1928)?

35. Who is the author of *The Blacker the Berry* (1929)? He was born on August 16, 1902 in Salt Lake City, Utah. His parents were Beulah and Oscar Thurman. He attended the University of Utah from 1919 through 1920, and the University of Southern California from 1922 through 1923. He also authored the novel *Infants of Spring* (1932), and he died in 1934.

36. Who is the editor of *Not Without Laughter* (1930), and author of the short story *Simple Speaks His Mind*? He was born in Joplin, Missouri in 1902. His parents were Carrie and James Hughes. Shortly after Hughes' birth, his father deserted the family and went

Figure 326—Claude McKay. Moorland Spingarn Research Center, Howard University.

to Mexico. James studied for about a year to take the bar exam to become a lawyer, but was denied the opportunity because he was African American. *Not Without Laughter* was written during his senior year at Lincoln University (Pennsylvania), and the Simple stories were a compilation of weekly newspaper columns Hughes wrote for the *Chicago Defender* newspaper. One example of Simple humor is as follows: "I knew a man that was so low, if he set on a dime, his feet would not touch the ground."

37. Who was a critic and chronicler of the Harlem Renaissance? He was born Alain Leroy Locke on September 13, 1886, in Philadelphia, Pennsylvania. His parents were Mary Hawkins and Pliny Ishmael Locke. He grew up and attended high school in Philadelphia. He graduated from Harvard in 1907, and studied at Oxford University in England, becoming the first African American Rhodes Scholar. After graduating from Oxford, he studied at the University of Berlin for one year. Locke worked at Howard University from 1912 to 1916 and from 1918 to 1952. From 1916 to 1918, Locke studied at Harvard. Books edited or authored by Locke include: *The New Negro* (1925), *The Negro and His Music* (1936), *The Negro in Art* (1941), and *When People Meet: A Study in Race and Culture Contacts* (1942). He died on June 10, 1954.

Figure 327—Alain Locke. Schomburg Center for Research in Black Culture, New York Public Library.

38. Who is the author of *The Chinaberry Tree* (1931)? She was born in 1882, in Fredericksville, New Jersey. Her parents were Annie Seamon and Redmon Fauset. In 1905, she graduated Phi Beta Kappa from Cornell University, with a major in classical languages. In 1919, she earned her Master's degree in French from the University of Pennsylvania. During the 1920s, she edited *The Brownies*, an NAACP publication for African American children. She was also the literary editor of the NAACP magazine, *Crises*. Fauset also wrote: *There Is Confusion* (1924), *Plum Bun: A Novel Without a Moral* (1929), and *Comedy, American Style* (1934).

Figure 328—Jessie Redmon Fauset. Reproduced from the Collections of the Library of Congress.

39. Who is the author of the novel *Black No More* (1931)?

40. What is the title of James Weldon Johnson's autobiography?

41. A poem by what poet is entitled "Give Me Strength" (1934)?

42. Who differed from most of his predecessors and contemporaries in that he addressed his poetry specifically to African American people? He received the 1960 Spingarn Medal.

43. Who wrote the play entitled *Mulatto* (1935)?

44. Who wrote the novel *Their Eyes Were Watching God* (1937)?

45. Samuel Coleridge-Taylor, the African English composer, was an idol to what composer?

46. Who is the main character in the novel *Their Eyes Were Watching God* (1937)?

47. Who does Janie Starks fall in love with in the novel *Their Eyes Were Watching God* (1937)?

48. Who is author of the book of poetry entitled *Tuntun de pasa y griferia* (Drumbeats of Kink and Blackness) (1937)?

Figure 329—Zora Neale Hurston. Schomburg Center for Research in Black Culture, New York Public Library.

49. Who is the author of the novel *To Make a Poet Black* (1939)? He was born in 1906, in Wilmington, Delaware. In 1928, he graduated from Brown University and in 1932, he earned a Master's degree from Brown University. Some of his books include: *No Day of Triumph* (1942), *Stranger and Alone* (1950), *On Being Negro in America* (1951), *They Came in Chains* (1951), *An American in India* (1954), *The Lonesome Road* (1958), and *The Negro* (1967).

50. Who is the author of the novel *Native Son* (1940), and the recipient of the 1941 Spingarn Medal?

51. Who is the main character in the novel *Native Son* (1940)?

52. How long did it take Richard Wright to write *Native Son* (1940)?

53. Langston Hughes' second autobiography is *I Wonder as I Wander* (1956). What is the name of his first autobiography? He was the 1960 Springarn Medal recipient. He died in Harlem on May 22, 1967, at age 67. At his funeral, his poem "Wake" was read to the mourners. The poem is as follows:

Figure 330—Richard Wright. Reproduced from the Collections of the Library of Congress.

> *Tell all my mourners*
> *To mourn in Red —*
> *Cause there ain't no sense*
> *In my bein' dead.*

Later, a jazz trio played, as he had asked, Duke Ellington's "Do Nothing Till You Hear From Me."

54. Who taught at Livingstone College (Salisbury, North Carolina), West Virginia College, and Jackson State University? One of her works is entitled *For My People* (1942). She was born on July 7, 1915, in Birmingham, Alabama. She earned her B.A. from Northwestern University (Illinois) and her M.A. from the University of Iowa. In 1943, she married Firnist James Alexander and remained active professionally until her death on November 30, 1998.

55. Zora Neale Hurston, whose autobiography is entitled *Dust Tracks on a Road* (1942), was a drama instructor at what college?

56. Who is the author of the volumes of poems entitled *Shakespeare in Harlem* (1942) and *Montage of a Dream Deferred* (1951)?

Figure 331—Margaret Walker Alexander. Schomburg Center for Research in Black Culture, New York Public Library.

57. What playwright received the Pulitzer Prize for a play about the investigation of an African American soldier sergeant killed at a Louisiana army base in 1944, entitled *A Soldier's Play* (1984)?

58. A novel by this author is *If He Hollers, Let Him Go* (1945), but he is best-known for detective novels featuring "Coffin" Ed Johnson and "Grave Digger" Jones. Some of these novels are *A Rage in Harlem* (1957), *Cotton Comes to Harlem* (1965), *Run Man Run* (1966), and *The Heat's On* (1966), sometimes referred to as *Come Back, Charleston Blue*. Who is this author? He was born Chester Bomar Himes on July 29, 1909, in Jefferson City, Missouri. His parents were Estelle Bomar and Joseph Sandy Himes. He entered Ohio State University in 1926, but was expelled. In 1928 at age 19, he was sentenced to 25 years in the Ohio penitentiary for the armed robbery of an elderly

Figure 332—Chester Himes. Reproduced from the Collections of the Library of Congress.

couple in Cleveland Heights. On April 21, 1930, a fire in the prison killed 320 inmates. Himes was influenced by the Black Mask writings of Dashiel Hammett and the gruesome events he witnessed in prison. While in prison, he began to write short stories and when he was released from prison, he went to Los Angeles, and in 1945 wrote his first novel. He moved to Paris in 1953 and then to Spain. In 1957, Marcel Duhamel asked Himes to write a detective novel for the French. His detective novels were an instant success in France. He died in Moravia, Spain, on November 12, 1984.

59. What author's first novel was entitled *The Street* (1945)? She was born Ann Lane in 1908, in Old Saybrook, Connecticut. In 1931, she graduated from the University of Connecticut with a degree in pharmacy. In 1938, she married George David Petry. The couple had a daughter named Elizabeth. Two of her other works are: *Tibuta of Salem Village* (1964) and *Harriet Tubman: Conductor on the Underground Railway* (1955).

60. What is the title of Richard Wright's autobiography?

61. Who is the author of the novel *The Foxes of Harrow* (1946)?

Figure 333—Ann Petry. Schomburg Center for Research in Black Culture, New York Public Library.

62. Who is the individual among whose best works is "Libretto for the Republic of Liberia" (1947)?

63. Who is the author of the novels *Knock on Any Door* (1947) and *Let No Man Write My Epitaph* (1960)?

64. Who received the Anisfield-Wolf Award for the book *Your Most Humble Servant* (1949), which is about Benjamin Banneker?

65. Who received the Pulitzer Prize in 1950 for the book of poems entitled *Annie Allen* (1949)? She was born June 7, 1917, in Topeka, Kansas and grew up in Chicago, Illinois. Her parents were David Anderson and Keziah Wims Brooks. She received the Pulitzer Prize—the first Pulitzer Prize awarded to an African American—for the book of poetry *Annie Allen*. She was invited by President John Kennedy to read poetry at the Library of Congress Poetry Festival in 1962. In 1968, she became the Poet Laureate of Illinois. She taught poetry workshops at Elmhurst College, Columbia College (Illinois), the University of Wisconsin, and other institutions of higher learning. In 1994, she was selected by the National Endowment for the Humanities as the 1994 Jefferson Lecturer. Other books by Brooks include: *Maud Martha* (1953), *Bronzeville Boys and Girls* (1956), and *In the Mecca* (1968). She died on December 3, 2000

Figure 334—Gwendolyn Brooks. Schomburg Center for Research in Black Culture, New York Public Library.

66. Who is the author of the plays *A Medal for Willie* (1951) and *In Splendid Error* (1954)?

67. Who wrote the novel *Invisible Man* (1952)?

68. What is the name of the main character in the novel *Invisible Man* (1952)?

69. Who is the author of the play *Take a Giant Step* (1953)?

70. Who was an international editor for *Ebony* magazine who, after visiting many African countries, authored the book *Africa, Land of My Father* (1953)?

71. Who is the author of *A Raisin in the Sun* (1954)?

Figure 335—Ralph Ellison. Reproduced from the Collections of the Library of Congress.

72. Who wrote the play *Trouble in Mind* (1955), which won the 1956 Obie Award, and wrote the novel *A Hero Ain't Nothin' but a Sandwich* (1973)?

73. Who is the author of the novel *The Third Door* (1955)?

74. Who is the author of the novel *The Long Night* (1958)?

75. Who was born on the island of Martinique and later wrote *The Wretched of the Earth* (1959)?

76. What novel by Paule Marshall deals with the dislocation of moving from the tropics to Brooklyn?

77. Who is the author of the novel entitled *A Different Drummer* (1960)?

78. Who is the author of the novels *The Fire Next Time* (1963), and *Nobody Knows My Name* (1961)?

79. Who is a prolific science fiction writer, one of whose works is entitled *Captives of the Flame* (1963)?

80. Who is the author of the book entitled *American Negro Poetry* (1963)?

81. Who is the author of the novels *And Then We Heard Thunder* (1963) and *Youngblood* (1954)?

Figure 336—Arna Bontemps. Fisk University Library's Special Collections.

82. What play by James Baldwin is roughly based on the story of Emmett Till in Mississippi?

83. Who is the author of the novel *Cotton Comes to Harlem* (1964)?

84. Who is the author of the novel *Manchild in the Promised Land* (1965)?

85. Who is the author of the novel *This Is My Country Too* (1965)?

86. Who is the author of *Preface to a Twenty Volume Suicide Note* (1965)?

87. Whose collection of poems is entitled *Selected Poems* (1966)?

88. Who is the author of *Soul on Ice* (1968)?

89. Who is the author of the novels *Bloodline* (1968), *The Autobiography of Miss Jane Pittman* (1971), and *In My Father's House* (1978)?

90. Who is the author of the books of poems entitled *Black Feeling* (1969), *Black Talk* (1968), and *Black Judgement* (1969)?

91. Who is the author of *I Know Why the Caged Bird Sings* (1969), and is the recipient of the 1994 Spingarn Medal?

92. Who is the author of the book entitled *Negro Poetry & Drama & the Negro in American Fiction* (1969)?

93. Who received the 1970 Pulitzer Prize in drama with the play *No Place to Be Somebody* (1969)?

94. What poet is known for her work entitled *I Am a Black Woman* (1970)?

95. Who teamed with Langston Hughes to author *The Poetry of the Negro, 1746–1970* (1970)?

96. Much of the last five years of poetry by what poet was thrown away by neighbors visiting her home after she became hospitalized, because the neighbors considered the pieces of scrap paper, on which her poetry was written, useless?

97. Who is the editor of *Black Literature in America* (1971)?

98. Who is the author of *Mumbo Jumbo* (1972), *Flight to Canada* (1976), and *The Terrible Twos* (1989)?

99. Who taught at Southern Illinois University in East St. Louis, Illinois, wrote a book of poetry entitled *Play Ebony, Play Ivory* (1974) and the novel *Rope of Wind* (1979), both published posthumously, and was killed in 1968 by a Harlem policeman in a case of mistaken identity?

100. Who is the author of the novel *If Beale Street Could Talk* (1974)?

101. What novel by James Baldwin is about Tish Rivers and Fonny Hunt, an African American Romeo and Juliet, whose love sustains them when Fonny is falsely accused and imprisoned for a crime he did not commit?

102. Who is a bibliographer and author of the book *I Have a Dream: The Life and Times of Martin Luther King, Jr.* (1975)?

103. A play written by what playwright is entitled *For Colored Girls Who Have Considered Suicide When the Rainbow is Enuf* (1975)?

104. The county library in Oklahoma City, Oklahoma, was named in whose honor in 1975?

Figure 337—James Baldwin. Schomburg Center for Research in Black Culture, New York Public Library.

105. Who wrote the play, *The Taking of Miss Janie* (1975)?

106. Who became a noted poet and playwright, one of whose works is entitled *Dimension of History* (1976)?

107. Who is the author of *Roots* (1976), and the recipient of the 1977 Spingarn Medal? He was born in Ithaca, New York on August 11, 1921. His parents were Bertha George Palmer and Simon Alexander Haley. In 1939, Haley enlisted in the U.S. Coast Guard. He retired from the Coast Guard in 1959 and started a career as a writer. His first book was *The Autobiography of Malcolm X: As Told to Alex Haley* (1965). In 1964, he began researching his ancestors, and traced them back to Kunta Kinte, who was kidnapped into slavery in West Africa. In 1976, he published *Roots: Saga of an American Family*. The book was made into a successful television miniseries. Haley died on February 10, 1992.

Figure 338—Alex Haley. Schomburg Center for Research in Black Culture, New York Public Library.

108. Who is the author of the science fiction novel *Survivor* (1978)?

109. Who received the Pulitzer Prize for the short story *Elbow Room* (1978)?

110. Who is the author of a volume of poems entitled *The Yellow House on the Corner* (1980), the novel *Fifth Sunday Stories* (1985), and the book of poems entitled *Thomas and Beulah Poems* (1986)?

111. Who is the author of the novels *Songs of Solomon* (1977) and *Tar Baby* (1981), and recipient of the 1988 Pulitzer Prize for the novel *Beloved* (1987)? She won the 1993 Nobel Prize in literature. She was born Chloe Anthony Wofford in 1931 and earned degrees from Howard and Cornell. She changed her name from Chloe to Toni because Toni was easier to pronounce. She taught at Texas Southern University, Howard University, the State University at Albany, and Princeton. She also wrote several other books.

112. Who is known for the works, *The Homewood Trilogy* (1981–1983)?

113. What novel by David Bradley is about thirteen escaped slaves who asked to be killed rather than recaptured?

Figure 339—Toni Morrison. Reproduced from the Collections of the Library of Congress.

114. Who is the author of *The Color Purple* (1983)?

115. Who is the author of the novel entitled *The Women of Brewster Place* (1983)?

116. Who is the author of the novel entitled *Daddy Was a Numbers Runner* (1986)?

117. Who is the author of *God Bless the Child* (1987), whose main character is Rosalie Fleming?

118. Who received the 1987 Pulitzer Prize for *Fences*?

Figure 340—Alice Walker. Copyright © 1990, Kim Komenich, San Francisco, California.

119. Whose final work was *Great Black Russian: A Novel on the Life and Times of Alexander Pushkin* (1988)?

120. Who is the author of the novel *Appalachee Red* (1989)?

121. Who founded the magazine *Encore* in 1972, and in 1984 was publisher of *Five Fifteen*, a newspaper with the subtitle "The First Black Women's Newspaper"?

122. Who is the author of the book entitled *Waiting to Exhale* (1992)?

123. Who is the author of the novel *The Wedding* (1995)?

124. Who received the 2002 Pulitzer Prize in drama for the play *Topdog/Underdog*?

Answers — 9 — Literature

1. Lucy Terry Prince (1730–1821)

2. Jupiter Hammon (1711–1806)

3. Phillis Wheatley (1753–1784)

4. Gustavus Vassa or Olaudah Equiano (c.1745–1797)

5. Alexander Pushkin (1799–1837)

6. Alexandre Dumas (1802–1870)

7. *The Life of Josiah Henson* (1849) by Josiah Henson (1789–1883)

8. William Wells Brown (1814–1884)

9. Samuel Ringgold Ward (1817–1866)

10. Harriet Jacobs (1813–1897)

11. *The Underground Railroad* (1872)

12. Octavia Albert (c.1853–1889)

13. Gertrude E.H. Bustill Mossell (1855–1948)

14. Francis James Grimké (1850–1925)

15. Paul Laurence Dunbar (1872–1906)

16. Charles Waddell Chesnutt (1858–1932)

17. Paul Laurence Dunbar (1872–1906)

18. William Stanley Braithwaite (1878–1962)

19. *The Brownsville Raid* (1986)

20. W.E.B. Du Bois (1868–1963)

21. James Weldon Johnson (1871–1938)

22. Angelina Weld Grimké (1880–1958)

23. Georgia Douglas Johnson (1880–1966)

24. Claude McKay (1889–1948)

25. James Weldon Johnson (1871–1938)

26. Anne Spencer (1882–1975)

27. Jean Toomer (1894–1967)

28. Countee Cullen (1903–1946)

29. Langston Hughes (1902–1967)

30. James Weldon Johnson (1871–1938)

31. Eulalie Spence (1894–1981)

32. Nella Larsen (1891–1964)

33. Helga Crane

34. Claude McKay (1889–1948)

35. Wallace Thurman (1902–1934)

36. Langston Hughes (1902–1967)

37. Alain L. Locke (1886–1954)

38. Jessie Redmon Fauset (1882–1961)

39. George Schuyler (1895–1977)

40. *Along This Way* (1933)

41. Esther Popel (1896–1958)

42. Langston Hughes (1902–1967)

43. Langston Hughes (1902–1967)

44. Zora Neale Hurston (1891–1960)

45. William G. Still (1895–1978)

46. Janie Crawford

47. Tea Cake

48. Luis Palés Matos (1898–1959)

49. Jay Saunders Redding (1906–1988)

50. Richard Wright (1908–1960)

51. Bigger Thomas

52. 15 years

53. *The Big Sea* (1940)

54. Margaret Walker Alexander (1915–1998)

55. North Carolina Central University in Durham, North Carolina

56. Langston Hughes (1902–1967)

57. Charles Fuller (1939–)

58. Chester Himes (1909–1984)

59. Ann Petry (1908–1997)

60. *Black Boy* (1945)

61. Frank Yerby (1916–1991)

62. Melvin Tolson (1898–1966)

63. Willard Motley (1909–1965)

64. Shirley Lola Graham Du Bois (between 1896 and 1904–1977), wife of W.E.B. Du Bois

65. Gwendolyn Brooks (1917–2000)

66. William Blackwell Branch (1927–)

67. Ralph Ellison (1914–1994)

68. Anonymous

69. Louis Peterson (1922–1998)

70. Era Bell Thompson (1905–1986)

71. Lorraine Hansberry (1930–1965)

72. Alice Childress (1920–1994)

73. Ellen Tarry (1906–)

74. Julian Mayfield (1928–1984)

75. Frantz Fanon (1925–1961)

76. *Brown Girl, Brownstones* (1959)

77. William Melvin Kelley (1937–)

78. James Baldwin (1924–1987)

79. Samuel R. Delany (1942–)

80. Arna Bontemps (1902–1973)

81. John Oliver Killens (1916–1987)

82. *Blues For Mister Charlie* (1964)

83. Chester Himes (1909–1984)

84. Claude Brown (1937–)

85. John A. Williams (1925–)

86. Imamu Amiri Baraka (1934–)

87. Robert Hayden (1913–1980)

88. Eldridge Cleaver (1935–1998)

89. Ernest J. Gaines (1933–)

90. Nikki Giovanni (1943–)

91. Maya Angelou (1928–)

92. Sterling Brown (1901–1989)

93. Charles Gordone (1925–1995)

94. Mari Evans (1923–)

95. Arna Bontemps (1902–1973)

96.   Anne Spencer (1882–1975)

97.   Houston A. Baker, Jr. (1943–)

98.   Ishmael Reed (1938–)

99.   Henry Dumas (1934–1968)

100. James Baldwin (1924–1987)

101. *If Beale Street Could Talk* (1974)

102. Lenwood G. Davis (1939–)

103. Ntozake Shange (1948–)

104. Ralph Ellison (1914–1994)

105. Edward Bullins (1935–)

106. Jay Wright (1935–)

107. Alex Haley (1921–1992)

108. Octavia E. Butler (1947–)

109. James A. McPherson (1943–)

110. Rita Dove (1952–)

111. Toni Morrison (1931–)

112. John Edgar Wideman (1941–)

113. *The Chaneysville Incident* (1981)

114. Alice Walker (1944–)

115. Gloria Naylor (1950–)

116. Louise Meriwether (1923–)

117. Kristin Hunter Lattany (1931–)

118. August Wilson (1945–2005)

119. John Oliver Killens (1916–1987)

120. Raymond Andrews (1934–1991)

121. Ida E. Lewis (1935–)

122. Terry McMillan (1951–)

123. Dorothy West (1907–1998)

124. Suzan-Lori Parks (1964–)

A Search of African American Life, Achievement and Culture

10 — Military History

1. What African American servant, who was wounded in 1756 while fighting Indians and died the same night, has a mountain (Negro Mountain) named in his honor? This mountain covers about a 30-mile area, and passes through Garrett County, Maryland and Somerset County, Pennsylvania, along U.S. Route 40.

2. What African American was one of five colonists killed in the Boston Massacre on March 5, 1770?

3. Who fought in the American Revolution at the Battle of Concord in Massachusetts (April 19, 1775), Battle of Bunker Hill in Massachusetts (June 17, 1775), Battle of Saratoga in New York (September 19, 1777 and October 7, 1777), and the Battle of Stoney Point in New York (July 16, 1779)? His last name, Salem, was given to him by his owner, Jeremiah Belknap. Salem, Massachusetts was Jeremiah's hometown; his hometown was Framingham, Massachusetts.

4. Who joined the regular forces and served with Ethan Allen's Green Mountain Boys during the capture of Fort Ticonderoga, New York, on May 10, 1775?

5. Who was a fifer in the Continental Army at the Battle of Bunker Hill on June 17, 1775?

6. During what battle did Peter Salem shoot the British Major Pitcairn when he claimed victory over the Americans on June 17, 1775?

7. Who, from New Hampshire, joined the Colonial Army as a slave and fought at the Battle of Bunker Hill (June 17, 1775), both Battles of Saratoga (September 19 and October 7, 1777), the Battle of Hubbardton in Vermont (July 7, 1777), and Valley Forge (not a battle, but an encampment around Philadelphia, Pennsylvania for six months, from December 19, 1777 to June 19, 1778)? He also fought at the Battle of Monmouth in New Jersey (June 28, 1778) and the General Sullivan expedition against the Iroquois, Battle of Newtown in New York (August 29, 1779), and served until the end of the war. He was freed due to his services in the army.

8. Fighting for the British, the Ethiopian Regiment of Lord Dunmore, born John Murray (1732–1809), was defeated on December 9, 1775 in what battle?

9. What African American stood his ground during the British attack at the Battle of Great Bridge, December 9, 1775, and sparked the American victory?

10.

Figure 341—*Washington Crossing the Delaware*, by Emanuel Gottlieb Leutze. Copyright © U.S. Postal Service. Reproduced with permission of the U.S. Postal Service.

What two prominent African Americans were in the boat when Washington crossed the Delaware on December 25, 1776? They were the starboard oarsman near George Washington's knee and the oarsman at the back of the boat.

11. What African American enlisted in Virginia's navy in 1776 and served on four different ships during the Revolutionary War?

12. In 1777, what African American enlisted at 18 years of age, and during his six-year enlistment in the American Revolutionary War, was an orderly to General Patterson, and to the Polish patriot Tadeuz Kosciusko?

13. What African American commando led a group that captured British Major Richard Prescott at his own headquarters on July 10, 1777? Major Prescott was exchanged for the American General Charles Lee.

14. During the Revolutionary War Battle of Brandywine (September 10 and 11, 1777), what African American saved his ammunition wagon and gathered arms that were later used by the Continental Army?

15. Who was considered a hero for his valor in the defense of Fort Donally, located near Lewisburg, West Virginia, during a May 1778 attack by Shawnee Indians?

16. What was the all-African American unit that participated in the August 1778 Revolutionary War Battle of Rhode Island? This unit held their ground against three assaults by Hessian troops.

17. During the American Revolution, what African American distinguished himself at the Battle of Kettle Creek in Georgia, February 14, 1779?

18. Who supplied the password that allowed General Anthony Wayne to capture Stoney Point, New York, on July 15, 1779, during the Revolutionary War?

19. What African American soldier collected information on Portsmouth, Virginia, that allowed the Continental Army to drive Cornwallis from this position in 1781? He was later given his freedom by the Virginia legislature.

20. What African American stabbed and killed the British commander Major Montgomery during the Battle of Groton Heights (near Groton, Connecticut), September 6, 1781, during the Revolutionary War? African Americans were not allowed to fire guns during this battle, and were given sharpened wooden pikes.

21. At the surrender of the Battle of Groton Heights, September 6, 1781, what African American was run through by a British officer as Colonel Ledyard surrendered to the Americans? Although wounded, this man stabbed and killed the officer with his sharpened wooden pike. He was subsequently killed by multiple bayonet wounds from the British troops.

22. During the Revolutionary War, what African American received the Gold Medal for valor from Lafayette, in the Battle of Yorktown (from late September 1781 to October 19, 1781), where Cornwallis' defeat marked the end of Britain's major war effort? He was later returned to slavery, fought in the War of 1812, and then again returned to slavery.

23. Who was a spy for America during the Revolutionary War, and risked his life behind enemy lines to collect information for General Marquis de Lafayette? These efforts helped defeat the British Navy at the Battle of Yorktown in October 1781. The Armistead family was compensated by the Virginia legislature and he was freed in 1787; he later assumed Lafayette as his surname.

24. Who was the pilot of the Virginia ship *Patriot* and captured the British ship *Fanny* during the Revolutionary War? He was given his freedom by the Virginia legislature on November 14, 1786 for his services during the Revolutionary War.

25. Who fought throughout the Revolutionary War with an African American Connecticut regiment, and was granted his freedom at the end of the war?

26. An African American regiment from Boston, Massachusetts, during the Revolutionary War was known by what name?

27. When Spain and France became allies of America during the Revolutionary War, what troops from Louisiana were used in combat?

28.   Who tried escaping slavery to join the British, was caught and convinced by his owner to fight for the Americans in order to win his freedom, and was present at the siege of Fort Catskill?

29.   During the Revolutionary War, Spanish, French, and what troops from New Orleans defeated the British at Baton Rouge, Louisiana; Mobile, Alabama; and Pensacola, Florida?

30.   There were no restrictions on the use of African Americans in what military branch during the Revolutionary War, and by both sides during the Civil War?

31.   Who was assigned to the U.S. Frigate *Sussex*, and later participated in the raid led by Jessie Elliot on October 8 and 9, 1812, which captured the British ships *Caledonia* and *Detroit*, anchored near Fort Erie, Ontario?

32.   During the War of 1812, aboard the schooner *Governor Tompkins* on Lake Ontario, what African American requested that his wounded body be thrown overboard and his shipmates keep fighting?

33.   General Andrew Jackson issued an urgent appeal for African Americans prior to what battle?

34.   Who was, at the age of 11, a free Black drummer who opened the Battle of New Orleans (December 1814 to January 1815) with reveille and at the end played taps? He also was a drummer in the Mexican-American War, which lasted from 1846 to 1848.

35.   What African American negotiated with the Cherokee Indians on behalf of Texas, and gained their neutrality during the Texas fight for independence from Mexico?

36.   What was the name of the African American killed at the Battle of the Alamo, which lasted from February 26, 1836 to March 6, 1836?

37.   What African American fought for Texas independence at the Battle of Goliad on March 27, 1836?

38.   What African American woman, known as the Yellow Rose of Texas, gathered Mexican troop information for Sam Houston that enabled the Texans to defeat Santa Anna at the Battle of San Jacinto on April 21, 1836?

39.   There were no African American combat units, only African American support personnel, during what war?

40.   What city supplied free African Americans to Louisiana's militia during the Civil War? They were not used in defense of the city, and were later absorbed into Union forces.

41. What group of African American soldiers defeated the Confederates at the Battle of Jacksonville on April 2, 1862, then were ordered to disband due to public protest?

42. What first official all-African American unit in the Civil War won its first victory at the Battle of Island Mound, Missouri on October 28, 1862?

43. What Louisiana Civil War battle on May 23, 1863, was the scene of numerous African American heroics of the 1st and 3rd Louisiana Native Guards, including those of their leader, Captain Andre Caillou, who was killed?

44. African American valor of the 1st Kansas Colored Troops was evident in what battle in Oklahoma, on July 17, 1863, which ended Confederate resistance in that territory?

45. Who was the first African American to receive the Congressional Medal of Honor for meritorious service? He carried the colors that rallied the troops during the battle of Fort Wagner, which occurred on July 18, 1863. He was awarded the medal in 1900.

46. What African American soldier from the 54th Massachusetts, chronicled the actions of the unit and wrote a letter to President Abraham Lincoln on September 28, 1863 (which was after the Emancipation Proclamation), protesting the inequity between pay for the African American soldiers and the White soldiers ($10 per month for African American soldiers and $13 per month for White soldiers)? This soldier was captured after being wounded in the thigh at the Battle of Olustee (Florida) on February 20, 1864, and was sent to the Andersonville, Georgia prison, where he died on July 19, 1864.

Figure 342—Sergeant William H. Carney. Moorland Spingarn Research Center, Howard University.

47. During the Civil War, the 25th Corps that served under General Grant was composed of what troops?

48. Who received the Navy Medal of Honor for distinguished service on December 25, 1863, aboard the *USS Marblehead*, during the Civil War?

49. Who was cited for valor in this Civil War battle in Florida on February 20, 1864, and became the first African American commissioned in the 54th Massachusetts? The 8th and 35th U.S. Colored Troops also participated in this battle.

50. During the Civil War, who was appointed surgeon of the 7th Regiment, U.S. Colored Volunteers, and is said to have become the first commissioned African American medical officer with the rank of major, on April 4, 1864? He was born in 1825, in Virginia. He earned his medical degree from Trinity Medical College in Canada, and returned to the United States in 1862. Although a major, he had to petition Senator Henry Wilson, Republican from Massachusetts, for assistance in getting comparable pay. Augusta was later transferred to the Freedmen's Hospital in Washington, D.C. Augusta maintained a private practice in Washington, D.C. and later taught at Howard University. He retired from Howard University in 1877.

Figure 343—Dr. Alexander Augusta. Moorland Spingarn Research Center, Howard University.

51. African American soldiers of the 6th U.S. Colored Heavy Artillery and 2nd U.S. Colored Light Artillery, were massacred during what Civil War battle in Tennessee on April 14, 1864?

52. African American soldiers of the 1st Kansas Colored were massacred during what Civil War battle in Arkansas on April 18, 1864?

53. Who received the Navy Medal of Honor for distinguished service aboard the *USS Kearsarge*, when the vessel destroyed the *CSS Alabama* off Cherbourg, France, on June 19, 1864, during the Civil War?

54. Who was a spy for the Union Army at the Confederate White House of Jefferson Davis in Richmond, Virginia, and played a significant role in the Union victory at Richmond in 1864? She was born a slave in Virginia around 1839. When she was a child, her master died and freed her. She was sent to a Quaker school in Philadelphia for education and later she returned to Richmond and married a free African American with the surname Bowser. Elizabeth Van Lew used her influence to get Bowser a servant position in Confederate President Jefferson Davis's White House. As Bowser cleaned, served, and waited on tables at official dinners, she made careful mental notes and recorded them later when she was alone. She would pass the information on to Elizabeth Van Lew or to a Union agent who worked out of a local bakery whose bakery wagon made periodic trips to the Confederate White House. After the Civil War, the Union Army destroyed personal information about her to protect her identity. Bowser also left a personal diary, but the diary was apparently destroyed by her family during the 1950s. She was inducted into the U.S. Army Military Intelligence Corps Hall of Fame in Fort Huachuca, Arizona in 1995.

55. Who received the Medal of Honor in the Battle of Petersburg, Virginia on July 30, 1864?

56.

THE CONGRESSIONAL MEDAL OF HONOR

JOHN LAWSON
1864

Figure 344—John Lawson. U.S. Department of the Navy.

John Lawson (1837–1919) received the Navy Medal of Honor for valor while serving aboard the *USS Hartford* during what battle on August 5, 1864?

57. In 1864, thirteen African Americans received Medals of Honor during what Civil War battle?

58. What soldier from the 6th Colored Infantry rescued his regimental colors and inspired the troops, was cited for valor, and received the Medal of Honor in the Civil War Battle of Chapin's Farm in Virginia, September 29, 1864?

59. During the Civil War, what soldier from Carthage, Texas, serving in the 5th U.S. Colored Troops unit, received the Congressional Medal of Honor for heroism during the Battle of Chapin's Farm (September 29, 1864)?

60. Who was awarded the Congressional Medal of Honor for valor during the Civil War, by carrying the colors through the battle during the Battle of Chaffin's Farm (September 29, 1864), which is located on the outskirts of Richmond, Virginia?

61. How many African Americans were awarded the Medal of Honor during the Civil War?

62. What African American woman was a spy for the Union forces during the Civil War?

63. Who was an officer in the 55th Massachusetts Regiment, and editor of the Boston *Guardian*?

64.   What song was a popular fighting song for African American troops during the Civil War?

65.   As a slave at age 7, who was permitted to live with her grandmother who taught her to read and write, and later became a well-known African American nurse during the Civil War? She was born in 1848, in Liberty County, Georgia. Her parents were Hagar and Raymond Baker. Her owner permitted her to move to her grandmother's house in Savannah, Georgia when she was 7 years old. Her grandmother secretly sent her to school. At 14 years old, she married Sergeant Edward King, a member of the South Carolina 33rd U.S. Colored Troops, one of the first all-African American groups mustered into the Union Army. Susie nursed soldiers, without pay, from January 1863 until the end of the Civil War. In 1866, Susie and Sergeant King moved to Savannah, Georgia, to have their first child. Susie's husband died before the child was born. In 1879 she married Russell Taylor. She privately published her autobiography *Reminiscences of My Life in Camp: A Black Woman's Civil War Memoirs* in 1902, and she died in 1912.

Figure 345—Susie King Taylor. Markus Wiener Publishing, Inc.

66.   Although the purpose of the Civil War from the Union side was to save the Union, or keep all the states together as one country, neither the Union nor the Confederacy could have won the Civil War without the use of what soldiers?

67.   Approximately how many African Americans participated in the Civil War in all positions, for example orderly, cook, building fortifications, burial details, and fighting?

68.   How many Navy Medals of Honor were awarded to African Americans during peace time?

69.   How many African Americans received Congressional Medals of Honor during the Indian Wars (1870–1890)?

70.   In 1870, who became the first African American to receive the Congressional Medal of Honor during the Indian Wars at Kickapoo Springs, Texas, for gallantry on scouting after Indians?

71.   Who received the Congressional Medal of Honor for gallantry at Pecos River, Texas in 1875?

72.   Who was the African American Army interpreter killed along with General Custer on June 25, 1876, at the Battle of the Little Big Horn?

73. Who documented his experience in the book entitled *The Colored Cadet at West Point* (1878), and was the first African American to graduate from West Point, in 1877? He was accused of embezzling funds and was court-martialed and dismissed from the army in 1881. In 1976, the Department of the Army issued his descendants a "Certificate of Honorable Discharge" dated June 30, 1882, in lieu of the dishonorable discharge he originally received.

Figure 346—Henry O. Flipper. Courtesy of the Texas Memorial Museum.

74. What Kansas fort was home to African American Buffalo soldiers?

75. What all-African American fighting unit during the Indian Wars had a buffalo in its insignia?

76. Who was awarded the Medal of Honor for valor at Las Animas Canyon, New Mexico, 1879?

77. How many African Americans received Medals of Honor during the Spanish-American War?

78. What two African American units led the charge on foot at the Battle of San Juan Hill, July 1, 1898, during the Spanish-American War?

79. During the Spanish-American War, who was awarded the Navy Medal of Honor for valor, for meritorious service aboard the *USS Iowa* off Santiago de Cuba?

80. What member of the "Rough Riders" received the Congressional Medal of Honor in the Spanish-American War, for valor in saving a fellow soldier during an attack?

81. Who was noted for operating a three-man Hotchkiss weapon during the Spanish American War in Cuba, after the other two-soldier crew had been killed?

Figure 347—Robert Penn. U.S. Naval Historical Center photograph, U.S. Department of the Navy.

82. What World War I African American unit was known to the Germans as "Hell Fighters"?

83.　Who were the first two African Americans, who served in France in World War I, to receive France's highest decoration, the Croix de Guerre, for heroism?

84.　During World War I, what all-African American unit in France created a record of 191 days of front-line action, in which the regiment did not lose any soldiers to capture, lose a trench, or lose a foot of ground?

85.　What African American lieutenant colonel, recipient of the 1916 Spingarn Medal, was declared physically unfit for the army at the start of World War I? He rode 500 miles on horseback from his home in Wilberforce, Ohio, to Washington, D.C. (in June 1918), to prove his fitness, because he wanted to participate in World War I, and was reinstated and assigned to Camp Grant, Illinois, and promoted to colonel. Later, this soldier was assigned to Liberia as a military attaché and sent on a mission to Lagos, Nigeria, where he died on January 8, 1922.

Figure 348—Charles Young. U.S. Army Military History Institute.

86.　During World War I, how many African Americans received the Croix de Guerre, the highest French military medal, from the French government for their military services?

87.　Who earned his wings as a pilot with the French during World War I? He was born Eugene Jacques Bullard on October 9, 1895, in Columbus, Georgia. His parents were William O. Bullard and Josephine Thomas Bullard, who was a Creek Indian. After the near lynching of his father in 1903, he ran away. He traveled to England in 1912 by stowing away on a German ship leaving from Norfolk, Virginia. He became a prizefighter in Britain and traveled to France and other countries. At the start of World War I, he joined the French army and he was later awarded the Croix de Guerre for his heroism at the Battle of Verdun, one of the bloodiest battles of the war. After being wounded twice, he was declared unfit for infantry service, so he asked to be assigned to flight training. He established a distinguished flying record, flying twenty missions and downing one German plane. He died on October 12, 1961, in New York City.

88.　How many African Americans received the Congressional Medal of Honor during World War I?

89.　Approximately how many African Americans participated in World War I?

90.　How many African Americans received the Congressional Medal of Honor during World War II?

91. Who was the first African American Army general in 1940? He was born Benjamin Oliver Davis on May 28, 1880, in Washington, D.C. He attended an integrated school. Later he attended M Street High School. He married his first wife, Elnora Dickerson Davis, in 1902. Some of his service included: assignment in the Philippines until 1901; assignment in Wyoming until 1905; professor of military science at Wilberforce University in Ohio, 1905–1909; military attache in Monrovia, Liberia until January 1912; 9th Cavalry in the West on border patrol until 1915; reassignment to Wilberforce University from 1915 to 1917; supply officer in the Philippines from 1915 to 1920; professor of military science and tactics at Tuskegee Institute until 1924; instructor in the Ohio National Guard until 1929; returned to Wilberforce University from 1929 to 1930; from 1930 to 1931 assigned to Liberia for the Department of State; reassigned to Tuskegee Institute from 1931 until 1937; reassigned to Wilberforce University until 1938; instructor and commanding officer of the 369th Infantry in New York City until January 1941; assistant to the Inspector General in June 1941; advisor on Negro problems in the European theater until 1944; special assistant to the commanding general, Communication Force in Paris, France in November 1944; and assistant to the Inspector General in Washington, D.C. He was awarded the Distinguished Service Medal on February 11, 1945. He was also awarded the Croix de Guerre with Palm by the French government and the Commander of the Order of the Star from the Liberian government. He died on November 26, 1970.

Figure 349—Benjamin O. Davis, Sr. U.S. Army Military History Institute.

92. Who grew up near Waco, Texas, and later received the Navy Cross for shooting down four Japanese airplanes during the attack on Pearl Harbor on December 7, 1941 while serving aboard the ship the *USS West Virginia*? He was assigned to the *USS Indianapolis* on December 13, 1941, and to the *USS Liscome Bay* in the spring of 1943. On November 24, 1943 the *Liscome Bay* was struck by a torpedo near Butaritari Island in the Pacific Ocean, and sank. On November 25, 1944, this sailor was listed as missing in action and presumed dead.

93. What African American was awarded the Navy Cross for valor while serving aboard the *USS Enterprise* during the Battle of Santa Cruz Islands on October 26, 1942?

Figure 350—Dorie Miller. U.S. Department of the Navy.

94.

Figure 351—Leonard Roy Harmon. U.S. Department of the Navy.

Who was awarded the Navy Cross for valor aboard the *USS San Francisco* in the Solomon Islands, November 1942? He was born on January 21, 1917, in Cuero, Texas. His parents were Nauita Mabry and Cornellius Harmon. He graduated from Daule High School and enlisted in the Navy in 1939. He trained in Norfolk, Virginia and was assigned to duty on the *USS San Francisco* in 1937 with the rank of Mess Attendant First Class. During the Battle of Guadalcanal in 1942, a damaged Japanese plane intentionally crashed into the radar and fire-control room of the *USS San Francisco*, killing and injuring numerous sailors. The next day the ship's bridge was struck by aircraft fire that nearly killed every officer on the bridge. Harmon helped evacuate the officers from the bridge and helped evacuate the wounded to a room for treatment. Harmon was killed while shielding the wounded with his body. He was posthumously awarded the Navy Cross on May 21, 1943. A Navy ship was named in his honor, the bachelor enlisted quarters at the Naval Air Station, North Island, California, is named in his honor, and the Cuero Municipal Park placed a state historical marker honoring Harmon in their park in 1977.

95.   What is the name of the first naval vessel named for an African American?

96.   Who was captain of the liberty ship *Booker T. Washington*, which carried many troops to Europe during World War II?

97.

Figure 352—99th Fighter Squadron (Tuskegee Airmen). P-51 Mustang Group pilots of the 15th Air Force in Italy kneel before the Mustang aircraft *Skipper's Darlin' III*. Smithsonian Institution, Washington, D.C.

What all-African American air fighter squadron had a distinguished military record during World War II?

98. What all-African American tank destroyer battalion had a distinguished military record during World War II? Captain Charles Thomas of this battalion was posthumously awarded the Medal of Honor by President Clinton in 1997 with this citation: "For extraordinary heroism in action on 14 December 1944, near Climbach, France. While riding in the lead vehicle of a task force organized to storm and capture the village of Climbach, France, then First Lt. Thomas's scout car was subjected to intense enemy artillery, self-propelled gun, and small arms fire. Although wounded by the initial burst of hostile fire, Lieutenant Thomas signaled the remainder of the column to halt and, despite the severity of his wounds, assisted the crew of the wrecked car in dismounting. Upon leaving the scant protection which the vehicle afforded, Lieutenant Thomas was again subjected to a hail of enemy fire which inflicted multiple gunshot wounds in his chest, legs, and left arm. Despite the intense pain caused by these wounds, Lt. Thomas ordered and directed the dispersion and emplacement of two antitank guns which in a few moments were promptly and effectively returning the enemy fire. Realizing that he could no longer remain in control of the platoon, he signaled to the platoon commander to join him. Lieutenant Thomas then thoroughly oriented him on enemy gun dispositions and the general situation. Only after he was certain that his junior officer was in full control of the situation did he permit himself to be evacuated. First Lt. Thomas's outstanding heroism was an inspiration to his men and exemplifies the highest traditions of the armed forces."

99.

Figure 353—Moving to a forward position in the combat zone, a tank from Company A, 761st Tank Battalion, U.S. Third Army, crosses a Bailey bridge in the town of Vic-Ser-Seille, France, November 1944. U.S. Army photo courtesy of the Patton Museum, Fort Knox, Kentucky.

What all-African American tank battalion helped General Patton win the Battle of the Bulge (December 16, 1944 to January 28, 1945), and rescued Jews and survivors of the concentration camps during World War II?

100. Where in the bay area of California was the site of a naval munitions explosion, and an African American work stoppage during 1944?

101. In World War II, who led the 99th Fighter Squadron (also referred to as the Tuskegee Airmen), which downed five enemy aircraft in four minutes over the Anzio Beachhead, which is located in Italy? The African American pilots of World War II were called Tuskegee Airmen because they were all trained in one location, Tuskegee Institute (now Tuskegee University), located in Tuskegee, Alabama.

102. During World War II, what soldier of the 761st Tank Battalion from Holtuka, Oklahoma, displayed extraordinary courage on November 15 through November 19, 1944 near Grebling, France as his lead tank ran over a mine and blew off the right track, severely injuring him in the leg? He refused medical attention and led Company A into Grebling. On the morning of November 19, 1944, the company began to advance toward Baugaktroff and his tank was hit by an anti-tank explosion, which killed him and wounded his crew. This Staff Sergeant was awarded the Silver Star and Purple Heart, and was awarded the Congressional Medal of Honor posthumously on January 13, 1997.

103. What book by Trezzvant Anderson, one of the soldiers of the famed World War II all-African American 761st Tank Battalion, was published in Germany in 1945, and used the battalion's motto as its title? Anderson was born in 1906. In 1928 and 1929, he worked as a contributing editor to the *Charlotte Post* and established the first African American press club in Washington, D.C. He was a railway clerk from 1930 to 1941, then was drafted into military service and served as a war correspondent. In 1947, went to work for the *Pittsburgh Courier*. He died in Georgia in 1963.

104. Who was the first African American sworn into the Navy Nurse Corps in 1945?

105. How many Distinguished Unit Citations did the 99th Fighter Squadron, part of the 332nd Fighter Group, earn during World War II?

106. Approximately how many African Americans participated in World War II?

107. Who was the first African American to graduate from the U.S. Naval Academy in 1949?

Figure 354—Wesley A. Brown. U.S. Naval Historical Center photograph, courtesy of the U.S. Naval Academy Library.

108. Who posthumously received the Congressional Medal of Honor in the Korean War, after fighting off the enemy single-handed during a withdrawal near the town of Haman, Korea?

109. Who was born in Hattiesburg, Mississippi, and became the first African American to be awarded the Navy's Distinguished Flying Cross for valor during the Korean War? He was awarded the medal for action on December 4, 1950, near the Chosin Reservoir, when his plane was hit by enemy fire and crashed while flying a support mission.

Figure 355—Ensign Jesse L. Brown. Naval Photographic Center, Naval Station, Washington, D.C.

110. The first U.S. victory in the Korean War was won by what all-African American unit?

111. How many African Americans received the Congressional Medal of Honor during the Korean War?

112. What was the last all-African American U.S. Army unit to serve in combat?

113. Who was the first African American Air Force general in 1954? He was born in 1912 in Washington, D.C. He graduated from West Point in 1936. In 1940, President Franklin Roosevelt created the 99th Fighter Squadron, an African American flying corps, with Davis in command. In 1944, from their base in Italy, Colonel Davis led 39 Thunderbolt airplanes escorting B-24 bombers, on a mission to Munich, Germany. They were attacked by German planes. For his leadership during the mission, he was awarded the Distinguished Flying Cross. The 99th Fighter Squadron or "Tuskegee Airmen" as they are often called, never lost an airplane they were escorting under Davis's leadership. He died in 2002, a hero.

Figure 356—Benjamin O. Davis, Jr. Western Reserve Historical Society, Cleveland, Ohio.

114. Whose autobiography, entitled *A Choice of Weapons* (1966), recounts his experiences with the all-African American 99th Fighter Squadron during World War II?

115. Who was the first African American to receive the Congressional Medal of Honor during the Vietnam War? A Chicago park is named in his honor.

116. How many African Americans received the Medal of Honor during the Vietnam War (1964–1973)?

117. Who became the first African American admiral in the U.S. Navy in July 1971?

118. Who became the first African American naval aviator in 1973, and has a frigate named in his honor?

119. Who became the first African American woman to qualify as a pilot in the U.S. Navy, in 1974?

120. Who became the first African American woman chaplain in the Army, in 1974?

Figure 357—Vice Admiral Samuel L. Gravely, Jr. Department of Defense, Still Media Records Center, Washington, D.C., U.S. Department of the Navy.

121. What four-star general was the first African American commander of the North American Air Defense Command, from September 1, 1975 to February 1, 1978? He was born in 1920 in Pensacola, Florida. He was a Tuskegee Airman and received his commission as a second lieutenant in July 1943. He was a fighter pilot in Korea and Vietnam and flew over 160 combat missions. In 1967, he became commander of Wheelus Air Force in Libya. Colonel Khadafy seized power via a coup in September 1969. Less than six weeks after the coup, Colonel Khadafy came to Wheelus and ordered a column of half-tracks onto the base. Colonel Davis was notified and immediately closed the gate. Colonel James saw Khadafy with his hand on his gun and ordered Khadafy to take his hand away; Khadafy complied and the half-tracks withdrew and did not attempt to re-enter the base. Wheelus Air Force Base was closed in 1970. James received a Distinguished Flying Cross in 1949 for rescuing a pilot after a flameout at Clark Air Force Base in the Philippines, and received a Distinguished Flying Cross in 1950 for flying a close air support mission for UN forces in Korea. Later, General James headed the North American Air Defense Command. He received honorary law degrees from various institutions and was named honorary commander of the Arnold Air Society. He died in 1978.

Figure 358—Daniel "Chappie" James. U.S. Army Military History Institute.

122. Who was the first African American Secretary of the Army, from February 14, 1977 through January 20, 1981?

123. Who became the first female African American general in 1980?

124. Who was the first African American Chairman of the Joint Chiefs of Staff (October 1989 to September 1993), the first African American U.S. Secretary of State (January 2001 through January 2005), and the recipient of the 1991 Spingarn Medal and the Presidential Medal of Freedom in 1991 and 1993? He also received the Congressional Gold Medal and the Distinguished Service Medal. He also has served as the chairman of America's Promise, Inc. Colin Powell was chairman of the Joint Chiefs of Staff during the Gulf War (1990–1991), and Secretary of State during the coalition entry into Afghanistan after the September 11, 2001 attacks and the coalition entry into Iraq in 2003.

Figure 359—Colin Powell. U.S. Pentagon.

125.

Figure 360—Black Revolutionary War Patriots Commemorative Silver Dollar Proof Coin. Courtesy U.S. Mint.

The Black Revolutionary War Patriots commemorative coin, sometimes referred to as the Crispus Attucks coin, was issued by the U.S. Mint in what year? These coins were issued in proofs and uncirculated silver dollars.

Answers — 10 — Military History

1. "Nemesis" or "Goliah," depending on the interpretation

2. Crispus Attucks (1723–1770)

3. Peter Salem (1750–1816)

4. Lemuel Haynes (1753–1833)

5. Barzillai Lew (1743–1822)

6. Battle of Bunker Hill

7. Jude Hall (1747–1827)

8. Great Bridge

9. William Flora (?–1818)

10. Prince Whipple (1750–1796) and Oliver Cromwell (1752–1852)

11. Joseph Ranger (?–?)

12. Agrippa Hull (1759–1838)

13. Tack Sisson (?–?)

14. Edward Hector (1744–1834)

15. Dick Pointer (17?–1827)

16. 1st Rhode Island Regiment

17. Austin Dabney (c.1760–1830)

18. Pompey Lamb (17?–?)

19. Saul Matthews (?–?)

20. Jordan Freeman (?–?)

21. Lambo Lathem (?–?)

22. James Robinson (c.1740–1797)

23. James Armistead Lafayette (1760–1832)

24. Caesar Tarrant (c.1740–1797)

25. Jeff Liberty

26. "The Bucks of America"

27. African American

28. Seymour Burr (17?–?)

29. Free African Americans

30. Continental Navy

31. Benjamin Fleming (1782–1870)

32. John Davis (?–1814)

33. Battle of New Orleans in 1814

34. Jordan B. Noble (c.1800–1880)

35. William Goyens (1794–1856)

36. John Du Sauge (?–1836)

37. Samuel McCullough, Jr. (1810–1893)

38. Emily Morgan (if slave owned by Colonial James Morgan) or Emily D. West (if indentured servant) (18?–?). Research appears to support indentured servant.

39. Mexican-American War

40. New Orleans, Louisiana

41. 1st South Carolina Volunteers

42. 1st Kansas Colored Troops

43. Battle of Port Hudson

44. Battle of Honey Springs

45. Sergeant William H. Carney (1840–1908)

46. Corporal James Henry Gooding (c.1837–1864)

47. African Americans

48. Robert Blake (?–?)

49. Stephen A. Swails (c.1832–1890) at the Battle of Olustee (Florida)

50. Dr. Alexander T. Augusta (1825–1890)

51. Fort Pillow, Tennessee

52. Poison Springs, Arkansas, near Camden, Arkansas

53. Joachim Pease (1842–?)

54. Mary Elizabeth Bowser (c.1839–?)

55. Sergeant Decatur Dorsey (1836–1891)

56. Battle of Mobile Bay

57. Battle of Chapin's Farm (sometimes referred to as Chaffin's Farm), Virginia, on September 29, 1864

58. Sergeant-Major Thomas Hawkins (1840–1870)

59. Milton M. Holland (1844–1910)

60. Christian Abraham Fleetwood (1840–1914)

61. 19; 16 Army Medals of Honor and 3 Navy Medals of Honor

Army:

Sergeant William H. Carney (1840–1908) of New Bedford (Bristol County), Massachusetts. Company C, 54th Massachusetts Colored Infantry. Place of action, July 18, 1863, Fort Wagner, South Carolina. Citation: when the color soldier (carrying the flag) was shot, Sergeant Carney picked up the flag and led the troops to the fortifications. When the troops fell back, Sergeant Carney carried the flag back under heavy fire, and was wounded twice.

Sergeant Decatur Dorsey (1836–1891) of Baltimore (Baltimore County), Maryland. Company B, 39th U.S. Colored Infantry. Place of action, July 30, 1864, Petersburg, Virginia. Citation: planted the color on Confederate position in advance of the troops and when the troops fell back, he carried colors and rallied the troops.

Private William Henry Barnes (1845–1866) of Norfolk (Norfolk County), Virginia. Company C, 38th U.S. Colored Infantry. Place of action, September 29, 1864, Chapin's Farm, Virginia. Citation: Private Barnes was among the first troops to reach the Confederate positions although he was wounded.

First Sergeant Powhatan Beaty (1837–1916) of Cincinnati (Hamilton County), Ohio. Company G, 5th U.S. Colored Infantry. Place of action, September 29, 1864, Chapin's Farm, Virginia. Citation: Sergeant Beaty took command of his company after all officers had been killed or wounded, and led the company valiantly.

First Sergeant James H. Bronson (1838–1884) of Trumbell County, Ohio. Company D, 5th U.S. Colored Infantry. Place of action, September 29, 1864, Chapin's Farm, Virginia. Citation: took command of his company, after all officers had been killed or wounded, and led the company valiantly.

Sergeant Major Christian A. Fleetwood (1840–1914) of Baltimore (Baltimore County), Maryland. 4th U.S. Colored Infantry. Place of action, September 29, 1864, Chapin's Farm, Virginia. Citation: rushed in advance of the troops, shot a Confederate officer who was on the fortifications rallying his troops, and then charged the officer with his bayonet.

Private James Gardiner (1839–1905) of Yorktown (York County), Virginia. Company I, 36th U.S. Colored Infantry. Place of action, September 29, 1864, Chapin's Farm, Virginia. Citation: seized the colors, after two color guards had been shot, and carried the colors throughout the fight.

Sergeant James H. Harris (1828–1898) of Great Mills (St. Mary's County), Maryland. Company B, 38th U.S. Colored Infantry. Place of action, September 29, 1864, New Market Heights, Virginia. Citation: valiant in the assault.

Sergeant Major Thomas R. Hawkins (1840–1870) of Philadelphia (Philadelphia County), Pennsylvania. 6th U.S. Colored Infantry. Place of action, September 29, 1864, Chapin's Farm, Virginia. Citation: rescue of his regimental colors.

Sergeant Alfred B. Hilton (1842–October 21, 1864, killed in action) of Baltimore (Baltimore County), Maryland. Company H, 4th U.S. Colored Infantry. Place of action, September 29, 1864, Chapin's Farm, Virginia. Citation: when the regimental color guard fell, Sergeant Hilton seized the colors and carried them forward with the national colors until disabled at the enemy's inner line of defense.

Sergeant Major Milton M. Holland (1844–1910) of Albany (Athens County), Ohio. 5th U.S. Colored Infantry. Place of action, September 29, 1864, Chapin's Farm, Virginia. Citation: took command of his company, after all

officers had been killed or wounded, and led the company valiantly.

First Sergeant Alexander Kelly (1840–1907) of Allegheny (Allegheny County), Pennsylvania. Company F, 6th U.S. Colored Infantry. Place of action, September 29, 1864, Chapin's Farm, Virginia. Citation: raised the colors, which had fallen near the enemy's line, and rallied the troops at a time of confusion and in an area of great danger.

First Sergeant Robert A. Pinn (1843–1911) of Massillion (Stark County), Ohio. Company I, 5th U.S. Colored Infantry. Place of action, September 29, 1864, Chapin's Farm, Virginia. Citation: took command of his company, after all officers had been killed or wounded, and led the company gallantly.

First Sergeant Edward Ratcliff (1835–1872) of Yorktown (York County), Virginia. Company C, 38th U.S. Colored Infantry. Place of action, September 29, 1864, Chapin's Farm, Virginia. Citation: commanded and valiantly led his company after the commanding officer had been killed, and was the first enlisted troop to enter the enemy's fortifications.

Private Charles Veal (1838–1872) of Baltimore (Baltimore County), Maryland. Company D, 4th U.S. Colored Infantry. Place of action, September 29, 1864, Chapin's Farm, Virginia. Citation: seized the national colors, after two color bearers had been shot down close to the enemy's fortifications, and carried them through the remainder of the battle.

Corporal Miles James (1829–1871) of Portsmouth (Portsmouth County), Virginia. Company B, 36th U.S. Colored Infantry. Place of action, September 30, 1864, Chapin's Farm, Virginia. Citation: having had his arm mutilated, making immediate amputation necessary, he loaded his weapon with one hand and urged his men forward, this within 30 yards of the enemy's fortifications.

Navy:

Contraband Robert Blake (?–?) of Port Royal (Caroline County), Virginia. *US Steam Gunboat Marblehead.* Place of action, December 25, 1863, off Legareville, Stono River, John's Island, South Carolina. Citation: Robert, an escaped slave, carried out his duties bravely, which forced the enemy to leave a caisson and one gun behind.

Seaman Joachim Pease (1842– ?) of New York, New York. *USS Kearsarge.* Place of action, June 19, 1864, off Cherbourg, France. Citation: acting as loader on the number two gun was recommended by his divisional commander for gallantry under fire, as the *USS Kearsarge* destroyed the *CSS Alabama.*

Landsman John Lawson (1837–1919) of Pennsylvania. *USS Hartford.* Place of action, August 5, 1864, Fort Morgan and Mobile Bay, Alabama. Citation: when a shell exploded near him, wounding him in the leg and killing or wounding the other five members of the crew, John remained at his station and continued his duties through out the remainder of the battle with the Confederate ram, *Tennessee* in Mobile Bay.

62. Harriet Tubman (1820–1913)

63. James Monroe Trotter (1842–1892)

64. "John Brown's Body"

65. Susie King Taylor (1848–1912)

66. African Americans

67. Over 200,000

68. One

69. Eighteen

70. Emanual Stance (1843–1887)

71. Pompey Factor (1849–1928)

72. Isaiah Dorman (18?–1876)

73. Henry O. Flipper (1856–1940)

74. Fort Leavenworth, Kansas

75. 10th Cavalry

76. Sergeant John Denny (1846–1901)

77. Six

78. 9th and 10th Cavalry, U.S. Regulars

79. Robert Penn (1872–1912)

80. Edward Lee Baker (1865–1913)

81. Horace W. Bivins (?–?)

82. 369th Infantry Regiment

83. Henry Johnson (1897–1929) and Needham Roberts

84. The 369th Infantry Regiment of the 93rd Division

85. Charles Young (1864–1922)

86. 171

87. Eugene Bullard (1894–1961)

88. One in World War I; Freddie Stowers (1896–1916), South Carolina, World War I, awarded April 1991

89. 367,000

90. Seven in World War II; six awarded posthumously on January 13, 1997 by President Clinton:

Major Charles L. Thomas (?–?), Detroit, Michigan

First Lieutenant John R. Fox (?–1944), Cincinnati, Ohio

Staff Sergeant Ruben Rivers (?–1944), Oklahoma City, Oklahoma

Staff Sergeant Edward A. Carter (?–1963), Los Angeles, California

Private First Class Willy F. James, Jr. (?–1945), Kansas City, Missouri

Private George Watson (?–1943), Birmingham, Alabama

Former First Lieutenant Vernon J. Baker of St. Maries, Idaho, received the Medal of Honor on January 13, 1997, from President Clinton.

91. Brigadier General Benjamin O. Davis, Sr. (1880–1970)

92. Dorie Miller (1919–1943)

93. William Pinckney (1915–1975)

94. Leonard Roy Harmon (1917–1942)

95. *USS Leonard Roy Harmon* (1943)

96. Hugh N. Mulzac (1886–1971)

97. 99th Fighter Squadron

98. 614th Tank Destroyer Battalion

99. 761st Tank Battalion

100. Port Chicago

101. Captain Clarence Jamison (?–)

102. Ruben Rivers (?–1944)

103. *Come Out Fighting!*

104. Phyllis Mae Dailey (?–), 1945

105. Three

106. One million

107. Wesley A. Brown (1927–)

108. PFC William Henry Thompson (1927–1951)

109. Ensign Jesse L. Brown (1926–1950)

110. 24th Infantry Regiment

111. Two. Sergeant Cornelius H. Charlton (1929–1951) of Bronx, New York. U.S. Army, Company C, 24th Infantry Regiment, 25th Infantry Division.

Private First Class William Thompson (1927–1951), Bronx, New York. U.S. Army, Company M, 24th Infantry Regiment, 25 Infantry Division.

112. 24th Infantry Regiment

113. Lieutenant General Benjamin O. Davis, Jr. (1912–2002)

114. Gordon Parks (1912–)

115. PFC Milton L. Olive, III (1946–1965)

116. 20:

Private First Class James Anderson, Jr. (1947–1967) of Los Angeles, California. U.S. Marine Corps, 2d Platoon, Company F, 2d Battalion, 3d Marine Division.

Sergeant Webster Anderson (1933–) of Winnsboro, South Carolina. U.S. Army, Battery A, 2d Battalion, 320th Field Artillery, 101st Airborne Infantry Division.

Sergeant Eugene Ashley, Jr. (1931–1968) of New York, New York. U.S. Army, Company C, 5th Special Forces Group, 1st Special Forces.

Private First Class Oscar P. Austin (1948–1969) of Phoenix, Arizona. U.S. Marine Corps, Company E, 2d Battalion, 7th Marines, 1st Marine Division.

Sergeant First Class William Maud Bryant (1933–1969) of Detroit, Michigan. U.S. Army, Company A, 5th Special Forces Group, 1st Special Forces.

Sergeant Rodney Maxwell Davis (1942–1967) of Macon, Georgia. U.S. Marine Corps, Company B, 1st Battalion, 5th Marines, 1st Marine Division.

Private First Class Robert H. Jenkins, Jr. (1948–1969) of Jacksonville, Florida. U.S. Marine Corps, 3d Reconnaissance Battalion, 3d Marine Division.

Specialist Sixth Class Lawrence Joel (1928–1984) of Winston-Salem, North Carolina. U.S. Army, Headquarters and Headquarters Company, 1st Battalion, 503d Infantry.

Specialist Fifth Class Dwight Johnson (1947–1971) of Detroit, Michigan. U.S. Army, Company B, 1st Battalion, 69th Armor, 4th Infantry Division.

Private First Class Ralph Johnson (1949–1968) of Oakland, California. U.S. Marine Corps, Company A, 1st Reconnaissance Battalion, 1st Marine Division.

Private First Class Garfield M. Langhorn (1949–1969) of Brooklyn, New York. U.S. Army, Troop C, 7th Squadron, 17th Cavalry, 1st Aviation Brigade.

Sergeant Matthew Leonard (1929–1967) of Birmingham, Alabama. U.S. Army, Company B, 1st Battalion, 16th Infantry, 1st Infantry Division.

Sergeant Donald Russell Long (1939–1966) of Ashland, Kentucky. U.S. Army, Troop C, 1st Squadron, 4th Cavalry, 1st Infantry Division.

Private First Class Milton Lee Olive, III (1946–1965) of Chicago, Illinois. U.S. Army, Company B, 2d Battalion, 503d Infantry, 173d Airborne Brigade.

Captain Riley L. Pitts (1937–1967) of Wichita, Kansas. U.S. Army, Company C, 2d Battalion, 27th Infantry, 25th Infantry Division.

Lieutenant Colonel Charles Calvin Rogers (1929–1990) of Institute, West Virginia. U.S. Army, 1st Battalion, 5th Artillery, 1st Infantry Division.

First Lieutenant Rupert L. Sargent (1938–1967) of Richmond, Virginia. U.S. Army, Company B, 4th Battalion, 9th Infantry, 25th Infantry Division.

Specialist Fifth Class Clarence Eugene Sasser (1947–) of Houston, Texas. U.S. Army, Headquarters Company, 3d Battalion, 60th Infantry, 9th Infantry Division.

Staff Sergeant Clifford Chester Sims (1942–1968) of Jacksonville, Florida. U.S. Army, Company D, 2d Battalion, 501st Infantry, 101st Airborne Division.

First Lieutenant John E. Warren, Jr. (1946–1969) of New York, New York. U.S. Army, Company C, 2d Battalion, 22d Infantry, 25th Infantry Division.

117. Vice Admiral Samuel L. Gravely, Jr. (1922–2004)

118. The *USS Jesse L. Brown* which was named in honor of Ensign Jesse L. Brown (1926–1950)

119. Jill Brown (1949–)

120. The Reverend Alice Henderson (?–)

121. General Daniel "Chappie" James, Jr. (1920–1978)

122. Clifford Alexander, Jr. (1933–)

123. Brigadier General Hazel W. Johnson-Brown (1927–), Army

124. General Colin Powell (1937–)

125. 1998

A Search of African American Life, Achievement and Culture

11 — Science

1. What African American slave described in 1721 how he was inoculated against smallpox using an African method of inoculation? Cotton Mather began to use the procedure in America. The method was used to protect the soldiers of the Revolutionary War, and was later adopted by the British.

2. Who arrived in Virginia as a slave in 1724 at the age of 14, and was noted for his math ability, although he could neither read nor write?

3. The beautiful malls and avenues of Washington, D.C., are partly due to whose photographic memory? After a dispute in 1792, Pierre Charles L'Enfant—who drew up the plans—returned to France with all the plans.

4. Who patented the pencil sharpener on November 23, 1807?

5. Who was the first African American to permanently settle in Cleveland, Ohio, in April 1809, and later invented a type of hand mill that was used to crush grain?

6. In 1832, who developed different ways of making ice cream?

Figure 361—Benjamin Banneker. Schomburg Center for Research in Black Culture, New York Public Library.

7. What African American obtained a patent for the corn planter in 1834, and a patent for the cotton planter in 1836?

8. In 1837, who was the first African American to receive a medical degree? He was born on April 18, 1813, in New York City. His father was freed by the Emancipation Act of New York and his mother worked her way out of bondage. He was denied admission to colleges in the United States because of his race, so he attended Glasgow University in Scotland. He returned to the United States in 1837 and wrote articles in medical journals regarding slavery and suffrage, and refuted racial theories. Frederick Douglass, John Brown, and Gerrit Smith also knew him and they all worked together on African American causes.

9. Who invented a working steam engine for a war ship—a sloop-of-war—in the late 1840s, while working at the U.S. Naval Academy in Annapolis, Maryland? He was not able to patent his steam engine invention because U.S. law prohibited slaves from patenting inventions. Nonetheless, he was able to purchase his freedom with the money he earned from his invention.

10. What African American developed a theory of multiple-effect evaporators, and a new sugar-refining process that cut fuel costs in half? He patented this process in 1846; the patent number was U.S. 4,879. He was born free in 1806 in New Orleans. His mother had been freed before he was born. His father, who was White, sent him to be educated at the Ecole Centrale in Paris, France. Rillieux studied engineering and taught at the school, publishing papers on steam power. He concentrated on the problem of making sugar, which was quite expensive at the time. He came back to the United States and worked on perfecting the process. He patented the process in 1846 and made money on the invention. The racial climate worsened in the United States prior to the Civil War, so he

Figure 362—Norbert Rillieux. Schomburg Center for Research in Black Culture, New York Public Library.

returned to Paris. Engineers there had misused his process and made it look ineffective, which harmed his reputation and Rillieux abandoned process engineering. In 1880, he met the author, Robert Hayden, in Paris, which re-ignited his interest in his process. In 1894, Rillieux patented (in Paris) a process that halved the cost of processing sugar beets. Rillieux died in Paris in 1894. Although the French refused to give him credit for his invention, Europe later recognized his contribution. In 1934 the International Sugar Cane Technologist created a memorial to Rillieux.

11. Who patented the toggle harpoon which improved whaling methods in 1848?

12. Who attended Harvard Medical School in 1850 and 1851, and after a protest by White students, was asked to leave? He was born in Charles Town, Virginia (now West Virginia) in 1812 of free parents. In 1843, he founded and edited a newspaper. In 1847 he teamed with Frederick Douglass to edit the *North Star* newspaper, and later he studied medicine at Harvard. In 1852, he published *The Condition, Elevation, Emigration and Destiny of the Colored People of the United States*. In 1856, he moved to Canada, established a medical practice, and wrote for Mary Ann Shadd Carey's *Provincial Freeman*. At one time he advocated emigration of African Americans to Central America and Africa. In 1863, he returned to the United States to recruit African American soldiers for the Union Army, and

Figure 363—Dr. Martin R. Delany. U.S. Army Military History Institute.

was commissioned a major in the Union Army during the Civil War.

13. Who received her early education in Salem, Massachusetts, traveled to England, and was known for her attempt to convince the English public not to purchase American cotton grown with slave labor, from the southern states from September 1858 to 1866? This woman left England and traveled to Florence, Italy, entered medical school, and became a doctor. She married an Italian and never returned to the United States.

Figure 364—Sara Parker Remond. Massachusetts Historical Society.

14. In 1862, what hospital was opened as a federally-funded health care facility for African Americans?

15. Who was the first African American woman to earn a medical degree in 1864?

16. Who received a passport from the state of Massachusetts because the Federal government did not consider him a citizen? He was noted for his medical assistance to ill fugitive slaves, and in 1865 became the first African American to practice law before the U.S. Supreme Court.

17. Who developed the potato chip in 1868?

18. Who was the first African American woman to receive a medical degree in 1870 from the state of New York?

19. Who was the first Canadian-born African American doctor from Toronto, Ontario, who joined the Union Army as a surgeon during the Civil War, and returned to Canada in 1871?

20. Who patented the fire extinguisher on October 26, 1872?

21. Who was born in Colchester, Ontario in Canada, and later invented the lubricating cup used to automatically oil machines without stopping them? This patent was issued on July 12, 1872, and the patent number was U.S. 129,843. And to whom does the expression "the real McCoy" refer?

22. Who patented the fire escape ladder on May 7, 1876?

Figure 365—Elijah McCoy. Schomburg Center for Research in Black Culture, New York Public Library.

23. Edward A. Bouchet, the first African American to receive a doctorate from Yale University in 1876, received his doctorate in what discipline?

24. Who was the first known African American to practice medicine in the state of North Carolina in 1878?

25. Who patented the street sprinkler on July 22, 1879 (patent number U.S. 217,843)?

26. In 1879, who became the first African American professional nurse?

27. Who patented the eye protector on November 2, 1880?

28. What college was the first to offer courses for African American nurses in 1881?

29. In Paris, France in 1881, what African American from New Orleans patented a process to apply his evaporating-pan process to make sugar from sugar beets?

30. Who patented a better way to attach the carbon filament in the Maxim electric lamp in 1882, and made the drawings for the first telephone, for Alexander Graham Bell? He was born in Chelsea, Massachusetts in 1848. His father was arrested as a slave fugitive and a judge ordered his return to slavery in Virginia; however, the local community raised money to buy his freedom. He enlisted in the Union Navy at age 15 by forging his birth certificate, and returned to Boston after serving. He died in 1928.

31. Who developed and patented a machine for making paper bags on April 25, 1882 (patent number U.S. 256,856), and patented the fountain pen on January 7, 1890 (patent number U.S. 419,065)?

32. Who became the first African American physician in the United States in 1883?

33. Who invented the lasting machine (to connect the upper part of the shoe to the sole), on March 20, 1883 (patent number U.S. 274,207), which revolutionized the shoe industry? He bequeathed all his holdings to the North Congregational Society Church of Lynn, Massachusetts; they were used to pay off its debt.

34. Who patented a mop on June 11, 1883?

35. Who patented a screw for the tobacco press in 1884?

Figure 366—Jan Matzeliger. Reproduced from the Collections of the Library of Congress.

36. Who patented the egg incubator, the air brake for railroad cars, and the railway telegraph, which allowed messages to be sent between moving trains, for which he received a patent on November 29, 1887 (patent number U.S. 373,915)?

37. Who patented the railway signal on January 1, 1888 (patent number U.S. 376,362)?

38. What U.S. Patent Office worker of the late 1800s and early 1900s used secret marks on the patent forms submitted by African Americans? These marks identified African American inventors, who would not have been recorded because there is no racial identity on the patent form.

Figure 367—Granville T. Woods. Schomburg Center for Research in Black Culture, New York Public Library.

39. Who patented the hand stamp?

40. On November 11, 1890, who patented the portable fire escape?

41. Who established a nursing school and hospital in Savannah, Georgia during the 1890s?

42. Who was in charge of installing street lights in New York, Philadelphia, and London, and in 1890 wrote the first book on lighting, entitled *Incandescent Electric Lighting*? He also improved the electric light bulb patented by Thomas Edison, by replacing the paper filament with a carbon filament that lasted much longer.

43. In 1891, who was the first woman to practice medicine in Alabama, and the first African American resident physician at Tuskegee Institute?

44. Who was a noted surgeon and gynecologist at Provident Hospital in Chicago, and became Surgeon-in-Chief at Provident Hospital in 1891?

Figure 368—Lewis H. Latimer. Schomburg Center for Research in Black Culture, New York Public Library.

45. Who patented compressed air refrigeration on July 14, 1891 (patent number U.S. 455,891)?

46. Who patented the ironing board on April 26, 1892 (patent number U.S. 473,653)?

47. Who patented the clothes dryer on June 6, 1892 (patent number U.S. 476,416)?

48. Who patented the horseshoe on August 23, 1892 (patent number U.S. 481,271)?

49. Who patented the letter box on October 4, 1892 (patent number U.S. 483,325)?

50. Who founded the first African American medical journal, *Medical and Surgical Observer* on December 1, 1892? This journal lasted until 1894. In 1900, this doctor established the University of West Tennessee, an African American medical school. The medical school closed in 1924 due to financial difficulties.

51. What African American doctor accomplished the first successful open-heart surgery in 1893 (removing a knife from the heart of a stabbing victim), and was the first African American member of the American College of Surgeons?

52. Who patented the cotton chopper in 1894?

53. Who founded the Douglass Hospital of Philadelphia in 1895? This hospital was later merged with the Mercy Hospital, becoming the Mercy-Douglass Hospital in 1948.

54. Who patented the street sweeper on May 12, 1896 (patent number U.S. 560,154)?

Figure 369—Daniel Hale Williams. Prints and Photographs Collection, History of Medicine Division, courtesy of National Archives.

55. Who patented the ice cream scoop in 1897?

56. Who submitted a patent on the lawn sprinkler on May 14, 1897?

57. Who developed and received a patent for the automatic railroad car coupler on November 23, 1897 (patent number U.S. 594,059), and patented the rotary engine on July 5, 1892 (patent number U.S. 478,271)?

58. Who was a professor of surgery at Howard University, and Chief Surgeon of Freedmen's Hospital from 1898 to 1938?

59. Who graduated from Harvard University, as a dentist invented a device to correct cleft palates, and also patented the golf tee in 1899?

60. Who patented the lawn mower on May 9, 1899 (patent number U.S. 624,749)?

61. Who taught school, was a part-time dentist in Washington, D.C., had a considerable interest in Lincolniana (collecting Lincoln memorabilia), and in 1905, became the first African American dentist licensed in Washington, D.C.?

62. Who published over 50 research papers on the nervous system, the ecology of invertebrate animals, and animal behavior while teaching biology and psychology at Sumner High School in St. Louis, Missouri? He was the first African American to earn a Ph.D. in biology from the University of Chicago in 1907.

63. In what year was the Mercy Hospital and School of Nurses founded in the city of Philadelphia, Pennsylvania?

64. The National Association of Colored Graduate Nurses was founded on August 25, 1908 by whom? The National Association of Colored Graduate Nurses voted in 1951 to merge with the American Nurses Association (ANA). The ANA also agreed to continue the Mary Mahoney Medal, which was started in 1936 in honor of the first African American graduate nurse. She was born in 1870. She was the only African American graduate in the 1897 class of the Women's Hospital Training School for Nurses in Philadelphia and became the first African American nurse in Connecticut (her home state) in 1908. She died in 1968 and was buried in the family plot with her brother, who died in 1905 and her mother, who died in 1934. It was later discovered that Franklin had outlived her family. As a result, her name was not added to the family gravestone in Meriden, Connecticut. The Chi Eta Phi sorority was concerned that someone of her stature would not have her name on the family tombstone. An anonymous donor contributed the funds, and her name was added.

65. Who was once a surgical assistant to Dr. Daniel Hale Williams in 1908, was editor of the *Journal of the National Medical Association*, and was elected president of the National Medical Association in 1915?

66. What engineer for Marsh Engineering in 1914 designed the Tidal Basin Bridge and the K Street Freeway of Washington, D.C., and later constructed the heating plant and power station at the University of Iowa?

67. Who patented the gas mask on October 14, 1914 (patent number U.S. 1,113,675)?

68. What did George Washington Carver develop from the clays of Alabama, that were used as replacement products for imported dyes and paints during World War I?

Figure 370—Archie Alexander. University of Iowa.

69. Who developed the intradermal smallpox vaccination in 1917, was the 1940 recipient of the Spingarn Medal Award from the NAACP, and had a Harlem hospital named in his honor in 1969? He was born in 1891 in La Grange, Georgia. His father, Dr. Ceah Ketcham, died when he was 4 years old. When Wright was 8, his mother married Dr. William Fletcher Penn, the first African American to graduate from Yale Medical School and Penn had a positive effect on Wright's life. Wright graduated from Clark University in 1911 and from Harvard Medical School in 1915, and he did his internship at the Freedmen's Hospital in Washington, D.C. In 1917, Wright entered the U.S. Army Medical Corps as a first lieutenant. His commander sent him to the front lines, hoping he would be killed. Wright returned, although he had been gassed. The chlorine or mustard gas effects lasted the rest of his life, eventually shortening his life. In 1918, he married Corrine Cook. When the war was over, he returned to New York City and began work at the Harlem Hospital as a clinical assistant visiting surgeon, and later he became director of surgery. Five years later, he became the president of the medical board. In 1948, he entered the field of cancer research and published 15 papers on his research. Wright's two daughters, Barbara and Jane, are both medical doctors. Jane began to work with him on his cancer research and later took it over. Wright died in 1952.

Figure 371—Dr. Louis T. Wright. Schomburg Center for Research in Black Culture, New York Public Library.

70. Who was a well-known nurse at Lincoln Hospital in New York City, and as a member of the National Association of Colored Graduate Nurses protested the exclusion of African American nurses by the American Red Cross and the Army Nurse Corps, prior to December 1918?

71. Who became the first licensed African American pilot in the United States? She earned her license on June 15, 1921 in Paris, France. On April 30, 1926, she fell out of the cockpit of an airplane while practicing stunts in Jacksonville, Florida, falling to her death. After the accident, it was discovered that a wrench used to service the plane had fallen into the gear box, which made the plane difficult to control.

Figure 372—Bessie Coleman. Schomburg Center for Research in Black Culture, New York Public Library.

72. Who patented the automatic traffic signal used throughout the world? In 1923 his patent was sold to General Electric for $40,000. He was born in 1877 in Paris, Kentucky. His parents were Sydney and Elizabeth Reed Morgan. At age 14, he traveled to Cincinnati, Ohio; because of the lack of opportunity there, he moved to Cleveland. His first job, in 1907, was repairing sewing machines. He opened his own sewing machine repair business and in 1909, he opened a tailoring shop. In 1911, by accident he discovered a chemical solution that caused hair to straighten. In 1912, he invented the gas mask or "breathing device" as he called it. He patented the device in 1914 (U.S. patent number 1,113,675). In 1916, Morgan rescued 32 men trapped by an explosion in a tunnel under Lake Erie, and

Figure 373—Garrett A. Morgan. Western Reserve Historical Society, Cleveland, Ohio.

later received a gold medal from the International Association of Fire Chiefs. The gas mask was modified and used by the U.S. Army during World War I. He patented the traffic light in 1923, U.S. patent number 1,475,024. He also obtained British and Canadian patents. He died in 1963 at age 86.

73. What former heavyweight boxing champion patented a wrench on April 18, 1922 (patent number U.S. 1,413,121)?

74. Who discovered that 325 different products could be made from the peanut, and received the 1923 Spingarn Medal?

75. Who was the first African American police surgeon in the New York City Police Department in 1929? He was known for his work on skull fractures.

76. Who became the first African American dean of the Howard University Medical School, June 14, 1929?

77. Who helped develop the method and apparatus for heating the 70-story Radio City Music Hall, which was built in New York City in 1932?

Figure 374—George Washington Carver. Reproduced from the Collections of the Library of Congress.

78. Who was issued a patent for the automatic gear shift on February 6, 1932?

79. Who was president of the National Asso-
ciation of Colored Graduate Nurses from
1934 to 1946, and received the Spingarn
Medal Award in 1951? She was born in
Barbados in 1890, and came to the United
States in 1903. In 1917, she graduated
from the Freedmen's Hospital School of
Nursing. She married James Max Keaton,
from Asheville, North Carolina, but they
soon divorced and in 1931, she married
Fritz C. Staupers of New York City. In
1934, she accepted a position with the
National Association of Colored Graduate
Nurses and worked to get African American nurses into the military. In 1936, she
resigned, but continued to work against
segregation. Her autobiography, *No Time
for Prejudice: A Story of the Integration
of Negroes in Nursing in the United
States*, was published in 1961. She died in 1989.

Figure 375—Mabel Keaton Staupers. Schomburg Center for Research in Black Culture, New York Public Library.

80. Who was known as the "soybean chemist,"
produced a physostigmine synthetic—a
significant medication for glaucoma—in
1935, produced a fire extinguishing foam
that was used to extinguish oil and gasoline
fires during World War II, and developed
a practical method to manufacture synthetic
cortisone (patent number, U.S.
2,752,339)—which relieves arthritis pain—
in 1949? He was the recipient of the 1947
Spingarn Medal.

81. Who was president of Tuskegee from 1935
to 1953, founder of the United Negro
College Fund in 1944, and became the first
African American member of the American
Red Cross in 1946?

Figure 376—Dr. Percy L. Julian. Schomburg Center for Research in Black Culture, New York Public Library.

82. Who was a well-known gastroenterologist
at the University of Illinois at Chicago, and a leading authority in gastric
analysis and biochemistry of the stomach during the 1930s and 1940s?

83. Who developed a test for syphilis, and later published the textbook *Syphilis
and its Treatment* (1936)?

84. What Liberian, grandson of an American slave and husband of Meta
Warrick, became a noted American psychiatrist and pathologist, and held
various positions at the Boston University School of Medicine until he
retired in 1937?

85. On June 27, 1939, who patented the ticket machine for movie theaters, the portable X-ray machine, and refrigeration for trucks (patent number U.S. 2,303,847, issued on July 12, 1940)? He was born in 1892 in Cincinnati, Ohio. He served in France during World War I and later worked as a garage mechanic. He conceived the self-starting gas motor and patented it in 1943. His inventions included adapting movie projectors to sound, and the air conditioner. His portable refrigeration unit was used in World War II to transport blood serum and medical supplies. Jones co-founded, with Joseph Numero, the Thermo King Corporation, a worldwide leader in the transport of temperature control equipment. In 1991, Jones received the National Medal of Technology, posthumously.

Figure 377—Frederick McKinley Jones. Photo: *Saturday Evening Post*. From the Collection of the Minnesota Historical Society.

86. Who wrote the book *Biology of Cell Surfaces* (1939), was recipient of the 1915 Spingarn Medal, and spent time in a Nazi concentration camp during World War II? He was born in 1883 in South Carolina. In 1912, he married Ethel Highwarden, whom he met at Howard University. They divorced in 1939 and he married Hedwig Schnetzler, a doctoral student from Berlin, Germany. When the Nazis overran France in 1940, he was probably put in the concentration camp at Chateaulin, France, but his wife's family got him out. Afterwards, he returned to the United States. Just was head of the Howard University Department of Zoology from 1912 to 1941 and from 1912 to 1920 he taught physiology at Howard Medical School. He died in 1941 in Washington, D.C.

Figure 378—Dr. Ernest E. Just. Schomburg Center for Research in Black Culture, New York Public Library.

87. Who was the only African American tropical disease specialist with the U.S. armed forces during World War II? He was born in 1901 in Alabama. He graduated from Lincoln University (Pennsylvania) in 1924, attended Dartmouth College 1926–1927, and received his MD from Harvard Medical School in 1929. He was head of the Medical College at Howard University from 1931 to 1943 and from 1947–1965 he worked for the U.S. Health Service. In 1948, he directed a mission to help the Liberian government plan sanitation and control infectious disease. He returned to Howard University, where he worked from 1965 to 1987. In 1973, he published his autobiography, *My World of Reality*. He died in 1987.

88.   Who developed techniques for pre-
       serving blood plasma, and on October
       1, 1940, was assigned medical director
       to gather plasma for Great Britain? He
       received the 1944 Spingarn Medal.

89.   Who arrived in the San Francisco Bay
       area in 1942, and became a noted
       dentist and researcher at the University
       of California in San Francisco? He has
       more than 25 published works.

90.   Who was a pioneer in the field of
       health physics, which protects people
       from the hazards of ionizing radiation,
       at Atomics International? Health
       physics became a field of study around
       1942.

Figure 379—Dr. Charles R. Drew.
Prints and Photographs Collection,
History of Medicine Division, courtesy
of National Archives.

91.   Who was the African American mathematician who helped develop the first
       atomic bomb, and received his Ph.D. in 1942 at the age of 19?

92.   Who was one of the U.S. Army's foremost radar scientists, and the first
       African American civilian employee to reach the grade of GS-16? He was
       responsible for the first lunar echo experiments in 1946.

93.   Who was a pioneer in the collection and processing of large quantities of
       blood? The blood bank of the Harlem Hospital is named in his honor.

94.   Who was a jet-and-rocket propulsion researcher at the National Aeronautics
       and Space Administration (NASA), specializing in solid fuels beginning in
       1954?

95.   Who was an internationally known der
       matologist from Chicago, Illinois, recip-
       ient of the Harmon Award for outstanding
       work in medicine, and in 1954, recipient
       of the Spingarn Medal Award? He was
       born in 1892 in Thibodeaux, Louisiana.
       His father was Dr. Alfred Lawless, Jr. He
       attended Talladega College, the Univer-
       sity of Kansas, Columbia University, and
       Howard University. He received his medi-
       cal degree from Northwestern University
       in Evanston, Illinois. He worked to find
       cures for leprosy and syphilis. He estab-
       lished the Lawless Department of Derma-
       tology in Belison Hospital, in Tel Aviv,
       Israel and was a noted philanthropist. He
       died in 1971.

Figure 380—Dr. Theodore K.
Lawless. Schomburg Center for
Research in Black Culture, New York
Public Library.

96. Who was a noted professor of statistics at the University of California at Berkeley, the first African American member of the National Academy of Sciences, and coauthor of the book *Theory of Powers and Statistical Decisions* (1954)?

97. Who was the first African American to be elected president of the American Association of Physical Anthropologists (1957 through 1959)? He also served as chairman of the anthropology section of the American Association for the Advancement of Science.

98. Who performed more than 500 kidney transplants, pioneered new techniques in preserving organs and reducing rejection, and organized organ transplant programs at several hospitals? In 1961, this doctor performed the first transplant in which the donor was not a twin.

99. Who patented a type of resistor used in many computers, radios, televisions, and other electronically controlled devices on February 21, 1961 (patent number U.S. 2,972,726)?

100. Who was an authority on polymer chemistry, fabric flammability, and fluorocarbons, and in 1962 was President of Riverside Research Laboratory?

101. Who was a noted ophthalmologist who researched eye damage caused by sickle-cell anemia and hypertension? This doctor also received awards in 1962 and 1964 for inner eye physiology.

102. Who invented the lunar surface ultraviolet camera, was an astronomy research physicist from 1964 to 1982, and directed the Ultraviolet branch of the Naval Research Laboratory? He was born in 1939 in Cincinnati, Ohio. He grew up on the south side of Chicago. At age 10, he built a telescope. He graduated from Englewood High School in Chicago, received his B.S. from the University of Illinois in 1961, and his M.S. in 1962. He received his Ph.D. from the University of Illinois in 1962. In 2003, he was inducted into the National Inventors Hall of Fame.

103. Who was appointed the first African American member of the U.S. Atomic Energy Commission in 1966, by President Lyndon Johnson?

104. Who was the first African American astronaut to be appointed to the Manned Orbiting Laboratory, in June 1967?

105. In 1967, Freedmen's Hospital was transferred to what university?

106. What clinical and research hematologist, who studied leukemia and sickle-cell anemia, was the first African American to graduate from the Duke University School of Medicine in 1967?

107. Who was a noted bacteriologist at Harvard University and the first African American to chair a department at the Harvard Medical School? He was chairman of the Bacteriology and Immunology Department (now known as the Department of Microbiology and Molecular Genetics) from 1968 to 1971, and again from 1971 to 1978.

108. Who patented an exhaust purifier (patent number U.S. 3,378,241) on April 16, 1968, that reduced gas and emissions from powerplants and furnaces?

Figure 381—Dr. Harold Amos. Photograph courtesy of Dr. Harold Amos.

109. Who was the first African American to receive a Ph.D. in computer science from the University of Illinois in 1969?

110. Who did extensive sickle-cell research, and was instrumental in the construction of the Howard University Hospital as director of the programs and facilities for the hospital in 1970?

111. Who was the co-discoverer of element 104 (Rutherfordium), in 1969, and element 105 (Hahnium), in 1970?

112. Who was a noted physicist at Brown University (professor—1970 to 1975, professor and dean 1975 to 1979) and the University of Chicago (1979 to 1982), Director of the National Science Foundation from 1990 to 1994, and president of Morehouse College beginning in 1995?

113. Who was a well-known microbiologist for the U.S. Army Tank Automotive Command (TACOM), and for 20 years starting in 1970, developed methods to prevent microorganisms from contaminating fuel and military storage materials?

Figure 382—Dr. Walter E. Massey. University Relations Photo Library, Brown University, Providence, Rhode Island.

114. Who is known for his research in protein structure, and was president of Lincoln University in Pennsylvania from 1970 until his retirement in 1985? He was born in Pocahontas, Virginia in 1914. He received his B.S. from Virginia State University in 1936 and his Ph.D. from the University of Cincinnati in 1939. He was a professor of physics and chemistry at Howard University from 1942 through 1944. Dr. Bronson was chair of the Physics Department at Howard University from 1941 to 1968 and president of Central State University from 1968–1970. He was a member of the National Research Council and wrote many articles on physical chemical studies of sickle anemic red blood cells. Dr. Branson was a co-inventor of the alpha helix in protein structure and perhaps deserved consideration for a share of the 1954 Nobel Prize in Chemistry. He died in 1995.

Figure 383—Dr. Herman Branson. Office of Public Relations, Lincoln University, Pennsylvania.

115. What doctor from New York City, noted for her research in cancer, joined the New York University faculty as an Associate Professor of Surgical Research and became the Director of Cancer Research? In 1971, she was elected president of the New York Cancer Society.

116. Who authored the book *Why Blacks Kill Blacks* (1972)?

117. Who did research on the structure and function of the inner ear, and in 1973 was appointed professor of anatomy at the University of Maryland College of Medicine?

Figure 384—Dr. Jane C. Wright Jones. Schomburg Center for Research in Black Culture, New York Public Library.

118. Who was the first African American woman to receive a Ph.D. in theoretical solid state physics from MIT in 1973?

119. Who is a noted geneticist, pathologist, and physician and, from 1973 through 1984, was the Director of the Comprehensive Sickle Cell Center at the University of Chicago?

120. What noted physician and activist had a hospital on Convent Avenue in Harlem named in his honor in 1974?

121. Who patented the disposable syringe on April 8, 1974 (patent number U.S. 3,802,434)?

122. Who grew up near Lansing, Michigan and in 1976, became the first woman and African American appointed to a residency at the University of Minnesota?

123. In 1976, who received a patent for a monitoring and energy control system, sometimes referred to as "Occustat" (patent number U.S. 4,000,400)? The device reduces energy consumption when a building is empty of people.

124. Who was a noted doctor who practiced medicine in New York City for more than 50 years before she retired in 1977?

125. Who was the first African American astronaut in August 1979?

126. Who invented the artificial heart stimulator (pacemaker) in 1981, and patented a variable resistor for guided missile parts?

127. Who is noted for her research in pigment cell research, and served as president of California State University, Fullerton from 1981 to 1990? Her photograph hangs in the National Academy of Sciences in Washington, D.C.

128. The physical science building at San Francisco State University, which was dedicated in April 1982, is named in honor of what physics professor?

129. Who was a co-inventor of the spin-flip turnable laser on July 1, 1985 (patent number U.S. 4,529,942)?

130. What African American astronaut was killed in 1986 when the Challenger spacecraft exploded?

131. Who is known for his contributions in missile research, including eight patents, one of which involves a method of fabricating an imaging X-ray spectrometer? That patent was awarded on September 18, 1986 (patent number U.S. 4,472,728).

Figure 385—Dr. Robert A. Thornton. San Francisco State University Library.

132. In 1987, what noted African American neurosurgeon led a 70-member surgical team at Johns Hopkins Hospital working to separate twins joined at the head?

133. Who is noted for his contributions in electrogas dynamics (EGD), which convert gas into electricity? In 1987, he patented a method for removing fog from airport runways.

134. Provident Hospital of Chicago closed in 1987, and later reopened in what year with an affiliation with Loyola University?

135. Who patented a method to remove cataracts from the eye via laser on May 17, 1988 (patent number U.S. 4,744,360)?

136. Who is a noted veterinarian, and has worked over 25 years at the Tuskegee Institute School of Veterinary Medicine? He was born on January 12, 1920, in Guthrie, Oklahoma. His parents were Lucille Owens and Clarence Adams. In 1941, he received his bachelor's degree from Wichita State University. In 1944, he earned his DVM (Doctor of Veterinary Medicine) from Kansas State University. On July 25, 1956, he married Myrtle Louise Evans. In 1957, he earned his Ph.D. from Cornell University.

137. In 1990, who began work on imaging products for computers?

138. What African American woman was a clinical professor of surgery at Meharry Medical College in 1994?

139. Who is best known for his contributions and achievements in advancing the accuracy of trace element analyses, and in 1995 patented a method of growing continuous diamond films?

140. Who was the 16th Surgeon General of the United States and was sworn in on February 13, 1998?

141. Who was noted for her new procedures for tracking manned and unmanned space missions, and was recognized in 1999 as the outstanding alumnus of the year at West Virginia State College (now West Virginia State University)? She was born in 1918 in West Virginia. She graduated summa cum laude from West Virginia State College with a degree in mathematics and French. She joined Langley Research Center as a mathematician on the leading edge technology for the National Aeronautics and Space Administration (NASA), and later transferred to the NASA flight research program. As a member of the NASA team, her mathematical calculations helped put the first American in space (John Glenn in 1962), and assisted in charting the course of Neil Armstrong, who first walked on the moon in 1969.

142. Who was a graduate of Norfolk State College (now Norfolk State University), became an aerospace technologist at NASA researching acoustics and dynamics, was a member of the National Technical Association (NTA), and in 2001 wrote a paper on Cryogenic Pressure for Wide Temperature Electronically Scanned Pressure (ESP) Modules?

Answers — 11 — Science

1. Onesimus (16?–17?)

2. Thomas Fuller (1710–1790)

3. Benjamin Banneker (1731–1806)

4. J.L. Love (?–?)

5. George Peake (1722–1827)

6. Augustus Jackson (c.1805–?)

7. Henry Blair (1807–1860)

8. Dr. James McCune Smith (1813–1865), who graduated from the University of Glasgow in Scotland

9. Benjamin Bradley (1830–?)

10. Norbert Rillieux (1806–1894)

11. Lewis Temple (1800–1854)

12. Dr. Martin R. Delany (1812–1885)

13. Sara Parker Remond (1826–1894)

14. Freedmen's Hospital

15. Dr. Rebecca Lee Crumpler (1833–1895), who graduated from the New England Medical College, located in Boston

16. John Sweat Rock (1825–1866)

17. Hyram S. Thomas (?–?)

18. Susan M. Stewart (1847–1918)

19. Anderson Ruffin Abbot (1837–1913)

20. T.J. Marshall (?–?)

21. Elijah McCoy (c.1844–1929)

22. J.W. Winters (?–?)

23. Physics

24. Dr. James Frances Shober (1853–1889)

25. M.W. Binka (?–?)

26. Mary Eliza Mahoney (1845–c.1926), who graduated from the New England Hospital for Women and Children (which is now the Dimock Community Health Center), located in Boston, Massachusetts

27. P. Johnson (?–?)

28. Spelman College

29. Norbert Rillieux (1806–1894)

30. Lewis H. Latimer (1848–1928)

31. William B. Purvis (?–?)

32. Dr. James Derham (1757–18?), 1883, New Orleans

33. Jan Matzeliger (1852–1889)

34. T.W. Stewart (?–?)

35. John P. Parker (1827–1900)

36. Granville T. Woods (1856–1910)

37. A.B. Blackburn (?–?)

38. Henry E. Baker (1827–1900)

39. William B. Purvis (?–?)

40. D. McCree (?–?)

41. Alice Woodby McKane (1865–1948)

42. Lewis H. Latimer (1848–1928)

43. Halle Tanner Dillon Johnson (1864–1901)

44. George Cleveland Hall (1864–1930)

45. J. Standard (?–?)

46. Sarah Boone (?–?)

47. G.T. Sampson (?–?)

48. Oscar E. Brown (?–?)

49. G.E. Becket (?–?)

50. Dr. Miles Vandahurst Lynk (1871–1957)

51. Dr. Daniel Hale Williams (1856–1931)

52. George W. Murray (1853–1926)

53. Nathan Francis Mossell (1856–1946)

54. C.B. Brooks (?–?)

55. A.L. Cralle (?–?)

56. J.W. Smith (?–?)

57. Andrew Jackson Beard (1849–1921)

58. Austin Maurice Curtis, Sr. (1868–1939)

59. Dr. George F. Grant (18?–1910)

60. J.A. Burr (?–?)

61. John Edwin Washington (?–?)

62. Dr. Charles H. Turner (1867–1923)

63. 1907

64. Martha Minerva Franklin (1870–1968)

65. Ulysses Grant Dailey (1885–1961)

66. Archie Alexander (1888–1958)

67. Garrett A. Morgan (1877–1963)

68. Dyes and paints

69. Dr. Louis T. Wright (1891–1952)

70. Adah B. Samuels Thoms (c.1870–1943)

71. Bessie Coleman (1892–1926), 1922

72. Garrett A. Morgan (1877–1963)

73. Jack Johnson (1878–1946)

74. George Washington Carver (1864–1943)

75. Dr. Louis T. Wright (1891–1952)

76. Numa Pompilius Garfield Adams (1885–1940)

77. David N. Crosthwait, Jr. (1898–1976)

78. Richard B. Spikes (18?–1962)

79. Mabel Keaton Staupers (1890–1989)

80. Dr. Percy L. Julian (1899–1975)

81. Frederick D. Patterson (1901–1988)

82. Dr. Leonidas H. Berry (1902–1995)

83. Dr. William A. Hinton (1883–1959)

84. Dr. Solomon Carter Fuller (1872–1953)

85. Frederick McKinley Jones (1892–1961)

86. Dr. Ernest E. Just (1883–1941)

87. Dr. Hildrus A. Poindexter (1901–1987)

88. Dr. Charles R. Drew (1904–1950)

89. Dr. Daniel A. Collins (1916–)

90. Roscoe L. Koontz (1922–)

91. Dr. J. Ernest Wilkins (1923–)

92. Dr. Walter McAfee (1914–1995)

93. Dr. Charles R. Drew (1904–1950)

94. Dr. Albert C. Antoine (1925–)

95. Dr. Theodore K. Lawless (1892–1971)

96. Dr. David H. Blackwell (1919–)

97. Dr. W. Montague Cobb (1903–1990)

98. Dr. Samuel L. Kountz (1930–1981)

99. Otis Boykin (1920–1982)

100. Henry A. Hall (1915–1979)

101. Dr. Maurice Rabb (1932–)

102. Dr. George R. Carruthers (1939–)

103. Dr. Samuel M. Nabrit (1905–2003)

104. Dr. Robert H. Lawrence, Jr. (1935–1967)

105. Howard University

106. Wilhelm Delano Meriwether (1943–)

107. Dr. Harold Amos (1919–2003)

108. Rufus Stokes (1924–1986)

109. Dr. Clarence A. Ellis (1943–)

110. Dr. Angella D. Ferguson (1925–)

111. James Harris (1932–)

112. Dr. Walter E. Massey (1938–)

113. Dorothy McClendon (1924–)

114. Dr. Herman Branson (1914–1995)

115. Dr. Jane C. Wright Jones (1919–)

116. Dr. Alvin Francis Poussaint (1934–)

117. Moses Wharton Young (1904–19?)

118. Dr. Shirley Ann Jackson (1946–)

119. Dr. James E. Bowman, Jr. (1923–)

120. Dr. Arthur C. Logan (1909–1973)

121. Phil Brooks (?–)

122. Dr. Alexa I. Canady (1950–)

123. Clarence L. Elder (1935–)

124. Dr. Mary Edward Chinn (1896–1980)

125. G.S. Bluford, Jr. (1942–)

126. Otis Boykin (1920–1982)

127. Jewel Plummer Cobb (1924–)

128. Robert A. Thornton (1898–1982)

129. Dr. Earl Shaw (1937–)

130. Ronald E. McNair (1950–1986)

131. George E. Alcorn (1940–)

132. Dr. Ben Carson (1951–)

133. Meredith Gourdine (1929–1998)

134. 1993

135. Dr. Patricia Bath (1942–)

136. Dr. Eugene W. Adams (1920–)

137. John P. Moon (1938–)

138. Dorothy L. Brown (1919–)

139. Dr. James W. Mitchell

140. Dr. David Satcher (1941–)

141. Katherine G. Johnson (1918–)

142. Nettie D. Faulcon (?–)

A Search of African American Life, Achievement and Culture

12 — Sports

1. Who was the first jockey to win the Kentucky Derby three times: in 1884, 1890, and 1891?

2. Who was the first African American to play major league baseball in the 1800s as a member of the Toledo Blue Stockings, which joined the major leagues in 1884?

3. What Canadian bantamweight boxing champion (1886 to 1906) was known as "Little Chocolate," and was elected to the Boxing Hall of Fame in 1956?

4. What team from Long Island, New York, established by Frank Thompson and S.K. Govern, were the Colored League Champions in 1887 and 1888?

Figure 386—Isaac Murphy. Reproduced from the Collections of the Library of Congress.

5. African American baseball teams existed prior to the formation of Negro leagues. One of the teams, which was established in 1895 by John W. Bud Fowler, was the Page Fence Giants, sponsored by the Page Woven Wire Fence Company. This team played in what city?

6. Who was the winning jockey in the Kentucky Derby in 1896 and 1898?

7. Who was the first African American to win the world bicycle championship in 1899?

8. Who was known as the "Father of Black Baseball," and played from 1902 to 1926?

9. What was the name of the Negro professional baseball team that played in Brooklyn, New York from 1905 until 1942?

10. Who lived in Galveston, Texas and became the first African American heavyweight boxing champion from 1908 to 1915?

11. What Hall of Fame pitcher who was born in Seguin, Texas, is mostly remembered for his days with the New York Lincoln Giants (1911 to 1923) and the Homestead Grays (1925 to 1932), both of the Negro Leagues?

12. What is the name of one of the Negro professional baseball teams that played in Chicago, Illinois from 1911 through 1950?

13. What was the name of the Negro professional baseball team that played in Philadelphia from 1916 to 1932?

14. What was the name of one of the Negro professional baseball teams that played in Baltimore from 1916 until 1934?

15. What label did the media give to the infield of Jud Wilson (first baseman), Frank Warfield (second baseman), Oliver "Ghost" Marcell (third baseman), and Richard Lundy (shortstop) of the Baltimore Black Sox?

16. In 1919, who was the first African American to become a college All-American football player, to play professional football, and to become a National Football League coach?

17. What was the name of the Negro professional baseball team that played in Detroit, Michigan from 1919 to 1931, 1933, 1954 to 1958, 1959 (when the name was changed to the Clowns), and 1960 (when their name changed back to the Stars)?

18. Who was an outstanding football player for Rutgers from 1915 through 1919?

19. During the period of the Negro professional baseball leagues, what city was represented by the Monarchs from 1920 through 1930, and 1937 through 1962? This city is also the home of the Negro Leagues Baseball Museum.

20. What Hall of Fame pitcher for the Kansas City Monarchs was given the nickname "Bullet"?

21. What Negro baseball league player played professionally from 1920 to 1947 and bore the nickname "Cool Papa"?

Figure 387—James "Cool Papa" Bell. Baseball Hall of Fame Library, Cooperstown, New York.

22. What was the name of the Negro professional baseball team that played in Nashville, Tennessee (1921 through 1934), Columbus (1935), Washington, D.C. (1936 to 1937), Baltimore (1938 to 1949), and Nashville (1950 to 1951)?

23. Who was the initial owner of the Nashville Elite Giants (1921 to 1934), who moved to Columbus, Ohio in 1935, Washington, D.C. from 1936 to 1937, Baltimore from 1938 to 1949, and back to Nashville from 1950 to 1951? He sold the team in 1946.

24.   Who was a noted home run hitter for the Detroit Stars for nine years, and played professionally from 1921 to 1942?

25.   What is the name of one of the Negro professional baseball teams that played in St. Louis, Missouri from 1922 to 1931, in 1937, and in 1939?

26.   What was the name of the Negro professional baseball team that played in Memphis, Tennessee from 1923 through 1962, and had its own stadium, which was named Martin Stadium?

27.   Between 1924 and 1967, for which of the following baseball teams did Negro professional baseball player Satchel Paige play the longest? Mobile Tigers, Chattanooga Black Lookouts, New Orleans Black Pelicans, Birmingham Black Barons, Baltimore Black Sox, Nashville Elite Giants, Cleveland Cubs, St. Louis Stars, Pittsburgh Crawfords, Trujilo All-Stars (Dominican Republic), Newark Eagles*, Kansas City Monarchs, Memphis Red Sox, New York Black Yankees, East Chicago Giants, Paige's All-Stars, Philadelphia Stars, Chicago American Giants, Cleveland Indians, St. Louis Browns, Kansas City Athletics, Miami Marlin, Portland Beavers, Peninsula Springfield Redbirds, Atlanta Braves, or the Indianapolis Clowns. *(Satchel did not report to the Newark Eagles, even though the Eagles owned his contract. Instead he went to Mexico to play baseball.)

28.   What was the name of the Negro professional baseball team that played in Birmingham, Alabama from 1924 through 1950?

29.   What third base player played for the Philadelphia Hilldale in the 1924 and 1925 Negro League World Series (NLWS), which was won by the Kansas City Monarchs in 1924 and the Philadelphia Hilldale in 1925? He played in the 1935 NLWS as a member of the Pittsburgh Crawfords, who defeated the New York Cubans?

30.   Who played professional baseball for the Chicago American Giants (1924 to 1925), the Bacharach Giants (1924 to 1925), the New York Lincoln Giants (1928), and other teams, and was considered the greatest baseball player of all time by Babe Ruth?

Figure 388—William Julius "Judy" Johnson. Baseball Hall of Fame Library, Cooperstown, New York.

31.   What Hall of Famer was born in Austin, Texas, and is best remembered for playing for the St. Louis Stars, the Chicago Leland Giants, and the Newark Eagles, and was referred to as the "Shakespeare of Shortstops"?

32.   Who won the 1926 and 1927 Negro League World Series? Both series were between the same two teams, the Chicago American Giants and the Atlantic

City Bacharach Giants. The Chicago American Giants were managed by Andrew "Rube" Foster during both series.

33.   Who won both games of an important doubleheader for the Chicago American Giants to help win the pennant in 1926, and also helped the Giants win the 1926 Negro League World Series?

34.   What Homestead, Pennsylvania team played their home games during 1930s and 1940s at both Forbes Field (home of the Pittsburgh Pirates), and Griffith Stadium (home of the Washington Senators)?

35.   What Negro professional baseball team played in Pittsburgh from 1932 through 1938?

36.   What is the name of one of the Negro professional baseball teams that played in New York City from 1932 to 1948, and from 1949 to 1959?

37.   Who was, at one time, a co-owner of the New York Black Yankees?

38.   Who set world records in the 220-yard, the 100-meter dash, and the 200-meter dash at the 1932 National Collegiate meet in Chicago? He later became a member of the Track and Field Hall of Fame, and a member of the U.S. House of Representatives?

39.   Who won the gold medal in the 100-meter dash at the 1932 Los Angeles Olympics?

Figure 389—Ralph Metcalf (right) and Jesse Owens. Reproduced from the Collections of the Library of Congress.

40.   What third baseman played in the Negro Leagues from 1933 to 1945, played for the Newark Eagles (a member of the Negro Leagues) for seven years, and played four years for the New York Giant's Triple-A Minneapolis club?

41.   Who was the first boxer to hold titles in three different weight divisions: welterweight (1935 to 1940), lightweight (1938 to 1939), and featherweight (1937 to 1938)? His 1956 biography was entitled *Gloves, Glory and God*.

42.   What was the name of the Negro professional baseball team that played in Newark, New Jersey from 1936 to 1948?

43. Who won four gold medals in the 1936 Olympics (100-meter dash, 200-meter dash, broad jump, and as a member of the 400-meter relay team), held in Berlin, Germany? His biography is entitled *I Have Changed* (1972). He received the Presidential Medal of Freedom in 1976, had a street in Berlin, Germany renamed in his honor in 1984, and was awarded the Medal of Honor posthumously in 1990 by President Bush? He was born James Cleveland Owens in 1913 in Oakville, Alabama and grew up in Cleveland, Ohio. He died in 1980.

Figure 390—Jesse Owens (USA). 1st place, Berlin 1936—100 Meters. Copyright © IOC/Olympic Museum Collections.

44. What Hall of Fame pitcher won 20 games from 1936 to 1948 in each of his 12 years with the Kansas City Monarchs?

45. Who held the heavyweight boxing championship longer than any other champion, from 1937 to 1949?

46. What was Joe Louis's full name?

47. What Cuban born baseball player played for the Cuban Stars, Homestead Grays, Philadelphia Hilldale, Baltimore Black Sox, and New York Cubans? He could play all nine positions in a baseball game, pitched the first no-hitter in 1938 in the Mexican League, where he was known as "El Maestro," and was known as "El Immortal" in Cuba? He was elected to the U.S. Baseball Hall of Fame, the Cuban Baseball Hall of Fame, and the Mexican Baseball Hall of Fame.

Figure 391—Joe Louis. Courtesy of National Archives.

48. What boxer, whose given name was Walker Smith, Jr., held boxing titles in three weight classes from 1940 through 1965?

49. Reece "Goose" Tatum and Meadowlark Lemon played from 1941 to 1942 and 1946 to 1956, for what basketball team from Harlem?

50. What is the name of one of the Negro baseball professional teams that played in Indianapolis, Indiana from 1946 to 1962?

51. Who won the 1943, 1944, and 1948 Negro League World Series between the Homestead Grays and the Birmingham Black Barons? All three series were between the same two teams.

52.   What was the name of the Negro professional baseball team that played in Cleveland, Ohio from 1943 until 1948, and 1950?

53.   What Baseball Hall of Fame pitcher, who pitched the only opening day no-hitter in Negro League history in 1946, had a winning percentage of .708?

54.   With the help of what two future major league players, who were Hall of Famers, did the Newark Eagles upset the Kansas City Monarchs in the 1946 Negro League World Series?

55.   What National Football League fullback was considered by Paul Brown, who coached the from 1946 to 1975, to be the greatest back to play for him?

56.   Who was one of the greatest hitters in the Negro professional baseball league's history, and died in 1947 at age 35? He was born in 1911 in Buena Vista, Georgia. His career started in Pittsburgh in 1930, when the Pittsburgh Grays' catcher, Buck Ewing, was injured during a game. Judy Johnson brought Gibson out of the stands to fill in for Ewing. Gibson is credited with almost 800 home runs in his 17-year career, and he was the Negro League's batting champion in 1936, 1938, 1942, and 1945. He was referred to by other players as "the Black Babe Ruth." Many of his feats could not be verified because of the lack of records in the Negro Leagues. In 1942, Gibson suffered from a brain tumor that put him in a coma. He died in 1947.

Figure 392—Josh Gibson. Baseball Hall of Fame Library, Cooperstown, New York.

57.   Who was the first athlete to letter in four sports (football, basketball, track and field, and baseball) while attending UCLA, played one season with the Kansas City Monarchs Baseball Team and was the first African American to play major league baseball in 1947? He was the recipient of the 1956 Spingarn Medal and received the Presidential Medal of Freedom posthumously in 1984.

58.   Who was the first African American to pitch in the major leagues, in 1947?

59.   Who won the gold medal in the high jump for women in the 1948 Olympics, held in London, England?

Figure 393—Jackie Robinson. Baseball Hall of Fame Library, Cooperstown, New York.

60. In 1948, who signed with the Cleveland Indians as a pitcher, and helped them win the pennant? He was born Leroy Robert Page in Mobile, Alabama in 1906. His mother changed the spelling of their last name to "Paige" around the 1920s because she wanted to distance the children and herself from her husband, John Page. Paige began pitching for a semi-pro team, Down the Bay Boys, and in the 9th inning was in a jam and the fans began booing him. He had the outfield come in and then worked his way out of the jam. His Baseball Hall of Fame plaque indicated that he pitched for the Negro Leagues 1826 through 1947, Cleveland Indians (American League) 1948 through 1949, St. Louis Browns (American League) 1951 through 1953, and Kansas City Athletics (American League) 1956. He struck out 21 major leaguers in an exhibition game and helped the Cleveland Indians win the pennant in 1948. He died in 1982.

Figure 394—Satchel Paige. Baseball Hall of Fame Library, Cooperstown, New York.

61. Who held the world heavyweight championship in 1949 and 1950?

62. Who played for the San Francisco Giants (1951 to 1973), and hit 660 career home runs? His auto-biography is entitled *Born to Play Ball* (1955). He was born in 1931 in Westfield, Alabama. In 1950 the Giants acquired Mays and sent him to their Trenton, New Jersey farm team. In 1951, he moved up to the Minneapolis Millers. With a batting average of .477, Mays was called up to play for the New York Giants baseball team and in 1951, Mays was named Rookie of the Year. He served in the U.S. Army, missing

Figure 395—Willie Mays. Baseball Hall of Fame Library, Cooperstown, New York.

part of the 1952 baseball season and all of the 1953 season. He returned to baseball in 1954. In the 1954 World Series, the Giants played the Cleveland Indians. The Giants won all four games, but Mays was known for "The Catch." In game 1 of the series, Vic Wertz hit a long fly ball to center field and Mays made a brilliant over-the-shoulder catch for an out. Midway in the 1972 baseball season Mays moved to the New York Mets. He played with the Mets until his retirement after the 1973 season. Some of the items mentioned on his Hall of Fame plaque include: first in putout by outfielder (7,095), first to top both 300 homers and 300 steals, led league in batting once, slugging five times, home runs and steals four seasons. Voted N.L. (National League) MVP in 1954 and 1965. Played in 24 all-star games.

63. Who was a catcher for the Brooklyn Dodgers (the team later moved to Los Angeles), and received the MVP award in 1951? He was born in Philadelphia, Pennsylvania on November 19, 1921. He was known a "Campy." He played in five World Series and won the Most Valuable Player award in 1951, 1953, and 1955. He played in the 1949, 1952, 1953, 1955, and 1956 World Series. On January 28, 1958, he was disabled permanently by an automobile accident.

64. Who held the world heavyweight boxing championship from 1951 to 1952?

65. Who held the world light-heavyweight boxing championship from 1952 through 1961?

Figure 396—Roy Campanella. Baseball Hall of Fame Library, Cooperstown, New York.

66. Who played for the Chicago Cardinals football team (which later moved to St. Louis and then to Arizona), and was traded to the Los Angeles Rams for eight players and a draft choice? He also played for the Los Angeles Rams (which later moved to St. Louis) and the Philadelphia Eagles, from 1952 through 1966.

67. Who played professional football for the Baltimore Colts (which later moved to Indianapolis) from 1953 through 1962, and was known as "Big Daddy"?

68. Who was one of the great hitters of the Negro professional baseball leagues, was known as "Charlie," and had a lifetime batting average of .353? He managed the Indianapolis Clowns to the 1954 American League title. He was born Oscar McKinley Charleston on October 14, 1896, in Indianapolis, Indiana, the seventh of eleven children. His father Tom was a Sioux Indian. Charleston joined the army in 1910 when he was 14 or 15 years old, and was stationed in the Philippines. In 1915, he began to play for the Indianapolis ABCs. In 1916, Charleston's team beat the Chicago American Giants in the Black World Series. Some of the other teams on which Charleston played are: New York Lincoln Giants, Chicago American Giants, Hilldale, Homestead Grays, Pittsburgh Crawfords, Toledo Crawfords, Indianapolis Crawfords, Harrisburg Giants, Philadelphia Stars, and the Indianapolis Clowns. He was elected to the Baseball Hall of Fame in 1976. He died on October 5, 1954, in Philadelphia, Pennsylvania.

Figure 397—Oscar Charleston. Baseball Hall of Fame Library, Cooperstown, New York.

69. What major league outfielder hit his 715th home run on April 18, 1974, and broke Babe Ruth's career record for home runs? His total career home runs were 755 (from 1954 to 1976). He was the recipient of the 1975 Spingarn Medal and the Presidential Medal of Freedom in 2002. He was born Henry Louis Aaron on February 5, 1934 in Mobile, Alabama. His parents were Herbert and Estella Aaron. Henry was the third of eight children. He was raised in Toulminville, Alabama, a suburb of Mobile. After seeing Jackie Robinson play and give a speech in Mobile, Aaron knew he wanted to become a major league player. He played for the

Figure 398—Henry Aaron. Photograph courtesy of the Atlanta Braves.

Mobile Black Bears and was signed by the Indianapolis Clowns in 1952. The Boston Braves purchased his contract, and he reported to the Braves farm team in Eau Claire, Wisconsin, then later to the Tars of Jacksonville, Florida. He played for Savannah, Augusta, and Columbus. He was brought to the Milwaukee (formerly Boston) Braves in 1954. Some of his accomplishments listed on his Hall of Fame plaque include: had 20 or more home runs for 20 consecutive years, at least 30 home runs in 15 seasons, and 40 or better home runs eight times. Set a record in games played (3,298), at-bat (12,364), long hits (1,477), total bases (6,856), runs batted in (2,297). Paced N.L. in batting twice and homers, runs batted in, and slugging percentage four times each. Won the Most Valuable Player Award in N.L. in 1957. His autobiography, *I Had a Hammer*, was published in 1991.

70. Who attended McClymonds High School in Oakland, California and San Francisco University, and later as a great player helped the Boston Celtics win eleven National Basketball Association titles (1956, 1959–1966, 1968, and 1969)? He was considered the greatest defensive player of all time. The title of his autobiography was *Go Up for Glory* (1966).

71. Who held the boxing heavyweight championship at various times each year from 1956 to 1959, and from 1960 to 1962? He was born on January 4, 1935, in Waco, North Carolina. He won the Olympic gold medal boxing as a middleweight in 1952 in Helsinki, Finland.

Figure 399—Bill Russell, Boston Celtics. Dick Raphael, Photographer.

72. In 1957, what woman won the Wimbledon tennis championship? Her autobiography is entitled *I Always Wanted to Be Somebody* (1958)? She was born on August 25, 1927, in Silver, South Carolina. Her parents were Annie and Daniel Gibson. The family moved to Harlem when she was 3 years old. In 1942, she won the New York State Open Championship of the American Tennis Association. In 1944 and 1945, she won the girl's singles of the American Tennis Association. Two doctors, Dr. Robert W. Johnson of Lynchburg, Virginia and Dr. Hubert A. Eaton of Wilmington, Delaware became her sponsors. She attended school at Dr. Eaton's residence because he had a tennis court, and Dr. Johnson arranged summer tournaments. In 1956, she won the French Tennis Championship. In 1957, she won Wimbledon and the U.S. championship, and repeated the feat in 1958. She retired after the 1958 tennis season.

Figure 400—Althea Gibson. Schomburg Center for Research in Black Culture, New York Public Library.

73. Who played for the Cleveland Browns from 1957 to 1965, and is considered one of football's greatest running backs?

74. Meadowlark Lemon, who was inducted into the Basketball Hall of Fame in 1990, played for what basketball team from 1957 to 1979?

Figure 401—Cleveland Browns player Jim Brown (1963). Copyright © Corbis.

75. What Football Hall of Famer, who was an offensive lineman of the Baltimore Colts from 1957 to 1967, protected Johnny Unitas and made many blocks for Lenny Moore?

76. Who was the National League's MVP (Most Valuable Player) in 1958 and 1959, and played for the Chicago Cubs?

77. Who led the Brazilian national team to the 1958, 1962, and 1970 world soccer championships, played for the New York Cosmos from 1975 to 1977, and led the Cosmos to the 1977 NASL championship?

78. Who played for the San Francisco Giants (1959–1973, 1977–1980), San Diego (1974–1976), Oakland Athletics (1976), and hit 521 career home runs? He was born Willie Lee McCovey in Mobile, Alabama on January 10, 1938. He made his major league debut with the Giants on July 30, 1959, with four hits in a 7–2 Giant victory. His nicknames were "Stretch" and "Big Mac." He was a great left-handed hitter.

Figure 402—Willie McCovey. Photograph courtesy of the San Francisco Giants.

79. Who played baseball for the Chicago Cubs and Oakland Athletics for over 18 seasons (1959–1976), and had 426 career home runs? He was born Billy Lee Williams on June 15, 1938 in Whistler, Alabama. He made his major league debut with the Chicago Cubs on August 6, 1959. He was a left-handed hitter and threw right-handed. He participated in six All-Star games.

80. Who led the National Basketball Association in scoring from 1960 to 1966? He was born Wilton Norman Chamberlain on August 21, 1936, in Philadelphia, Pennsylvania. He attended Overbrook High School in Philadelphia and led the school to three winning seasons. In 1955, he announced his college choice, the University of Kansas. Freshmen could not play with the varsity team, but he played the following year and led the University of Kansas to the 1957 college finals against North Carolina. Kansas lost in triple overtime. In 1958, Chamberlain decided to skip his senior year to play for the Harlem Globetrotters. In 1959, he was signed by the Philadelphia Warriors and during the 1959-60 season, he won Rookie of the Year and MVP awards.

Figure 403—Wilt Chamberlain (center) and Bill Russell (left). Photograph courtesy of Dick Raphael Associates.

He played for the Philadelphia Warriors from 1959–1962, the San Francisco Warriors from 1963–1964, the Philadelphia 76ers from 1964–1968, and the Los Angeles Lakers from 1968–1973. Chamberlain won National Basketball Association championships in 1967 as a member of the Philadelphia 76ers, and in 1972 as a member of the Los Angeles Lakers. His autobiography, *A View from Above*, was published in 1991. He died in Bel Air, California on October 12, 1996.

81.   Who suffered from polio as a child, attended Burt High School in Clarksville, Tennessee and Tennessee State University, and
won three gold medals in the 1960 Olympics? She was born Wilma Glodean Rudolph in 1940, in Clarksville, Tennessee.
As a child, she contracted polio, and doctors told her mother she would never walk
again. Her mother found out that she could
be treated at Meharry Hospital in Nashville, Tennessee and drove the 50 miles
twice a week for two years for Rudolph's
treatment. The doctors taught her mother
how to do all the exercises at home and her
brothers and sisters helped. By age 12,
Wilma was able to walk normally. She
played basketball at Burt High School,
attended Tennessee State on a track
scholarship, and graduated from Tennessee

Figure 404—Wilma Rudolph.
Reproduced from the Collections of
the Library of Congress.

in 1963. In 1960, Rudolph became the first African American woman to win
3 gold medals, for the 100-meter dash, 200-meter dash, and anchor on the
400-meter relay team. She wrote her autobiography, *Wilma*, in 1977 and was
inducted into the U.S. Olympic Hall of Fame in 1983. She died in 1994.

82.   Who was the decathlon gold medalist in the 1960 Olympics?

83.   Who won the 1960 Olympic broad jump?

84.   Who was known as the best "small man" in the NBA, and played for the
Cincinnati Royals from 1960 to 1970, and the Milwaukee Bucks from 1970
to 1974?

85.   In the 1960s, who had the reputation as a
noted African American bowler?

86.   What pitcher for the St. Louis Cardinals in
the 1960s was known as their "Ace"? He
was born in 1935, in Omaha, Nebraska. He
played for the St. Louis Cardinals from
1959–1975 and had nine 200-strikeout
seasons, World Series MVP in 1964 and
1967, and 13 shutout games in 1968. He
was the second major league pitcher to
strike out over 3,000 batters.

87.   What professional football player's nickname was "Deacon"? During his professional career (1961 to 1974), he played for
the Los Angeles Rams, the San Diego
Chargers, and the Washington Redskins.

Figure 405—Bob Gibson.
Baseball Hall of Fame Library,
Cooperstown, New York.

88. Who played cornerback for the Green Bay Packers from 1961 to 1972, and later became a member of the National Football League Hall of Fame? He was born on June 8, 1937, in Philadelphia, Pennsylvania. He played football at Michigan State University and was an offensive star. He was the first-round draft choice of the Green Bay Packers in 1961, to play halfback and flanker. After seeing that his play would be limited because of starters Paul Hornung and Jim Taylor, he moved to defense as a cornerback to replace an injured player. He played cornerback for the Green Bay Packers from 1962–1969, and was traded to the Dallas Cowboys, where he played from 1970–1972. He played in Super Bowls I (1967), II (1968), V (1971), and VI (1972). Adderley was on the winning Super Bowl team, except for Super Bowl V. He was elected to the Professional Football Hall of Fame in 1980.

Figure 406—Herb Adderley. Photograph courtesy of the Green Bay Packers, Vernon J. Biever, Photographer.

89. In 1962, who helped organize the Rocky Mount (Carolina League) club and served as its vice president? He was inducted into the Baseball Hall of Fame in 1972. He died November 27, 1977.

90. What ball player was known as "Pops" and spent his entire 21 professional baseball seasons (1962 to 1982) with the Pittsburgh Pirates?

91. Who was a linebacker for the Kansas City Chiefs from 1963 to 1974, and became a member of the National Football Hall of Fame?

92. What professional football player, who played in the National Football League from 1964 to 1974 for the Cleveland Browns, and from 1976 to 1977 for the Miami Dolphins, was nicknamed "The Ghost"?

Figure 407—Buck Leonard, Baseball Hall of Fame Library, Cooperstown, New York.

93. Who was one of the greatest wide receivers to play for the Washington Redskins from 1964 to 1977?

94. What St. Louis Cardinal outfielder led the National League in stolen bases eight times (1966 through 1969 and 1971 through 1974), and played in the World Series in 1964, 1967, and 1968?

95. Who won the Olympic 100-meter dash for women in 1964 and 1968?

96.   Who won an Olympic gold medal for boxing in 1960 as a light heavyweight, and was heavyweight champion from 1964–1967, 1974–1978, and 1978–1979? He was inducted into the Olympic Hall of Fame in 1983 and the International Boxing Hall of Fame in 1991. He was convicted of draft evasion and lost his title and boxing license from 1967–1970. He appealed his conviction on religious reasons, the Supreme Court overturned his sentence, and in 1970, he returned to boxing.

Figure 408—Muhammad Ali. Reproduced from the Collections of the Library of Congress.

97.   Who won a gold medal in the 100-meter dash in the 1964 Olympics with a record time of 10.05 seconds, and a gold medal in the same Olympics as the anchor of the U.S. 400-meter relay team with a time of 8.6 seconds? He played for the Dallas Cowboys (1965–1974) and the San Francisco 49ers (1975), and was inducted into the National Track and Field Hall of Fame in 1976.

98.   Who attended Central High School in Omaha, Nebraska, played football at the University of Kansas where he was known as the "Kansas Flash," and was one of the all-time rushing leaders of the Chicago Bears from 1965–1971?

99.   What middleweight boxer spent 19 years (1966–1985) in prison for a crime he did not commit, and published a book entitled *The Sixteenth Round* (1974), which details his accounts of the crime and his life in prison? In 1975 he sent a copy of his book to Bob Dylan, who wrote a song about the ordeal.

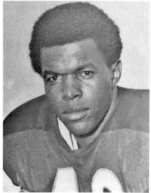

Figure 409—Gale Sayers. Courtesy of the Chicago Bears.

100.   In 1966, what college was the first to win the NCAA Division I championship with an all-African American starting-five lineup, defeating the University of Kentucky?

101.   Who played for the Baltimore Colts and the San Diego Charges (1966 to 1978), and is arguably the greatest tight end to ever play professional football?

102.   Who was one of the great middle linebackers, playing for the Kansas City Chiefs from 1967 to 1977?

103.   Who played professional football as a defensive tackle (number 88) for the Minnesota Vikings and the Chicago Bears, from 1967 to 1981?

104. Who pitched for the Philadelphia Phillies, Chicago Cubs, Texas Rangers, and Boston Red Sox, had 6 consecutive 20-game winning seasons (1967 to 1972), and was 25–13 with the Texas Rangers in 1974?

105. What Detroit Pistons player led the National Basketball Association in scoring in 1967–1968?

106. Who played for the Pittsburgh Steelers from 1968 to 1981, and was known as "Mean Joe"? He was on the winning team in Super Bowls IX (1975), X (1976), XIII (1979), and XIV (1980).

107. Who was known for his "skyhook" shot in basketball? He played for the Milwaukee Bucks (1969 to 1975), the Los Angeles Lakers (1975 to 1989), and was on NBA championship teams in 1971 (with the Milwaukee Bucks), 1981, 1982, 1985, 1987, and 1988 (with the Lakers). His autobiography is entitled *Giant Steps* (1983).

108. What football player, known as "the Juice," played professionally from 1969 to 1979 for the Buffalo Bills and the San Francisco 49ers?

Figure 410—Joe Greene. Photograph courtesy of the Pittsburgh Steelers.

109. What professional basketball player nicknamed "Clyde" led the New York Knicks to the NBA championships in 1970 and 1973?

110. Who helped lead the New York Knicks to the NBA championship in 1970 and 1973? He was NBA MVP in 1970 and NBA Finals MVP in 1973.

111. Who won an Olympic gold medal in 1964 as a heavyweight boxer, won the heavyweight championship in 1971, and was known as "Smokin' Joe"?

112. What professional basketball player, whose nickname was "Dr. J," played for the American Basketball Association (ABA) Virginia Squires (1971–1973), the New York Nets (1973–1976), the NBA 76ers (1976–1987), and led the 76ers to the NBA championship in 1983? He was born Julius Winfield Erving, II in 1950, in Hempstead (Long Island), New York. His family later moved to Roosevelt, where he was a star player on the high school basketball team and acquired the nickname "Dr. J." He attended the University of Massachusetts and in 1971, left after his junior year to play for the Virginia Squires.

Figure 411—Julius Erving. Photograph courtesy of the Philadelphia 76ers Basketball Club, Incorporated.

113. Who led the American League in batting from 1972 to 1975, and from 1977 to 1978?

114. Roberto Clemente, a Pittsburgh Pirate out-fielder, won four batting titles. He died in 1972, while taking relief supplies to Nicaraguan earthquake victims, which was what type of a mission? Roberto received the Presidential Medal of Freedom posthumously in 2003. He was born August 18, 1934 in Carolina, Puerto Rico. He was the youngest of four children. He first played baseball for the Santurce Grabbers, a Puerto Rican winter league team. He started playing for the Pittsburgh Pirates in 1955 and played his entire 18-year career with the Pirates. He won twelve Golden Glove Awards, had 3,000 hits, was voted National League MVP in 1966, and MVP of the 1971 World Series. In 1964, he married Vera Cristena Zabala; they have three children.

Figure 412—Roberto Clemente. Baseball Hall of Fame Library, Cooperstown, New York.

115. Who was known as "Mr. October," and led the American League in home runs in 1973, 1975, and 1980? His autobiography, *Reggie*, was published in 1984.

116. Who was known as the "Pearl" when he played basketball in the National Basketball Association and on the 1973 New York Knicks championship team?

117. Who won a gold medal in the 1968 Olympics as a heavyweight, and held the boxing heavyweight championship in 1973 and 1994?

Figure 413—Reggie Jackson. Photograph courtesy of the Oakland Athletics.

118. What college football player was the first player to win the Heisman trophy twice, in 1974 and 1975?

119. In 1975, who won the men's Wimbledon tennis championship, and was awarded a posthumous Presidential Medal of Freedom in 1993?

120. Who was the first African American major league baseball manager in 1975, working as manager of the Cleveland Indians?

121. Who was the first African American to play in the Masters golf tournament in 1975?

122. Who was the NBA MVP in 1975 as a member of the Buffalo Braves (who later moved to Los Angeles and became the Los Angeles Clippers), and won two NBA championships with the Los Angeles Lakers in 1982 and 1985?

123. What National Football League player who played for the Chicago Bears from 1977 to 1989, attended John J. Jefferson High School in Columbia, Mississippi? He also attended Jackson State University and Southern University, and the title of his autobiography is *Sweetness*. He was elected to the National Football Hall of Fame in 1993; his son made the presentation speech.

124. What National Basketball Association (NBA) player's nickname was the "Iceman"? He led the NBA in scoring in 1977 to 1978, 1978 to 1979, and 1979 to 1980?

Figure 414—Walter Payton. Photograph courtesy of the Chicago Bears.

125. What Boston Red Sox outfielder led the American League in home runs in 1977, 1978, and 1983?

126. What player known as "Big E" played basketball at the University of Houston, and later helped lead the Washington Bullets to the 1978 NBA championship?

127. What Baseball Hall of Famer played short stop for the San Diego Padres (1978 to 1981) and the St. Louis Cardinals (1982 to 1996), had 13 Golden Glove awards, helped St. Louis win the 1982 World Series, and played in the 1985 and 1987 World Series? He was known as "The Wizard of Oz."

128. Earl Campbell played for what National Football League teams from 1978 to 1985?

129. Who was the MVP in the National Basketball Association in 1979, 1982, and 1983?

130. Who held boxing championship titles in five weight divisions from 1979 to 1991, and was nicknamed "Sugar"?

131. What boxer nicknamed "Marvelous" held boxing championship titles from 1979 to 1987? His name was changed legally to make Marvelous part of his name.

132. What former basketball player whose nickname is "Magic," played with the Los Angeles Lakers, NBA champions in 1980, 1982, 1985, 1987, and 1988?

133. What boxer's nickname was "Hitman"? He was the WBA Welterweight Champion (1980 to 1981), WBC Superwelterweight Champion (from 1982 to 1986), NABF Middleweight Champion (1986), WBC Light Heavyweight Champion (1987), and WBC Middleweight Champion (from 1987 to 1988).

134. Who played defensive tackle at the University of Tennessee from 1980 to 1983, and was inducted into the College Football Hall of Fame in 2002? He played professionally for the Memphis Showboats, Philadelphia Eagles, Green Bay Packers, and Carolina Panthers.

135. Who won four gold medals in track, at the 1984 Olympics?

136. Who led the New York Giants to Super Bowl titles in 1986 and 1990?

137. In 1986, who was the world figure skating champion for women?

138. When he retired from the Dallas Cowboys after the 1987 season, who was the all-time rushing leader for the Cowboys?

139.

Figure 415—Seoul 1988—200m. From left to right: Florence Griffith-Joyner (USA) 1st, Katrin Krabbe (GDR) 3rd, Merlene Ottey (JAM). Copyright © IOC/Olympic Museum Collections, photographer J. Widener.

Who won three gold medals in the 1988 Olympics, and holds the world outdoor record for women for the 100-meter run and 200-meter run, both set in 1988?

140. Who led the Detroit Pistons to the 1989 and 1990 National Basketball Association championships?

141. Who held various world heavyweight championships from 1990 to 2001?

142. Who attended Laney High School in Wilmington, North Carolina and the University of North Carolina, is known as "Air Jordan," and led the Chicago Bulls to NBA championships in 1991, 1992, 1993, 1996, 1997, and 1998? Jordan played for the Washington Wizards during 2001–2002 and 2002–2003. In 2001–2002, he donated his one million dollar salary to the victims of the September 11, 2001 attacks.

Figure 416—Michael Jordan. Photograph courtesy of the Chicago Bulls.

143. Who was the first African American to enter the Indianapolis 500 automobile race in 1991?

144. Who won the women's heptathlon gold medal in the 1992 Summer Olympics held in Barcelona, Spain?

145. Who won the women's 100-meter gold medal in the 1992 Olympics held in Barcelona, Spain?

146. Who played his entire career in the major leagues, playing for the San Diego Padres, New York Yankees, California Angels, Minnesota Twins, Toronto Blue Jays, and Cleveland Indians? He was born on October 3, 1951, in St. Paul, Minnesota. Later, he earned a scholarship to the University on Minnesota where he played basketball and baseball. He helped the Toronto Blue Jays win the World Series in 1992, and was inducted into the Baseball Hall of Fame in 2001.

147. Who attended Auburn University, played basketball for the Philadelphia 76ers, and led the Phoenix Suns to the 1993 National Basketball Association Finals?

148. Who holds the world outdoor record for men for the 200-meter run, set in 1996, and the 400-meter run, set in 1999? He was born Michael Duane Johnson on September 13, 1967, in Dallas, Texas. He attended Atwell Junior High School and Skyline High School, graduating in 1986. In 1990, he graduated from Baylor University. In the 1996 Olympics in Atlanta, Johnson won the gold medal in the 200 meters and 400 meters. In 2000, Johnson repeated the feat in Sydney and also won a gold medal as a participant on the 4x400 meter relay team.

Figure 417—Atlanta, 1996—400m, Michael Johnson (USA), 1st. IOC/ Olympic Museum Collections, copyright © Allsport, photograph: Mike Powell.

149.

Figure 418—Jackie Robinson Commemorative Silver Dollar Proof Coin. Courtesy U.S. Mint.

Figure 419—Jackie Robinson Commemorative Five Dollar Gold Proof Coin. Courtesy U.S. Mint.

The Jackie Robinson commemorative silver dollar and five dollar gold coins were issued by the U.S. Mint in what year? These coins were issued in proofs and uncirculated coins. On the silver dollar, Jackie Robinson is pictured as he stole home plate during the 1955 World Series between the New York Yankees and the Brooklyn Dodgers.

150. Who won the Masters Tournament in 1997, 2001, and 2002?

151. What duo lead the San Antonio Spurs to NBA titles in 1999 and 2003?

152. Who was the most valuable player (MVP) of the National Basketball Association in 1999?

153. What Detroit Lions player was the second all-time rusher in the NFL, and retired prior to the 1999 NFL season?

154. Who won gold medals in the 2000 Olympics in the women's 100-meter dash, 200-meter dash and the 4x400-meter relay?

155. What duo led the Los Angeles Lakers to NBA championships in 2000, 2001 and 2002?

156. Who was the 2000–2001 Wimbledon singles woman champion? Who was the 2002 Wimbledon singles woman champion?

157. Who led the National Basketball Association in scoring during the 2001–2002 season?

Figure 420—Los Angeles Lakers Kobe Bryant (L) and Shaquille O'Neal chat during the Lakers' 103–101 loss to the Sacramento Kings, in Los Angeles, February 26, 2004. Copyright © Lucy Nicholson/Reuters/Corbis.

158. Who led the National Football League through 2004 as the all-time leading receiver and touchdown scorer? When he retired in 2005, he had amassed in his career 197 touchdowns, 22,895 receiving yards, and 1,549 receptions, and played in four Super Bowls: XXIII (1989), XXIV (1990), XXIX (1995), and XXXVII (2003).

159. What Dallas Cowboys player was the all-time leading rusher in the National Football League, and left the Cowboys in 2003 to play for the Arizona Cardinals?

160. Prior to the start of the 2004 baseball season, what San Francisco Giants outfielder was in fourth place on the all-time home runs list with 613 home runs?

161. Prior to the start of the 2004 baseball season, what Chicago Cubs outfielder from the Dominican Republic had a career total of 499 home runs?

Figure 421—Emmitt Smith. Photograph courtesy of the Dallas Cowboys.

162. What Cincinnati Reds outfielder hit his 500th career home run on June 20, 2004?

163. Who, along with Rasheed Wallace, Richard Hamilton, Chauncey Billups, Tayshaun Prince, and Corliss Williams led the Detroit Pistons to the 2004 NBA Championship?

164. What NBA finals MVP led the San Antonio Spurs to the 2005 NBA championship?

Answers — 12 — Sports

1. Isaac Murphy (1861–1891)

2. Moses Fleetwood Walker (1856–1924)

3. George Dixon (1870–1909)

4. Cuban Giants

5. Adrian, Michigan

6. Willie Simms (1870–1927)

7. Marshall Taylor (1878–1932)

8. Andrew "Rube" Foster (1879–1930)

9. Brooklyn Royal Giants

10. Jack Johnson (1878–1946)

11. Joe "Smokey" Williams (1885–1951)

12. Chicago American Giants

13. Philadelphia Hilldale

14. Baltimore Black Sox

15. "The Million Dollar infield," because of what they would have been paid if they had been White.

16. Fritz Pollard (1894–1986), Akron Indians, 1919

17. Detroit Stars

18. Paul Robeson (1898–1976)

19. Kansas City, Missouri

20. Joe Rogan (1889–1967)

21. James "Cool Papa" Bell (1903–1991)

22. Nashville Elite Giants

23. Thomas T. Wilson (1883–1947)

24. Norman "Turkey" Steames (1901–1979)

25. St. Louis Stars

26. Memphis Red Sox

27. Pittsburgh Crawfords (1932–1937)

28. The Birmingham Black Barons

29. William Julius "Judy" Johnson (1899–1989). He acquired the nickname "Judy" because he reminded people of Judy Gans, who played for the Chicago American Giants.

30. John Henry "Pop" Lloyd (1884–c.1965)

31. Willie Wells (c.1906–1989)

32. Chicago American Giants

33. William "Willie" Foster (1904–1978), half-brother of Andrew "Rube" Foster

34. Homestead Grays

35. Pittsburgh Crawfords

36. New York Black Yankees

37. Bill "Bojangles" Robinson (1878–1949)

38. Ralph Metcalf (1910–1978)

39. Eddie Tolan (1909–1967)

40. Ray Dandridge (1913–1994)

41. Henry Armstrong (1912–1988)

42. Newark Eagles

43. Jesse Owens (1913–1980)

44. Hilton Smith (1907–1983)

45. Joe Louis (1914–1981)

46. Joseph Louis Barrow (1914–1981)

47. Martin Dihigo (1905–1971)

48. Sugar Ray Robinson (1920–1989)

49. Harlem Globetrotters

50. Indianapolis Clowns

51. Homestead Grays

52. Cleveland Buckeyes

53. Leon Day (l916–1995)

54. Larry Doby (1923–2003) and Monte Irvin (1919–)

55. Marion Motley (1920–1999)

56. Josh Gibson (1911–1947)

57. Jackie Robinson (1919–1972)

58. Dan Bankhead (1920–1976), Brooklyn Dodgers, 1947

59. Alice Coachman (1923–)

60. Satchel Paige (1906–1982)

61. Ezzard Charles (1921–1975)

62. Willie Mays (1931–)

63. Roy Campanella (1921–1993)

64. Joe Walcott (1914–1994)

65. Archie Moore (1913–1998)

66. Ollie Matson (1930–)

67. Gene Lipscomb (1931–2002)

68. Oscar Charleston (1896–1954)

69. Henry Aaron (1934–)

70. Bill Russell (1934–)

71. Floyd Patterson (1935–)

72. Althea Gibson (1927–)

73. Jim Brown (1936–)

74. Harlem Globetrotters

75. Jim Parker (1934–)

76. Ernie Banks (1931–)

77. Pelé (Edson Arantes do Nascimento) (1940–)

78. Willie McCovey (1938–)

79. Billy Williams (1938–)

80. Wilt Chamberlain (1936–1999)

81. Wilma Rudolph (1940–1994)

82. Rafer Johnson (1935–)

83. Ralph Boston (1939–)

84. Oscar Robinson (1938–)

85. J. Wilbert Sims (?–)

86. Bob Gibson (1935–)

87. David "Deacon" Jones (1938–)

88. Herb Adderley (1939–)

89. Buck Leonard (1907–1997)

90. Willie Stargell (1940–2001)

91. Bobby Bell (1940–)

92. Paul Warfield (1942–)

93. Charley Taylor (1941–)

94. Lou Brock (1939–)

95. Wyomia Tyus (1945–)

96. Muhammad Ali (1942–)

97. Robert "Bob" Hayes (1942–2002)

98. Gale Sayers (1943–)

99. Rubin "Hurricane" Carter (1937–)

100. Texas Western College (later became the University of Texas at El Paso [UTEP])

101. Lenny Moore (1933–)

102. Willie Lanier (1945–)

103. Alan Page (1945–)

104. Ferguson Jenkins (1943–)

105. Dave Bing (1943–)

106. Joe Greene (1946–)

107. Kareem Abdul-Jabbar (1947–)

108. O.J. Simpson (1947–)

109. Walt Frazier (1945–)

110. Willis Reed (1942–)

111. Joe Frazier (1944–)

112. Julius Erving (1950–)

113. Rod Carew (1945–)

114. A humanitarian mission

115. Reggie Jackson (1946–)

116. Earl Monroe (1944–)

117. George Foreman (1949–)

118. Archie Griffin (1954–)

119. Arthur Ashe (1943–1993)

120. Frank Robinson (1935–)

121. Lee Elder (1934–)

122. Bob McAdoo (1951–)

123. Walter Payton (1954–1999)

124. George Gervin (1952–)

125. Jim Rice (1953–)

126. Elvin Hayes (1945–)

127. Ozzie Smith (1954–)

128. Houston Oilers (which later became the Tennessee Titans) and the New Orleans Saints

129. Moses Malone (1955–)

130. Sugar Ray Leonard (1956–)

131. Marvelous Marvin Hagler (1954–)

132. Earvin "Magic" Johnson (1959–)

133. Thomas Hearns (1958–)

134. Reggie White (1961–2004)

135. Carl Lewis (1961–)

136. Lawrence Taylor (1959–)

137. Debi Thomas (1967–)

138. Tony Dorsett (1954–)

139. Florence Griffith-Joyner (1959–1998)

140. Isaiah Thomas (1961–)

141. Evander Holyfield (1962–)

142. Michael Jordan (1963–)

143. Willy T. Ribbs (1959–)

144. Jackie Joyner-Kersee (1962–)

145. Gail Devers (1966–)

146. David M. Winfield (1951–)

147. Charles Barkley (1963–)

148. Michael Johnson (1967–)

149. 1997

150. Eldrick "Tiger" Woods (1975–)

151. Tim Duncan (1976–) and David Robinson (1965–)

152. Karl Malone (1963–)

153. Barry Sanders (1968–)

154. Marion Jones (1975–)

155. Shaquille O'Neal (1972–) and Kobe Bryant (1978–)

156. Venus Williams (1980–) and Serena Williams (1981–)

157. Allen Iverson (1975–)

158. Jerry Rice (1962–)

159. Emmitt J. Smith, III (1969–)

160. Barry Bonds (1964–)

161. Sammy Sosa (1968–)

162. Ken Griffey, Jr. (1969–)

163. Ben Wallace (1974–)

164. Tim Duncan (1976–)

A Search of African American Life, Achievement and Culture

Select Bibliography

Adolescence

Altman, Susan. *Extraordinary Black Americans*. Chicago: Children's Press, 1989.

Brownmiller, Susan. *Shirley Chisholm, A Biography*. Garden City, New York: Doubleday & Company, 1971.

Burt, Olive. *Jim Beckwourth, Crow Chief*. New York: Julian Messner, 1957.

David, Jay. *Growing Up Black*. New York: Pocket Books, 1969.

Fenderson, Lewis H. *Daniel Hale Williams, Open-Heart Doctor*. New York: McGraw-Hill, 1971.

Gilman, Michael. *Black Americans of Achievement, Matthew Henson*. New York: Chelsea House Publishers, 1988.

Graham, Shirley. *Booker T. Washington, Educator of Hand and Heart*. New York: Julian Messner, 1955.

————. *Dr. George Washington Carver, Scientist*. New York: Julian Messner, 1965.

————. *Paul Robeson, Citizen of the World*. New York: Julian Messner, 1971.

————. *The Story of Phillis Wheatley*. New York: Julian Messner, 1949.

————. *There Was Once a Slave*. New York: Julian Messner, 1947.

Hamilton, Virginia. *In the Beginning, Creation Stories from Around the World*. New York: Harcourt Brace Jovanovich, 1988.

————. *M.C. Higgins, the Great*. New York: Macmillan, 1974.

————. *The Planet of Junior Brown*. New York: Macmillan, 1971.

————. *W.E.B. Du Bois, A Biography*. New York: Thomas Y. Crowell, 1972.

Hansen, Joyce. *Which Way Freedom*. New York: Walker and Company, 1986.

Haskins, James. *Lena Horne*. New York: Coward-McCann, 1983.

————. *Ralph Bunche, A Most Reluctant Hero*. New York: Hawthorn Books, Inc., 1974.

Hayden, Robert C. and Jacqueline Harris. *Famous Negro Heroes of America*. New York: Dodd, Mead & Company, 1958.

Hughes, Langston. *Famous Negro Heroes of America*. New York: Dodd, Mead & Company, 1958.

Hunter, Kristin. *Soul Brothers and Sister Lou*. New York: Charles Scribner's Sons, 1968.

Jackson, Jesse. *Make a Joyful Noise Unto the Lord! The Life of Mahalia Jackson, Queen of Gospel Music*. New York: Thomas Y. Crowell, 1974.

Johnson, Charles S. *Growing Up in the Black Belt*. New York: Schocken Books, 1967.

Jones, Reginald L. *Black Adolescents*. Berkeley, California: Cobb & Henry, 1989.

Lewis, Claude. *Benjamin Banneker, The Man Who Saved Washington*. New York: McGraw-Hill, 1970.

Libby, Bill. *Joe Louis, The Brown Bomber*. New York: Lothrop, Lee & Shepard Books, 1980.

Mathews, Marcia M. *Richard Allen*. Baltimore: Helicon Press, 1963.

Melzer, Milton. *Langston Hughes, A Biography*. New York: Thomas Y. Crowell, 1968.

Petry, Ann L., *Harriet Tubman, Conductor on the Underground Railroad*. New York: Thomas Y. Crowell, 1955.

Rollins, Charlemae H. *Black Troubadour: Langston Hughes*. New York: Rand McNally, 1970.

———. *Famous American Negro Poets*. New York: Dodd, Mead & Company, 1965.

———. *They Showed the Way, Forty American Negro Leaders*. New York: Thomas Y. Crowell, 1964.

Rubin, Robert. *Satchel Paige, All-Time Baseball Great*. New York: G.P. Putnam's Sons, 1974.

Standford, Barbara Dodds and Karima Amin. *Black Literature for High School Students*. Urbana: National Council of Teachers of English, 1978.

Sterne, Emma Gelders. *Mary McLeod Bethune*. New York: Alfred A. Knopf, 1957.

Stull, Edith. *Unsung Black Americans*. New York: Grosset & Dunlap, 1971.

Taylor, Mildred D. *Let the Circle Be Unbroken*. New York: Dial Press, 1981.

———. *Roll of Thunder, Hear My Cry*. New York: Dial Books, 1976.

———. *The Road to Memphis*. New York: Dial Books, 1990.

Woodson, Carter G. and Charles H. Wesley. *Negro Makers of History*. Washington, D.C.: Associated Publishers, 1986.

Yates, Elizabeth. *Amos Fortune, Free Man*. New York: E.P. Dutton & Co., 1962.

Art

Adams, Alexander B. *John James Audubon*. New York: G.P. Putnam's Sons, 1966.

Ailey, Alvin. *Alvin Ailey, City Center Dance Theatre*. New York: Souvenir, 1973.

Alinder, James, ed. *Roy DeCarava Photographs*. Carmel, California: The Friends of Photography, 1981.

Anacostia Neighborhood Museum. *The Barnett Aden Collection*. Washington, D.C.: Smithsonian Institution Press, 1974.

Bearden, Romare and Harry Henderson. *History of African-American Artists: From 1792 to the Present*. New York: Pantheon Books, 1993.

——. *Six Black Masters of American Art*. New York: Zenith Books, Doubleday & Company, 1972.

Biggers, John, Carroll Simms, John Edward Weems. *Black Art in Houston, The Texas Southern University Experience*. College Station: Texas A&M University Press, 1978.

Bontemps, Arna A. *Forever Free: Art by African American Women 1862–1980*. Alexandria, Virginia: Stephenson, 1980.

Brown, Milton W. *Jacob Lawrence*. New York: Dodd, Mead & Company, 1974.

Cederholm, Theresa Dickason. *Afro-American Artists, A Bio-bibliographical Directory*. Boston: Trustees of the Boston Public Library, 1973.

Davis, Lenwood G. and Janet L. Sims. *Black Artists in the United States, An Annotated Bibliography of Books, Articles, and Dissertations on Black Artists, 1779–1979*. Westport, Connecticut: Greenwood Press, 1980.

Dover, Cedric. *American Negro Art*. New York: New York Graphic Society, 1970.

Driskell, David C. *Hidden Heritage: Afro-American Art, 1800–1950*. Bellevue, Washington: Nissha Printing, 1987.

——. *Two Centuries of Black American Art*. New York: Alfred A. Knopf, 1976.

Fax, Elton C. *Black Artists of the New Generation*. New York: Dodd, Mead & Company, 1977.

Foresta, Merry A. *A Life in Art: Alma Thomas, 1891–1978*. Washington, D.C.: Smithsonian Press, 1981.

Hartingan, Lynda Roscoe. *Sharing Traditions, Five Black Artists in Nineteenth-Century America*. Washington, D.C.: Smithsonian Institution Press, 1985.

Hudson, Ralph. *Black Artists/South*. Huntsville, Alabama: Huntsville Museum of Art, 1979.

Igoe, Lynn Moody and James Igoe. *250 Years of Afro-American Art, An Annotated Bibliography*. New York: R.R. Bowker, 1981.

Lewis, Samella. *The Art of Elizabeth Catlett*. Los Angeles: Hancraft Studios, 1984.

Livington, Jane and John Beardsley. *Black Folk Art in America, 1930–1980*. University, Mississippi: Corcoran Gallery of Art, 1983.

Locke, Alain Leroy. *The Negro in Art*. Washington, D.C.: Association in Negro Folk Education, 1940.

Mathews, Marcia M. *Henry Ossawa Tanner, American Artist*. Chicago: University of Chicago Press, 1969.

McElroy, Guy C. *African American Artists 1880–1987*. Washington, D.C.: Smithsonian Institution Press, 1989.

National Portrait Gallery, Smithsonian Institution. *National Portrait Gallery, Smithsonian Institution, Permanent Collection Illustrated Checklist, Twenty-Fifth Anniversary Edition*. Washington, D.C.: Smithsonian Institution Press, 1989.

Patterson, Lindsay, ed. *The Negro in Music and Art*. New York: Publishers Company, 1968.

Porter, James A. *Modern Negro Art*. New York: Arno Press, 1969.

Powell, Richard J. *Homecoming, The Art and Life of William H. Johnson*. Washington, D.C.: National Museum of Art, Smithsonian Institution, 1991.

Rhodes, Bertha N. *Guide to African-American Museums and Galleries*. Baltimore, Maryland: Bertha N. Rhodes, 1988.

Rodman, Selden and Carol Cleaver. *Horace Pippin, the Artist as a Black American*. Garden City, New York: Doubleday & Company, 1972.

Rubinstein, Charlotte S. *American Women Artists from Early Indian Times to the Present*. Boston and New York: G.K. Hall and Avon Books, 1982.

Washington, M. Bunch. *The Art of Romare Bearden*. New York: Henry N. Abrams, 1973.

Business and Professional Associations

Anderson, Jarvis A. *Philip Randolph, A Biographical Portrait*. New York: Harcourt Brace Jovanovich, 1973.

Bundles, A'Lelia Perry, *Madam C.J. Walker*. New York: Chelsea House, 1991.

Buni, Andrew. *Robert L. Vann of the Pittsburgh Courier*. Pittsburgh: University of Pittsburgh Press, 1974.

Cross, Theodore L. *Black Capitalism*. New York: Atheneum, 1969.

Davis, Daniel S. *Mr. Black Labor*. New York: E.P. Dutton & Co., 1972.

Douty, Ester M. *Forten, The Sailmaker*. New York: Rand McNally, 1968.

Foner, Philip S. *Organized Labor and the Black Worker, 1619–1981*. New York: International Publishers, 1982.

Harris, Sheldon H. *Paul Cuffe, Black America and the African Return*. New York: Simon and Schuster, 1972.

Hope, John, II. *Equality of Opportunity, A Union Approach to Fair Employment.* Washington, D.C.: Public Affairs Press, 1956.

Johnson, John H. *Succeeding Against the Odds.* New York: Warner Books, 1989.

Ottley, Roi. *The Lonely Warrior, The Life and Times of Robert S. Abbott.* Chicago: Henry Regnery, 1955.

Seder, John and Berkeley G. Burrell. *Getting It Together, Black Businessmen in America.* New York: Harcourt Brace Jovanovich, 1971.

Walker, Juliet E.K., ed. *Encyclopedia of African American Business History.* Westport, Connecticut: Greenwood Press, 1999.

Weare, Walter B. *Black Business in the New South, A Social History of the North Carolina Mutual Life Insurance Company.* Urbana: University of Illinois Press, 1994.

Children

Aardema, Verna. *Why Mosquitoes Buzz in Peoples Ears.* New York: Dial Books for Young Readers, 1975.

Adler, David A. *Martin Luther King, Jr., Free at Last.* New York: Holiday House, 1986.

Baker, Augusta. *The Black Experience in Children's Books.* New York: New York Public Library, 1971.

Barclay, Pamela. *Charley Pride.* Mankato: Creative Educational Society, 1975.

Brooks, Gwendolyn. *Bronzeville Boys and Girls.* New York: Harper & Brothers, 1956.

Bryan, Asley. *I'm Going to Sing Black American Spirituals.* Vol. 2. New York: Atheneum, 1984.

Burt, Olive W. *Black Women of Valor.* New York: Julian Messner, 1974.

Caines, Jeannette. *Just Us Women.* New York: Harper & Row, 1982.

Clifton, Lucille. *Don't You Remember.* New York: E.P. Dutton & Co., 1973.

Cummings, Pat. *Jimmy Lee Did It.* New York: Lothrop, Lee & Shepard Books, 1985.

Davis, Burke. *Black Heroes of the American Revolution.* New York: Harcourt Brace Jovanovich, 1976.

Deegan, Paul J. *Michael Jordan, Basketball's Soaring Star.* Minneapolis: Lerner Publications, 1988.

Felton, Harold W. *Edward Rose, Negro Trail Blazer.* New York: Alfred A. Knopf, 1950.

———. *Jim Beckwourth, Negro Mountain Man.* New York: Dodd, Mead & Company, 1966.

———. *John Henry and his Hammer.* New York: Alfred A. Knopf, 1950.

———. *Mumbet, The Story of Elizabeth Freeman.* New York: Dodd, Mead & Company, 1970.

———. *Nat Love, Negro Cowboy.* New York: Dodd, Mead & Company, 1969.

Gause-Jackson, Arlene and Barbara Banks-Hayes. *Champions of Change.* Irvine, California: Steck-Vaughn, 1989.

Gentry, Tony. *Paul Laurence Dunbar.* New York: Chelsea House, 1989.

Giles, Lucille H. and Louis F. Holmes. *Color Me Brown.* Chicago: Johnson Publishing Company, 1976.

Giovanni, Nikki. *Ego-Tripping.* Chicago: Lawrence Hill Books, 1973.

———. *Spin a Soft Black Song.* New York: A Sunburst Book, Hill and Wang, 1985.

Goodman, Michael E. *Magic Johnson.* New York: Crestwood House, 1988.

Goss, Linda and Clay Goss. *The Baby Leopard, An African Folktale.* New York: Bantam Books, 1989.

Greenfield, Eloise, *Grandpa's Face.* New York: Philomel Books, 1988.

———. *Mary McLeod Bethune.* New York: Thomas Y. Crowell, 1977.

Haskins, James and Kathleen Bentson. *Space Challenger, The Story of Guion Bluford.* Minneapolis: Carol Rhonda Books, 1984.

Hess, Debra. *Thurgood Marshall, The Fight for Equal Justice.* Englewood Cliffs, New Jersey: Silver Burdett Press, 1990.

Hopson, Derek S. and Darlene Powell-Hopson. *Different and Wonderful: Raising Black Children in a Race-Conscious Society.* New York: Prentice-Hall, 1991.

Hughes, Langston. *Don't You Turn Back.* New York: Alfred A. Knopf, 1969.

Johns, Bessie and Bess Lomax Hawes. *Step It Down, Games, Plays, Songs & Stories from the Afro-American Heritage.* Athens: University of Georgia Press, 1987.

Jordan, June. *Fannie Lou Hamer.* New York: Thomas Y. Crowell, 1972.

Knowlton, Jack. *Geography from A to Z.* New York: Thomas Y. Crowell, 1988.

Kunjufu, Jawanza. *Developing Positive Self-Images and Discipline in Black Children.* Chicago: African-American Images, 1984.

Laflin, Edward Beecher. *Sojourner Truth and the Struggle for Freedom.* New York: Barron's Educational Series, 1987.

Lawrence, Jacob. *Harriet and the Promised Land.* New York: Windmill Books, 1968.

Lester, Julius. *The Tales of Uncle Remus: The Adventures of Br'er Rabbit.* New York: Dial Books, 1987.

———. *To Be a Slave*. New York: Dell Publishing, 1968.

Manber, David. *Wizard of Tuskegee*. New York: Macmillan, 1967.

Martinello, Marian L. and Melvin M. Sance. *A Personal History: The Afro-American Texans, Stories for Young Readers*. San Antonio: University of Texas, 1982.

McKissack, Patricia C. *Jesse Jackson, A Biography*. New York: Scholastic, 1989.

———. *Mirandy and Brother Wind*. New York: Alfred A. Knopf, 1988.

——— and Fredrick McKissack. *Frederick Douglass, The Black Lion*. Chicago: Children's Press, 1987.

———. *W.E.B. Du Bois*. New York: Franklin Watts, 1990.

Meltzer, Milton. *Mary McLeod Bethune, Voice of Black Hope*. New York: Viking Kestrel, 1987.

Meriwether, Louise. *The Heart Man*. Englewood Cliffs: Prentice-Hall, 1972.

Millender, Dharathula H. *Crispus Attucks, Boy of Valor*. New York: Bobbs-Merrill, 1965.

Musgrove, Margaret. *Ashanti to Zulu*. New York: Dial Press, 1976.

Patterson, Lillie. *Sure Hands Strong Heart, The Life of Daniel Hale Williams*. Nashville, Tennessee: Abingdon, 1981.

Petry, Ann. *Harriet Tubman, Conductor on the Underground Railroad*. New York: Thomas Y. Crowell, 1955.

Rollins, Charlemae, ed. *We Build Together*. Champaign, Illinois: National Council of Teachers of English, 1967.

Shepard, Betty. *Mountain Man, Indian Chief, The Life and Adventures of Jim Beckwourth*. New York: Harcourt, Brace & World, 1968.

Steptoe, John. *Mufaro's Beautiful Daughters*. New York: Lothrop, Lee & Shepard Books, 1987.

———. *Stevie*. New York: Harper & Row, 1969.

———. *The Story of the Jumping Mouse*. New York: Lothrop, Lee & Shepard Books, 1984.

Sterling, Dorothy. *Captain of the Planter*. Garden City, New York: Doubleday & Company, 1958.

Taylor, Mildred D. *The Friendship*. New York: Dial Books for Young Readers, 1987.

Walker, Alice. *Langston Hughes, American Poet*. New York: Thomas Y. Crowell, 1974.

Walter, Mildred P. *My Momma Needs Me*. New York: Lothrop, Lee & Shepard Books, 1983.

Winslow, Eugene. *Afro-American '76, Black Americans in the Founding of Our Nation.* Chicago: Afro-Am Publishing, 1973.

Woods, Harold. *Bill Cosby, Making America Laugh and Learn.* Minneapolis: Dillion Press, 1983.

Education

Butler, Addie Louise Joyner. *The Distinctive Black College: Talladega, Tuskegee and Morehouse.* Metuchen, New Jersey: Scarecrow Press, 1977.

Campbell, Clarice T. and Oscar Allen Rogers, Jr. *Mississippi: The View From Tougaloo.* Jackson: University Press of Mississippi, 1979.

Chambers, Frederick, comp. *Black Higher Education in the United States.* Westport, Connecticut: Greenwood Press, 1978.

Children's Books: Awards & Prizes, Including Prizes for Young Adult Books. New York: Children's Book Council, 1986.

Davis, John P. *The American Negro Reference Book.* Englewood Cliffs, New Jersey: Prentice-Hall, 1966.

Du Bois, W.E.B. *The Souls of Black Folk.* New York: Avon Books, 1965.

Forten, Charlotte L. *Journal of Charlotte Forten, A Free Negro in the Slave Era.* New York: W.W. Norton, 1953.

Hicks, Florence Johnson. *Mary McLeod Bethune, Her Own Words of Inspiration.* Washington, D.C.: Nuclassics and Science Publishing, 1975.

Holt, Rackham. *Mary McLeod Bethune, A Biography.* Garden City, New York: Doubleday & Company, 1964.

Hughes, William Hardin and Frederick D. Patterson. *Robert Russa Moton of Hampton and Tuskegee.* Chapel Hill: University of North Carolina Press, 1956.

Mays, Benjamin E. *Born To Rebel.* Athens: University of Georgia Press, 1987.

Mitzel, Harold E., ed. *Encyclopedia of Educational Research.* New York: Free Press, 1982.

Ohles, John F. and Shirley M. Ohles. *Private Colleges and Universities.* Westport, Connecticut: Greenwood Press, 1982.

Peterson, Linda Kaufman and Maryland Leathers Solt. *Newberry and Caldecott Medal and Honor Books.* Boston: G.K. Hall & Co., 1982.

Rhodes, Lelia Gaston. *Jackson State University, The First Hundred Years 1877–1977.* Jackson: University Press of Mississippi, 1979.

Richardson, Joe M. *A History of Fisk University, 1865–1946.* University, Alabama: University of Alabama Press, 1980.

Schlachter, Gail C. *Directory of Financial Aids for Minorities*. San Carlos, California: Reference Service Press, 1989.

Summerville, James. *Educating Black Doctors, A History of Meharry Medical College*. University, Alabama: University of Alabama Press, 1983.

Torrence, Ridgely. *The Story of John Hope*. New York: Arno Press and New York Times, 1969.

Walker, Alyce B., ed. *Alabama, A Guide to the Deep South*. New York: Hastings House, 1975.

Washington, Booker T. *Up from Slavery*. New York: Avon Books, 1965.

Weinberg, Meyer. *The Education of Poor and Minority Children, A World Bibliography, Supplement, 1979-1985*. Westport, Connecticut: Greenwood Press, 1981.

————, comp. *The Education of Poor and Minority Children, A World Bibliography*. Vols. 1–2. Westport, Connecticut: Greenwood Press, 1981.

————, comp. *The Education of the Minority Child*. Chicago: Integrated Education Associates, 1970.

Wesley, Charles H. *The Quest for Equality from Civil War to Civil Rights*. New York: Publishers Company, 1969.

Woodson, Carter G. *The Education of the Negro Prior to 1861*. New York: Arno Press and New York Times, 1968.

————. *The Mis-Education of the Negro*. New York: AMS Press, 1977.

Entertainment

1990 International Television & Radio Almanac. New York: Quigley Publishing, 1990.

Anderson, Marian. *My Lord, What a Morning, An Autobiography*. New York: Viking Press, 1956.

Arvey, Verna. *In One Lifetime*. Fayetteville: University of Arkansas Press, 1984.

Bailey, Pearl. *The Raw Pearl*. New York: Harcourt, Brace & World, 1968.

Baker, Josephine and Jo Bouillon. *Josephine*. New York: Paragon House Publishers, 1988.

Bogle, Donald. *Blacks in American Films and Television, An Encyclopedia*. New York: Garland Publishing, 1989.

Brown, Scott E. *James P. Johnson, A Case of Mistaken Identity*. Scarecrow Press and Institute of Jazz Studies, Rutgers University, 1960.

Bryan, Ashley. *I'm Going to Sing Black American Spirituals*. Vol. 2. New York: Atheneum, 1960.

Davis, Sammy, Jr., Jane Boyar, and Burt Boyar. *Why Me?* New York: Warner Books, 1989.

Ellington, Duke. *Music Is My Mistress*. Garden City, New York: Doubleday & Company, 1973.

Fuller, Charles. *A Soldier's Play*. New York: Hill and Wang, 1985.

Hampton, Lionel and James Haskins. *Hamp*. New York: Warner Books, 1989.

Handy, William C. *Father of the Blues*. New York: Macmillan, 1941.

————, ed. *A Treasury of the Blues*. New York: Simon and Schuster. 1949.

Haskins, James. *Black Music in America*. New York: Thomas Y. Crowell Junior Books, 1987.

Haskins, Jim and N.R. Mitgang. *Mr. Bojangles, The Biography of Bill Robinson*. New York: William Morrow and Company, 1988.

Holiday, Billie and William Dufty. *Lady Sings the Blues*. New York: Penguin Books, 1984.

Horne, Lena and Richard Schickel. *Lena*. Garden City, New York: Doubleday & Company, 1965.

Jackson, Jesse. *Make a Joyful Noise Unto the Lord! The Life of Mahalia Jackson, Queen of Gospel Music*. New York: Thomas Y. Crowell, 1974.

Kernfield, Barry, ed. *The New Grove Dictionary of Jazz*, Vols. 1–3. New York: MacMillan Publishers Limited, London Grove's Dictionaries, 2002.

Kitt, Eartha. *Alone with Me, A New Autobiography by Eartha Kitt*. Chicago: Henry Regnery, 1976.

Lee, George W. *Beale Street*. New York: Robert O. Ballou, 1934.

Lieb, Sandra. *Mother of the Blues: A Study of Ma Rainey*. Amherst: University of Massachusetts Press, 1981.

Locke, Alain. *The Negro and His Music*. Washington, D.C.: Associates in Negro Folk Education, 1936.

Marsh, J.B.T. *The Story of the Jubilee Singers; With Their Songs*. New York: AMS Press, 1971.

Moore, Carmen. *Somebody's Angel Child, The Story of Bessie Smith*. New York: Thomas Y. Crowell, 1969.

Patterson, Lindsay, ed. and comp. *Anthology of the American Negro in the Theatre*. New York: Publishers Company, 1968.

Schauffler, Robert A. *Beethoven, The Man Who Freed Music*. New York: Doubleday & Company, 1951.

Taylor, Frank C. *Alberta Hunter, A Celebration in Blues*. New York: McGraw-Hill, 1987.

Thomas, J.C. *Chasin' the Trane, The Music and Mystique of John Coltrane*. Garden City, New York: Doubleday & Company, 1975.

Troupe, Quincy. *Miles, The Autobiography*. New York: Simon and Schuster, 1989.

Waters, Ethel. *His Eye Is on the Sparrow*. Garden City, New York: Doubleday & Company, 1951.

Geography

Cloyd, Iris, ed. *Who's Who Among Black Americans 1990/91*. New York: Gale Research, 1990.

Graham, Shirley. *Jean Baptiste Pointe du Sable, Founder of Chicago*. New York: Julian Messner, 1953.

Hansen, Harry. *The Chicago*. New York: Farrar & Rinehart, 1942.

Henson, Matthew A. *A Black Explorer at the North Pole*. New York: Walker and Company, 1969.

Holtzclaw, Robert Fulton. *Black Magnolias*. Shaker Heights, Ohio: Keeble Press, 1984.

Johnson, Daniel M. and Rex R. Campbell. *Black Migration in America*. Durham, North Carolina: Duke University Press, 1981.

Katz, William Loren. *The Black West*. Garden City, New York: Doubleday & Company, 1971.

Lewis, Captain Meriwether and Sergeant John Ordway. *The Journals of Captain Meriwether Lewis and Sergeant John Ordway*. Madison: State Historical Society of Wisconsin, 1965.

Madariaga, Salvador de. *Christopher Columbus*. New York: Frederick Ungar, 1967.

McAdoo, Harriette Pipes, ed. *Black Families*. Beverly Hills, California: Sage Publications, 1988.

Poloski, Harry A. and James Williams, eds. and comp. *The Negro Almanac, A Reference Work on the African American*. Detroit: Gale Research, 1989.

Porter, Kenneth W. *The Negro on the American Frontier*. New York: Arno Press and New York Times, 1971.

Terrell, John Upton. *Estivanico, The Black*. Los Angeles: Westernlore Press, 1968.

Wilson, Elinor. *Jim Beckwourth, Black Mountain Man and War Chief of the Crows*. Norman: University of Oklahoma Press, 1972.

History and Civil Rights

Barr, Alwyn. *Black Texans*. Austin, Texas: Jenkins Publishing, 1982.

Baskin, Wade and Richard N. Runes. *Dictionary of Black Culture*. New York: Philosophical Library, 1973.

Bennett, Lerone, Jr. *Before the Mayflower, A History of Black America*. Chicago: Johnson Publishing, 1987.

Blassingame, John W. *Black New Orleans, 1860–1880*. Chicago: University of Chicago Press, 1973.

Boyd, Herb and Robert L. Allen, eds. *Brotherman: The Odyssey of Black Men in America*. New York: One World/Ballantine Books, c.1995.

Bradford, Sarah. *Harriet Tubman, The Moses of Her People*. Secaucus, New Jersey: Citadel Press, 1961.

Cheek, William and Aimee Lee Cheek. *John Mercer Langston and the Fight for Black Freedom*. Chicago: University of Illinois Press, 1989.

Christopher, Maurine. *America's Black Congressmen*. New York: Thomas Y. Crowell, 1971.

Corbin, Raymond M. *1990 Facts About Blacks*. Providence, Rhode Island: Beckham House, 1986.

Cutler, John Henry. *Ed Brooke, Biography of a Senator*. New York: Bobbs-Merrill, 1972.

Dannett, Sylvia G.L. *Profiles of Negro Womanhood, 20th Century*. Yonkers, New York: Educational Heritage, 1966.

Davis, Joe Tom. *Legendary Texans*. Austin, Texas: Eakin Press, 1986.

Dickerson, M. Ashley. *Delayed Justice for Sale*. Anchorage: Al-Acres, 1991.

Douglass, Frederick. *Life and Times of Frederick Douglass*. New York: Collier Books, 1962.

———. *My Bondage and My Freedom*. New York: Arno Press and New York Times, 1968.

Du Bois, W.E.B. *Black Reconstruction in America*. New York: Russell & Russell, 1935.

Durant, Will. *The Story of Philosophy, The Lives and Opinions of the Greater Philosophers*. New York: Simon and Schuster, 1961.

Duster, Alfreda M., ed. *Crusade for Justice, The Autobiography of Ida B. Wells*. Chicago: University of Chicago Press, 1970.

Dwight, Margeret L. *Mississippi Black History*. Oxford: University Press of Mississippi, 1984.

Farmer, James. *Freedom-When?* New York: Random House, 1965.

Fehrenbacher, Don E. *The Dred Scott Case, Its Significance in American Law and Politics*. New York: Oxford University Press, 1978.

Foner, Philip S. *History of Black Americans, from Africa to the Emergence of the Cotton Kingdom*. Westport, Connecticut: Greenwood Press, 1975.

————. *History of Black Americans, from the Compromise of 1850 to the End of the Civil War.* Westport, Connecticut: Greenwood Press, 1983.

Franklin, Jimmie Lewis. *The Blacks in Oklahoma.* Norman: University of Oklahoma Press, 1980.

Franklin, John Hope. *From Slavery to Freedom.* New York: Vintage Books, 1967.

Frazier, Edward Franklin. *The Negro Family.* Chicago: University of Chicago Press, 1969.

Garvey, Marcus. *The Philosophy and Opinions of Marcus Garvey, or Africa for the Africans/Compiled by Amy Jacques.* Dover, Massachusetts: Majority Press, 1986.

Gilbert, Olive. *Narrative of Sojourner Truth.* Salem, New Hampshire: Ayer Company, 1967.

Haskins, James. *Pinckney Benton Stewart Pinchback.* New York: Macmillan, 1973.

Hicks, Nancy. *The Honorable Shirley Chisholm.* New York: Lion Books, 1971.

Jackson, Miles M. *And They Came A Brief History and Annotated Bibliography of Blacks in Hawaii.* Kaneohe: FOUR-G Publishers, 2000.

Jordan, Barbara and Shelby Hearon. *Barbara Jordan, A Self-Portrait.* Garden City, New York: Doubleday & Company, 1979.

Karenga, Maulana. *The African American Holiday of Kwanzaa.* Los Angeles: University of Sankore Press, 1988.

Katz, William Loren. *Teacher's Guide to American Negro History.* Chicago: Quadrangle Books, 1971.

————. *The Black West.* Seattle, Washington: Open Hand Publishing 1987.

Khan, Lurey. *One Day, Levin ... He Be Free, William Still and the Underground Railroad.* New York: E.P. Dutton & Co., 1972.

King, Martin Luther, Jr. *The Words of Martin Luther King, Jr.* New York: Newmarket Press, 1987.

Klingman, Peter D. *Josiah Walls, Florida's Black Congressman of Reconstruction.* Gainesville: University Presses of Florida, 1976.

Logan, Rayford W. and Michale R. Winston, eds. *Dictionary of American Negro Biography.* New York: W.W. Norton & Company, 1982

Low, W. Augustus, and Virgil A. Clift, eds. *Encyclopedia of Black America.* New York: McGraw-Hill, 1981.

Lynch, John R. *Reminiscences of an Active Life, The Autobiography of John Roy Lynch.* Chicago: University of Chicago Press, 1970.

Mullins, Joseph G. *Hawaiian Journey.* Honolulu: Mutual Publishing Company, 1978.

Overstreet, Everett Louis. *Black on a Background of White.* Anchorage: Alaska Black Caucus, 1988.

Pease, Jane H. and William H. Pease. *Those Who Would Be Free, Blacks' Search for Freedom, 1830–1861*. New York: Atheneum, 1974.

Powell, Adam Clayton, Jr. *Adam by Adam*. New York: Dial Press, 1971.

Quarles, Benjamin. *Black Abolitionists*. New York: Oxford University Press, 1969.

Richardson, Ben and A. Fahey. *Great Black Americans*. New York: Thomas Y. Crowell, 1976.

Robinson, Wilhelmena S., ed. *Historical Negro Biographies*. New York: Publishers Company, 1968.

Rogers, J. A. *100 Amazing Facts About the Negro*. St. Petersburg, Florida: Helga M. Rogers, 1957.

Rowan, Carl T. *Breaking Barriers*. Boston: Little, Brown and Company, 1991.

Schweninger, Loren. *James T. Rapier and Reconstruction*. Chicago: University of Chicago Press, 1978.

Smith, Jessie Carney, ed. *Notable Black American Women*. Detroit: Gale Research, 1992.

Sterling, Dorothy. *We Are Your Sisters, Black Women in the Nineteenth Century*. New York: W.W. Norton & Company, 1984.

Thurman, Howard. *Jesus and the Disinherited*. Boston, Massachusetts: Beacon Press, c.1996.

Turner, Martha Anne. *The Yellow Rose of Texas, Her Saga and Her Song*. Austin, Texas: Shoal Creek Publishers, 1976.

Wesley, Charles H., ed. *The Quest for Equality*. New York: Publishers Company, 1969.

Williams, Juan. *Eyes on the Prize*. New York: Viking Penguin, 1987.

Woodson, Carter G. *The History of the Negro Church*. Washington, D.C.: Associated Publishers, 1945.

World Book Encyclopedia. Chicago: World Book, 1970.

X, Malcolm and Alex Haley. *The Autobiography of Malcolm X*. New York: Grove Press, 1966.

Literature

Albert, Octavia. *The House of Bondage*. New York: Oxford University Press, 1988.

Angelou, Maya. *I Know Why the Caged Bird Sings*. New York: Random House, 2002.

Baldwin, James. *Blues for Mister Charlie*. New York: French, c.1964.

———. *Giovannie's Room*. New York: Dell, 1988.

———. *Go Tell It on the Mountain.* New York: Bantam Doubleday Dell Publishing Group, 1985.

———. *If Beale Street Could Talk.* New York: Bantam Doubleday Dell Publishing Group, 1974.

———. *Nobody Knows My Name.* New York: Dial Press, 1961.

———. *The Fire Next Time.* New York: Vintage International, 1993.

Bontemps, Arna. *We Have Tomorrow.* Boston: Houghton Mifflin, 1945.

Bradley, David. *The Chaneysville Incident.* New York: Harper & Row, c.1981.

Brawley, Edward M. *The Negro in Literature and Art.* New York: AMS Press, 1971.

Brooks, Gwendolyn. *Annie Allen.* Westport, Connecticut: Greenwood Press, 1971.

———. *Bronzeville Boys and Girls.* New York: Harper, c.1956.

Butler, Octavia E. *Kindred.* Garden City, New York: Doubleday, 1979.

———. *Survivor.* Garden City, New York: Doubleday, 1978.

Chase-Riboud, Barbara. *Sally Hemings.* New York: Viking Press, 1979.

Contemporary Authors, Autobiography Series. New York: Gale Research, 1992.

Cooper, Wayne. *The Passion of Claude McKay.* New York: Schocken Books, 1973.

Cullen, Countee. *On These I Stand.* New York: Harper & Brothers, 1947.

Davis, Ursula Broschke. *Paris Without Regret, James Baldwin, Kenny Clark, Chester Himes, and Donald Byrd.* Iowa City: University of Iowa Press, 1986.

DeCarava, Roy and Langston Hughes. *The Sweet Flypaper of Life.* New York: Hill and Wang, 1955.

Dictionary of Literary Biography, American Poets, 1880–1945. Second Series, Vol. 46. Detroit: Gale Research, 1986.

Dumas, Henry. *Play Ebony, Play Ivory.* New York: Random House, 1974.

Dunbar, Paul Laurence. *Lyrics of Lowly Life.* Upper Saddle River, New Jersey: Gregg Press, 1968 [first published in 1896 by Dodd, Mead & Company].

———. *The Sport of Gods.* New York: Dodd, Mead & Company, 1981.

Ellison, Ralph. *Invisible Man.* New York: Vantage Books, Division of Random House, 1989.

Fanon, Frantz. *Black Skin, White Masks.* New York: Grove Press, 1967.

Gaines, Ernest J. *A Lesson Before Dying.* New York: Vintage Contemporaries, 1994.

———. *Bloodline*. New York: Norton, 1976.

———. *In My Father's House*. New York: Knopf; distributed by Random, 1978.

———. *The Autobiography of Miss Jane Pittman*. New York: Bantam Books, 1972.

Genovese, Eugene D. *Roll, Jordan, Roll, The World the Slaves Made*. New York: Pantheon Books, 1974.

Greenlee, Sam. *The Spook Who Sat by the Door*. Detroit: Wayne State University Press, 1990.

Griggs, Sutton. *Imperium in Imperico*. New York: Arno Press and New York Times, 1969.

Haley, Alex. *Roots: Saga of an American Family*. Garden City, New York: Doubleday and Company, 1976.

Hercules, Frank. *I Want a Black Doll*. New York: Simon and Schuster, 1967.

Himes, Chester B. *Cotton Comes to Harlem*. New York: Vintage Books, 1988.

———. *If He Hollers Let Him Go*. New York: Thunder's Mouth Press (Berkeley, California), distributed by Publishers Group West, 2002.

Hughes, Langston. *Not Without Laughter*. New York: Scribner Paperback Fiction, 1995.

———. *Selected Poems of Langston Hughes*. New York: Vintage Books Edition, Random House, 1974.

———. *Simple Speaks His Mind*. Mattituck, New York: Aeonian Press, 1976.

———. *The Best of Simple*. New York: Hill and Wang, 1961.

———. *The Big Sea*. New York: Thunder's Mouth Press, 1989.

——— and Arna Bontemps, eds. *The Book of Negro Folklore*. New York: Dodd, Mead & Company, 1958.

———. *The Poetry of the Negro 1746–1970*. Garden City, New York: Doubleday & Company, 1970.

Hunter, Kristin. *God Bless the Child*. New York: Charles Scribner's Sons, 1964.

Hurston, Zora Neale. *Dust Tracks on a Road*. New York: Harper Perennial, 1991.

———. *Their Eyes Were Watching God*. New York: Perennial Classics, 1998.

Johnson, James W. *The Autobiography of an Ex-Colored Man*. New York: Avon Books, 1965.

Johnson, James Weldon. *Along This Way*. New York: Viking Press, 1967.

———. *God's Trombones*. New York: Penguin Books, 1990.

———. *The Book of American Negro Poetry*. New York: Harcourt Brace Jovanovich, 1969.

Kadiner, Abram and Lionel Ovesey. *The Mark of Oppression*. Cleveland: World Publishing, 1962.

Larsen, Nella. *Quicksand*. New York: Negro Universities Press, 1969.

Locke, Alain. *Plays of Negro Life*. Westport, Connecticut: Greenwood Press, 1970.

Marshall, Paule. *Brown Girl, Brownstones*. New York: Feminist Press at the City University of New York, 1981.

Morrison, Toni. *Beloved*. Thorndike, Maine: Thorndike Press, c.1987.

———. *Song of Solomon*. New York: Plume, 1987.

———. *Tar Baby*. New York: Alfred A. Knopf, 1990.

Motley, Willard. *Knock on Any Door*. New York: Appleton-Century-Crofts, 1947.

Patterson, Lindsay, comp. and ed. *An Introduction to Black Literature in America*. New York: Publishers Company, 1969.

Petry, Ann. *The Street*. Boston, Massachusetts: Beacon Press, 1985.

Redding, Jay Saunders. *To Make a Poet Black*. Chapel Hill: University of North Carolina Press, 1939.

Robeson, Paul. *Here I Stand*. Boston: Beacon Press, 1971.

Thurman, Wallace. *The Blacker the Berry*. New York: Simon and Schuster, 1996.

Turner, Darwin T., comp. *Afro-American Writers*. New York: Appleton-Century-Crofts, Meredith Corporation, 1970.

Walker, Alice. *The Color Purple*. New York: Washington Square Press, 1982.

Walker, Margaret. *For My People*. New Haven: Yale University Press, 1939.

———. *Jubilee*. New York, Toronto: Bantam Books, 1967.

Ward, Samuel Ringgold. *Autobiography of a Fugitive Negro*. Chicago: Johnson Publishing, 1970.

Williams, John A. *The Man Who Cried I Am*. Boston: Little, Brown and Company, 1967.

Wilson, August. *Fences*. New York: New American Library, 1986.

Woodson, Carter G. *The Works of Francis J. Grimké*. Washington, D.C.: Associated Publishers, 1942.

Wright, Richard. *Black Boy*. New York: Harper & Row, 1945.

———. *Native Son*. New York: Harper & Row, 1966.

Military History

Adler, Bill. *The Black Soldier, From the American Revolution to Vietnam.* New York: William Morrow, 1971.

Allen, Robert L. *The Port Chicago Mutiny.* New York: Warner Books, 1989.

Anderson, Trezzvant W. *Come Out Fighting!* Tersendorf, Germany: Salzburger Bruckerei und Verlag, 1945.

Brown, William Wells. *The Negro in the American Rebellion, His Heroism and His Fidelity.* New York: Citadel Press, 1974.

Cashin, Herschel V., ed. *Under Fire with the Tenth U.S. Cavalry.* New York: Arno Press and New York Times, 1969.

Cornish, Dudley Taylor. *The Sable Arm.* Lawrence: University Press of Kansas, 1987.

Davis, Benjamin O., Jr. *Benjamin O. Davis, Jr., American.* Washington, D.C.: Smithsonian Institution Press, 1991.

Drotning, Phillip T. *Black Heroes in Our Nation's History.* New York: Cowles Book Company, 1969.

Emilio, Luis F. *A Brave Black Regiment, A History of the Fifty-Fourth Regiment of Massachusetts Volunteer Infantry, 1863–1865.* New York: Arno Press and New York Times, 1969.

Ferguson, William C. *Black Flyers in World War II.* Los Angeles: William C. Ferguson, 1987.

Fletcher, Marvin E. *America's First Black General.* Lawrence: University Press of Kansas, 1989.

Flipper, Henry O. *Negro Frontiersman, The Western Memories of Henry O. Flipper, First Negro Graduate of West Point.* El Paso: Texas Western College Press, 1963.

Golstein, Ernest. *Emanuel Leutze, Washington Crossing the Delaware.* Champaign, Illinois: Garrard Publishing Company, 1983.

Hartke, Vance and the Committee on Veterans' Affairs, United States Senate. *Medal Of Honor Recipients, 1863–1973.* Washington, D.C.: U.S. Government Printing Office, 1973.

Lang, George, M.H., Raymond Collins, and Gerard White. *Medal of Honor Recipients 1863–1994, Volume 1, Civil War to 2nd Nicaraguan Campaign.* New York: Facts on File, 1995.

———. *Medal of Honor Recipients 1863–1994, Volume 2, World War II to Somalia.* New York: Facts on File, 1995.

Leckie, William H. *The Buffalo Soldiers.* Norman: University of Oklahoma Press, 1981.

Lee, Irvin H. *Negro Medal of Honor Men.* New York: Dodd, Mead & Company, 1967.

Nell, William C. *The Colored Patriots of the American Revolution*. New York: Arno Press and New York Times, 1968.

Quarles, Benjamin. *The Negro in the American Revolution*. Chapel Hill: University of North Carolina Press, 1961.

———. *The Negro in the Civil War*. New York: Russell & Russell, Division of Atheneum Publishers, 1953.

Robinson, Wilhelmena S. *Historical Negro Biographies*. New York: Publishers Company, 1968.

Taylor, Joe Gray. *Louisiana, A Bicentennial History*. New York: W.W. Norton & Company, 1976.

Taylor, Susie King. *Black Woman's Civil War Memoirs, Reminiscences of My Life in Camp with the 33rd U.S. Colored Troops Late 1st South Carolina*. New York: Markus Weiner Publishing, 1988.

Uya, Okon Edet. *From Slavery to Public Service: Robert Smalls, 1839–1915*. New York: Oxford University Press, 1971.

Wesley, Charles H. and Patricia W. Romero, eds. *Negro Americans in the Civil War*. New York: Publishers Company, 1968.

Science

Adams, Russell L. *Great Negroes, Past and Present*. Chicago: Afro-Am Publishing, 1964.

Baker, Henry E. *The Colored Inventor*. New York: Arno Press and New York Times, 1969.

Brawley, Benjamin. *Negro Builders and Heroes*. Chapel Hill: University of North Carolina Press, 1965.

Buckler, Helen. *Doctor Dan, Pioneer in American Surgery*. Boston: Little, Brown and Company, 1954.

Burt, McKinley, Jr. *Black Inventors of America*. Portland, Oregon: National Book Company, 1989.

Carwell, Hattie. *Blacks in Science: Astrophysicist to Zoologist*. Hicksville, New York: Exposition Press, 1977.

Graham, Shirley. *Your Most Humble Servant*. New York: Julian Messner, 1967.

Haber, Louis Haber. *Black Pioneers of Science & Invention*. New York: Harcourt Brace Janovich, 1970.

Hardesty, Von and Dominik Pisano. *Black Wings, The American Black in Aviation*. Washington, D.C.: National Air and Space Museum, Smithsonian Institution, 1983.

Hartwick, Richard. *Charles Richard Drew, Pioneer in Blood Research*. New York: Charles Scribner's Sons, 1967.

Hayden, Robert C. *Eight Black American Inventors*. Reading, Massachusetts: Addison-Wesley, 1972.

————. *Seven Black American Scientists*. Reading, Massachusetts: Addison-Wesley, 1970.

———— and Jacqueline Harris. *11 African American Doctors*. New York: Twenty-First Century Books, 1970.

————. *Nine Black American Doctors*. Reading, Massachusetts: Addison-Wesley, 1976.

Holt, Rackham. *George Washington Carver, An American Biography*. Garden City: Doubleday, Doran and Company, 1943.

Klein, Aaron E. *The Hidden Contributors: Black Scientists and Inventors in America*. Garden City: Doubleday & Company, 1971.

Krapp, Kristine, ed. *Notable Black American Scientist*. Detroit: Gale Research, 1999.

Lichello, Robert. *Pioneer in Blood Plasma*. New York: Julian Messner, 1968.

Manning, Kenneth R. *Black Apollo of Science, The Life of Ernest Everett Just*. New York: Oxford University Press, 1983.

Morais, Herbert M., ed. *The History of the Negro in Medicine*. New York: Publishers Company, 1968.

Ott, Virginia and Gloria Swanson. *Man With a Million Ideas, Fred Jones Genius/Inventor*. Minneapolis: Lerner Publications, 1977.

Sammons, Vivian Ovelton. *Blacks in Science and Medicine*. Washington D.C.: Hemisphere Publishing, 1990

Sertima, Ivan Van, ed. *Blacks in Science, Ancient and Modern*. London: Transaction Books, 1990.

Sports

Aaron, Henry and Lonnie Wheeler. *I Had a Hammer*. New York: HarperCollins, 1991.

Abdul-Jabbar, Kareem. *Giant Steps*. New York: Bantam Books, 1985.

Banks, Ernie and Jim Enright. *"Mr. Cub."* Chicago: Follett Publishing, 1971.

Barrow, Joe Louis, Ida Rust and Art Rust, Jr. *Joe Louis: My Life*. New York: Harcourt Brace Jovanovich, 1978.

Brown, Jim. *Out of Bounds*. New York: Zebra Books, 1989.

Duckett, Alfred. *I Never Had It Made: The Autobiography of Jackie Robinson*. New York: Putnam, 1972.

Gibson, Althea. *I Always Wanted to Be Somebody*. New York: Harper & Brothers, 1958.

Henderson, Edwin B., ed., and the Editors of *Sport* magazine. *The Black Athlete*. New York: Publishers Company, 1969.

Holway, John. *Blackball Stars Negro League Pioneers*. Westport, Connecticut: Meckler Books, 1988.

————. *Voices From The Great Black Baseball Leagues*. New York: Dodd, Mead & Company, 1975.

Jackson, Bo and Dick Schaap. *Bo Knows Bo*. New York: Doubleday, 1989.

Lemon, Meadowlark and Jerry B. Jenkins. *Meadowlark*. Nashville, Tennessee: Thomas Nelson Publishers, 1987.

Owens, Jesse. *I Have Changed*. New York: William Morrow & Company, 1972.

Paige, LeRoy (Satchel). *Maybe I'll Pitch Forever*. New York: Curtis Publishing Company, 1962.

Payton, Walter. *Sweetness*. Chicago: Contemporary Books, 1978.

Robinson, Sugar Ray and Dave Anderson. *Sugar Ray*. New York: Viking Press, 1970.

Russell, Bill and William McSweeny. *Go Up for Glory*. New York: Coward-McCann, 1966.

Sayers, Gale and Al Silverman. *I Am Third*. New York: Viking Press, 1970.

Webb, Spud and Reid Slaughter. *Flying High*. New York: Harper & Row, 1988.

Index

1st Kansas Colored Troops, 243, 244, 257
1st Louisiana Native Guards, 243
1st Rhode Island Regiment, 257
1st South Carolina Volunteers, 257, 331
2nd Kansas Colored Troops, 174
2nd U.S. Colored Light Artillery, 244
3rd Louisiana Native Guards, 243
3rd U.S. Colored Infantry, 193
4th U.S. Colored Infantry, 258, 259
5th Artillery, 262
5th Dimension, 168
5th Marines, 262
5th Massachusetts Cavalry Regiment, 87
5th Special Forces Group, 262
5th U.S. Colored Troops, 245, 258, 259
6th U.S. Colored Heavy Artillery, 244
6th U.S. Colored Infantry, 245, 259
7th Regiment, U.S. Colored Volunteers, 244
8th U.S. Colored Troops, 174, 243
9th Cavalry, U.S. Regulars, 249, 260
10th Cavalry, U.S. Regulars, 260, 330
15th Air Force, **251**
24th Infantry Regiment, 176, 261
25th Corps, 243
25th Infantry Division, 261, 262, 263
33rd U.S. Colored Troops, 246, 331
35th U.S. Colored Troops, 243
36th U.S. Colored Infantry, 259
38th U.S. Colored Infantry, 258, 259
54th Massachusetts Regiment, 32, 174, 245, 259
55th Massachusetts Infantry Regiment, 87, 245
59th U.S. Colored Troops, 174
99th Fighter Squadron, 16, **251**, 252, 253, 254, 261
99th Pursuit Squadron Air Base, 66
101st Airborne, 119, 261
332nd Fighter Group, 253
369th Infantry Regiment of the 93rd Division, 249, 260
372nd Infantry, 115
614th Tank Destroyer Battalion, 261
761st Tank Battalion, **252**, 253, 261

Aardema, Verna, 317
Aaron, Estella, 295
Aaron, Henry Louis, 25, **295**, 309, 332
Aaron, Herbert, 295
Abbot, Anderson Ruffin, 282

Abbott, Robert S., 66, 90, 317
Abdul-Jabbar, Kareem, 25, 310, 332
Abele, Julian, 77
Abernathy, Ralph David, 220
Abraham, 23
Abraham Rosenberg Scholarship, 44
Abyssinian Baptist Church, 186
Academy Award, 138, 148, 149, 156, 160, 161, 162, 163, 164
Accra, Ghana, 183, 199
Adams, Clarence, 281
Adams, Eugene W., 284
Adams, John Quincy, 187
Adams, Numa Pompilius Garfield, 283
Adderley, Herb, **299**, 309
Adderley, Julian "Cannonball," 168
Adger, Robert Mara, 76
Adrian, Michigan, 308
Aesop, 103
Afghanistan, 255
Africa, 3, 6, 23, 27, 83, 86, 172, 182, 187, 266, 325
African American funeral businesses, 77
African American Museum, 61
African Methodist Church, 59, 191
African Methodist Episcopal Church, 3, 110, 122, 186; First African Methodist Episcopal Church, 107
African Methodist Episcopal Zion Church, 122
Afro American Newspaper, 65, 77
Aguanum, Switzerland, 197
Aiken, South Carolina, 193
Ailey, Alvin, **100**, 105, 162, 167, 314
Ajile, Dan, 163
Akron Indians, 308
Alabama, 99, 119, 188, 191, 194, 196, 202, 215, 219, 269, 271, 275, 321
Alabama A&M College, 128
Alabama State University, 181
Albany, Georgia, 150
Albany, Ohio, 259
Albert, Octavia, 235, 326
Alberto Culver Corporation, 77
Albuquerque, New Mexico, 13, 93
Alcorn College, 191
Alcorn, George E., 284
Alcorn, James L., 109, 196
Alcorn State University, 109, 122
Aldridge, Ira, 14, 165
Alexander and Repass, 177

Alexander, Archie, **177**, **271**, 283
Alexander, Clifford, Jr., 263
Alexander, Firnist James, 229
Alexander, James, 154
Alexander, Margaret Walker, **229**, 236
Alexander, Mary Hamilton, 177
Alexander, Price, 177
Alexander, Sadie T.M., 104
Ali, Muhammad, **300**, 310
Allegheny, Pennsylvania, 259
Allen, Annie, 327
Allen, Anthony, 76
Allen, Richard, 23, 110, 121, 218, 314
Allen, Tina, 61
Allen University, 110, 181
Allensworth, Allen, **176**
Allensworth, California, 176, 182
Allensworth, Levi, 176
Allensworth, Phyllis, 176
Allensworth State Historical Park, 176
Allison, Verne, 145
Along This Way, 235, 329
Alpha Kappa Alpha Sorority, 89
Alpha Phi Omega, 93
Alston, Charles, 43, **53**, 60
Alston, Henry, 53
Alta California, 187
Alton, Illinois, 150
Alvarez, Juan, 218
Alvin Ailey American Dance Theater, 162, 314
Amelia County, Virginia, 114
American Association of Physical Anthropologists, 277
American Baptist Home Mission Society, 110, 122
American Basketball Association (ABA), 301
American College of Surgeons, 9, 270
American Colonization Society, 187
American Conservatory Theater, 162
American Express Corporation, 79
American Indians, 39, 90
American Missionary Association, 108, 122
American Negro Academy, 57
American Nurses Association, 271
American Red Cross, 93, 272, 274
American Tennis Association, 296
America's Promise, Inc., 255
Amherst College/University, 93, 94, 123
Amistad, 187
Amos, Harold, **278**, 284
Amos n' Andy, 139
Amsterdam News, 66

Anacostia Museum, 61, 315
Anchorage, Alaska, 68, 204
Anderson, Carl, 97
Anderson, David, 230
Anderson, Eddie "Rochester," 166
Anderson, James H., 76
Anderson, James, Jr. (Private First Class), 261
Anderson, Katherine, 148
Anderson, Marian, 24, **133**, 152, 165, 321
Anderson, Osborne Perry, 103
Anderson, Trezzvant W., 253, 330
Anderson, Webster (Sergeant), 261
Andersonville prison, 243
Andover, Massachusetts, 3
Andrews, Raymond, 237
Angelou, Maya, 236, 326
Anita Bush Players, 129
Anna T. Jeanes Fund, 123
Annapolis, Maryland, 203, 265
Antoine, Albert C., 284
Antoine, Caesar C., 76
Anzio Beachhead (Italy), 252
Apollo Records, 144
Apollo Theater, 17, 96, 137, 160, 180
Archie Bell and The Drells, 169
Arizona, 171, 294
Arizona Cardinals, 294, 307
Arkansas, 95, 119, 174, 178, 244
Arkansas City, Arkansas, 70
Arlington National Cemetery, 7
Armstrong, Henry, 308
Armstrong, Lillian "Lil" Hardin, 165
Armstrong, Louis, **11**, 24, 54, 132, **133**, 165
Armstrong, Neil, 281
Army Medals of Honor, 258
Arnae, 163
Arnaz, Desi, 69
Arnold Air Society, 255
Arrested Development, 169, 170
Arrington, Richard, Jr., **213**, 221
Art Institute of Chicago, 11, 33, 44, 46, 51, 55, 58
Ashanti tribe, 76, 319
Ashe, Arthur, 310
Ashford, Rosalind, 149
Ashland, Kentucky, 262
Ashley, Eugene, Jr. (Sergeant), 262
Ashley, John, 81
Ashmun Institute, 107
Asheville, North Carolina, 274
Associated Negro Press (ANP), 200
Association for the Study of Negro Life and History, 115

Association of Black Anthropologists, 77
Association of Black Cardiologists, 78
Association of Black Psychologists, 77
Asuo, Kwesi, 163
Athens, Georgia, 112
Athens, Ohio, 65
Atherton, St. John, 76
Atlanta Baptist College, 6, 115
Atlanta Braves, 289
Atlanta, Georgia, 6, 9, 23, 32, 73, 85, 108, 134, 162, 183, 201, 211, 305
Atlanta Life Insurance Company, 66
Atlanta, Texas, 90
Atlanta University, 6, 12, 20, 43, 87, 89, 108, 110, 111, 112, 113, 115, 123, 199, 207, 211
Atlantic City, New Jersey, 17, 51
Atlantic Records, 100, 144
Attucks, Crispus, 18, 103, **185**, 218, **256**, 257, 319
Auburn Avenue, 178
Auburn, New York, 183
Auburn University, 305
Augusta, Alexander T., **244**, 258
Augusta, Georgia, 6, 108, 189, 295
Aurora, Illinois, 9
Austin, Oscar P. (Private First Class), 262
Austin, Texas, 89, 183, 289
Australia, 156
Ayers, Louisa, 203
Aztec Indians, 185

Bacener, Pio Casimiro, 59
Badeau, Aminda, 12
Bahamas, 149
Bailey, Ella Mae, 143
Bailey, Frederick Augustus Washington, 4 (*see also* Douglass, Frederick)
Bailey, Joseph James (Rev.), 143
Bailey, Pearl, **143**, 166, 321
Bailey, Philip, 159
Bainter, Fay, **138**
Baja Men, 170
Baker, Anita, 170
Baker, Edward Lee, 260
Baker, Ella, 220
Baker, George, 220
Baker, Hagar, 246
Baker, Henry, 282, 331
Baker, Houston A., Jr., 237
Baker, Josephine, 24, 93, 104, **131**, 165, 321
Baker, Raymond, 246
Baker, LaVern, 167

Baker, Vernon J., 261
Baker, Willie, 93
Baldwin, David, 19
Baldwin, James, **19**, 25, 179, 232, **233**, 236, 237, 326
Baldwin, Mississippi, 41
Ball, J.P., 30
Ball, Lucille, 69
Ball, William, **82**, 103
Ballard, Florence, **152**
Ballard, Hank, and the Midnighters, 167
Baltimore Black Sox, 288, 289, 291, 308
Baltimore Colts, 294, 296, 300
Baltimore, Maryland, 4, 16, 64, 65, 73, 93, 94, 103, 107, 110, 127, 139, 176, 183, 200, 203, 258, 259, 288
Bancroft, Ann, **149**
Bankhead, Dan, 309
Banks, Ernie, 309, 332
Banks, Homer, 158
Banneker, Benjamin, **81**, 103, 230, **265**, 282, 314
Bannister, Edward Mitchell, **29**, **30**, 59, 103
Bar-Kays, 168
Baraka, Imamu Amiri, 236
Barbados, 186, 210, 274
Barbett, Charlie, 141
Barcelona, Spain, 305
Barkley, Charles, 311
Barksdale, Charles, 145
Barnard College, 9
Barnes, William Henry (Private), 258
Barnett, Claude A., 220
Barnett, Ferdinand, 198
Barnett, Ida B. Wells (*see* Wells-Barnett, Ida)
Barons of Rhythm, 13
Barrow, Joseph Louis, **16**, 17, 25, 50, 97, **291**, 309, 314, 332
Barthé, Richmond, 24, **51**, 60, 180
Baseball Hall of Fame, 293, 294, 295, 299, 305
Basie, Count, 13, 24, **131**, 165
Basie, Harvey Lee, 13
Basie, Lilly Ann, 13
Bass, Fontella, 168
Basset, Ebenezer Don Carlos, 219
Bates, Daisy, 125, **206**, 220
Bath, Patricia, 284
Baton Rouge, Louisiana, 83, 184, 242
Battle Creek, Michigan, 183
Battle of Brandywine, 240
Battle of Brices Crossroads, 182

Battle of Bunker Hill, 3, 82, 239, 257
Battle of Chapin's (Chaffin's) Farm, 245, 258
Battle of Charleston, 239
Battle of Concord, 239
Battle of Cowpens, **82**
Battle of Fort Wagoner, 173
Battle of Goliad, 242
Battle of Great Bridge, 239
Battle of Groton Heights, 241
Battle of Guadalcanal, 250
Battle of Honey Springs, 257
Battle of Hubbardton, 239
Battle of Island Mound, Missouri, 243
Battle of Jacksonville, 243
Battle of Kettle Creek, Georgia, 241
Battle of Mobile Bay, 258, 260
Battle of Monmouth, 239
Battle of New Market Heights, Virginia, 259
Battle of New Orleans, 83, 242, 257
Battle of Newtown, 239
Battle of Olustee, Florida, 243, 258
Battle of Petersburg, Virginia, 244, 258
Battle of Port Hudson, 257
Battle of Rhode Island, 171, 240
Battle of San Jacinto, 242
Battle of San Juan Hill, 247
Battle of Santa Cruz Island, 249
Battle of Saratoga, 239
Battle of Savannah, Georgia, 23
Battle of Stoney Point, 239
Battle of the Alamo, 172, 242
Battle of the Bulge, 252
Battle of the Little Big Horn, 246
Battle of Verdun, 248
Battle of Yorktown, 241
Baumfree, Isabella, 186
Bay St. Louis, Mississippi, 11
Baylor University, 305
Beal, Earl, 167
Beale Street, 5, 66, 178, 322, 327
Beard, Andrew Jackson, 283
Beard, Annette, 149
Bearden, Romare, **54**, 60, 315, 316
Beasley, Delilah I., 24
Beaty, Powhatan (First Sergeant), 258
Beaufort, South Carolina, 84, 87
Beavers, Louise, 104
bebop, 139, 166
Bechet, Sidney, **132**, 165
Becket, G.E, 283
Beckwourth, James P., **83**, 103, **173**, 182, 313, 317, 319, 323
Beckwourth Pass, 173

Beckwourth Trail, 173
Bel Air, California, 297
Belafonte, Harry, 169
Belison Hospital, 276
Belknap, Jeremiah, 82
Bell, Bobby, 309
Bell, George, 121
Bell, James "Cool Papa," **288**, 308
Bell, Robert "Kool," 160
Bell, Ronald, 160
Benedict College, 92, 110
Benin, Nigeria, 223
Benny Goodman Quartet, 140
Benny, Jack, 137
Benson, Renaldo "Obie," 151
Benton, Alabama, 39
Benton, Brook, 147, 169
Berea College, 121
Berea, Kentucky, 121
Berean Savings Association, 78
Berger, Flora Batson, 165
Berkeley, California, 15
Berkshire County, Massachusetts, 81
Berlin, Germany, 96, 132, 275, 291
Berlin International Congress of Women, 203
Berry, Chuck, 166
Berry, Edwin C., 76
Berry, Halle, 170
Berry, Leonidas H., 283
Bethune, Albert, 88
Bethune, "Blind Tom," 165
Bethune, Mary McLeod, 23, 47, **88**, **113**, 123, 125, 178, 314, 318, 319, 320
Bethune-Cookman College, 88, 123, 178
Beverly Hills, California, 69
Biddle Memorial Institute, 123
Biddle University, 123
Bidwell's Bar, 173
Big Sea, The, 92, 236, 328
Bigger Thomas (*see* Thomas, Bigger)
Biggers, John, **55**, 61, 315
Biggie Smalls, 170
Bill of Rights, 81
Billops, Camille, 25
Billy Ward and the Dominoes, 100
Bing, Dave, 310
Binga, Jesse, 76
Binka, M.W., 282
Birmingham, Alabama, 14, 69, 73, 74, 140, 183, 184, 208, 213, 229, 261, 262
Birmingham Black Barons, 99, 289, 291, 308
Bishop College, 7, 65, 125, 133

Bivins, Horace W., 260
BlackAmericaWeb.com, 164
"Black Babe Ruth," 292
Black Boy, 236, 330
"Black City Hall," 189
black codes, 219
Black Culinary Alliance, 78
Black Enterprise magazine, 71, 78
Black Entertainment Television network, 72, 78
Black Filmmakers Hall of Fame, 139
Black History Month, 201, 220
Black Journalists' Lifetime Achievement Award, 70
Black, Julian, 16
Black Revolutionary War Patriots commemorative coin, **256**
Black Revolutionary War Patriots' Memorial, 179
Black Star Line, 200
Black World, 70
Black World Series, 294
Blackburn, A.B., 282
Blackfeet Indians, 59
Blackfeet Indians, 173
Blackwell, David H., 284
Blair, Henry, 282
Blake, James Hubert "Eubie," **89**, 104, **127**, 140, 165
Blake, Robert, 258, 260
Bland, Bobby "Blue," 167
Bland, James, 165
Bledsoe, Henry, 133
Bledsoe, Julius, 165
Blind Blake, 142
Blind Boy Fuller, 15
Blind Joe Taggart, 142
Blind John Henry Arnold, 142
Blind Lemon Jefferson, 142, 165
Bluefield State College, 122
Blues for Mister Charlie, 236, 327
Blues Vocalist of the Year Award, 160
Bluford, Guion S., Jr., 105, 284, 318
Bo Diddley, 166
Boley, Oklahoma, 183
Bolivar County, Mississippi, 196
Bomar, Estelle, 229
Bond, Horace Mann, 124
Bond, Julian, 117, 221
Bonds, Barry, 311
Bonga, George, **186**, 218
Bonga, Stephen, **173**, 182
Bonner, Thomas D., 173
Bontemps, Arna, 104, **231**, 236, 315, 327, 328

Booker T. (Jones) and the MGs, 168
Booker T. Washington and George Washington Carver commemorative coin, 39, **119**
Booker T. Washington Business College, 69
Booker T. Washington commemorative coin, **118**
Booker T. Washington High School, 17, 89
Booker T. Washington Insurance Company, 69, 78
Boone, Sarah, 283
bop, 150
Born to Play Ball, 293
Boston Bank of Commerce, 79
Boston Braves, 295
Boston Celtics, 295
Boston Herald, 199
Boston, Massachusetts, 23, 29, 31, 38, 44, 75, 87, 91, 107, 183, 186, 223, 241, 268, 282
Boston Massacre, 81, 185, 239
Boston, Ralph, 309
Boston Red Sox, 301, 303
Boston University, 211, 274
Bouchet, Edward, 122, 268
Bowles, Charles, 23
Bowman, James E., Jr., 284
Bowser Mary Elizabeth, 258
Boyd, Richard Henry, 65, 76
Boykin, Cloyd L., 42
Boykin, Otis, 284
Boyz II Men, 170
Braddock, Jim, 17
Bradley, Benjamin, 282
Bradley, Crenner, 212
Bradley, David, 234, 327
Bradley, Lee, 212
Bradley, Tom, **212**, 221
Braithwaite, William Stanley, **225**, 235
Branch, Mary E., 104
Branch, William, 236
Branson, Herman, **279**, 284
Brazil, 185, 201, 296
Br'er Rabbit, 319
Brevard, North Carolina, 129
Bright, Ronnie, 146
Brimmer, Andrew F., 77
British Army, 82
Broadway Federal Savings and Loan Association, 78
Brock, Lou, 309
Bronson, James H. (First Sergeant), 258
Bronx, New York, 19, 261

Brook, Harvey, 91
Brooke, Edward, **209**, 221, 324
Brooklyn College, 210
Brooklyn Dodgers, 97, 294, 306, 309
Brooklyn Law School, 214
Brooklyn, New York, 9, 141, 161, 210, 231, 262, 287
Brooklyn Royal Giants, 308
Brooks, C.B., 283
Brooks, Gwendolyn, **230**, 236, 317, 327
Brooks, Keziah Wims, 230
Brooks, Pat, 16
Brooksville, Mississippi, 19
Brotherhood of Sleeping Car Porters, 11
Brothers Johnson, 169
Brown, Aunt Clara, **174**, 182
Brown, Carl, 78
Brown, Charlotte Hawkins, 24, **113**, 123
Brown, Claude, 236
Brown, Dorothy L., 285
Brown, Emily, 114
Brown, Fay, 94
Brown, George, 160
Brown Girl, Brownstones, 236, 329
Brown, Grafton Tyler, 59
Brown, James, 168
Brown, Jesse L. (Ensign), **253**, 261, 263
Brown, Jill, 263
Brown, Jim, **296**, 309, 332
Brown, John, 47, 189, 265
Brown, Lee P., Jr., 222
Brown, Linda, 124
Brown, Oscar E., 283
Brown, Ronald H., 78
Brown, Sterling, 24, 236
Brown University, 111, 228, 278
Brown v. Board of Education, Topeka, Kansas, 12, 94, 119, 120, 124, 203
Brown, Wesley A., **253**, 261
Brown, William (of the Mad Lads), 168
Brown, William Wells, 235, 330
Brown, Willie L., Jr., 222
Brownhelm Township, 198
Brownsville Raid, 235
Brownsville, Tennessee, 73
Brownsville, Texas, 225
Bruce, Blanche Kelso, 23, **196**, 219
Bruce, John Edward, 57
Bryant, Kobe, **307**, 311
Bryant, William Maud (Sergeant First Class), 262
Buckminister, Lawson, 82
"Bucks of America," 257
Buena Vista, Georgia, 95, 292
Buffalo Bills, 301

Buffalo Braves, 303
Buffalo, New York, 36
Buffalo soldiers, 247, 331
Bullard, Eugene Jacques, 260
Bullard, Josephine Thomas, 248
Bullard, William O., 248
Bullins, Edward, 237
Bunche, Fred, 13
Bunche, Olive Johnson, 13
Bunche, Ralph, **13**, 24, 104, **116**, 220, 313
Burke, Selma Hortense, 24
Burke, Solomon, 167
Burleigh, Harry T., 128, 165
Burnett, Chester Arthur "Howlin' Wolf," **95**, 104, 166
Burr, J.A., 283
Burr, Seymour, 257
Burroughs, James, 112
Burroughs, Margaret, 61
Burroughs, Nannie Helen, 104, 123
Bush, George H.W., 291
Bush, George W. (President), 206, 217
Bush, George Washington, 52, 172, 182
Bussa, 218
Butler, Jerry "The Iceman," 149
Butler, Octavia E., 237, 327

Caesar (Cesar), 218
Caillou, Andre Captain, 243
Cain, Richard H., 192
Caines, Jeanette, 101, 317
Cairo, Georgia, 97
Cairo, Illinois, 44, 94
Caldecott Medal, 320
Caldwell, Ronnie, 154
Caleb, Joseph, 79
Califa, Queen, 182
California, 15, 32, 43, 69, 92, 120, 171, 173, 176, 187, 188, 189, 218, 220, 252
California Angels, 305
California State College, 20
California State University, 280
Calloway, Cab, 166
Calvert, Texas, 212
Cambridge, England, 112
Cambridge, Massachusetts, 8
Camden, Arkansas, 183, 258
Cameo, 170
Camero, Manual, 171
Camp Grant, Illinois, 248
Campbell, E. Simms, 166
Campbell, Earl, 303
Campbell, "Little" Milton, Jr., 168
Campeche, José, 59

Campenella, Roy, 294, 309
Canaan, New Hampshire, 112
Canada, 28, 32, 107, 124, 172, 186, 189, 201, 218, 244, 266, 267; Canada West, 186; Lower Canada, 186; Upper Canada, 86
Canady, Alexa I., 284
Capitol Records, 98
Carey, Jake, 147
Carey, Mariah, 170
Carey, Mary Ann Shadd, 121, 218, 266
Carew, Rod, 310
Carey, Rick, 163
Carey, Zeke, 147
Carmichael, Hoagy, 137
Carmichael, Stokely, 221
Carnegie Hall, 15
Carnegie Library, 66
Carney, William H. (Sergeant), 243, 257, 258
Carolina League, 299
Carolina Panthers, 304
Carolina, Puerto Rico, 302
Caroline County, Maryland, 83
Caroll, Diahann, 105
Carroll County, Mississippi, 133
Carroll, Earl, 146
Carruthers, George R., 284
Carson, Ben, 284
Carson, Eddie, 93
Carteaux, Christina, 29
Carter, Clarence, 168
Carter, Edward A. (Staff Sergeant), 261
Carter, Jimmy, 25, 212
Carter, Johnnie, 145
Carter, Rubin "Hurricane," 310
Carthage, Texas, 245
Carver Federal Savings Bank, 78
Carver, George Washington, 39, 47, **86**, 103, **111**, 124, 178, 180, 271, **273**, 283, 313, 332
Carver National Monument, 180
Cascade, Montana, 200
Cash, Fred, 149
Casino Theater, 129
Cass, Melnea, 104
Catholic saint, 197
Cauley, Ben, 154
Cedartown, Georgia, 130
Central America, 266
Central Baptist Church, 89
Central City, Colorado, 174
Central State University, 279
Centralia, Washington, 182
Cesar (Caesar), 218

Cézanne, Paul, 44, 50
Chamberlain, Wilt(on) Norman, **297**, 309
Chambers County, Alabama, 16
Chambers, Paul, 151
Chaney, James, 208
Chaney, Lon, 69
Chaneysville Incident, 237, 327
Charles County, Maryland, 3, 86
Charles, Ezzard, 17
Charles, Ray, **150**, 164, 168
Charles Town, Virginia, 266
Charleston, Oscar, **294**, 309
Charleston, South Carolina, 5, 46, 89, 186, 190, 192, 193, 195
Charleston, West Virginia, 217
Charlotte, North Carolina, 53, 54, 86, 184
Charlotte Post, 253
Charlton, Cornelius H. (Sergeant), 261
Chateaulin, France, 275
Chatfield, Texas, 7
Chatsworth, California, 10
Chattanooga Black Lookouts, 289
Chattanooga, Tennessee, 9, 130
Cheatham, Henry P., 196, **197**, 219
Checker, Chubby, 167
Chelsea, Massachusetts, 268
Chenault, Kenneth I, **75**, 79
Cheraw, South Carolina, 140
Cherbourg, France, 244, 260
Cherokee Indians, 44, 242
Cherry Hill, New Jersey, 144
Chesapeake Marine Railway and Dry Dock Company, 64
Chesnutt, Charles Wadell, 224, 235
Chester County, Pennsylvania, 107
Chester, Pennsylvania, 10
Cheyenne, Wyoming, 64
Cheyney State College, 49, 114
Cheyney University, 107
Chi Eta Phi sorority, 271
Chi-Lites, 169
Chicago American Giants, 289, 290, 294, 308
Chicago Bears, 300, 303
Chicago Bee, 67
Chicago Board of Trade, 4, 5
Chicago Bulls, 305
Chicago Cardinals, 294
Chicago Cubs, 296, 297, 301, 307
Chicago Defender, 75, 76, 90, 140, 226
Chicago, Illinois, 4, 5, 8, 14, 15, 38, 51, 66, 67, 68, 69, 73, 83, 84, 88, 90, 94, 96, 98, 120, 129, 131, 139, 140, 144, 145, 147, 164, 175, 179, 182, 183, 184, 194, 197, 198, 200, 205, 209,

213, 220, 230, 254, 262, 269, 276, 277, 287, 290, 323
Chicago Leland Giants, 289
Chief League, 197
Children's Defense Fund, 212
Childress, Alice, 236
Chinese Exclusion Act of 1878, 196
Chinn, Mary Edward, 284
Chippewa Indian, 31
Chisholm, Conrad, 210
Chisholm, Shirley Anita, 25, 204, **210**, 221, 313, 325
Christian Methodist Episcopal (CME) Church, 110, 122
Christian, Timothy, 162
Christmas "Gif," 91
Christophe, Henri, 3
Church of England, 110
Church, Robert, 203
Church, Robert, Sr., 76
Churchill, Winston, 225
Cincinnati Enquirer, 15
Cincinnati, Ohio, 4, 7, 15, 28, 30, 92, 258, 261, 273, 275, 277
Cincinnati Reds, 307
Cincinnati Royals, 298
Cinque, Joseph, 218
Citizens Federal Savings and Loan, 69, 78
Citizens Savings Bank and Trust Company, 65, 78
Citizens Trust Bank, 78
City College of New York, 11, 200
City National Bank of New Jersey, 78
Civil Rights Act of 1866, 189
Civil Rights Act of 1875, 195
Civil Rights Act of 1968, 209
Civil War, 22, 32, 40, 63, 65, 89, 116, 121, 122, 127, 128, 174, 175, 176, 187, 188, 189, 193, 194, 195, 196, 197, 242, 243, 244, 245, 246, 266, 267, 321, 330, 331
Clara Ward Singers, 143, 166
Clark Air Force Base, 255
Clark Atlanta University, 44
Clark, Dee, 167
Clark, Joe, 22
Clark, Kenneth B., 124, 327
Clark, Mark, 209
Clark, Peter H., 23
Clark, Septima, 220
Clark University, 9, 59, 110, 113, 272
Clark, York, **172**, 182
Clarksburg, Virginia, 95

Clarksdale, Mississippi, 130, 147, 183, 184
Clarksville, Tennessee, 298
Claverack, New York, 81
Clayton, Eva M., 221
Clearview, Oklahoma, 181
Cleaver, Eldridge, 236
Clemente, Roberto, **20**, 25, **302**
Cleveland Browns, **296**, 299
Cleveland Buckeyes, 309
Cleveland Cubs, 289
Cleveland, Grover, 176
Cleveland Heights, 229
Cleveland Indians, 289, 293, 302, 305
Cleveland, James (Reverend), 167
Cleveland, Ohio, 7, 16, 88, 92, 96, 97, 129, 183, 184, 224, 265, 273, 291, 292
Climbach, France, 251
Clinton, DeWitt, 27
Clinton, William Jefferson, 251, 261
Clio, South Carolina, 58
Club Nouveau, 170
Clyde McPhatter and the Drifters, 100
Coachman, Alice, 309
Coahoma Community College, 181
Coasters, 167
Cobb, Jesse, 133
Cobb, Jewel Plummer, 284
Cobb, W. Montague, 104, 284
Cochran, Johnnie, 222
Coincoin, Marie Therese, 63, 172
Coke, Thomas, 115
Cole, Johnnetta, 125
Cole, Nat "King," **98**, 105, **141**, 166, 170
Cole, Natalie, 170
Colechester, Ontario, 267
Coleman, Bessie, **90**, 104, **272**, 283
Coleman, Cordelia, 139
Coleridge-Taylor, Samuel, 165, 228
Coley, Doris, 146
College of Educational and Industrial Arts, 152
Collins, Addie M., 208
Collins, Daniel A., 25, 284
Collins, Marva, 125
Color Me Brown, 318
Colored Industrial and Agricultural School, 112
Coltrane, John, **99**, 105, **151**, 168, 323
Coltrane, Ravi, 151
Columbia College (Illinois), 230
Columbia, Mississippi, 303

Columbia Presbyterian, 123
Columbia, South Carolina, 10, 184
Columbia University, 9, 20, 50, 53, 58, 91, 93, 123, 133, 135, 156, 210, 214, 276
Columbus, Christopher, 171, 323
Columbus County, North Carolina, 68
Columbus, Georgia, 6, 134, 199, 248, 295
Columbus, Ohio, 41, 68, 288
Commander of the Order of the Star, 249
Come Out Fighting!, 261, 330
Committee for the Negro in Arts, 51
Commodores, 169
Concordia Parrish, Louisiana, 194
Confederacy, 246
Confederate, 190, 192, 193, 194, 244, 258, 259, 260
Confederate States of America, 4
Congo, 6
Congress of Racial Equality (CORE), 203
Congressional Gold Medal, 206, 255
Congressional Medal of Honor, 243, 245, 246, 247, 248, 252, 253, 254
Conkling, Roscoe, 196
Connecticut, 191, 218, 221, 271
Consolidated Bank and Trust Company, 65, 78
Continental Army, 3, 82, 239, 240, 241
Continental Navy, 257
Cook, Corrine, 272
Cooke, Sam, **147**, 167
Coolidge, Calvin, 200
Cooper, Anna J., 23
Cooper Union, 42
Copenhagen, Denmark, 148
Coptic Christian soldiers, 197
Coretta Scott King Award, 101, 102, 105
Cornell University, 117, 227, 234, 281
Cornish, Samuel E., 63
Cornwallis, Charles (Lieutenant General), 82
Cortez, Hernando, 171
Cortor, Eldzier, 60
Cortor, John, 46
Cortor, Ophelia, 46
Cosby, Bill, 32, 161, 170, 320
Cosby, Camille, 105
Costa Chica, 184
Cotton Club, 18, 135, 141
Cotton Comes to Harlem, 232, 328
Cotton Plant, Arkansas, 96, 137
Cotton States Exposition, 85
Cottrell, Comer J., Jr., **72**, 77
Cottrell, Elias (Bishop), 113
Couchman, Texas, 131

Council for Minorities in Engineering, Inc. (*see* National Action Council for Minorities in Engineering, Inc.)
Count Basie, **13**
Couvent, Madame Bernard, 23
Covington, Tennessee, 86, 156
Cowart, Juanita, 148
Cox, Adler, 130
Cox, Ida, 165
Craft, Ellen, 122
Craft, Juanita J., 220
Craft, William, 122
Cralle, A.L., 283
Crane, Helga, 235
Crawford, Janie, 236
Creek Indians, 122, 248
Crescent City, Florida, 11
Cresson, Sara Emlen, 107
Crichlow, Ernest, 61
Crises magazine, 12, 227
Crite, Allan Rohan, **46**
Croatan Indian, 191
Crockett, Texas, 183
Croix de Guerre, 131, 248, 249
Cromwell, Oliver, 23, **240**, 257
Crosthwait, David N., Jr., 283
Crow Indians, 83, 173, 313
Crum, William D., 23
Crummell, Alexander, 57, **112**, 123
Crump, Jesse, 130
Crumpler, Rebecca Lee, 282
CSS Alabama, 244, 260
CSS Planter, 84, 192
Cuba, 187
Cuban Giants, 308
Cuban Stars, 291
Cuernavaca, Mexico, 98
Cuero, Texas, 250
Cuffee, Paul, 3, 179
Cullen, Countee, 19, 50, **226**, 235, 327
Cummings, Elijah E., 210
Cummings, Pat, 105, 317
Cunningham, Carl, 154
Curtis, Austin Maurice, Sr., 283
Curtis, King, 146
Cuyahoga River, 178

Dabney, Austin, 257
Dailey, Phyllis Mae, 261
Dailey, Ulysses Grant, 283
Dallas County, Alabama, 192
Dallas Cowboys, 299, 300, 304, 307
Dallas, Texas, 7, 58, 120, 131, 152, 164, 206, 211, 216, 217, 305
Dance Theater of Harlem, 145

Dandridge, Dorothy, 25
Dandridge, Ray, 308
Danforth, John, 215
Daniel Payne College, 110, 181
Daniels, Jerry, 166
Danville, Illinois, 41
Darlington, South Carolina, 17, 92
Dartmouth College, 8, 30, 275
Davidson County, Tennessee, 84
Davidson, Olivia A., 85
Davis, Allison, **12**, 24, **117**, 124
Davis, Angela, 221
Davis, Benjamin O., Jr. (Lieutenant
    General), 24, **254**, 261, 330
Davis, Benjamin O., Sr. (Brigadier
    General), **89**, 104, **249**, 255, 261
Davis, Billie Louise Barbour, 61
Davis, Billy, Jr., 154
Davis, Elnora Dickerson, 249
Davis, Gabrielle, 12
Davis, Jefferson, 4, 175, 191, 244
Davis, John, 12
Davis, John, 257, 320
Davis, Joseph, 175
Davis, Lenwood G., 237, 315
Davis, Miles, 98, **150**, 151, 168
Davis, Ossie, 105
Davis, Rodney Maxwell (Sergeant), 262
Davis, Sammy, Jr., 167, 321
Dawson, William L., **202**, 220
Day, Bobby, 102, 167
Day Home Clubs, 5
Day, Leon, 309
Day, Tom, 63
Dayton, Ohio, 87, 103
Dayton Tattler, 234
Daytona Beach, Florida, 183
Daytona Normal and Industrial Institute
    for Negro Girls, 88
De Leon, Ponce, 171
De Olano, Nuflo, 182
De Priest, Oscar, **202**
De Vaca, Cabeza, 171
Deadwood Dick, 84, 199, 219
Deadwood, South Dakota, 84, 199
DeCarava, Roy, 61, 315, 327
Decca Records, 96, 137
Dee, Ruby, 105
deGaulle, Charles, 131
Delaney, Beauford, 61
Delany, Martin R., **266**, 282
Delany, Samuel R., 25, 236
DeLarge, Robert C., **191**, 192, **193**, 219
Delaware, 111
Delaware River, 240, 330

Delaware State University, 122
Dells, 167
Delta Blues (style of guitar playing), 95
Delta Blues Museum, 178
Delta, Louisiana, 5
Delta Sigma Theta Sorority, 90
Denison, Texas, 7
Denmark, 177
Denmark, South Carolina, 111, 183
Denny, John (Sergeant), 260
Denver, Colorado, 64, 66, 184
Department of Agriculture, 196
Department of State, 249
Depauw University, 92
Depriest, James, 105
Derham, James, 282
Des Moines, Iowa, 177
Destiny's Child, **164**
Detroit Lions, 306
Detroit, Michigan, 13, 16, 21, 28, 71, 73,
    75, 78, 98, 135, 144, 197, 212, 261,
    262, 288
Detroit Pistons, 301, 304, 307
Detroit School of Dramatic Art, 135
Detroit Stars, 289, 308
Dett, Robert Nathaniel, 165
Devers, Gail, 310
DeWitt Clinton High School, 19
Dexter Avenue Baptist Church, 183
Diamond, Missouri, 183
Dickerson, M. Ashley, 221, 324
Dickey, John Miller, 107
Dickinson School of Law, 139
Dihigo, Martin, 309
Dillard University, 12, 58, 116, 180
Dinkins, David, **214**, 221
Diocletian, 197
Distinguished Flying Cross, 254, 255
Distinguished Service Medal, 249, 255
District of Columbia, 107, 174, 189, 221
District of Columbia Board of Education,
    88
District of Columbia Teachers' College,
    121
Dixon, Dean, **156**, 169
Dixon, George, 308
Dobbins, Georgia, 148
Dobbs, Irene, 211
Doby, Larry, 309
Dodds, Julia, 95
Doggett, Bill, 167
Dominican Republic, 289, 307
Domino, Antoine "Fats," **146**, 167
Don, Rasha, 163
Dorantes, Estivanico (Stephen), **171**

Dorchester County, Missouri, 52
Dorman, Isaiah, 260
Dorsett, Tony, 310
Dorsey, Decatur (Sergeant), 258
Dorsey, Thomas A., **134**, 136, 137, 166
Douglas, Aaron, 39, 46, **50**, 60, 104
Douglass, Anna Murray, 103
Douglass Bank, 78
Douglass, Frederick, 12, 16, 23, 39, 47,
    76, 83, **84**, 87, 162, 178, 188, **189**,
    203, 218, 219, 265, 266, 319, 324
Douglass Hospital of Philadelphia, 270
Dove, Rita, 237
Dover, Delaware, 111
Down the Bay Boys, 293
Dream Girls, 168
Drew, Charles R., **93**, 115, 118, 124, **276**,
    284, 332
Drifters, 144, 166
Drinkwater, John, 129
Du Bois, Shirley Graham, 236
Du Bois, W.E.B., **15**, 38, 40, 57, 103,
    111, 114, 123, 178, **199**, 219, 235,
    236, 313, 319, 320, 324
Du Sable High School, 213
Du Sable, Jean Baptiste Pointe, **83**, 103,
    171, 172, 323
Du Sauge, John, 182, 257
Dudly, James, 135
Duhamel, Marcel, 229
Duke University, 69, 134; School of
    Medicine, 277
Dumas, Alexandre, 235
Dumas, Henry, 237, 327
Dunbar High School, 12
Dunbar, Joshua, 87
Dunbar, Mathilda, 87
Dunbar, Paul Laurence, 39, **87**, **224**, 235,
    318, 327
Duncan, Cleveland, 145
Duncan, Tim, 311
Duncanson, Robert Scott, **28**, **29**, 59
Dunham, Albert, 14
Dunham, Fanny, 14
Dunham, Katherine, 24, **149**, 167
Dunn, Larry, 159
Dunn, Oscar J., 219
Durham, North Carolina, 7, 68, 74, 76,
    100, 113, 144, 184, 236
Dutch (language), 85

Eakins, Thomas, 86
Earth, Wind & Fire, 169
East Chicago Giants, 289
East Nashville, Tennessee, 7

East St. Louis, Illinois, 149, 150, 183, 232
Eaton, Hubert A., 296
Easton, Pennsylvania, 51
Eatonton, Georgia, 100
Eatonville, Florida, 9
Eau Claire, Wisconsin, 295
Ebenezer Baptist Church, 178
Ebony magazine, 70, 77, 231
Eckstein-Norton University, 88
Eckstein, William Clarence (*see* Eckstine,
    Billy)
Eckstine, Billy, 105, **142**, 150, 166
Ecole Centrale, 266
Edelman, Marian Wright, 221
Edenton, North Carolina, 223
Edinburgh, Scotland, 183
Edmondson, William, 45, 60
Edwards, Raymond, 167
Edwards Sisters, 137
Einstein, Carl, 44
Eisenhower, Dwight D., 119
Elder, Clarence, 284
Elder, Lee, 310
Elders, Jocelyn, 221
Eldridge, Roy, 140
Ellington, Daisy Kennedy, 91
Ellington, Duke, 13, 54, **91**, 98, 104, **135**,
    166, 228, 322
Ellington, James Edward, 91
Elliott, Robert Brown, **191**, 192
Ellis, Clarence A., 284
Ellison, Ralph, **231**, 236, 237, 327
Elmhurst College, 230
Emancipation Act of New York, 265
Emancipation Proclamation, 31, 41, 189,
    219, 243
Emmy Award, 160, 161
Emory Neighborhood Law Office, 211
England, 227, 248
Englewood High School, 277
Equal Employment Opportunity
    Commission, 215
Erie, Pennsylvania, 128
Erving, Julius Winfield, II, **301**, 310
Eshe, Montsho, 163
Estivanico, **171**, 323
Etaples, Normandy, 36
Ethiopia(n), 41, 81, 214, 239
Euclid Avenue, 178
Europe, 6, 29, 44, 47, 49, 132, 139, 143,
    156, 197, 249, 266
Europe, James R., 24
Europeans of African descent, 182
Evans, Bill, 151
Evans, Gil, 151

Evans, Julius Caesar, 56
Evans, Lillian, 129
Evans, Mari, 236
Evans, Minnie, 61
Evans, Myrtle Louise, 281
Evanston, Illinois, 276
Evanti, Lillian, 129, 165
Evers, Medgar W., **208**, 220
Evers-Williams, Myrlie, 222
Ewing, Buck, 292
expressionism, 60

Factor, Pompey, 260
Fagan, Sadie, 96
Fairfield, Alabama, 99
Fakir, Abdul "Duke," 151
Fanon, Frantz, 236, 327
Farmer, James, 220, 324
Farmer, Karen, 221
Farmville, Virginia, 89, 196
Farris, Dionne, 163
Father Divine, 202
Faulcon, Nettie D., 285
Fauset, Jessie Redmon, **227**, 235
Fauset, Redmon, 227
Fayetteville, North Carolina, 4, 191, 224
Federal Arts Project, 44, 53
Federal Reserve Board, 71
Felton, William McDonald, 76
Ferguson, Angella D., 284
Ferguson, Washington, 112
Ferrer, Ramon, 187
Fields, Mary, **200**, 220
Fifteenth Amendment to the U.S.
    Constitution, 219
First Baptist Church, 7
First Independence National Bank of
    Detroit, 78
First Methodist Church, 69
Fisk, Clinton B. (General), 121
Fisk Jubilee Singers, 165
Fisk University, 46, 50, 57, 66, 89, 92,
    110, 118, 121, 165, 178, 199, 321
Fitzgerald, Ella, 25, **137**, 166
Fitzgerald, Temperance, 137
Fitzgerald, William, 137
Flack, Roberta, 169
Flamingoes, 167
Fleetwood, Christian Abraham (Sergeant
    Major), 258, 259
Fleming, Benjamin, 257
Fleming, Lethia C., 104
Fletcher Henderson Band/Orchestra, 133,
    139
flight of the Holy Family, 59

Flipper, Henry O., **247**, 260, 330
Flora, William, 257
Florence, Alabama, 7, 183
Florence, Italy, 267
Florence, South Carolina, 47
Florida, 7, 8, 111, 171, 174, 182, 191,
    193, 243, 258
Florida A&M University, 19, 122, 181
Florida School for the Deaf and Blind,
    150
Florville, William, 76
Floyd, Eddie, 168
Foley, 163
Folies Bergere, 131
Ford, Barney L., **64**, 76
Ford, Harold, Sr., **212**
Ford Motor Company, 16
Ford, Tennessee Ernie, 136
Fordham University, 162
Foreman, George, 310
Forest City, Arkansas, 157
Forriest, Sonny, 146
Fort Blakely, Alabama, 195
Fort Des Moines, Iowa, 123
Fort Donally, West Virginia, 240
Fort Erie, Ontario, 242
Fort Huachuca, Arizona, 244
Fort Leavenworth, Kansas, 260
Fort McIntosh, Texas, 108
Fort Negro, Florida, 172
Fort Pillow, Tennessee, 22, 258
Fort Ticonderoga, New York, 239
Fort Valley High and Industrial School,
    111
Fort Valley State College, 111, 117
Fort Wagner, 174, 243, 258
Fort Worth, Texas, 74
Forten, Charlotte L., 121, 320
Forten, James, 76, 316
Fortress Monroe, 174
Fortune, Amos, 172, 314
Fortune, T. Thomas, 219
Foster, Andrew "Rube," 290, 308
Foster, Denzil, 162
Foster, William "Willie," 308
Founders National Bank, 79
Four Tops, 168
Fourteenth Amendment to the U.S.
    Constitution, 122, 193
Fox, John R., 261
Foxx, Charles, 168
Foxx, Inez, 168
Foxx, Jamie, 170
Foxx, Redd, 169
Framingham, Massachusetts, 81, 82, 239

France, 42, 90, 241, 248, 265, 275
Frankfort, Kentucky, 183
Frankfort Radio Symphony Orchestra, 156
"Frankie and Johnny," 25
Franklin, Aretha, **154**, 168
Franklin County, Virginia, 85
Franklin, Jennie E., 105
Franklin, John Hope, 25, 115, 194, 222, 325
Franklin, Martha Minerva, 283
Franklin, Melvin, **153**
Franklin Normal and Industrial Institute, 113
Franklin, Virginia, 113
Frazier, E. Franklin, 124, 325
Frazier, Joe, 310
Frazier, Walt, 310
Frederick Douglass Monument, 178
Frederick, Virginia, 173
Fredericksville, New Jersey, 227
Free Library of Philadelphia, 69
Free Speech, 23
Freedman's Bank, 64, 76
Freedman's Bureau, 121, 122
Freedman's Journal, 76
Freedmen's Aid Society, 28, 121
Freedmen's Hospital, 244, 270, 272, 274, 277, 282
Freedom Farms Corporation, 208
Freedom National Bank, 77
Freeman, Elizabeth, 81, 103, 318
Freeman, Jordan, 257
Freeman, Morgan, 22, 170
French National Radio Orchestra, 156
French Red Cross, 131
Friendship Baptist Church, 211
Fry, Theodore, 94
Fuller, Charles, 225, 236, 322
Fuller, Meta Warrick, **40**, **41**, 60, 104
Fuller Products Company, 69, 70
Fuller, Samuel B., 77
Fuller, Solomon Carter, 283
Fuller, Thomas, 195, 282
Fuqua, Charles, 166

Gabor, Zsa Zsa, 69
Gaines, Ernest J., 236, 327
Gaines, Lloyd, 116, 124
Gaines, Matthew, 122
Gainesville, Florida, 193
Galveston, Texas, 287
Gandhi, Mahatma, 202
Gantt, Harvey, **181**
Gap Band, 169

Gardiner, James (Private), 259
Gardner, Carl, Jr., 146
Garland, Red, 151
Garner, Erroll, **98**, 105, **158**, 169
Garnet, Henry H., 103
Garnet Mimms and the Enchanters, 168
Garnet, Sarah J., 122
Gammon Theological Seminary, 115
Garrett County, Maryland, 239
Garrido, Juan, 182
Garrison, William Lloyd, 31
Garvey, Marcus, 58, **200**, 207, 220, 325
Gaston, Arthur G., **69**, 77
Gaye, Marvin, 167
General Electric, 273
Genovese, Eugene, 328
George, Barbara, 167
George Smith College, 6
George Washington Carver commemorative coin, 39
George Washington Carver Museum, 179
George Washington University, 19
Georgetown, Maryland, 86
Georgetown, South Carolina, 190
Georgia, 43, 76, 111, 190, 191, 209, 222, 241
Germany, 39, 135, 248, 253
Gershwin, George, 152
Gervin, George, 310
Ghana, 199
Giant Steps, 301, 332
Gibbs, Mifflin, 76
Gibson, Althea, 25, **296**, 309, 332
Gibson, Annie, 296
Gibson, Bob, **298**, 309
Gibson, Daniel, 296
Gibson, Josh, **95**, 104, **292**, 309
Gibson, Kenneth, 221
Gillespie, Dizzy, 138, 139, **140**, 150, 166
Gillespie, Frank L., 77
Gillespie, James, 140
Gillespie, Lattie, 140
Gilliam, Sam, **56**, 61
Gilpin, Charles, 129, 165
Gilpin Players, 129
Giovanni, Nikki, 25, 236, 318
Glacier National Park, 39
Gladys Knight and the Pips, 169
Glasgow, Scotland, 28, 265
Glasgow, University, 265
Glen Ellyn, Illinois, 14
Glenn, John, 281
Glory, 162
Glover, Danny, 170
Go Up for Glory, 295, 333

Goldberg, Whoopi, **163**, 170
Golden Circle Insurance Company, 78
Golden Globe Award, 161
Golden Glove award, 302, 303
Golden State Mutual Life Insurance
    Company, 43, 68, 69, 78
Gone with the Wind, 138, 165
Goode, Woodrow Wilson, 213, 221
Gooden, Samuel, 149
Gooding, Cuba, Jr., 170
Gooding, James Henry (Corporal), 258
Goodman, Andrew, 208
Goodman, Benny, 140
Goodman, Shirley, 167
Gordon, Dexter, 167
Gordon, Nora Antonia, 23
Gordone, Charles, 236
Gordy, Barry, Jr., 77
Goshen, New York, 9
Gossett, Louis, Jr., **160**, 170
Goteberg Symphony, 156
Gottschalk, Louis Moreau, 23
Gourdine, Meredith, 284
Goyens, William, 257
Graham, Billy, 10
Graham, Johnny, 159
Grambling, Louisiana, 123
Grambling, P.G., 123
Grambling State University, 112
Grammy Award, 137, 150, 152, 154, 161,
    164
Grand Rapids, Michigan, 157
Grant, George F., 283
Grant, Ulysses S. (General), 175
Granz, Norman, 139
Gravely, Samuel L., Jr. (Vice Admiral),
    254, 263
Graves, Earl G., Sr., 77
Gray, Dobie, 169
Great Barrington, Massachusetts, 15, 86,
    199
Great Bridge, 257
Great Depression, 42, 67
Great Mills, Maryland, 259
Great Northern Railroad, 39
Grebling, France, 252
Green, Al, **157**, 169
Green Bay Packers, 299, 304
Green Cove Springs, Florida, 42
Green, Julius, 168
Green Mountain Boys, 239
Greene, Joe, **301**, 310
Greene, Nancy, 92
Greene, Nathaniel (Major General), 82
Greene, Sylvester, 92

Greener, Richard Theodore, 122
Greenfield, Elizabeth Taylor, 165
Greenfield, Eloise, 105, 318
Greensboro, North Carolina, 183
Greenville, South Carolina, 17, 21, 142
Gregory, Dick, 25, 168
Grice, Francis, 59
Griffey, Ken, Jr., 311
Griffin, Archie, 310
Griffith-Joyner, Florence, 25, **304**, 310
Griggs, Sutton, 7, 23, 328
Grimes, Ting, 136
Grimké, Angelina, 220, 235
Grimké, Archibald, 220
Grimké, Charlotte L. Forten, 121, 320
Grimké, Francis James, 108, 235, 330
Groton, Connecticut, 241
Guerrero, Mexico, 184
Guggenheim Fellowship, 58
Gulf War, 255
Guillaume, Robert, 22
Gunter, Cornell, 146
Guthrie, Oklahoma, 281
Guy, Billy, 146

Hagler, Marvelous Marvin, 310
Haiti, 14, 30, 52, 83, 115, 182, 191, 198
Hale, Millie E., 104
Hales Ford, Virginia, 112
Haley, Alex, 58, 161, **233**, 237, 326, 328
Haley, Simon Alexander, 233
Halifax County, North Carolina, 192
Hall, Arsenio, 181
Hall, Henry A., 284
Hall, Jude, 257
Hall, Lloyd A., 24
Hall, Prince, 57, 121, 218
Hamer, Fannie Lou, 105, **208**, 220, 318
Hamilton, Virginia, 25, 313
Hamlet, North Carolina, 151
Hammer, M.C., 170
Hammett, Dashiel, 229
Hammon, John, 138
Hammon, Jupiter, 235
Hammonds, David, 60
Hampton, Carl, 158
Hampton, Fred, 209
Hampton Institute, 5, 12, 32, 85, 114, 122
Hampton University, 58
Hampton, Lionel, 21, 24, **140**, 166, 322
Handy, William C., **7**, 23, 98, **128**, 141,
    165, 178, 180, 322
Hansberry, Lorraine, 236
Haralson, Jeremiah, 192
Harbor Bank of Maryland, 78

Harlem, 11, 18, 19, 21, 42, 54, 55, 71, 86, 96, 138, 180, 226, 228, 229, 232, 272, 279, 291, 296, 328
Harlem Art School, 17
Harlem Artist Guild, 50
Harlem Community Art Center, 42
Harlem Globetrotters, 297, 309
Harlem Hospital, 53, 272, 276
Harlem Renaissance, 5, 41, 89, 225, 227
Harlem School for the Arts, 119
Harleston, Edwin, 46, 104
Harleston, Elise Forrest, 46, 60
Harmon, Cornellius, 250
Harmon (Foundation) Award, 42, 44, 47, 276
Harmon, Leonard Roy, **250**, 261
Harper, Fenton, 176
Harper, Francis Ellen Watkins, 176
Harper, William, 59
Harper's Bazaar, 45
Harper's Ferry, Virginia, 188
Harrell, Vernon, 146
Harriet and the Promised Land, 105, 318
Harriet Tubman Home for the Aged, 179
Harris, Addie "Micki," 146
Harris, James, 284
Harris, James H. (Sergeant), 259
Harris, Judia C. Jackson, 123
Harris, Patricia Roberts, **19**, 25
Harris Prize, 59
Harris, Ruth Ethel, 13
Harris, Samuel, 112
Harrisburg Giants, 294
Harrisburg, Pennsylvania, 193
Harrison, Benjamin, 203
Harrison, Richard B., 41, 135, 166
Harrison, Wilbert, 167
Hartford, Connecticut, 27, 30, 41, 49
Harvard University, 12, 13, 32, 58, 69, 89, 92, 109, 111, 112, 115, 124, 133, 199, 201, 227, 270, 278; Harvard University Divinity School, 115; Harvard Medical School, 266, 272, 275, 278
Harvey, Steve, 163, 170
Haskins, James, 313, 318, 322, 325
Hastie, William Henry, 124, 220
Hathaway, Isaac, 39, 59
Hattiesburg, Mississippi, 95, 253
Haughton, Aaliyah, 170
Hawaii, 66, 325, 326
Hawaiian Kingdom, 63
Hawkins, Coleman, **93**, 104, **139**, 166
Hawkins, Mary, 227

Hawkins, Thomas (Sergeant-Major), 258, 259
Hawthorne, Nina, 194
Hayden, Belle, 6
Hayden, Della Irving, 123
Hayden, Palmer C., **42**, 160
Hayden, Robert, 236, 266, 313, 332
Hayes, Charles, 202
Hayes, Elvin, 310
Hayes, Isaac, **156**, 169
Hayes, Robert "Bob," 310
Hayes, Roland, 165
Hayes, Rutherford B., 199
Haynes, Lemuel, 257
Hazelhurst, Mississippi, 95
HBO, 161
Headliner, D.J., 163
Heard, Josephine D., 103
Hearns, Thomas, 310
Hector, Edward, 257
Hedgeman, Peyton Cole, 41
Height, Dorothy I., 24, 220
Heisman trophy, 302
Helena, Arkansas, 94
Hempstead, New York, 301
Henderson, Alice (Reverend), 263
Henderson, Fletcher, 165
Hendrix, Jimi, 168
Henry, John, 41, **84**, 103, 318
Henson, Josiah, 23, 235
Henson, Matthew A., **86**, 103, **176**, 182, 313, 323
Hercules, Frank, 328
Herenton, Willie, **216**, 221
Herndon, Alonzo, **66**, 76
Herring, James V., 61
Herron Art Institute, 44
Hickman, Robert T., 219
Hield, Omerit, 163
Higginbotham, A. Leon, Jr., 221
High Point, North Carolina, 99, 151
Highland Community Bank, 78
Highwarden, Ethel, 275
Hill, Leslie Pinckney, 123
Hill, Z.Z., **160**, 170
Hilton, Alfred B. (Sergeant), 259
Hilyer, Amanda Gray, 103
Himes, Chester Bomar, **229**, 236, 327, 328
Himes, Joseph Sandy, 229
Hines, Earl, 13
Hines, Gregory, 169
Hines, Wilber, 14
Hinton, William A., 283

Hirsch, Stanley, 45
Hodge, Alex, 145
Hogeboom, Hannah, 81
Hogeboom, Pieter, 81
Holiday, Billie, **96**, 105, **138**, 166, 322
Holiday, Clarence, 96
Holland, Jerome Heartwell, 77
Holland, Milton, 258, 259
Holland, William H., 122
Holly Springs, Mississippi, 113, 122, 183, 198
Holtuka, Oklahoma, 252
Holtzclaw, William H., 123
Holy Land, 13, 32
Holyfield, Evander, 310
Homestead Grays, 287, 291, 294, 308, 309
Homestead, Pennsylvania, 290
Honolulu, Hawaii, 217
Hood, William, 212
Hooker, John Lee, 169
Hooks, Benjamin, **211**, 221
Hooks, Julia, 23
Hoover, Herbert, 201
Hope, John, 23, 103, 111, 123, 321
Hopewell Baptist Church, 7
Horace Trumbaur and Associates, 69
Horne, Lena, 14, **141**, 166, 313, 322
Hornung, Paul, 299
Horton, Bill, 167
Horton, George Moses, 23
Horton, Gladys, 148
Houeston, Cornelia, 41
House, Son, 166
Houston, Charles Hamilton, **116**, 124
Houston, Norman O., **68**
Houston Oilers, 310
Houston, Texas, 55, 100, 211, 214, 217, 262, 315
Houston, Whitney, 170
Howard, Oliver Otis (General), 122, 123
Howard University, 5, 9, 13, 19, 31, 45, 58, 68, 89, 91, 98, 108, 112, 114, 115, 116, 117, 119, 121, 123, 124, 141, 142, 175, 195, 198, 214, 227, 234, 244, 270, 273, 275, 276, 279, 284; Howard University Hospital, 278; Howard University Law School, 94; Howard University Medical School, 87, 275; Howard University School of Music, 129; Howard University School of Religion, 203
Howells, William Dean, 224
Hudlun, Anna, 23
Hudlun, Joseph Henry, Sr., 23

Hughes, Carrie, 226
Hughes, James, 226
Hughes, Langston, **39**, 55, **92**, 101, 104, 228, 232, 235, 236, 313, 314, 318, 320, 327, 328
Hughes, Leon, 146
Hull, Agrippa, 257
Humphrey, Daisy Elizabeth, 142
Humphreys, Richard, 121
Hunt, Henry Alexander, 123
Hunt, Henry Alexander, Sr., 111
Hunt, Mariah, 111
Hunt, Tommy, 147
Hunter, Alberta, 132, 165, 323
Hunter, Clementine, 104
Hunter College, 120
Hunter, Ivory Joe, 167
Hunter, Jane Edna, 47
Hunter, Kristin, 21, 22, 237, 313, 328
Hurricane Plantation, 175
Hurston, John, 9
Hurston, Zora Neale, **9**, 24, **228**, 229, 236, 328
Hurt, Mississippi John, 165
Huston-Tillotson College, 89, 178
Hyman, John Adams, **196**

I Have Changed, 291, 333
IBM Corporation, 74
If Beale Street Could Talk, 233, 237, 327
Illinois, 197, 201, 202, 213, 217, 218, 220, 230
Illinois Service Federal S & L, 78
Imitation of Life, 92, 165
Impact Magazine, 164
impressionism, 59; impressionistic, 60
Impressions, 168
Independence Federal Savings Bank, 78
Indiana, 4, 197, 215, 218, 221
Indianapolis ABCs, 294
Indianapolis Clowns, 289, 294, 295, 309
Indianapolis Crawfords, 294
Indianapolis, Indiana, 66, 138, 291, 294
Indians, 83, 239, 246
Industrial Bank of Washington, 78
Ingram, Luther, 169
Ink Spots, 166
Institute for Colored Youth, 69
Institute of Race Relations, 13
Institute, West Virginia, 262
Internal Revenue Service, 195
International Association of Fire Chiefs, 273
International Association of Professional Fire Fighters, 77

International Boxing Hall of Fame, 300
International League, 97
International Sugar Cane Technologist, 266
International Transport Service Employee Union, 69
Iowa State College/University, 111, 117, 122
Iraq, 255
Irby, Ray, 78
Irvin, Monte, 309
Isley Brothers, 168
Isley, O'Kelly, 150
Isley, Ronald, 150
Isley, Rudolph, 150
Isley, Vernon, 150
Italy, 251, 252, 254
Ithaca, New York, 233
Itta Bena, Mississippi, 118, 183
Iverson, Allen, 311

Jackie Robinson commemorative coins, **306**
Jackson 5, 169
Jackson, Alfred, 112
Jackson, Augustus, 282
Jackson, Bo, 333
Jackson, Chuck, 167
Jackson, Jackie, 157
Jackson, Janet, 170
Jackson, Jermaine, 157
Jackson, Jesse, 25, 202, **209**, 221, 314, 319, 322
Jackson, J.J., 168
Jackson, Louise Terrell, 112
Jackson, Mahalia, **16**, 25, 136, **144**, 166, 314, 322
Jackson, Marlon, 157
Jackson, Mary Howard, 44
Jackson, Maynard, Jr., 211, 221
Jackson, Maynard, Sr., 211
Jackson, Michael, 157, 170
Jackson, Mississippi, 8, 14, 110, 113, 208
Jackson, Patterson & Parks, 211
Jackson, Raymond, 158
Jackson, Reggie, **302**, 310
Jackson, Shirley Ann, 284
Jackson State University, 120, 122, 229, 303, 320
Jackson, Tennessee, 110, 183
Jackson, Tito, 157
Jacksonville, Florida, 7, 42, 262, 272, 295
Jacksonville Tars, 295
Jacobs, Adolph, 146
Jaffrey, New Hampshire, 182

Jakes, T.D., 222
Jamaica, 14, 200
James, Daniel "Chappie," Jr. (General), **255**, 263
James, Elmore, 166
James, Etta, 169
James Hubert Blake High School, 127
James, Joe Willie, 143
James, Miles (Corporal), 259
James, Rick, 169
James, Willy F., Jr., 261
Jamestown Tercentennial, 40
Jamison, Clarence (Captain), 261
Jamison, Judith, 170
Jasper, John, 219
Jeanes, Anna T., 88, 123
Jefferson, Blind Lemon, 165
Jefferson City, Missouri, 17, 108, 182, 229
Jefferson Lecturer, 230
Jemison, Mae C., 105
Jemmy, 218
Jenkins, Robert H., Jr. (Private First Class), 262
Jersey City, New Jersey, 156
Jerusalem, 59
Jimmy's Chicken Shack, 18
"Joe Turner," 165
Joel, Lawrence (Specialist Sixth Class), 262
"John Brown's Body," 260
John, Daymond, 78
John, "Little" Willie, 167
John's Island, South Carolina, 260
Johnson Brothers, 144
Johnson C. Smith University, 114
Johnson, Carolyn, 115
Johnson, Charles Spurgeon, 57, 104, **118**, 124, 314
Johnson, Clarence, 157
Johnson, Dwight (Specialist Fifth Class), 262
Johnson, Earvin "Magic," 310, 318
Johnson, Eddie Bernice, 211, 221
Johnson, George E., **71**, 77
Johnson, Georgia Douglas, 235
Johnson, Halle Tanner Dillon, 283
Johnson, Henry, 260
Johnson, Jack, 283, 308
Johnson, James P., 13, **91**, 104, **130**, 134, 165, 321
Johnson, James Weldon, 7, **225**, 227, 235, 328
Johnson, John H., **70**, 71, 77, 317
Johnson, Judy, 292

Johnson, Katherine G., 285
Johnson, Lyndon B., 94, 277
Johnson, Malvin Gray, **46**
Johnson, Michael Duane, **305**, 311
Johnson, (Wyatt) Mordecai, **115**, 123
Johnson, Noah, 95
Johnson, P., 282
Johnson Products Company, Inc., 71
Johnson Publishing Company, 70
Johnson, Rafer, 309
Johnson, Ralph (musician), 159
Johnson, Ralph (Private First Class), 262
Johnson, Robert (musician), **95**, 104, 166
Johnson, Robert L., 78
Johnson, Robert W., 296
Johnson, Sargent, **44**
Johnson, Terry, 147
Johnson, William H., **47**, **48**, **49**, 316
Johnson, William Julius "Judy," **289**, 308
Johnson, William T., 76
Johnson, Wyatt, 115
Johnson-Brown, Hazel W. (Brigadier
 General), 263
Johnston, Joshua, **27**, 59
Joint Chiefs of Staff, 255
Joliet, Illinois, 14
Jones, Creadel "Red," 157
Jones, David "Deacon," 309
Jones, Emma, 40
Jones, Frederick McKinley, 24, **275**, 283,
 332
Jones, James Earl, 167
Jones, Jane C. Wright, **279**, 284
Jones, John, 103
Jones, Lois Mailou, 50, 60
Jones, Marion, 311
Jones, Minnie Eva, 56
Jones, Orville "Hoppy," 166
Jones, Phalin, 154
Jones, Philly Joe, 151
Jones, Quincy, 170
Jones, Ruth Lee (*see* Washington, Dinah)
Jones, Virginia Lacy, 104
Jones, Will "Dub," 146
Joplin, Missouri, 226
Joplin, Scott, **6**, 23, **128**, 180
Jordan, Ben, 211
Jordan, Arlyne, 211
Jordan, Barbara, **211**, 325
Jordan, Michael "Air," **305**, 310, 317
Jordan, Vernon, 221
Joseph, Ronald, 61
Journal of Negro Education, 116, 124
Journal of Negro History, 115

Joyner, Tom, Sr., 170
Joyner-Kersee, Jackie, 310
Julian, Percy L., **92**, **274**, 283
Julius Rosenwald Fellowship, 58
Julius Rosenwald Fund, 60, 81
Julliard School of Music, 150, 152, 156
Juneteenth, 174
Junior, Marvin, 145
Junior Walker and the All Stars, 168
Just, Ernest E., **8**, 24, 104, **275**, 283, 332
Just Us Women, 101, 317

K-Doe, Ernie, 167
Kaiser, Ernest D., 9
Kansas, 67, 87, 175, 196, 197, 219, 247
Kansas City Athletics, 289, 293
Kansas City Call, 12
Kansas City Chiefs, 299, 300
Kansas City, Kansas, 18, 73
Kansas City, Missouri, 18, 134, 261, 308
Kansas City Monarchs, 288, 289, 291,
 292
Kansas State University, 28
Karamu Players, 129
Katherine Dunham Dance Company, 99
Kay, Ulysses, 170
Keaton, James Max, 274
Keith, Damon J., 221
Kelley, William Melvin, 236
Kelly, Alexander (First Sergeant), 259
Kendricks, Eddie, **153**
Kennedy, John F., 94, 230
Kent County, Maryland, 83
Kentucky, 58, 87, 108, 121, 189
Kentucky Derby, 287
Kentucky Normal and Industrial Institute,
 58
Kentucky State Industrial College, 207
Kentucky State University, 58, 180
Ketcham, Ceah, 272
Keys, Alicia, 170
Khadafy, Moammar, 255
Kickapoo Springs, Texas, 246
Killens, John Oliver, 236, 237
Kimball Union Academy, 30
King, Albert, 170
King, B.B., **157**, 160, 169
King, Ben E., 144, 167
King, Bennie, 222
King Cole Trio, 98, 141
King, Coretta Scott, 25, 101, 102
King, Edward (Sergeant), 246
King George's War, 223
King, Jay, 162

King, Jimmy, 154
King, Martin Luther, Jr., 12, 20, 25, 61, **99**, 105, 117, 120, 178, 179, 180, 205, 206, **214**, 221, 233, 317, 325
"King of Swing," 165
King, William, 169
Kirby, Colonial Jack, 122
Kirk, Ronald, 222
Kitt, Eartha, 105, 167, 322
Knight, Gwendolyn, 52
Knight, Marie, 137
Knox College, 191
Knoxville College, 122
Knoxville, Tennessee, 109, 130, 183, 190
Knowles, Beyoncé, **164**, 170
Kool & The Gang, 169
Koontz, Elizabeth Duncan, 125
Koontz, Roscoe L., 284
Korea, 255
Korean War, 253
Kosciusko, Mississippi, 184
Kosciusko, Tadeuz, 240
Kountz, Samuel L., 284
Krabbe, Katrin, **304**
Krake, Holca, 47
Krupa, Gene, 140
Kwanzaa, 221, 325
KWEM radio station, 95

La Grange, Georgia, 6, 272
Lafayette, James Armistead, 241, 257
Lafayette Players, 129
Lagos, Nigeria, 207
Lake Erie, 273
Lake Ontario, 242
Lake Oroville, 173
Lakeside, 169
Lamar, Lucius Q.C., 196
Lamb, Pompey, 257
Lampkin, Daisy, 104
Lance, J.W., 146
Lane, Ann, 230
Lane College, 110, 122, 178
Lane, Isaac (Bishop), 122
Lane, Pinkie Gordon, 25
Laney, Lucy, 121
Langhorn, Garfield M. (Private First Class), 262
Langley Research Center, 281
Langston, Lucy, 198
Langston, John Mercer, 122, **198**, 219, 324
Langston, Oklahoma, 90, 182
Lanier, Willie, 310
Lansing, Michigan, 207, 280

LaPread, Ronald, 169
Larsen, Nella, 235, 329
LaRue, Florence, 154
Las Animas Canyon, New Mexico, 247
lasting machine, 85
Lathem, Lambo, 257
Latifah, Queen, 170
Latimer, Catherine A., 24
Latimer, Lewis H., **269**, 282, 283
Lattany, Kristin Hunter, 25, 237
Laurel, Mississippi, 19, 152
Laurinburg Institute, 140
Lawless, Alfred, Jr., 276
Lawless, Theodore K., **276**, 284
Lawrence, Jacob, 25, **52**, **53**, 60, 101, 180, 315, 318
Lawrence, Kansas, 196
Lawrence, Margaret M., 25
Lawrence, Martin, 170
Lawrence, Robert H., Jr., 284
Lawson, John, **245**, 260
Lawson, Pearl, 44
League on Non-violent Civil Disobedience, 11
Lean on Me, 25
"Lean on Me," 159, 161
Ledbetter, Huddie "Leadbelly," **8**, 24, **129**, 131, 165
Lee, Barron, 13
Lee, Beverly, 146
Lee, Canada, 165
Lee, Leonard, 167
Lee, Spike, 162, 170
Lee, Tom, **177**
Leflore County, Mississippi, 118
Legacy Bank, 78
Legion d'Honneur, 32, 131
Leidesdorff, William A., **187**, 218
Leland, George Thomas "Mickey," 211, 221
Leland, Mississippi, 148
Lemon, Meadowlark, 291, 296, 333
LeMoyne-Owen College, 121
Leonard, Buck, **299**, 309
Leonard, Matthew (Sergeant), 262
Leonard, Sugar Ray, 310
Lester, Robert, 157
Let the Circle Be Unbroken, 101, 314
Leutze, Emanuel Gottlieb, 240
Lew, Barzillai, 257
Lewis, Arthur, 78
Lewis, Bobby, 167
Lewis, Carl, 310
Lewis, Edmonia, 23, **31**, **32**, 59
Lewis, Ida E., 77, 237

Lewis, John, 190, 222
Lewis, Ramsey, 167
Lewis, Rich, 167
Lewis, Rudy, 144
Lewis, Samella Sanders, 25, 315
Lewisburg, West Virginia, 240
Lexington, Kentucky, 39
Liberia, 27, 30, 83, 112, 187, 218, 230, 248, 249, 274, 275
Liberty Bank and Trust, 78
Liberty City, 179
Liberty County, Georgia, 246
Liberty, Jeff, 257
Liberty Life Insurance Company, 67, 68
Library of Congress, 90, 224, 230
Libya, 255
Life and Times of Frederick Douglass, 218, 324
Lincoln, Abraham, 31, 47, 63, 174, 192, 243, 271
Lincoln College, 182
Lincoln Hospital, 272
Lincoln Institute, 18, 207
Lincoln Memorial, 133
Lincoln Players, 139
Lincoln Ridge, Kentucky, 18, 207
Lincoln University (Missouri), 17, 121
Lincoln University (Pennsylvania), 49, 94, 117, 121, 124, 226, 275, 279
Linden, Texas, 6
Lion, Jules, 59
Lionel Hampton School of Music, 140
Lippincott Prize, 59
Lipscomb, Gene, 309
Little, Earl, 207
Little Eva, 167
Little, Louise, 207
Little, Malcolm (*see* X, Malcolm)
Little Richard, 166
Little Rock, Arkansas, 8, 10, 63, 119, 175, 183, 206
Livingston, Alabama, 213
Lloyd, John Henry "Pop," 24, 308
Locke, Alain Leroy, 24, 57, 123, **227**, 235, 316, 322, 329
Locke, Pliny Ishmael, 227
Logan, Arthur C., 284
Logan, Rayford W., **115**, 123, 325
Lomax, Alan, 90
London, England, 6, 129, 132, 152, 223, 269, 292
Long Creek, North Carolina, 56
Long, Donald Russell (Sergeant), 262
Long Island, New York, 151, 187, 301
Long, Jefferson Franklin, **190**, **191**, 219

Longfellow, Henry Wadsworth, 32
Longworth, Nicolas, 28
Lorain County, Ohio, 219
Lorman, Mississippi, 109
Los Angeles, California, 13, 16, 20, 21, 51, 69, 74, 79, 98, 107, 121, 138, 140, 158, 182, 212, 229, 261, 290, 294, 303, 307
Los Angeles Clippers, 303
Los Angeles Community College, 164
Los Angeles Lakers, 21, 297, 301, 303, 307
Los Angeles Rams, 294, 298
Lou Gehrig's disease, 98
Louis, Joe (*see* Barrow, Joseph Louis)
Louisa County, Virginia, 198
Louisiana, 18, 64, 76, 83, 112, 172, 189, 194, 215, 229, 241, 242, 243, 331
Louisiana National Guard Corps d'Afrique, 194
Louisville Defender, 78
Louisville, Kentucky, 73, 140, 176
Louvre, 32
Love, J.L., 282
Love, Nat, 103, **199**, 219, 317
Lowell Institute, 29
Lowell, John, 29
Lowell, John, Jr., 29
Loyola University (Illinois), 280
LTD, 169
Lubbock, Texas, 214
Lumby Indian, 191
Lundy, Richard, 288
Luxemburg, 19
Lynch, David, 145
Lynch, John R., 23, **194**, 219, 325
Lynch, Patrick, 194
Lynchburg, Virginia, 113, 225, 296
Lynk, Miles Vandahurst, 283
Lynn, Massachusetts, 85, 268

Mabley, Jackie "Moms," 165
Mabry, Nauita, 250
Mackinac Island, 182
Macon, Georgia, 20, 190, 262
Macon, Mississippi, 6
Mad Lads, 168
Madison, Wisconsin, 154
Mahoncy, Mary Eliza, 271, 282
Maine, 218
Malden, West Virginia, 85, 182
Malone, Annie M. Turbo, **67**, 76
Malone, Karl, 311
Malone, Moses, 310
Malone, Vivian, 125

Mandela, Nelson, 216, 221
Manhasset, New York, 142
Manhattan State Hospital, 6
"Maple Leaf Rag," 164
Marcell, Oliver "Ghost," 288
Marciano, Rocky, 17
Marconi Award, 164
Marion, Alabama, 20
Marley, Bob, 169
Marsh Engineering Company, 177
Marshall, John, 82
Marshall, Paule, 231, 329
Marshall, Texas, 184, 203
Marshall, Thurgood, **94**, 104, **203**, 220,
   318
Marshall, T.J., 282
Martha and the Vandellas, 168
Martin, J. Alexander, 78
Martin, Roberta, **94**, 104, 167
Martin, William, 94
Martinique, 14
Marvelettes, 167
Mary Allen Junior College, 179
Mary Lou Williams Center for Black
   Culture, 134
Mary Mahoney Medal, 271
Mary McLeod Bethune Memorial, 178
Maryland, 4, 16, 52, 78, 176, 179, 189,
   221
Mason, Biddy, **107**, 121
Mason, John Young, 27
Mason, Michigan, 19
Masons, 57
Massachusetts, 12, 81, 83, 85, 123, 179,
   209, 218, 223, 239, 244, 267
Massey, Walter E., **278**, 284
Massillion, Ohio, 259
Matadors, 151
Mather, Cotton, 265
Mathis, Johnny, 167
Matos, Luis Palés, 236
Matson, Ollie, 309
Matthews, Saul, 257
Matthews, Victoria Earle, 103
Matzeliger, Jan, **85**, **268**, 282
Mayan Indians, 185
Maybe I'll Pitch Forever, 333
Mayfield, Curtis, 149
Mayfield, Julian, 236
Mayfield, Kentucky, 58
Maynor, Dorothy, 125
Mays, Benjamin E., 124, 320
Mays, Willie, 105, **293**, 309
Maysville Presbyterian Mission School,
   88

Maysville, South Carolina, 88
McAdoo, Bob, 310
McAfee, Walter, 284
McCabe, Edward, **175**
McCary, Michael, 163
McCauley, James, 205
McCauley, Leona, 205
McClendon, Dorothy, 284
McClendon, Rosalie "Rose," 24
McComb, Mississippi, 145
McCoo, Marilyn, 154
McCovey, Willie Lee, **297**, 309
McCoy, Elijah, 24. 64, 180, **267**, 282
McCree, D., 282
McCullough, Geraldine, 61
McCullough, Samuel, 257
McDaniel, Hattie, **138**, 166
McDonald, Carrie, 93
McDonald, Freda Josephine (*see* Baker,
   Josephine)
McElroy, Thomas, 162
McGhee, Brownie, 15
McGhee, Howard, **150**
McGill, Michael, 145
McGill University (Montreal, Quebec),
   93, 123
McGovern, George, 210
McKane, Alice Woodby, 282
McKay, Al, 159
McKay, Claude, 104, **226**, 235, 327
McKissack and McKissack, 76
McKissack, Moses, 76
McKissack, William, 76
McLary, Thomas, 169
McLemore, Lamonte, 154
McLeod, Patsy, 88
McLeod, Samuel, 88
McMillan, Terry, 237
McNair, Denise, 208
McNair, Ronald E., 284
McNeil, Herman Atkins, 42
McPhatter, Clyde, **100**, 105, 144
McPherson, James Alan, 237
Mechanics and Farmers Bank, 78
Medal of Honor, 251
Medal of the Resistance, 131
Meharry brothers, 122
Meharry Hospital, 298
Meharry Medical College, 86, 110, 281,
   321
Melrose, Louisiana, 63, 76, 182
Memphis City Schools, 125
Memphis Free Speech and Headlight, 23
Memphis Red Sox, 289, 308
Memphis Showboats, 304

Memphis, Tennessee, 5, 6, 7, 8, 14, 17, 18, 66, 67, 69, 70, 73, 75, 89, 95, 108, 125, 133, 145, 154, 160, 164, 177, 182, 183, 194, 198, 203, 209, 215, 216, 289
Men's Sunday Club, 57
Mercer County, Virginia, 84
Meredith, James, 125
Meriden, Connecticut, 271
Meridian, New Hampshire, 8, 30
Meriwether, Louise, 237, 319
Meriwether, W. Delano, 284
metallurgy, 27
Metcalf, Ralph, **290**, 308
Methodist Church, 110
Metropolitan Opera, 100, 152
Mexican-American War, 242, 257
Mexico, 39, 58, 171, 181, 185, 186, 187, 188, 199, 226, 242, 289
Miami Dolphins, 299
Miami, Florida, 74, 79, 149, 183
Miami Marlin, 289
Micheaux, Oscar, 24
Michigan, 28, 172, 218, 220
Michigan State University, 299
Mickens, Robert, 160
Milan, Italy, 152
Miles College, 110, 113, 180, 213
Miles, William H. (Bishop), 123
Miller, Dorie, **249**, 261
Miller, Johnny, 16
Miller, May, 24
Miller, Thomas E., 172
Mills, Florence, 104
Milton, North Carolina, 63
Milwaukee Braves, 295
Milwaukee Bucks, 21, 298, 301
Milwaukee, Wisconsin, 73
Mims, Florida, 204
Miner Teachers' College, 107
Mingus, Charles, **98**, 105, 169
Minneapolis Millers, 293
Minneapolis, Minnesota, 99
Minnesota, 173, 186, 218
Minnesota Twins, 305
Minnesota Vikings, 300
Miracles, **151**, 167
Mississippi, 4, 5, 6, 12, 23, 41, 97, 109, 110, 145, 174, 175, 181, 191, 194, 196, 232, 320, 324
Mississippi Freedom Democratic Party (MFDP), 206, 208
Mississippi Industrial College, 123
Mississippi Levee Board, 196
Mississippi River, 177, 196

Mississippi Valley State University, 118, 124, 179
Mississippi Vocational College, 118
Missouri, 108, 180, 188, 189, 196, 197, 215, 218, 221, 243
Mitchell, Arthur, 167, 202
Mitchell, Clarence M., Jr., 221
Mitchell, James W., 285
Mitchell, Juanita, 24
Mitchell, Parren H., 210
Mitchell, Willie, 157, 169
Mobile, Alabama, 146, 242, 295, 297
Mobile Bay, Alabama, 260, 293
Mobile Black Bears, 295
Mobile Tigers, 289
Monaco, 131
Monette's (Harlem), 138
"Money," 147
Money, Mississippi, 205
Monk, Thelonious Sphere, **17**, 25, **146**, 151, 167
Monroe, Earl, 310
Monroe, George, **188**, 218
Monroe, Louisiana, 67, 73, 100
Monrovia, Liberia, 249
Monsanto Corporation, 215
Montana, 39
Montgomery, Alabama, 13, 20, 40, 92, 97, 98, 104, 179, 184, 205
Montgomery, Benjamin, 175
Montgomery County, Mississippi, 208
Montgomery, Isaiah Thornton, **175**
Montgomery, Wes, 168
Montgomery, William Thornton, 175
Montreal Royals, 97
Moody Bible Institute, 88
Moon, John P., 285
Moon, Mollie, 104
Moore, Aaron McDuffie, 65, 76, 77
Moore, Archie, 309
Moore, Harry T., 220
Moore, Johnny, 144
Moore, Lenny, 296, 310
Moore, Oscar, 141
Moore, Pete, 151
Moore, Sam, 168
Moore, Warren "Pete," **151**
Moorhead, Scipio, 59
Mooringsport, Louisiana, 8
Mora, Elizabeth Catlett, 51, **58**, 315
Mora, Francisco, 58
Moravia, Spain, 229
Morehouse College, 6, 111, 113, 115, 117, 277, 278
Morehouse, Henry L., 121

Morgan, Daniel (Brigadier General), 82
Morgan, Elizabeth Reed, 273
Morgan, Emily, 257
Morgan, Garrett A., 23, 180, **273**, 283
Morgan, Lyttleton F., 121
Morgan, Norma, 61
Morgan, "Sister" Gertrude, **57**
Morgan State College/University, 93,
    108, 116, 179, 213
Morgan, Sydney, 273
Morganfield, McKinley, **97**, 105, **145**,
    166 (*see also* "Muddy Waters")
Morial, Ernest, 221
Morocco, 59
Morris Brown College, 110, 180
Morris, Greg, 169
Morris Island, South Carolina, 182
Morris, Nathan, 163
Morris, Wanya, 163
Morrison, Toni, **234**, 237, 329
Morse, Alvin, 146
Morton, Ferdinand "Jelly Roll," **90**, 104,
    128, 160, 165
Moseley-Braun, Carol, **216**, 221
Moss, Tom, 203
Mossell, Gertrude E.H. Bustill, 235
Mossell, Nathan Francis, 283
Moten, Buster, 13
Moten, Lucy Ellen, 121
Motley, Archibald, 60
Motley, Constance Baker, 220
Motley, Marion, 309
Motley, Willard, 236, 329
Moton, Booker, 114
Moton, Robert Russa, 23, **114**, 123, 320
Motown Industries, 71
Mound Bayou, Mississippi, 175, 182, 208
Mount Lebanon Singers, 100
Mount Meigs, Alabama, 14
Mount Vernon, New York, 162
Mt. Sinai, Alabama, 16
"Muddy Waters," **97**, **145**, 166
Mufaro's Beautiful Daughters, 101, 105,
    319
Muhammad, Elijah, 220
Muir Technical High School, 97
Mulzac, Hugh N., 261
Munich, Germany, 39, 254
Murphy, Carl, 67, 123
Murphy, Eddie, 170
Murphy, Gertrude Mae, 99
Murphy, Isaac, **287**, 308
Murphy, John Henry, 76
Murray, Charles D., Sr., 77
Murray, Donald Gaines, 94

Murray, George W., 192, 219, 283
Murray, Margaret James, 85
Muse, Clarence, 139, 166
Museum of Modern Art, 45
My Bondage and My Freedom, 218, 324
Myers, Isaac, 76

Nabrit, James M., Jr., 125
Nabrit, Samuel M., 284
Nail, John E., 77
Nantucket, Massachusetts, 189
Napier, Nettie Langston, 23
Naples, Texas, 160
Nash, Charles Edward, 195, 219
Nash, Johnny, 169
Nashville Elite Giants, 288, 289, 308
Nashville Songwriters International Hall
    of Fame, 136
Nashville, Tennessee, 5, 21, 44, 45, 65,
    66, 74, 76, 89, 108, 110, 114, 176,
    183, 197, 199, 288, 298
Natchez, Mississippi, 5, 63, 110, 194
Natchitoches, Louisiana, 89
National Academy of Design, 36, 51, 60
National Academy of Sciences, 277, 280
National Action Council for Minorities in
    Engineering, Inc., 79
National Aeronautics and Space
    Administration (NASA), 276, 281
National African American Museum, 61
National Alliance of Black Educators, 77
National Association for the Advance-
    ment of Colored People (NAACP),
    24, 46, 51, 199, 200, 201, 224, 227
National Association of Black
    Accountants (NABA), 77
National Association of Black Journalists,
    78
National Association of Black Social
    Workers, 77
National Association of Black Telecom-
    munications Professionals, 78
National Association of Blacks in
    Criminal Justice, 78
National Association of Broadcasters, 164
National Association of Colored Graduate
    Nurses, 271, 272, 274
National Association of Colored Women,
    175, 200, 203
National Association of Independent Real
    Estate Brokers, 79
National Association of Women Printers
    and Sculptors, 42
National Autonomous University of New
    Mexico, 58

National Baptist Convention, 88, 99
National Bar Association, 77
National Basketball Association (NBA),
  295, 297, 298, 301, 302, 303, 304,
  305, 306, 307
National Black MBA Association, 77
National Black Nurses Association, 77
National Black Police Association, 77
National Civil Rights Museum, 178, 221
National Conservatory Music School, 128
National Council of Negro Women, 15,
  206
National Dental Association, 78
National Education Association (NEA),
  120
National Endowment for the Humanities,
  230
National Endowment of the Arts, 41
National Football Hall of Fame, 303
National Football League (NFL), 288,
  292, 299, 303, 306, 307
National Funeral Directors & Morticians
  Association, 77
National Heritage Fellowship, 41
National Inventors Hall of Fame, 277
National Labor Relations Board, 211
National Medal of Technology, 275
National Medical Association, 76, 271
National Museum of American Art, 31,
  47
National Negro Business League, 76
National Organization for the
  Professional Advancement of Black
  Chemists and Chemical Engineers, 78
National Public Welfare League, 7
National Research Council, 279
National Society of Black Physicists, 78
National Technical Association (NTA),
  281
National Urban League, 76
National Women's Hall of Fame, 206
Naval Academy, 235, 265
Naval Research Laboratory, 277
Navy Cross, 249, 250
Navy Distinguished Flying Cross, 253
Navy Medal of Honor, 243, 244, 245,
  246, 247, 258
Naylor, Gloria, 237
Nazis, 275
Negro Digest, 70, 77
Negro History Week, 302
Negro League World Series, 289, 290,
  291, 292
Negro Leagues (Baseball), 95, 287, 290,
  292, 293, 333

Negro Leagues Baseball Museum, 288
Negro Mountain, 239
Negro Society for Historical Research, 57
Nelson, Annie Greene, 104
Nelson, Dave, **134**
Nelson, Nate, 147
Nelson, Willie, 150
"Nemesis," 257
Nevada, 32, 219
Neville, Aaron, 168
New Bedford, Massachusetts, 4, 258
New Brunswick, Canada, 29, 84
New Brunswick, New Jersey, 91, 130
New Canton, Virginia, 88
New England, 28, 29
New Hampshire, 172, 218, 239
New Haven, Connecticut, 30, 56, 82
New Jersey, 3, 31, 78, 188, 218, 221
New Market Heights, Virginia, 259
New Mexico, 171
New Orleans Black Pelicans, 289
New Orleans Feetwarmers, 133
New Orleans, Louisiana, 3, 4, 11, 19, 27,
  44, 74, 83, 90, 132, 133, 146, 173,
  183, 194, 195, 209, 242, 257, 266,
  268, 282, 324
New York Age, 70
New York Black Yankees, 289, 290, 308
New York Cancer Society, 279
New York City, 6, 8, 15, 17, 18, 19, 20,
  21, 27, 31, 36, 38, 39, 42, 47, 50, 51,
  53, 54, 56, 57, 58, 65, 66, 67, 73, 79,
  83, 86, 91, 94, 95, 112, 121, 128, 129,
  131, 132, 133, 134, 135, 136, 137,
  139, 141, 150, 152, 153, 156, 158,
  160, 172, 183, 186, 191, 194, 200,
  207, 214, 220, 248, 249, 274, 260,
  262, 269, 272, 273, 279, 280, 290
New York City Board of Elections, 214
New York Cubans, 289, 291
New York Giants, 99, 293
New York Knicks, 301, 302
New York Library, 57
New York Lincoln Giants, 287, 289, 294
New York Mets, 293
New York Nets, 301
New York (State), 196
New York State Centennial, 60
New York Stock Exchange, 71, 72
New York University, 44, 45, 54
New York Yankees, 305, 306
Newark Eagles, 289, 290, 292, 309
Newark, New Jersey, 19, 68, 74, 210, 290
Newberry Medal, 21, 320
Newburyport, Massachusetts, 91

Newport Jazz Festival, 143, 150
Newport News, Virginia, 137, 143
Newton, Huey P., 221
Nicaragua, 176
Nice, France, 129
Nicodemus, Kansas, 182
Nino, Pedro Alonzo, 182
Nkrumah, Kwame, 199
Nobel Peace Prize, 13, 93, 204, 214, 216
Nobel Prize in economics, 72
Nobel Prize in literature, 234
Noble, Jordan B., 103, 257
Norfolk State College (University), 183, 281
Norfolk, Virginia, 179, 248, 250, 258
Normal, Alabama, 128
Norman, Jimmy, 146
North Africa, 32
North African School, 30
North American Air Defense Command, 255
North Carolina, 28, 56, 82, 108, 140, 195, 197, 201, 213, 216, 219, 268
North Carolina A&T State University, 135, 178
North Carolina Central College (University), 123, 181, 211, 236
North Carolina Mutual and Provident Association, 68
North Carolina Mutual Life Insurance Company, 65, 68, 76, 77, 317
North Congregational Church, 85
North Island, California, 250
North Pole, 176
North Star (newspaper), 266
North, South Carolina, 99
Northampton County, North Carolina, 4
Northwestern University, 213, 229, 276
Norwood, Massachusetts, 94
Noyes Academy, 112
Nubin, Katie Bell, 96
Numero, Joseph, 275
Nunn, Bobby, 146

O'Hara, James E., **195**, 196, 219
O'Neal, Frederick, 24
O'Neal, Shaquille, **307**, 311
Oahu, Hawaii, 66
Oak Park Vocational High School, 152
Oakland, California, 15, 107, 262, 295
Oakland Tribune, 15
Oakville, Alabama, 291
Obama, Barack, 222
Oberlin College, 31, 198, 203

Ohio, 4, 28, 31, 176, 191, 194, 203, 218, 219, 221
Ohio National Guard, 249
Ohio State University, 96, 229
Oje, Baba, 163
Ojibway Indians, 173
Oklahoma, 90, 175, 179, 181, 222, 243
Oklahoma City, Oklahoma, 93. 233. 261
Oklahoma Territory, 175
Old Saybrook, Connecticut, 230
Olive, Milton L., III (PFC), 261, 262
Oliver, Joe "King," 13, 133, 165
Olmec, 185, 218
Olssen, Jessie, 36
Olustee, Florida, 182, 243, 258
Olympia, Washington, 172
Olympics, 16, 21, 96, 290, 291, 292, 295, 298, 299, 300, 302, 304, 305, 307
Omaha, Nebraska, 19, 207, 298, 300
Oneida Institute, 30, 112
Onesimus, 282
OneSource, 79
Ontario, 186, 267
Opelousas, Louisiana, 195
Orange, Walter, 169
Orangeburg, South Carolina, 5, 184
Order of Honor and Merit, 115
Organization of Afro American Unity, 207
Otis Art Institute, 51
Otis Day and the Knights, 169
Ottey, Merlene, **304**
Ottumwa, Iowa, 177
Overbrook High School, 297
Overton, Anthony, 77
Owens, Jesse, **96**, 104, **290**, **291**, 309, 333
Owens, Lucille, 281
Owens, Shirley, 146
Oxford, Pennsylvania, 117
Oxford University, 227

Pace, Harry H., 77
Page, Alan, 310
Page Fence Giants, 287
Page, John, 293
Paige, LeRoy "Satchel," **14**, 24, 289, **293**, 309, 314, 333
Paige's All-Stars, 289
Palm Springs Tennis Club, 69
Palm, Zetta, 41
Palmer, Bertha George, 233
Palmer Memorial Institute, 8, 113
Palmer, Thomas, 146
Paramount Records, 134

Pararibo, Surinam, 85
Paris, France, 14, 32, 33, 36, 38, 40, 41, 42, 50, 59, 88, 115, 129, 131, 132, 183, 229, 249, 266, 268, 272
Paris, Kentucky, 273
Paris, Tennessee, 115
Parker, Addie Boyley, 18
Parker, Charles Sr., 18
Parker, Charlie, **18**, 25, 98, **139**, 150, 158, 166
Parker, Jim, 309
Parker, John J., 201
Parker, John P., 63, 76, 282
Parker, Junior, 167
Parker, Ray, 170
Parks, Gordon, 61, 261
Parks, Rosa, 101, **205**, 220
Parks, Suzan-Lori, 237
Pasadena, California, 92, 97
Patterson, Floyd, 309
Patterson, Frederick D., 124, 283, 320
Patton, Charlie, 95
Patton, Georgia E.L., 103
Paul Quinn College, 110, 125
Paul, Thomas, 218
Payne, Daniel A., 121
Payne, Ethel L., **15**, 24
Payton, Lawrence, 151
Payton, Walter, **303**, 310, 333
Peake, George, 282
Pearl Harbor, 249
Peary, Robert, **86**, 176
Pease, Joachim, 258, 260
Pecos River, Texas, 246
Pekin Company, 129
Pelé, 309
Pendergrass, Teddy, 169
Penguins, 166
Peninsula Springfield Redbirds, 289
Penn, Robert, **247**, 260
Penn, William Fletcher, 272
Pennsylvania, 13, 17, 28, 32, 108, 139, 218, 220, 260, 279
Pennsylvania Academy, 88
Pennsylvania Academy of Fine Arts, 86
Pennsylvania Anti-slavery Society, 188
Pennsylvania Museum, 69
Pennsylvania School of Industrial Art, 40, 69
Pensacola, Florida, 242, 255
People United to Save Humanity (PUSH), 21, 209
Peoples Bank of Commerce, 79
Peoples, John A., Jr., **120**, 125
Peoples National Bank of Commerce, 79

Peoria, Illinois, 158
Perkins, Marion, **55**
Perrin, Keith, 78
Perris, California, 139
Peru, 171
Petersburg, Virginia, 7, 89, 184, 244, 258
Peterson, Louis, 236
Petry, Ann, **230**, 236, 314, 319, 329
Petry, George David, 230
Phi Beta Kappa, 13, 115, 227
Philadelphia 76ers, 297, 301, 305
Philadelphia Building and Loan Association, 63
Philadelphia Centennial Exposition, 29
Philadelphia Eagles, 294, 304
Philadelphia Hilldale, 289, 291, 294, 308
Philadelphia, Mississippi, 208
Philadelphia Museum of Art, 69
Philadelphia, Pennsylvania, 10, 18, 20, 38, 40, 69, 74, 78, 85, 86, 88, 96, 99, 107, 110, 127, 133, 137, 140, 143, 172, 182, 183, 184, 191, 213, 227, 239, 244, 259, 269, 270, 271, 288, 294, 297, 299
Philadelphia Phillies, 301
Philadelphia Stars, 289, 294
Philadelphia Warriors, 297
Philander Smith College, 178
Philippines, 249, 255, 294
Phillips Gallery, 180
Phillips, Robert, 168
Phoenix, Arizona, 262
Phoenix Suns, 305
Phyllis Wheatley High School, 211
physics, 276, 279, 280, 282
Picasso, 44
Picken, Andrew, 82
Pickett, Bill, **87**, 103, **178**
Pickett, Wilson, 168
Pico, Pio, **187**, 218
Pierce, Elijah, 60
Pierce, Willie, 41
Pin Point, Georgia, 215
Pinchback, Nina, 225
Pinchback, Pinckney Benton Stewart, **194**, 215, 219, 225, 325
Pinckney, William, 261
Pinewood Tom (*see* White, Josh)
Pinkney, Bill, 144
Pinn, Robert A. (First Sergeant), 259
Pippin, Horace, 24, **45**, 104, 316
Pitts, Riley L. (Captain), 262
Pitts, Zasu, 69
Pittsburgh Courier, 70, 253
Pittsburgh Crawfords, 289, 294, 308

Pittsburgh Grays, 292
Pittsburgh, Pennsylvania, 54, 66, 86, 90, 96, 98, 134, 142, 158, 290, 292
Pittsburgh Pirates, 20, 290, 299, 302
Pittsburgh Steelers, 301
Pizarro, Francisco, 171
Platters, 166
Pleasant, Mary Ellen, 219
Plessy v. Furgeson, 123, 124
Pocahontas, Virginia, 279
Poindexter, Hildrus A., 284
Pointer, Anita, 160
Pointer, Bonnie, 160
Pointer, Dick, 257
Pointer, June, 160
Pointer, Ruth, 160
Pointer Sisters, 169
Poison Springs, Arkansas, 178, 258
Poitier, Sydney, **149**, 168
Pollard, Fritz, 308
Pollock, Ed, **134**
Ponca City, Oklahoma, 178
Pond, Harry, 11
Pontotoc, Mississippi, 145
Poor, Salem, **3**, 23
Popel, Esther, 235
Poro College, 67
Port Chicago, California, 179, 203, 261, 330
Port Royal, South Carolina, 108, 179
Port Royal, Virginia, 260
Port-au-Prince, Haiti, 30
Porter, Charles Ethan, 60
Porter, David (Admiral), 175
Porter, James A., **45**, 60, 316
Portland Beavers, 289
Portland, Maine, 42
Portrait of a Cleric, 27
Portsmouth, Rhode Island, 182
Portsmouth, Virginia, 241, 259
Potts, Lucy Ann, 9
Poussaint, Alvin Francis, 284
Powell, Adam Clayton, Jr., **204**, 326
Powell, Colin (General), **255**, 263
Powell, Earl "Bud," 98, 166
Prairie View, Texas, 122
Prairie View A&M University, 109, 110
Prater, Dave, 168
Prater, Ida, 130
Pratter, Samuelle, 162
Presbyterian Church of the United States, 114
Presbyterians, 109, 122, 123, 224
Presidential Medal of Freedom, 143
Presley, Elvis, 136

Price, Florence, 24
Price, James, 152
Price, Kate, 152
Price, Leontyne, 25, **152**, 168
Price, Lloyd, 167
Price, Sammy, 137
Pride, Amelia Perry, 123
Pride, Charley, 105, 169, 317
Pridgett, Ella, 134
Pridgett, Thomas, 134
Prince, Lucy Terry, 235
Prince, Wesley, 141
Princeton University, 234
Pro-Line Corporation, 72, 77
Professional Football Hall of Fame, 299
Prosper, Marvin, 163
Prosser, Gabriel, 218
Protective Industrial Insurance Co. of Alabama, Inc., 78
Prout, Mary Ann, 121
Providence Art Club, 29
Providence, Rhode Island, 29, 84
Provident Hospital, 84, 179, 269, 280
Pryor, Richard, 169
Puerto Rico, 20, 27, 57, 171, 302
Pullman Company, 11
Purvis, William B., 282
Pushkin, Alexander, 234, 235

Quachita Parish, Louisiana, 69
Quarles, Benjamin A., 124, 326, 331
Quarles, Ralph, 198
Queen Victoria, 127, 186
Queen's College, 112
Quincy, Illinois, 197
Quinn, Anthony, 69

Rabb, Maurice, 284
Radio City Music Hall, 273
Radio Hall of Fame, 164
Rainey, Edward, 190
Rainey, Gertrude Malissa "Ma," **10**, 24, **134**, 166, 322
Rainey, Joseph H., 64, **190**, **191**, 192, 219
Rainey, William "Pa," 134
Raleigh, North Carolina, 5
Ramsey Lewis Trio, 168
Randolph, A. Philip, **11**, 24, 58, 77, 316
Randolph, Virginia, 103
Ranger, Joseph, 257
Rankin, John, 63
Rankin, Pennsylvania, 15
Ranney, William, 82
Ransier, Alonzo J., 192, **195**, 219
Rapier, James T., 192, 326

Ratcliff, Edward (First Sergeant), 259
Rawls, Lou, **159**, 169
Ray, Charlotte E., 103
Raymond, Usher, 170
Reach Media, 164
Reagan, Ronald, 214
Real Times, Inc., 79
Reason, Charles L., 121
Reason, Patrick Henry, 23, 59
Record, Eugene, 157
Red Bank, New Jersey, 198
Redding, Jay Saunders, 236, 329
Redding, Otis, **20**, 25, **154**, 168
Reed, Herb, 145
Reed, Ishmael, 237
Reed, Mathis James "Jimmy," **148**, 167
Reed, Willis, 310
Reeves, Martha, 149
Regal Theater, 180
Reiss, Winold, 39
Reliable Life Insurance Company, 78
Remond, Sara Parker, **267**, 282
Reno, Nevada, 173
replevin, 81
Republic of Equatorial Guinea, 97
Revels, Hiram, 23, **109**, 122, 180, **191**, 219
Reverend George Lisle Monument, 171
Revolutionary War, 3, 81, 82, 171, 172, 179, 212, 240, 241, 242, 256, 265
Reyneau, Betsy Graves, **51**
Rhode Island, 30, 171, 218
Rhodes Scholar, 227
Ribbs, Willy T., 310
Rice, Condoleezza, 222
Rice, Jerry, 311
Rice, Jim, 310
Richland, Mississippi, 143
Richmond, Virginia, 46, 65, 78, 88, 129, 136, 189, 206, 215, 244, 245, 262
Rick, Branch, 97
Riggs, Robert, 60
right to vote, 191
Riles, Wilson C., 125
Rillieux, Norbert, 180, **266**, 282
Ripley, Ohio, 63
Ritchie, Lionel, 169
Rivers, Ruben, 261
Roach, Max, 139
Roberta Martin Singers, 94
Roberts, Joseph Jenkins, 187
Roberts, Needham, 260
Robertson, Carole, 208
Robeson, Paul, **10**, 24, 101, 114, **135**, 166, 308, 313, 329

Robinson, Bill (Luther) "Bojangles," 24, 129, **136**, 166, 308, 322
Robinson, David, 311
Robinson, Frank, 310
Robinson, Jackie, 71, **97**, 105, **292**, 295, 309, 333
Robinson, James, 257
Robinson, Jerry, 97
Robinson, Mallie, 97
Robinson, Oscar, 309
Robinson, Percy, 136
Robinson, Sugar Ray, 309, 333
Robinson, William, 218
Robinson, William "Smokey," **151**, 168
Robinsonville, Mississippi, 95
Rochester, New York, 183
Rock, John Sweat, 282
Rockefeller grants, 45
Rockville, Maryland, 183
Rocky Mount club, 299
Rocky Mountains, 173
Rodin, Auguste, 41
Rogan, Joe, 308
Roger Williams University, 65
Rogers, Bobbie, **151**
Rogers, Charles Calvin (Lieutenant Colonel), 262
Rogers, Claudette, 151
Rogers, Texas, 100, 155
Rohan, Nanette, 54
Rolling Fork, Mississippi, 97, 145
Rollins, Charlemae Hill, 104, 314, 319
Rollins, Sonny, 170
Rome, Italy, 27, 31
Rookie of the Year, 293
Roosevelt College, 213
Roosevelt, Franklin Delano, 10, 142, 254
Roosevelt, Theodore, 225
Roots, 233
Rose, Edward, 103, 175, 318
Rosenwald Fellowship, 14
Rosenwald, Julius, 60, 123
Ross, Araminta, 218 (*see also* Tubman, Harriet)
Ross, Diana, **152**
Rowan, Carl T., 221, 326
Rowland, Kelly, **164**
Roxborough, John, 16
Roxbury, 91, 178
Rudolph, Wilma Glodean, **298**, 309
Ruffin, David **153**, 168
Ruffin, Jimmy, 168
Ruiz, José, 58, 187
Ruleville, Mississippi, 208
Rushing, Jimmy, **93**, 104, **155**, 168

Russell, Bill, 105, **295**, **297**, 309, 333
Russell, Nipsey, 167
Russwurm, John B., 76
Rust College, 108, 121, 122
Rust, Richland S., 121
Rustin, Bayard, 206, 220
Rutgers University, 123, 135, 288

Sacramento, California, 107
Saint-Gaudens, August, 40
Saks Fifth Avenue building, 69
Salem, Massachusetts, 239, 267
Salem, North Carolina, 262
Salem, Peter, **82**, 103, 230, 257
Salisbury, North Carolina, 110, 229
Salon Award, 59
Sam and Dave, **153**, 168
Sampson, G.T., 283
San Antonio Spurs, 306, 307
San Antonio, Texas, 182
San Bernardino, California, 20
San Diego, California, 183
San Diego Padres, 303, 305
San Francisco 49ers, 300, 301
San Francisco Art Association, 44
San Francisco Bay area, 183, 276
San Francisco, California, 17, 32, 36, 44,
    107, 152, 162, 187, 189, 202, 217,
    276
San Francisco Giants, 293, 297, 307
San Francisco State University, 280
San Francisco Warriors, 297
Sanders, Barry, 311
Sanderson, Jeremiah Burke, 121
sanitation workers, 120, 145
Santurce Grabbers, 302
Sargent, Rupert L. (First Lieutenant), 262
Sash, Moses, 103
Sasser, Clarence Eugene (Specialist Fifth
    Class), 262
Satcher, David, 285
Savage, Augusta, **42**, **43**, 60
Savannah, Georgia, 23, 109, 182, 215,
    246, 269, 295
Sayers, Gale, **300**, 310, 333
Schenectady, New York, 63
Schmeling, Max, 16, 17
Schnetzler, Hedwig, 275
Schomburg, Arthur P., 9, **57**, 61
Schomburg Center for Research in Black
    Culture, New York Public Library,
    61, 178
Schuyler, George, 235
Schuyler, Philippa, 168
Schwerner, Michael, 208

Scotia Seminary, 88, 109
Scotland, 6, 28
Scott, Dred, 219, 325
Scottsboro, Alabama, 220
Scottsboro Boys, 220
Seale, Bobby, 221
Seamon, Annie, 227
Searles, Joseph L., III, 77
Seattle, Washington, 52
Seaway National Bank, 78
Second Baptist Church, 69
Secretary of State, 255
Sedalia, Missouri, 6
Sedalia, North Carolina, 113
Sedgwick, Theodore, 81
Seguin, Texas, 287
Seifert, Charles, 52
Selma, Alabama, 20, 192
Seminole Indians, 3
Seneca County, New York, 28
Seneca Village, 182
Senegal, 182
Shabazz, Betty, 25
Shadd, Mary Ann (*see* Carey, Mary Ann
    Shadd)
Shakoor, Nadirah, 163
Shakur, Tupac, 170
Shange, Ntozake, 237
Shannon, Charles, 40
Sharp, Granville, 27
Shaw, Earl, 284
Shaw, Patricia Walker, 70
Shaw, Robert Gould (Colonel), 32
Shaw University, 68, 110, 116, 121
Shawnee Indians, 240
Shelby, North Carolina, 15
Sheridan, Arkansas, 182
Shirelles, 167
Shober, James Frances, 282
Sierra Leone, 182, 187
Silhouettes, 167
Silver, South Carolina, 19, 296
Silver Spring, Maryland, 127
Simkins, Modjeska, 24
Simms, Willie, 308
Simon, Joe, 168
Simone, Nina, 169
Simpson College, 111
Simpson, O.J., 216, 310
Sims, Clifford Chester (Staff Sergeant),
    262
Sims, J. Wilbert, 309
Sims, Naomi, 78
Sinatra, Frank, 69
Singleton, Benjamin "Pap," **197**, 219

Sioux Indian, 294
Sissel, Nobel, 14, 165
Sisson, Tack, 257
Sixth Zion Baptist Church, 189
Sixteenth Avenue Church, 208
Sklarek, Norma Merrick, 25
Sledge, Mississippi, 100
Sledge, Percy, 168
Slowe, Lucy Diggs, 104
Sly and the Family Stone, 169
Small, Herschel, 163
Smalls, Robert, 103, **192**, 331
Smith, Bessie, **9**, 24, **130**, 165, 181, 322
Smith, Bragg, 219
Smith, Charles, 160
Smith, Emmitt J., III, **307**, 311
Smith, Fannie N., 85
Smith, Gerrit, 265
Smith, Hilton, 309
Smith, James McCune, 282
Smith, J.W., 283
Smith, Mamie, 24
Smith, Maxine, 221
Smith, Nolle, 76
Smith, O.C., 168
Smith, Ozzie, 310
Smith, Vasco, 221
Smith, Will, 170
Smithsonian American Art Museum, 47
Smokey Robinson and the Miracles, **151**, 168
Smythe-Haithe, Mabel Murphy, 105
Somerset County, PA, 239
Somerville, New Jersey, 10
Sosa, Sammy, 311
Soul Brothers and Sister Lou, 20, 25
South Africa, 200, 216
South Carolina, 10, 64, 82, 88, 111, 183, 185, 186, 190, 191, 193, 195, 198, 219, 246, 260, 275
South Carolina Leader, 195
South Carolina State University, 181
South Parkway, 183, 201
South Side Community Art Center, 51
Southeast Fort Worth Federal Credit Union, 74
Southern Christian Leadership Conference (SCLC), 206, 209
Southern Illinois University, 14, 232
Southern Methodist University, 216
Southern University, 181, 303
Sowell, Thomas, 215
Spain, 229, 241
Spanish-American War, 176, 247
Sparta, Georgia, 111

Spaulding, Charles Clinton, 23, 65, **68**, 76, 77
Speech, 163
Spelman College (Seminary), 6, 97, 110, 120, 122, 161, 282
Spelman, Harvey Buel, 122
Spelman, Lucy Henry, 122
Spence, Eulalie, 235
Spencer, Anne, 235, 237
Spikes, Richard B., 283
Spingarn Award, 220
Spingarn, Joel Elias, 220
Springfield, Illinois, 63
Springfield, Massachusetts, 94
St. Andrews, New Brunswick, Canada, 29
St. Ann's Bay, Jamaica, 200
St. Augustine, Florida, 150
St. Georges, Bermuda, 190
St. Hill, Shirley (*see* Chisholm, Shirley)
St. Joseph, Missouri, 139
St. Jude Hospital, 69
St. Louis Browns, 289, 293
St. Louis Cardinals, 298, 299, 303
St. Louis, Missouri, 12, 14, 20, 67, 83, 89, 93, 124, 173, 184, 197, 204, 271, 289, 294, 303
St. Louis Stars, 289, 308
St. Luke's Episcopal Church, 112
St. Maries, Idaho, 261
St. Maurice, 197
St. Moritz, 197
St. Paul, Minnesota, 12, 189, 305
St. Paul Urban League, 207
Stance, Emanual, 260
Standard, J., 283
Staple Singers, **158**, 169
Staples, Cleotha, **158**
Staples, Mavis, **158**
Staples, Roebuck "Pops," **158**
Star, Nina Howells, 56
Stargell, Willie, 309
State University at Albany, 234
Staupers, Fritz C., 274
Staupers, Mabel Keaton, **274**, 283
STAX Records, 154
Steames, Norman "Turkey," 308
Steptoe, John, 101, 105, 319
Stevens, Ray, 100
Stevie, 101, 319
Steward, Slam, 136
Stewart, Ella P., 77
Stewart, Susan M., 282
Stewart, T.W., 282
Still, William Grant, 24, **136**, 163, 166, 175, 236

Still, William Lloyd, **188**, 223, 325
Stillman, Charles A., 122
Stillman College, 109, 179
Stockman, Shawn, 163
Stockton, California, 107, 188
Stokes, Lottie, 6
Stokes, Louis, 210
Stokes, Rufus, 284
Story family, 31
Stout, Juanita K., 25
Stowe, Harriet Beecher, 3, 63, 223
Stowers, Freddie, 260
Strong, Barrett, 167
Stubs, Levi, 151
Student Nonviolent Coordinating
    Committee (SNCC), 206, 209
Succeeding Against the Odds, 70, 317
Sugar Hill, 183
Sullivan, Leon (Reverend), 78
Summit, Oklahoma, 181
Super Bowl, 299, 301 304, 307
Superior City, Wisconsin, 173
Supreme Court of Pennsylvania, 17
Supreme Insurance Company, 70
Supreme Liberty Life Insurance
    Company, 68
Supreme Life and Casualty Company, 68
Supreme Life Insurance Company of
    America, 67, 72, 78
Supremes, **152**, 160, 168
Surinam, 103
Surry, Virginia, 7
Sutton, Percy Eliis, 221
Swails, Stephen A.
Swanson, Zula, 77
Swarthmore College, 13
Sweden (Swedish), 44. 156
Switzerland, 156
Sydney, Australia, 305
Symantec Corporation, 74
Syracuse University, 58

Tabernacle Baptist Church, 7, 89
Taft Museum of Art, 59
Taft, Oklahoma, 181
Talbert, Mary B., 220
"Talented Tenth," 123
Talladega, Alabama, 184
Talladega College, 43, 44, 110, 181, 276,
    320
Tallahassee, Florida, 111, 184
Tallahatchie County, Mississippi, 196
Tanner, Henry O., **32**, **33**, **34**, **35**, **36**, **37**,
    38, **39**, 40, 50, 51, **86**, 103, 316
Tanner, Jesse, 36

Tanner, Jessie M. Olssen, 36, 59
Tanneyhill, Ann, 104
Taree, Aerle, 163
Tarleton, Banastre (Lieutenant Colonel),
    82
Tarrant, Caesar, 257
Tarry, Ellen, 236
Tate, Bruce, 145
Tatum, Arthur "Art," 18, 98, 136, 166
Tatum, Reece "Goose," 291
Taylor, Charley, 309
Taylor, Isaiah, 163
Taylor, James, 160
Taylor, Jim, 299
Taylor, Johnnie, **155**, 168
Taylor, Lawrence, 310
Taylor, Marshall, 308
Taylor, Mildred D., 101, 103, 314, 319
Taylor, Russell, 246
Taylor, Susie King, **246**, 260, 331
Taylor, Texas, 182
Tazewell, Virginia, 88
Tea Cake, 236
Teachers College of Columbia
    University, 50
Tel Aviv, Israel, 276
Temple Black, Shirley, 7, 136
Temple, Lewis, 282
Temptations, **153**, 168
Tennessee, 76, 86, 114, 121, 189, 221,
    244
Tennessee State University, 66, 123, 298
Terrell, Mary Church, 175, **203**, 220
Terrell, North Carolina, 15
Terrell, Saunders (*see* Terry, Sonny)
Terrell, Texas, 164
Terry, Sonny, **15**, 24, 166
Tex, Joe, 168
Texarkana, Texas, 6
Texas, 65, 90, 109, 110, 111, 116, 178,
    182, 211, 216, 221, 242, 326
Texas A&M University, 109
Texas Christian University, 216
Texas College, 110, 181
Texas Rangers, 301
Texas Southern University, 124, 211,
    214, 234, 315; Texas Southern School
    of Law, 2003
Texas Western College, 310
Tharpe, Sister Rosetta, **96**, 105, **137**, 166
Theban Legion, 197
Thermo King Corporation, 275
Thibodeaux, Louisiana, 276
Thirteenth Amendment to the U.S.
    Constitution, 219

Thomas, Alma Woodsey, 49, **56**, 315
Thomas, Bigger, 133, 236
Thomas, Carla, **148**, 167
Thomas, Charles L., 261
Thomas, Charlie, 144
Thomas, Clarence, **215**, 221
Thomas, Debi, 310
Thomas, Dennis, 160
Thomas, Hyram S., 282
Thomas, Isaiah, 310
Thomas, John, 220
Thomas, Leola Williams, 215
Thomas, M.C., 215
Thomas, Rufus, 25, **148**, 168
Thompson, Era Bell, 236
Thompson, John W., 78
Thompson, Marshall, 157
Thompson, William (PFC), 261
Thoms, Adah B. Samuels, 283
Thornton, Robert A., **280**, 284
Thrash, Dox, 60
Thrasher, Andrew, 144
Thrasher, Gerhart, 144
Three Marys, 60
Thurgood Marshall School of Law, 203
Thurman, Beulah, 226
Thurman, Howard, 115, 220, 326
Thurman, Oscar, 226
Thurman, Wallace, 235, 329
Till, Emmet, **205**, 220, 232
Till, Mamie, **205**
Tillman, Georgeanna, 148
Tisby, Dexter, 145
Tixtla, Guerrero, 186
TLC Beatrice International Holdings, Inc., 79
Tobias, Channing H., 220
Toccoa, Georgia, 130
Todd, Beverly, 22
Tokyo, Japan, 20
Tolan, Eddie, 308
Toledo Blue Stockings, 287
Toledo Crawfords, 294
Toledo, Ohio, 67, 136
Toledo School of Music, 136
Tolson, Melvin, 236
Tolton, Augustus (Father), 219
Tone Loc, 170
Tony Award, 147, 160
Tony! Toni! Tone!, 170
Toomer, Jean, 235
Toomer, Nathan, 225
Toon, Earl, 160
Topeka, Kansas, 12, 67, 91, 92, 119, 120, 124, 139, 230

Toronto Blue Jays, 305
Toronto, Ontario, 267
Tougaloo College, 110, 181
Tougaloo, Mississippi, 184, 320
Toulminville, Alabama, 295
Toussaint, Pierre, 103
Toussaint-L'Ouverture, Pierre Dominique, 51, 52
Townsend, Ella, 208
Townsend, Jim, 208
Townsend, Willard, 77
Towson, Ron, 154
Trans-Atlantic Society, 197
Travis, Virginia, 95
Traylor, Bill, **40**, 60
Trenton, New Jersey, 99, 214, 293
Tri-State Bank, 77, 78
Tri-State Defender, 75
Triannon Lyrique, 129
Trinidad, 14
Trinity Medical College, 244
Trotter, Geraldine "Deenie" Pindell, 103
Trotter, James Monroe, 260
Trotter, William Monroe, 87, 180, 219, 260
Troy, New York, 175
Trujilo All-Stars, 289
Truman, Harry, 11
Trumbell County, Ohio, 258
Trumbull, John, 82
Truth, Sojourner, **4**, 51, 103, 179, **186**, 318, 325
Tubman, Harriet, **4**, 18, 47, 52, 58, 103, 179, 186, **189**, 218, 219, 260, 314, 319, 324
Tuckahoe, Maryland, 84
Tulsa, Oklahoma, 17, 220
Tupelo, Mississippi, 182
Turner, Benjamin S., **191**, **192**
Turner, Charles H., 283
Turner, Ike, 169
Turner, Nat, 218
Turner Theological Seminary, 110
Turner, Tina, 170
Tuscaloosa, Alabama, 21, 183
Tuskegee Airmen, 251, 252, 254, 255
Tuskegee, Alabama, 38, 66, 122, 183, 205, 252
Tuskegee Institute, 39, 84, 110, 111, 114, 115, 117, 120, 122, 124, 177, 199, 249, 252, 269, 274, 281, 319, 320
Tuskegee Normal and Industrial Institute, 85
Tuskegee University, 125, 179, 252
Twain, Mark (Samuel Clemens), 41

Twenty-fourth Amendment to the U.S. Constitution, 221
Twenty-third Psalm, 59
Tyler, Texas, 146, 184
Tyus, Wyomia, 310

UCLA, 13, 21, 97, 292
Underground Railroad, 52, 82, 84, 188, 189, 223, 235, 314, 319, 325
Union Army, 193, 194, 195, 244, 246, 266
Union Navy, 192, 268
United Bank of Philadelphia, 79
United Colored Links, 197
United Kingdom, 201
United Nations, 13, 255
United Negro College Fund, 117, 274
United Republic of Cameroon, 97
United States, 20, 31, 32, 44, 61, 112, 115, 121, 127, 133, 136, 139, 149, 155, 172, 177, 186, 187, 189, 191, 198, 200, 201, 209, 210, 225, 244, 265, 266, 267, 268, 272, 274, 275, 281
Universal Life Insurance Company, 66, 67, 70
Universal Negro Improvement Association (UNIA), 200
University of Berlin, 199, 227
University of California, Berkeley, 277
University of California, San Francisco, 276
University of Chicago, 12, 14, 91, 112, 124, 201, 271, 278
University of Cincinnati, 279
University of Connecticut, 230
University of Detroit, 213
University of Glasgow, Scotland, 282
University of Houston, 303
University of Idaho, 140
University of Illinois at Chicago, 274, 277, 278
University of Iowa, 58, 177, 229, 271
University of Kansas, 276, 297, 300
University of Kentucky, 300
University of Maryland, 100, 279; University of Maryland Law School, 94
University of Massachusetts, 301
University of Michigan, 147
University of Minnesota, 12, 207, 280, 305
University of Mississippi, 119
University of Missouri, 116, 124
University of North Carolina, 4, 297, 305

University of Oklahoma, 213
University of Pennsylvania, 69, 112, 123, 213, 227
University of South Carolina, 5, 109, 226
University of Southern California, 69
University of Tennessee, 304
University of Texas, Austin, 211
University of Texas, El Paso, 310
University of the District of Columbia, 121
University of Utah, 226
University of Vienna, 92
University of West Tennessee, 270
University of Wisconsin, 230
Up from Slavery, 123
Upper Missouri River, 83
Urban League, 18, 76, 94, 95, 118, 212, 220
Usher (*see* Raymond, Usher)
U.S. Air Force, 156, 164
U.S. Army, 17, 97, 176, 213, 273, 293
U.S. Army Medical Corps, 272
U.S. Army Military Intelligence Corps Hall of Fame, 244
U.S. Coast Guard, 233
U.S. Congress, 5, 64, 108, 190, **191**, 195, 197, 198, 216, 222, 324, 325
U.S. Constitution, 81
U.S. Court of Appeals, 94
U.S. Health Service, 275
U.S. House of Representatives, 64, 190, 192, 193, 194, 195, 196, 198, 202, 204, 205, 206, 208, 210, 211, 212, 213, 214, 215, 216, 217, 290
U.S. Navy, 176, 192, 250
U.S. Olympic Hall of Fame, 298, 300
U.S. Senate, 109, 191, 194, 196, 209, 216
U.S. State Department, 13
U.S. Supreme Court, 12, 94, 116, 124, 187, 188, 195, 201, 203, 205, 215, 267, 300
USS Enterprise, 249
USS Hartford, 245, 260
USS Indianapolis, 249
USS Iowa, 247
USS Jesse L. Brown, 263
USS Kearsarge, 244, 260
USS Leonard Roy Harmon, 261
USS Liscome Bay, 249
USS Marblehead, 243
USS Norman, 177
USS San Francisco, 250
USS Washington, 187
USS West Virginia, 249
Utica College, 113

Vai, 218
Van Buren, Martin, 187
Van Der Zee, James, 61
Van Lew, Elizabeth, 244
Van Peebles, Melvin, 169
Vandross, Luther, 170
Vann, Robert L., 76, 316
Vassa, Gustavus, 223, 235
Vaughan, Sarah, 25, 142, **161**, 170
Veal, Charles (Private), 259
Veracruz, Mexico, 184, 185
Vermont, 218, 239
Vesey, Denmark, 218
Vic-Ser-Seille, France, **252**
Vicksburg, Mississippi, 5, 175
Victory Life Insurance Company, 67
Vienna, 152
Vietnam, 143, 255
Vietnam War, 153, 254, 330
Virgin Islands, 57, 177, 221
Virginia, 4, 127, 175, 182, 186, 187, 189, 198, 201, 221, 241, 244, 245, 258, 259, 260, 265, 268
Virginia Historical Society, 27
Virginia Normal and Collegiate Institute, 198
Virginia Squires, 301
Virginia State College (University), 89, 179, 181, 198, 279
Virginia Union University, 110, 115, 133
Voorhees College, 92, 111, 179
Voorhees Industrial School, 111
Voorhees, Ralph, 111
vote/voting, 60, 109, 123, 191, 204, 208, 216, 271

Waco, North Carolina, 295
Waco, Texas, 133, 216, 249
Waddy, Henrietta, 166
Walcott, Joe, 309
Walker, A. Maceo, **70**, 77
Walker, A'Lelia, 104
Walker, Aaron Thibeaux "T-Bone," 166
Walker, Alice, 105, **234**, 237, 319, 329
Walker, David, 180
Walker, J.E. (Joseph Edison), **67**, 70, 77
Walker, Junior, 168
Walker, Lelia, 24
Walker, Madam C.J., **5**, 23, **66**, 76, 316
Walker, Maggie Lena, **65**, 76
Walker, Moses Fleetwood, 308
Wallace, Ben, 311
Wallace, Christopher, 170
Wallace, Rasheed, 307
Waller, Thomas "Fats," 13, 165

Walls, Josiah T., **191**, **193**, 219, 325
Wanamaker, Rodman, 32
War of 1812, 241, 242
Ward, Clara M., **99**, 105, **143**, 166
Ward, Samuel Ringgold, 235, 329
Ward Trio, 99
Ward, Willarene, 99, 166
Warfield, Frank, 288
Warfield, Paul, 309
Waring, Laura Wheeler, **49**
Waring, Walter, 49
Warren County, North Carolina, 196
Warren, John E. (First Lieutenant), 262
Warrenton, North Carolina, 196
Warwick, Dionne, 168
Washburn College, 67
Washington, Augustus, 30, 59
Washington, Bertha Jones, 213
Washington, Booker T., 6, 17, 23, 38, 39, 51, 59, 73, 84, **85**, 103, 109, 111, **112**, 114, 124, 174, 179, 198, 199, 250, 313, 321
Washington Bullets, 303
Washington, D.C., 5, 7, 10, 11, 12, 32, 38, 40, 45, 58, 64, 66, 73, 81, 84, 87, 88, 89, 91, 93, 100, 104, 107, 112, 113, 115, 129, 176, 182, 183, 192, 194, 196, 198, 200, 201, 203, 207, 211, 217, 224, 244, 248, 249, 253, 265, 271, 272, 275, 280, 288
Washington, Denzel, **162**, 170
Washington, Dinah, **21**, **147**, 167
Washington, Ernest Davidson, 85
Washington, Gabriel, **134**
Washington, George, **174**
Washington, George (President), 82
Washington, Harold, 202, **213**, 221
Washington, John Edwin, 283
Washington, Margaret Murray, 23
Washington, Olivia Davidson, 103
Washington Redskins, 298, 299
Washington, Roy Lee, Sr., 213
Washington Senators, 91, 290
Washington Technical Institute, 121
Washington University, 204
Washington Wizards, 305
Waters, Ethel, **10**, 24, 54, **132**, 165, 323
Waters, Maxine, 208
Watkins, William, 176
Watson, Deek, 166
Watson, George, 261
Watson, Louvenia, 22
Watson, Valerie, 162
Watts, California, 98
Watts, J.C., 217

Waxahachie, Texas, 90
Waycross, Georgia, 97
Weaver, Robert C., 220
Webb, Spud, 333
Webb, Wellington, 181
Wells, Mary, 168
Wells, Willie, 308
Wells-Barnett, Ida B., **6**, 111, 179, **198**, 324
Wellston, Oklahoma, 181
Wertz, Vic, 293
Wesley, Charles Harris, 124, 314, 321, 326, 331
Wesley, Cynthia, 208
Wesley, John, 110
West Africa, 233
West, Dorothy, 237
West Indies, 195
West Memphis, Arkansas, 95
West Palm Beach, Florida, 42
West Point, 254
West Point, Mississippi, 95
West Virginia, 111, 219, 266, 281
West Virginia College, 229
West Virginia State College/University, 281
Westfield, Alabama, 99, 293
Westmart, Illinois, 145
Westport, Massachusetts, 183
"What a Difference a Day Makes," 25
Wheatley, Laura Frances, 220
Wheatley, Phillis, 3, 27, 171, **223**, 235, 313
Wheeler, Mary, 49
Wheeler, Robert, 49
Wheelus Air Force Base, 255
Which Way Freedom, 25, 313
Whipper, Frances Rollin, 87
Whipper, Ionia Rollin, 103
Whipper, William J., 87
Whipple, Prince, 23, **240**, 257
Whistler, Alabama, 297
White, Barry, 169
White, Charles W., **51**
White, Dennis, 142
White, Fred, 159
White, George L., 165
White, George W., 196
White House, 142
White, Josh, **17**, 25, **142**, 166
White, Maurice, 159
White, Reggie, 310
White, Ronnie, **151**
White Rose Home, 86
White Station Baptist Church, 95

White, Verdine, 159
White, Walter Francis, 12, **201**, 220
White, William Jefferson (Reverend), 108
Whitesboro, New York, 50, 112
Whitmore, B. Franklin, 190
Whitney Museum of American Art, 11
Whitney School of Fine Arts, 56
Why Me?, 322
Wichita, Kansas, 262
Wichita State University, 281
Widener Library, 69
Widewater, Virginia, 41
Wiess, Julius, 6
Wiggins, Dwayne, 162
Wiggins, Raphael, 162
Wilberforce, Ohio, 152, 203, 248
Wilberforce University, 65, 108, 110, 121, 123, 150, 199, 249
Wilberforce, William, 121
Wilder, Lawrence Douglas, **215**, 221
Wiley College, 181, 203
Wilkins, J. Ernest, 284
Wilkins, Roy, **12**, 24, **206**, 220
Williams, Bert, 165
Williams, Billy Lee, 297, 309
Williams, Billy Dee, 25
Williams, Charles Melvin "Cootie," 167
Williams College, 12, 115
Williams, Corliss, 307
Williams, Curtis, 145
Williams, Daniel Hale, 103, 123, 180, **270**, 271, 283, 313, 319
Williams, Eugene, 130
Williams, George W., 219
Williams, Joe "Smokey," 308
Williams, John, 134
Williams, John A., 236, 329
Williams, John Gary, 168
Williams, Lucie Campbell, 104
Williams, Marion, 166
Williams, Mary Lou, **134**, 166
Williams, Michelle, **164**
Williams, Milan, 169
Williams, Otis, **153**
Williams, Paul, **153**
Williams, Paul R., **69**, 77
Williams, Serena, 311
Williams, Sonny Boy, 95
Williams, Tony, 145
Williams, Venus, 311
Williams, William Taylor Burwell, 123
Williamson County, Texas, 87
Willis, Chuck, 167
Wilmington, Delaware, 121, 228, 296
Wilmington, North Carolina, 305

Wilson, August, 237, 329
Wilson, Charlie, 160
Wilson, Eliza Mae, 144
Wilson, Ellis, 61
Wilson, Flip (Clerow), 169
Wilson, Henry, 244
Wilson, Jack, 144
Wilson, Jackie, 100, **144**, 166
Wilson, Jud, 288
Wilson, Margaret Bush, 220
Wilson, Mary, **152**
Wilson, Paul, 147
Wilson, Robert, 160
Wilson, Ronnie, 160
Wilson Teachers' College, 121
Wilson, Teddy, 140
Wilson, Thomas T., 308
Wimbledon, 19, 296, 302, 307
Winchester, Virginia, 193
Windsor, Ontario, 188
Winfield, David M., 310
Winfrey, Oprah, 25, 170, 181
Winnsboro, South Carolina, 260
Winston, Anna, 94
Winters, J.W., 282
Wisconsin, 84, 173, 218
Withers, Bill, 169
The Wiz, 25, 141, 158
Women's Convention, 88
Women's Hospital Training School for
    Nurses, 271
Wonder, Stevie, 169
Woodruff, Hale, **43**, **44**, 60
Wofford, Chloe Anthony (*see* Morrison,
    Toni)
Woods, Granville T., **269**, 282
Woods, Tiger, 311
Woodson, Carter G., 57, **88**, 103, 115,
    180, **201**, 314, 321, 326, 329
Woodson, Jacqueline, 101
Woodville, Mississippi, 182
Woolfolk, Andrew, 159
Worcester, Massachusetts, 6
Works Progress Association (WPA), 50,
    53
World Series, 294, 298, 305
World War I, 36, 45, 51, 114, 115, 140,
    201, 247, 248, 260, 271, 273, 275

World War II, 16, 17, 45, 117, 131, 205,
    225, 248, 250, 251, 252, 253, 254,
    261, 274, 275, 330, 331
World's Columbian Exposition, 87
Wormley, James, 76
Wright, Betty, 169
Wright, Elizabeth "Lizzie," 123
    Wright, Jay, 237
Wright, Louis T., 24, **272**, 283
Wright, Orville and Wilbur, 224
Wright, Richard, 12, 24, 179, **228**, 230,
    236, 329
Wynn, Al, **134**
Wyoming, 249

X, Malcolm, **19**, 21, 25, 58, 161, 204,
    207, 220, 233, 326

Yale Medical School, 272
Yale University, 82, 91, 122, 215, 268
Yanga, Gaspar, 218
Yankee Stadium, 16, 17
Yazoo City, Mississippi, 91
Yellow Rose of Texas, 242, 326
Yellow Tavern, 76
Yerby, Frank, 236
Yergan, Max, 220
Yosemite National Park, 188
Young, Andrew, 190, 221
Young, Charles, **248**, 260
Young, Coleman, 221
Young, Laura Ray, 207
Young Men's Christian Association
    (YMCA), 15, 200, 201
Young, Moses Wharton, 284
Young, Whitney Moore, Jr., **18**, 25, **207**
Young, Whitney Moore, Sr., 207
Young Women's Christian Association
    (YWCA), 55
Ypsilanti, Michigan, 8
Yucca Plantation, 63, 172

Zabala. Vera Cristena, 302
Zadkine, Ossip, 58
Zapata, Emiliano, 220
Zumbi, 218
Zuni Indians, 171